*Historical Readings in
Developmental Psychology*

THE CENTURY PSYCHOLOGY SERIES

Kenneth MacCorquodale

Gardner Lindzey

Kenneth E. Clark

Editors

Historical Readings in
Developmental Psychology

Edited by
WAYNE DENNIS

APPLETON-CENTURY-CROFTS
Educational Division
MEREDITH CORPORATION   New York

Copyright © 1972 by MEREDITH CORPORATION
All rights reserved

BF
721
D379

This book, or parts thereof, must not be used or reproduced without written permission. For information address the publi Century-Crofts, Educational Division, Meredith Corporation, 4 South, New York, N. Y. 10016.

72 73 74 75 76 / 10 9 8 7 6 5 4 3 2 1

Library of Congress Card Number: 74–189127

PRINTED IN THE UNITED STATES OF AMERICA
390–26299–4

ACKNOWLEDGMENTS:

3. From Dietrich Tiedeman, *Observations on the Mental Development of a Child* (1787), trans. Suzanne K. Langer and Carl Murchison, *The Pedagogical Seminary,* 34 (1927), 205–230.
4. From Jean Marc Gaspard Itard, *First Developments of the Young Savage of Aveyron* (1801), trans. George and Muriel Humphrey (New York: Appleton-Century-Crofts, 1932), pp. 3–10, 20–23, 31–35, 52–53, 67–73, 85–86, 96–100.
22. From Alfred Binet and Theophile Simon, *The Development of the Binet-Simon Scale* (1905–1908), (American Institute for Mental Studies, Training School Unit, Vineland, New Jersey, 1916).
25. From Sigmund Freud, "Infantile Sexuality," *American Journal of Psychology,* 22 (1910), 26–33.
26. From Lewis M. Terman, *The Measurement of Intelligence* (Boston: Houghton Mifflin & Co., 1916), pp. 51–56, 65–67, with permission.
27. From John B. Watson, *Psychology from the Standpoint of a Behaviorist* (Philadelphia: J. B. Lippincott Company, 1919), pp. 199–213. Used with permission of the publisher.
29. From Jean Piaget, *The Language and Thought of the Child* (London: Routledge and Kegan Paul, Ltd., 1926; New York: Humanities Press, Inc.), pp. 80–102. Used by permission of the publishers.
30. Reprinted from *Mental and Physical Traits of a Thousand Gifted Children,* Genetic Studies of Genius, Volume 1, pp. v–vii, 631–641, by Lewis Terman et al., with the permission of the publishers, Stanford University Press, Copyright © 1925, 1926 by Stanford University Press. Copyright renewed 1954 by Board of Trustees of Leland Stanford Junior University.
31. From Bronislaw Malinowski, *The Sexual Life of Savages* (New York: Harcourt, Brace, and World, 1929), pp 52–69. Copyright 1929 by Bronislaw Malinowski. Used by permission.
33. From Willis C. Beasley, "Visual Pursuit in 109 White and 142 Newborn Negro Infants," *Child Development,* 4 (1933), 106–120. With permission of The Society for Research in Child Development, Inc., and the author.
34. From H. H. Newman, F. N. Freeman, and K. J. Holzinger, *Twins: A Study of Heredity and Environment* (Chicago: University of Chicago Press, 1937), pp. 132–136, 142, 143, 145, 350–363. Copyright © 1937 by The University of Chicago.
35. From Myrtle B. McGraw, *The Neuromuscular Maturation of the Human Infant* (New York: Columbia University Press, 1943), pp. 27–36. Copyright © 1943 by The Columbia University Press.
36. From Donald O. Hebb, "On the Nature of Fear," *Psychological Review* (1946), 259–276. Copyright 1946 by American Psychological Association and reproduced by permission.
37. From Alfred C. Kinsey, Wardell B. Pomeroy, and Clyde E. Martin, *The Sexual Behavior in the Human Male* (Bloomington, Ind. and Philadelphia: Institute for Sex Research and W. B. Saunders Company, 1948), pp. 182–192.

Contents

	Preface	ix
1.	WILLIAM CHESELDEN (1688–1752)	1
	An account of some observations made by a young gentleman, who was born blind, or lost his sight so early, that he had no remembrance of ever having seen, and was couched between 13 and 14 years of age *(1728)*	
2.	DAINES BARRINGTON (1727–1800)	5
	Account of a very remarkable young musician *(1770)*	
3.	DIETRICH TIEDEMANN (1748–1803)	11
	Observations on the mental development of a child *(1787)*	
4.	JEAN MARC GASPARD ITARD (1775–1838)	32
	First developments of the young savage of Aveyron *(1801)*	
5.	JEAN MARC GASPARD ITARD (1775–1838)	41
	A report made to his Excellency the Minister of Interior *(1806)*	
6.	JAMES WARDROP (1782–1838)	50
	History of James Mitchell, a boy born blind and deaf, with an account of the operation performed for the recovery of his sight *(1813)*	
7.	SAMUEL GRIDLEY HOWE (1801–1876)	62
	The education of Laura Bridgman *(Published 1837 and later)*	
8.	THE PEDAGOGICAL SOCIETY OF BERLIN	68
	The contents of children's minds on entering school at the age of six years *(1870)*	
9.	CHARLES DARWIN (1809–1882)	75
	The expression of the emotions in man and animals *(1872)*	
10.	FRANCIS GALTON (1822–1911)	80
	The history of twins, as a criterion of the relative power of nature and nurture *(1876)*	
11.	FRANCIS GALTON (1822–1911)	93
	Psychometric experiments *(1879)*	

12. MELVILLE BALLARD (1839–1912) 101
    Recollections of a deaf-mute (1881)
13. WILHELM PREYER (1842–1897) 106
    The mind of the child. (1882)
14. WILHELM PREYER (1842–1897) 117
    Observations on a newborn acephalic child (1884)
15. G. STANLEY HALL (1846–1924) 119
    The contents of children's minds (1883)
16. JOSEPH JASTROW (1863–1944) 138
    The dreams of the blind (1888)
17. JOSEPH JACOBS (1854–1916) 144
    Experiments on "prehension" (1887)
18. LOUIS ROBINSON (1857–1925) 148
    Darwinism in the nursery (1891)
19. JOSEPH JASTROW (1863–1944) 154
    Psychological notes on Helen Keller (1894)
20. MILLICENT SHINN (1859–1940) 160
    The biography of a baby (1900)
21. EDWARD L. THORNDIKE (1874–1949) 168
    Some data concerning the value of Latin as a secondary school subject (1900)
22. ALFRED BINET (1857–1911) and THEOPHILE SIMON (1873–1961) 177
    The development of the Binet-Simon Scale (1905–1908)
23. DUDLEY KIDD (1858–1916) 188
    African childhood (1906)
24. N. I. KRASNOGORSKI (1882–1962) 198
    The formation of conditioned reflexes in young children (1907)
25. SIGMUND FREUD (1856–1939) 201
    Infantile sexuality (1910)
26. LEWIS M. TERMAN (1877–1956) 208
    The measurement of intelligence (1916)
27. JOHN B. WATSON (1878–1958) 219
    Watson on fear (1919)
28. HUGH GORDON (1863–1934) 228
    Mental and scholastic tests among retarded children. (1923)
29. JEAN PIAGET (b. 1896) 237
    The language and thought of the child (1926)
30. LEWIS M. TERMAN (1877–1956) and associates 253
    Mental and physical traits of a thousand gifted children (1925)
31. BRONISLAW MALINOWSKI (1884–1942) 263
    The social and sexual life of Trobriand Children (1929)
32. ARNOLD L. GESELL (1880–1961) 273
    Maturation and infant behavior pattern (1929)
33. WILLIS C. BEASLEY (b. 1901) 282
    Visual pursuit in white and Negro infants (1933)
34. HORATIO H. NEWMAN (1875–1957), FRANK N. FREEMAN (1880–1961) and KARL J. HOLZINGER (1892–1954) 297
    Twins: A study of heredity and environment (1937)

35. MYRTLE M. MCGRAW (b. 1899) 310
    The neuromuscular maturation of the human infant (1943)
36. DONALD O. HEBB (b. 1904) 318
    On the nature of fear (1946)
37. ALFRED C. KINSEY (1894–1956), WARDELL B. POMEROY (b. 1913), and CLYDE E. MARTIN (b. 1917) 339
    The sexual behavior of boys (1948)

Name Index 351

Subject Index 353

Preface

This book has been prepared for students of human development in order to make available to them materials which are hard for them to come by. I am much in favor of direct experience with children for students of child behavior, but the possibilities of observing or examining many kinds of children are not available to them. Few are likely to see cases of congenital cataract before and after operation, child musicians as precocious as Mozart, or cases such as the wild boy of Aveyron, or deaf-blind persons such as James Mitchell, Laura Bridgman, and Helen Keller. Nor can they interrogate children of the Berlin schools of 1870 or of the Boston schools of 1883.

Reading primary sources is essential to intellectual life. But to find the *Philosophical Transactions of the Royal Society of London* for 1728 and 1770, or the *Annual Report* of the Perkins Institution for the Deaf and Blind for 1889, the *Princeton Review* for 1881, or the *Report of the U. S. Commissioner of Education* for 1900–1901 is not easy, and for many students not possible.

It took a long time to find Wardrop's monograph on James Mitchell and Hugh Gordon's monograph on the canal boat children and the gypsy children of England in the 1920s, and then I was able to do it only with the help of others. These are important studies, mentioned by many authors, but the copies are scarce.

Most of our current textbooks and books of readings in child psychology begin their primary coverage at about 1948, or even later. Little attention is given to earlier work. If there is an historical section it is perfunctory. I believe that there is a need for a collection of historical materials to supplement and give background for the current scene.

If an instructor wished to assign any title which is in the present book, he would find that the library has only one copy, or none, that the journal or book in which the selection occurs is out of print and is not likely to be reprinted.

I have attempted to include in this book some of the most important historical contributions to child psychology, chronologically arranged from 1728 to 1948.

In my opinion a knowledge of historical background is essential in the study of human development. If this book contributes to that understanding, it will have served its purpose.

Wayne Dennis

Doswell, Va.
January 2, 1972

*Historical Readings in
Developmental Psychology*

WILLIAM CHESELDEN (1688–1752)

An account of some observations made by a young gentleman, who was born blind, or lost his sight so early, that he had no remembrance of ever having seen, and was couched between 13 and 14 years of age (1728)

The history of child psychology is similar to the history of science in general. To most persons, the ordinary course of events requires no explanation. The usual is as things are and should be. If the sun and moon shine, no one asks that they be investigated. But an eclipse attracts attention, and astronomers are asked to explain it. Similarly, a volcano attracts more attention than erosion. In human life, too, the unusual was the first to be described.
 The observation of child behavior began long before there were psychologists. The early observations often were made by physicians who came in contact with children in their practice of medicine. Usually they were concerned with some type of what we now call "exceptional children" and their reports dealt with individual cases, including cases of blindness.
 Blindness is not rare. In ancient and medieval times, blindness caused by injury or disease was taken for granted, and was considered incurable. But for a child to be born blind was and is a rare event. Such cases are often due to a condition described by the word cataracts.
 This term refers to a condition in which the lenses of the eyes are semi-opaque. The appearance of the pupils suggests the whiteness or turbulence of cascading water, hence the name. When this condition is fully developed, the lenses admit some light, but do not permit clear vision.

When the cataractous condition is present at birth, it is referred to as congenital cataract.

At some time in history, it is not known just when, it was discovered that cataractous lenses could be removed. When the person was given spectacles, moderately clear vision was attained. In the case of congenital cataracts this meant that a person might achieve his first useful vision when several years of age, or even as an adult. This situation seems to provide the possibility of determining the extent to which visual perception is learned or innate.

Naturally this near-miraculous medical cure claimed the attention of philosophers as well as of the surgeons. What does the world look like to one who sees for the first time? Does he recognize by sight anything he formerly knew only by other senses? Does he have to learn to see?

William Cheselden, a famous British surgeon in his day, was not the first to remove congenitally cataractous lenses, but he was the first to publish a description of the experiences of a patient. His account appeared in the Philosophical Transactions of the Royal Society of London in 1728 on pages 447–451, which is reproduced here in its entirety.

In his first sentence, Cheselden speaks of "ripe cataracts." By this phrase he is referring to the fact that there is a progressive increase in the opaqueness of the lenses. Hence, unless the eyes are carefully examined at birth, it is not known whether or not a period of good vision occurred before eyesight became seriously obscured by cataracts. This is one of the uncertainties often associated with the study of these cases.

The obscurity produced by cataractous lenses may be removed in several ways. Cheselden used "couching," which refers to freeing the lens and pushing it into the eye below the line of sight.

Cheselden's operation was performed long before the advent of local and general anesthesia. He does not refer to the difficulty of performing such operations, but a description of such difficulties occurs in selection 6.

Since Cheselden's account of his patient's experiences, many other such case reports have appeared, usually in medical journals and usually written by surgeons. In general they corroborate Cheselden's report, except that no other patient has reported that immediately after his bandages were removed, he thought that all objects he saw touched his eyes. It is likely that, unaccustomed to visual terms, this was an inaccurate report on his part.

The reaction of the subject, whose name is not given, to his first sight of a Negro is mentioned in the last sentence of paragraph one of this selection. Before this, in his brief visual experience, he had seen only whites. For comparative purposes, the description by Kidd (selection 23) of African children's emotional response to their first views of a white man should be consulted. Selection 36, "On the nature of fear" by Hebb deals with the general phenomenon of reaction to the strange.

In populous countries many children with congenital cataracts are born each year. At the present time the cataractous lenses are usually removed before two years of age. Since the operation is now "routine," and since two-year-olds cannot give reports on their experiences, few reports of these cases have appeared recently. But the determination of the after effects of varying periods of early blindness is potentially an important topic for research today.

The most extensive survey of case reports of vision after operations for congenital cataracts was published by a German psychologist, Marius Von Senden, in German in 1932 as Raum-und Gestalt auffassung bei Operierten Blindgeborenen. *It was published in English, with some revisions and additions, as* Space and Sight *(The Free Press, 1961).*

Though we say of the gentleman that he was blind, as we do of all people who have ripe cataracts, yet they are never so blind from that cause, but they can discern day from night; and for the most part in a strong light, distinguish black, white and scarlet; but they cannot perceive the shape of anything; for the light by which these perceptions are made, being let in obliquely through the aqueous humor, or the anterior surface of the chrystalline (by which the rays cannot be brought into a focus upon the retina) they can discern in no other manner, than a sound eye can through a glass of broken jelly, where a great variety of surfaces so differently refract the light, that the several distinct pencils of rays cannot be collected by the eye into their proper foci; wherefore the shape of an object in such a case, cannot be at all discerned, though the color may. And thus it was with this young gentleman, who though he knew these colors asunder in a good light, yet when he saw them after he was couched, the faint ideas he had of them before, were not sufficient for him to know them afterwards; and therefore he did not think them the same, which he had before known by those names. Now scarlet he thought the most beautiful of all colors, and of others the most gay were the most pleasing, whereas the first time he saw black, it gave him great uneasiness, yet after a little time he was reconciled to it; but some months after, seeing a Negro woman, he was struck with great horror at the sight.

When he first saw, he was so far from making any judgment about distances, that he thought all objects whatever touched his eyes, (as he expressed it) as what he felt, did his skin; and thought no objects so agreeable as those which were smooth and regular, though he could form no judgment of their shape, or guess what it was in any object that was pleasing to him. He knew not the shape of anything, nor any one thing from another, however different in shape, or magnitude; but upon being told what things were, whose form he before knew from feeling, he would carefully observe, that he might know them again; but having too many objects to learn at once, he forgot many of them; and (as he said) at first he learned to know, and again forgot a thousand things in a day. One particular only (though it may appear trifling) I will relate; having often forgot which was the cat, and which the dog, he was ashamed to talk; but catching the cat (which he knew by feeling) he observed to look at her steadfastly, and then setting her down, said, so puss! I shall know you another time. He was very much surprised, that those things which he had liked best, did not appear most agreeable to his eyes, expecting those persons would appear most beautiful that he loved most, and such things to be most agreeable to his sight that were so to his taste. We thought he soon knew what pictures represented, which were shown to him, but we found afterwards we were mistaken; for about two months after he was couched, he discovered at once, they represented solid bodies; when to that time he considered them only as colored planes, or surfaces diversified with variety of paint; but even then he was no less surprised, expecting the pictures would feel like the things they represented, and was amazed when he found those parts, which by their light and shadow appeared now round and uneven, felt only flat like the rest; and asked which was the lying sense, feeling, or seeing?

Being shown his father's picture in a locket of his mother's watch, and told what it was, he acknowledged a likeness, but was vastly surprised; asking, how it could be, that a large face could be expressed in so little room, saying, it should have seemed as impossible to him, as to put a bushel of anything into a pint.

At first, he could bear but very little sight, and the things he saw, he thought extremely large; but upon seeing things larger, those first seen he conceived less, never being able to imagine any lines beyond the bounds he saw; the room he was in he said he knew to be but part of the house, yet he could not conceive that the whole house could look bigger. Before he was couched, he expected little advantage from seeing worth undergoing an operation for, except reading and writing; for he said, he thought he could have no more pleasure in walking abroad than he had in the garden, which he could do safely and readily. And even blindness he observed, has this advantage, that he could go anywhere in the dark much better than those who can see; and after he had seen, he did not soon lose this quality, nor desire a light to go about the house in the night. He said every new object was a new delight, to express it; but his gratitude to his operator he could not conceal, never seeing him for some time without tears of joy in his eyes, and other marks of affection; and if he did not happen to come at any time when he was expected, he would be so grieved, that he could not forbear crying at his disappointment. A year after first seeing, being carried upon Epsom Downs, and observing a large prospect, he was exceedingly delighted with it, and called it a new kind of seeing. And now being lately couched of his other eye, he says, that objects at first appeared large to this eye, but not so large as they did at first to the other; and looking upon the same object with both eyes, he thought it looked about twice as large as with the first couched eye only, but not double, that we can anyways discover.

2

DAINES BARRINGTON (1727–1800)

Account of a very remarkable young musician (1770)

Here is another early case study of an exceptional child, in this case a musical genius, Mozart.

Mozart's subsequent career is so well-known that it need not be related here. Barrington, who wrote the report, was an English gentleman, scholar and lawyer. This account, republished in full, appeared in the Philosophical Transactions of the Royal Society of London, *in 1770, pages 54–64. This, the same journal in which Cheselden published, was the only British journal of science for many years.*

Another account of Mozart's childhood will be found in Early Mental Traits of Three Hundred Geniuses *(1926) by Catherine M. Cox, pages 592–594. In Cox's study Mozart's IQ in childhood was estimated to have been 150. It was not lower when he was an adult. Mozart died at age 35.*

If I was to send you a well attested account of a boy who measured seven feet in height, when he was not more than eight years of age, it might be considered as not undeserving the notice of the Royal Society.

The instance which I now desire you to communicate to that learned body, of as early an exertion of most extraordinary musical talents, seems perhaps equally to claim their attention.

Joannes Chrysostomus Wolfgangus Theophilus Mozart, was born at Saltzbourg in Bavaria, on the 17th of January, 1756.

I have been informed by a most able musician and composer, that he frequently saw him at Vienna, when he was little more than four years of age.

By this time he not only was capable of executing lessons on his favorite instrument, the harpsichord, but composed some in an easy style and taste, which were much approved of.

His extraordinary musical talents soon reached the ears of the present empress dowager, who used to place him upon her knees while he played on the harpsichord.

This notice taken of him by so great a personage, together with a certain consciousness of his most singular abilities, had much emboldened the little musician. Being therefore the next year at one of the German courts, where the elector encouraged him, by saying, that he had nothing to fear from his august presence; little Mozart immediately sat down with great confidence to his harpsichord, informing his highness that he had played before the empress.

At seven years of age his father carried him to Paris, where he so distinguished himself by his compositions that an engraving was made of him.

Upon leaving Paris, he came over to England, where he continued more than a year. As during this time I was witness of his most extraordinary abilities as a musician, both at some public concerts, and likewise by having been alone with him for a considerable time at his father's house; I send you the following account, amazing and incredible as it may appear.

I carried to him a manuscript duet, which was composed by an English gentleman to some favorite words in Metastasio's opera of Demosoonte.

The whole score was in five parts, viz. accompaniments for a first and second violin, the two vocal parts, and a bass.

I shall here likewise mention, that the parts for the first and second voice were written in what the Italians style the contralto cleff; the reason for taking notice of which particular will appear hereafter.

My intention in carrying with me this manuscript composition, was to have an irrefragable proof of his abilities, as a player at sight, it being absolutely impossible that he could have ever seen the music before.

The score was no sooner put upon his desk, than he began to play the symphony in a most masterly manner, as well as in the time and style which corresponded with the intention of the composer.

I mention this circumstance, because the greatest masters often fail in these particulars on the first trial.

The symphony ended, he took the upper part, leaving the under one to his father.

His voice in the tone of it was thin and infantile, but nothing could exceed the masterly manner in which he sung.

His father, who took the under part in this duet, was once or twice out, though the passages were not more difficult than those in the upper one; on which occasions the son looked back with some anger, pointing out to him his mistakes, and setting him right.

He not only however did complete justice to the duet, by singing his own part in the truest taste, and with the greatest precision; he also threw in the accompaniments of the two violins, wherever they were most necessary, and produced the best effects.

It is well known that none but the most capital musicians are capable of accompanying in this superior style.

As many of those who may be present, when this letter may have the honor of being read before the society, may not possibly be acquainted with the difficulty of playing thus from a musical score, I will endeavor to explain it by the most similar comparison I can think of.

I must at the same time admit that the illustration will fail in one particular, as the voice in reading cannot comprehend more than what is contained in a single line. I must suppose, however, that the reader's eye, by habit and quickness, may take in other lines, though the voice cannot articulate them, as the musician accompanies the words of an air by his harpsichord.

Let it be imagined, therefore, that a child of eight years old was directed to read five lines at once, in four of which the letters of the alphabet were to have different powers.

For example, in the first line A, to have its common powers.

In the second that of B.

In the third of C.

In the fourth of D.

Let it be conceived also, that the lines so composed of characters, with different powers, are not ranged so as to be read at all times one exactly under the other, but often in a desultory manner.

Suppose then, a capital speech in Shakespeare never seen before, and yet read by a child of eight years old, with all the pathetic energy of a Garrick.

Let it be conceived likewise, that the same child is reading, with a glance of his eye, three different comments on this speech tending to its illustration; and that one comment is written in Greek, the second in Hebrew, and the third in Etruscan characters.

Let it be also supposed, that by different signs he could point out which comment is most material upon every word; and sometimes that perhaps all three are so, at others only two of them.

When all this is conceived, it will convey some idea of what this boy was capable of, in singing such a duet at sight in a masterly manner from the score, throwing it at the same time all its proper accompaniments.

When he had finished the duet, he expressed himself highly in its approbation, asking with some eagerness whether I had brought any more such music.

Having been informed, however, that he was often visited with musical ideas, to which, even in the midst of the night, he would give utterance, on his harpsichord; I told his father that I should be glad to hear some of his extemporary compositions.

The father shook his head at this, saying that it depended entirely upon his being as it were musically inspired, but that I might ask him whether he was in humor for such a composition.

Happening to know that little Mozart was much taken notice of by Manzoli, the famous singer, who came over to England in 1764, I said to the boy, that I should be glad to hear an extemporary love song such as his friend Manzoli might choose in an opera.

The boy on this (who continued to it at his harpsichord) looked back with much archness, and immediately began five or six lines of a jargon recitative proper to introduce a love song.

He then played a symphony which might correspond with an air composed to the single word, *Assetto.*

It had a first and second part, which, together with the symphonies, was of the length that opera songs generally last; if this extemporary composition was not amazingly capital, yet it was really above mediocrity, and showed most extraordinary readiness of invention.

Finding that he was in humor, and as it were inspired, I then desired him to compose a Song of Rage, such as might be proper for the opera stage.

The boy again looked back with much archness, and began five or six lines of a jargon recitative proper to precede a song of anger.

This lasted also about the same time with the song of love; and in the middle of it, he had worked himself up to such a pitch, that he beat his harpsichord like a person possessed, rising sometimes in his chair.

The word he pitched upon for this second extemporary composition was, Persido.

After this he played a difficult lesson, which he had finished a day or two before; his execution was amazing, considering that his little fingers could scarcely reach a fifth on the harpsichord.

His astonishing readiness, however, did not arise merely from great practice; he had a thorough knowledge of the fundamental principles of composition, as, upon producing a treble he immediately wrote a bass under it, which when tried had a very good effect.

He was also a great master of modulation, and his transitions from one key to another were excessively natural and judicious; he practised in this manner for a considerable time with an handkerchief over the keys of the harpsichord.

The facts which I have been mentioning I was myself an eye witness of, to which I must add that I have been informed by two or three able musicians, when Bach the celebrated composer had begun a fugue and left off abruptly, that little Mozart hath immediately taken it up, and worked it after a most masterly manner.

Witness as I was myself of most of these extraordinary facts, I must own that I could not help suspecting his father imposed with regard to the real age of the boy, though he had not only a most childish appearance but likewise had all the actions of that stage of life.

For example, while he was playing to me, a favorite cat came in, upon which he immediately left his harpsichord, nor could we bring him back for a considerable time.

He would also sometimes run about the room with a stick between his legs by way of a horse.

I found likewise that most of the London musicians were of the same opinion with regard to his age, not believing it possible that a child of so tender years could surpass most of the masters in that science.

I have therefore for a considerable time made the best inquiries I was able from some of the German musicians resident in London, but could never receive any further information than that he was born near Saltzbourg, till I was so fortunate as to procure an extract from the register of that place, through his excellence Count Haslang.

It appears from this extract, that Mozart's father did not impose with regard to his age when he was in England, for it was in June, 1765, that I was witness to what I have above related, when the boy was only eight years and five months old.

I have made frequent inquiries with regard to this very extraordinary genius since he left England, and was told last summer, that he was then at Saltzbourg, where he had composed several oratorios, which were much admired.

I am also informed, that the prince of Saltzbourg, not crediting that such masterly compositions were really those of a child, shut him up for a week during which he was not permitted to see any one, and was left only with music paper, and the words of an oratorio.

During this short time he composed a very capital oratorio, which was most highly approved of upon being performed.

Having stated the above mentioned proofs of Mozart's genius, when of almost an infantile age, it may not be improper perhaps to compare them with what hath been well attested with regard to other instances of the same sort.

Amongst these, John Barratier hath been most particularly distinguished, who is said to have understood Latin when he was but four years old, Hebrew when six, and three other languages at the age of nine.

This same prodigy of philological learning also translated the travels of Rabbi Benjamin when eleven years old, accompanying his version with notes and dissertations. Before his death, which happened under the age of twenty, Barratier seems to have astonished Germany with his amazing extent of learning; and it need not be said, that its increase in such a soil, from year to year, is commonly amazing.

Mozart, however, is not now much more than thirteen years of age, and it is not therefore necessary to carry my comparison further.

The Rev. Mr. Manwaring (in his *Memoirs of Handel*) hath given us a still more apposite instance, and in the same science.

This great musician began to play on the clavichord when he was but seven years of age, and is said to have composed some church services when he was only nine years old, as also the opera of Almeris, when he did not exceed fourteen.

Mr. Manwaring likewise mentions that Handel, when very young, was struck sometimes while in bed with musical ideas, and that, like Mozart, he used to try their effect immediately on a spinnet, which was in his bedchamber.

I am the more glad to state this short comparison between these two early prodigies in music, as it may be hoped that little Mozart may possibly attain to the same advanced years as Handel, contrary to the common observation that such *ingenia praecocia* are generally short lived.

I think I may say without prejudice to the memory of this great composer that the scale most clearly preponderates on the side of Mozart in this comparison, as I have already stated that he was a composer when he did not much exceed the age of four.

3

DIETRICH TIEDEMANN (1748–1803)

Observations on the mental development of a child (1787)

The two preceding selections were studies of exceptional children: a boy born blind who at age 13 was enabled to see and a musical genius.

In the case reported in the present selection, for the first time in human history, someone thought it worthwhile to record and publish a record of the behavioral development of a normal child. In a sense, this publication represents the beginning of normal child psychology.

The subject was a son, the first child of a German historian of philosophy. He made observations on the development of his son from birth to the age of about two and one-half years. Then, as he says in his last paragraph, "Other business prevented me from their continuation." He refers to his second child, a daughter, but his references to her are concerned only with her impact upon her brother.

It is a careful naturalistic description, unprejudiced by a theoretical bias. While Tiedemann was an educated and highly intelligent man, he was probably somewhat naive in respect to child development at the time he began the observation of his first child. Yet all of his observations have been replicated by subsequent observers, many of whom were unacquainted with Tiedemann's monograph.

Many aspects of child behavior mentioned by Tiedemann have become areas of research for present-day workers. If one translates Tiedemann into the current psychologese, he sounds most modern. Child behavior is much the same today as it was in 1781–1783, but a professional language has been developed around it which sometimes obscures the similarities.

For the convenience of the reader, we have numbered each of Tiedemann's paragraphs. Using these numbers we will indicate many respects in which Tiedemann on the basis of one child anticipated many modern researches and interpretations. Relevant paragraphs will be denoted by number.

The following list is not complete but it may serve to show how much Tiedemann saw:

Behavioral development follows a sequence which is much the same for all children, but children differ in the rate at which they progress through the sequence. This is most explicitly stated in (2) but is implicit throughout the monograph.

The methods by which food can be taken at birth are variable and are affected by experience (3). Tiedemann is probably the first to refer to cup feeding (3), to the fact that cup feeding (and other forms of non-sucking ingestion) reduces sucking responses (3) and that the reception of food via sucking reinforces sucking (3).

Reference is made to the grasp reflex (6) and the sequence by which this reflex eventuates into intentional and precise prehension is described (12,14,15,17).

Reaction to restraint (5) fear of falling (16) and the causes of laughter (11,14) are dealt with.

It is indicated that the child's interest in the visual and auditory environment (4) is not dependent upon organic reinforcement.

Variability and novelty in stimuli is observed to be an important aspect of their effectiveness (14,17,22,27,33). For example, (20) when not hungry, the child preferred to be with the caretaker who took him for walks rather than with his mother who breast-fed him.

Operant conditioning, in different words, was referred to, and it was noted that the reinforcement of crying increased the frequency of the response (13).

The animistic and anthropomorphic aspects of the child's thinking are illustrated (43,44), thus anticipating parts of Piaget's Child's Conception of the World *(1929) by 142 years.*

Several developmental items of behavior which are now standard items in developmental scales were first recorded by Tiedemann. They are: visual pursuit (4), various forms of prehension (6,12,14,15,17), imitates a sound (24), executes commands (28), points to familiar objects in pictures (31), points to parts of own body when requested (36), reaction to mirror (32), names objects (35), uses two-word sentences (36), uses three-word sentences (40). The rank order correlation between the dates of appearance of these items in Tiedemann's record and their placement in current infant scales is quite high.

Tiedemann's small monograph was published in German in 1787. Later it was translated into French. The present and only English version was prepared by Carl Murchison and Susanne Langer, and was published in the Journal of Genetic Psychology *34 (1927): 205–230. It is reprinted here in full by permission of Powell Murchison editor of the* Journal Press.

Though several "baby biographies" intervened, no fuller account of the behavioral development of an individual child was published until the advent of Preyer's two volumes in 1882 (see selection 13).

1. The fact that experience and practice teach us to use our senses and perceive correctly has been proved by Cheselden's blind man; observations on persons who were found in forests, speechless, reared by animals, have shown that the mental faculties develop slowly, successively, and confusedly. Yet that part of mental philosophy which purports to teach the development of the mind's powers, important though it be both for pedagogy and for a rightful understanding of the soul, has been little pursued; undoubtedly for the reason that there is a dearth of exact and sufficiently numerous observations upon children's souls. Whatever I have had opportunity to remark in this matter, that I will relate, not as though I considered it sufficient and complete, but in order to encourage as well as possible, by my example, keener and more conscientious observers to impart their own material and rectify mine. There is among men a great deal of information which is therefore not disseminated and at the disposal of those who could elaborate it, because its possessor knows not its importance, and regards it as not worthy of any public exhibition.

2. The boy with whom the following monograph deals was born August 23, 1781; which fact is stated for this reason, that the determination of time-periods is of fundamental importance in the progress of development and just this matter has been least observed. I grant that what has here been observed cannot be taken as a general law, since children, just like adults, progress variously, the one with speed, the other more slowly; but at least it informs us of *one* among the possible rates of progress, and allows us to put some determination upon the previously indefinite subject. When we shall have several such records it will be possible by means of comparison to strike an average for the common order of nature.

3. It is a matter of common knowledge that children immediately after birth, and thereafter always upon awaking, turn their eyes to the light, a proof that light makes upon them a pleasing impression; a pleasure no longer observed by adults because habit and more absorbing impressions have made it imperceptible. Yet we can experience it by attention to the effect that is wrought upon the soul by a sunbeam descending through clouds in a stormy sky. On the day after his birth, when the nurse placed her finger in the boy's mouth, he sucked at it, but not continuously, only in a smacking fashion. When, however, a sweet, tied in a cloth, was placed in his mouth, he sucked continuously; a proof I think, that sucking is not instinctive, but acquired. The first smacking action of the lips is a mechanical motion of the mouth, actuated by the feeling of hunger and thirst, combined with the stimulation of the glands that is caused by the presence of a foreign body; this is not to be called sucking. But as soon as it has been understood that this motion has brought to the tongue a new sensation which alleviates the former uneasiness, the motion is increased, the smacking becomes a genuine sucking, as the organs gradually assume the postures required for this purpose. The following may serve as corroboration: when children who have never sucked are relieved of hunger and thirst by the administration of liquids, then they refuse thereafter to suck, and it is hard to accustom them to draw at the breast; undoubtedly because they know not the proper use of lips and tongue,

and since they are not forced by hunger, which they have other means of appeasing, they will not inconvenience themselves by any attempt.

4. The eyes [of the infant] were now moved in all directions, not unsteadily, but from the first as though they were in search of objects, and they rested first upon moving objects. And indeed all moving objects, because they produce in us constant variation and modification, attract our senses, so that merely sensuous persons find therein the greatest entertainment. Before reflection and contemplation, through inward autonomous motion, have found occupation also with inert objects, these are little observed; therefore such things as are in motion must primarily attract the childish mind. Here I think we can trace human nature even to the infant soul. The animal observes only what serves his physical needs, being unable to take interest in aught else; wherefore one is not apt to see animals follow with their eyes things that are not in relation to their bodily wants. But man, being ordained for higher purposes, seeks from the beginning to expand his ideas without regard to his physical needs, and finds entertainment even where he is not driven by sensuous desires. The reason probably lies in nothing else than the higher degree of activity, and the autonomic nature of that activity, which looks continually for occupation and is alert even after the physical desires are satisfied.

5. The boy liked to be free. Reluctantly and with evident repulsion he would let himself be swaddled; but in the motion of his limbs one could detect no purpose, nothing save, perhaps, a sense of pain which put the body into involuntary and unintended motion. Motion of the body usually reduces pain because it distracts the attention from the perception of it. In the very mechanism of the body there lies a tendency to move as soon as we experience a lively pain, and it is in accordance with this reflex that children in pain move their bodies unintentionally. Partly for this reason, and partly because motion affords occupation and entertainment, children love to be free, and hate to be swaddled. Besides pain, there are other causes of instinctive motion: accumulation of blood and secretions in certain places, free circulation of the secretions generally, some stimuli in certain parts of the body which arouse all dark sensations and involuntary desires to action.

6. Are, then, all the movements of children at this age unintentional? Or could there already be some purpose and acquired knowledge? One circumstance I think, indicates that even at such an early stage some learning process may occur. The mother was yet unable to offer the child the food which nature intended for him; artificial feeding was so far avoided for the reason mentioned above, so he had to suffer some want, and, as he was healthy, some hunger. For relief he sought to put his own and, if possible, other people's fingers into his mouth in order to suck them, though indeed he did not find his mouth save after many vain attempts. Herein methinks we can discern something learned, something intentional. From experience the child already knew that when something enters the mouth, the sensation of hunger is reduced. These two ideas were already associated. Also he had learned even then to distinguish that part of his own body where hunger and thirst are chiefly perceived, and sought to

direct his hands thereto, though through lack of conception of his own face, as also inexperience in the use of arms and hands, he could not accurately locate the place. He had no idea as yet of purposely grasping anything; grasping occurred only by instinctive reflex, by which the fingers, like the leaves or flowers of certain sensitive plants, contract when their inner surfaces are touched by a foreign object.

7. Tickling sensations were not yet present. When the soles of the feet were gently touched, the feet were withdrawn but without any tendency to laughter. Neither could one detect in his eyes or the motion of his mouth anything that might have related to pleasure or to pain. Thus his impressions were not yet differentiated; everything that caused an impression was apprehended only under the general character of attraction or repulsion, without distinction of the specific sorts of pleasure and displeasure. Even the special sensations of taste, which must certainly have been the first in evidence, were not yet distinguished, and even less, of course, those of smell. This appeared conclusively on August 25th. On account of an indisposition the boy was given a medicine of unpleasant taste and pungent odor; he took it without any sign of objection, like his usual food. Thus even our common and most plainly distinguishable sensations require practice and comparison before they are separated and clearly conceived.

8. On August 28th he showed the first sign of laughing, but without special provocation, indeed without a sensation of pleasure, merely because his mechanism would have it so. In sleep children do often assume this expression, or when they are about to fall asleep, therefore without relevant thoughts and feelings. Likewise young children will often make other motion in their sleep, or utter sounds, as though they were dreaming, howbeit very probably they do not dream, but stir only by bodily reaction. I at least have observed nothing from which one could infer with any confidence the existence of ideas of non-present objects; even sensory association does not appear until later. Maids, nurses, and others usually take this phenomenon for dreaming; but they do not distinguish the mechanical from mental activity, and ascribe to the latter whatever resembles it, or is usually due to it in the case of adults.

9. On the 5th of September, i.e., thirteen days after his birth, the boy showed some traces of acquired ideas, in clearer sensations and affections of his soul. Some medicines were now unwillingly taken, with evident reluctance, yes, were even spewn forth again, but not immediately, rather upon being tasted several times. So now the boy distinguished the taste of medicines from that of his regular food, and could foretell, either by smell or by the manner of feeding, whether something unpleasant or his nourishment was to be given him. Yet this distinction was still uncertain, for again the physic was taken without objection. In his eyes and expressions one could now detect signs of pain and pleasure; heretofore the eyes had not spoken, the mouth known no contortion but for crying. Previously all objects had received the same attention; now one could see continued attention given to those who spoke to him, also his crying could be somewhat hushed by soothing speech. Before, he had cried only for pain, now

he wept when he found it uncomfortable to let himself be handled. All this proves the presence of some gathered ideas, recognition of beings that were human like himself, and preciser discretion between sensations. The first quarter year is popularly known as the age of stupor, and this is correct if it means only that thereafter appear the clearest evidences of human sensations and ideas; wrong, however, if it is to imply that within this period there be no such evidence whatever.

10. On September 10th all this was more definitely remarked, and with a few novel conditions. If, when he was crying, the boy was laid upon his side in the position of nursing, or if he felt a soft hand upon his face, he subsided and sought the breasts. Here the association of ideas is visible: the feeling of the particular posture or of the soft hand awakened the image of nursing and of the breasts; so he had formed thereof a definite image, that is to say, he had retained a few traces of previous impressions, which were revived upon receiving a proper sensory stimulus, and through the inner mental powers were transformed into images again. Thus it appeared he had now so far distinguished his sensory impressions that he could imagine them separately. But of his own body and of distances he had as yet very faulty conceptions, if any. Faulty ones, because if now for short periods his hands were released from their swathings, he beat and scratched himself painfully, so he plainly could not distinguish his own body from others, nor the parts thereof from one another. None at all, for of distance he knew nothing, else he would not, even after several efforts, have struck his own face. One may also gather from this that he little knew how to control his limbs, much less to give their motions the required amount of force. Moreover, one could see in the motions of his hands no intention, save possibly that in the event of hunger they were placed in the mouth, which, however, was due more to mechanical reflex and some association of ideas than to any premeditated purpose. The first bodily movements are merely mechanical, according to physical stimulations; from this the mind obtains ideas of motions to be performed with the limbs; then desires awaken, which by the help of association produce intentional actions; experience imparts a knowledge of the various sorts of motion, and teaches us to project our energies into the requisite parts of the body. Only then are we able to move each limb properly according to our purposes.

11. On the 28th of the same month it was observable that the boy did not beat or scratch himself with his hands as frequently as before; so it seemed that painful, oft repeated experience had taught him to draw some distinction between himself and foreign bodies, and to recognize some distances. This corroborates what Cheselden observed upon his blind man, that sight alone does not teach us a knowledge of distances, since all objects appear as though lying directly upon the eye; so that touch must aid sight in forming a conception of external and remote bodies. But I gravely doubt whether children could not earlier acquire knowledge of distances and a better use of the hands. In that we bind their hands from the beginning in swathings, we undoubtedly hinder them from gaining through movement a much earlier conception of their own bodies and of

external objects. At this time, also, the period of sleeping diminished. As a matter of common knowledge, healthy children in earliest infancy sleep almost all day, awaking only from the pangs of hunger. This need of sleep is gradually decreased, so that even when one would lull them to sleep, they will not come to rest. Why is this? From purely physical causes, or from increased activity of the soul? The former alternative is unlikely. For animals, if they have abundance of food, so that they are not moved to action by hunger and thirst, sleep the livelong day. The dog, commonly so alert, lies calmly in his corner when no physical need spurs him to action. Caged birds, indeed, do not sleep by day, but their food is of such a nature that they can partake of it only by particles, and can never become perfectly satiated; their digestion, too, appears to be more rapid. Not so the human being and the child. Both may assuage their hunger at once and for several hours to come. So the reduction of sleep must rise from increased activity of the soul. The more the young mind gathers ideas, the more it is stirred to action, the less will it permit the body to rest. Another proof of the superior original activity of the human soul! At this time also one could note the first smiles of pleasure, for by talking to the boy or performing all sorts of mimicry one could move him to smile. Just why he took pleasure in these things cannot well be determined. Was it merely the variety of motions, or the dawning of sympathies, or the unexpectedness of gestures in rapid succession, or perhaps all this together? That sympathy played no small part therein seems evident from the following: if one spoke to the boy, he tried also to produce sounds, simple ones indeed, without articulation, but none the less responsive. The impulse to imitation develops very early and seems to have its original source in an instinct [Mechanismus] which is aided by the association of ideas. Whenever we entertain a lively image and with rapt attention watch the actions of someone else, we cannot refrain from imitating them according to our powers, and we feel a strong impulse to do precisely the same thing; an impulse oft hard to resist, which reflection must hold in check. This is partly grounded in the system itself, since the organs which function in the production of a lively image assume just the position required that they may perform their office; partly also in the association of ideas, since the idea of an action is directly accompanied by that action itself, and is its first beginning. In this way infants who have already learned to produce sounds and to employ the vocal organs are involuntarily led to the imitation of sounds. And herein lies the first source of sympathy; for by looking upon others, who are stirred by some emotion, the soul projects itself into the same situation, wherein it has once experienced that feeling, and thereby the old emotion itself is renewed. Thus though the boy, who had already formed some ideas of pleasant and unpleasant sensations, might not yet have known or conceived of their expression in the human physiognomy, yet he was moved to smiles by a cheerful and pleasant look, just because the sight of it created in him the circumstances proper to such emotion. For between expression and emotion there is a natural connection, wherefore the same feeling is always accompanied by the same expression, and likewise any expression, even though we may not have met with it before, will at once awaken within us its proper feeling, provided this feeling has at some time entered our experience. The rapid change of expressions was also conducive to the boy's smile. Young children laugh at everything that is sudden and subject to unexpected change, a proof that matters of surprise, as long as they do not produce any terror, make a pleasing impression.

12. He now began to distinguish precisely and positively certain sensations, especially those of taste; for on October 2nd he took his medicine with obvious repulsion every time. He learned also to distinguish external objects from himself, which fact appeared from his first attempts to reach for things, expressed by stretching forth the hands and inclining his entire body. But he knew not as yet the correct use of his fingers. If indeed he grasped something, it was more by chance than by successful attempt, because the object came to lie between his fingers so that it could be grasped. How much practice, indeed, and vain effort, is required even for those motions which we consider most facile and well-nigh instinctive! The desire of the mind to make ideas of its sensations was now clearly apparent. Heretofore no object had long held his attention, and any new phenomenon had served at once to distract him; but now his gaze followed after things quite steadily, and in his eyes one could read an inner desire to comprehend what he saw.

13. By October 19th he had ceased entirely to beat and scratch his face with his hands, so he had differentiated completely between his body and other objects. Distances, at least in the case of very nearby objects, had become known to him, and he had learned some control of his arms and hands. The impulse to gather ideas became more evident, for only new, unfamiliar objects attracted his eyes for a prolonged period. Also his inner appreciation of the pleasure afforded by his own activity developed visibly, and was plainly shown by the extreme pleasure with which he viewed new objects especially such as were in motion. He made more effort to observe the gestures of persons addressing him in order to learn their attitude toward him, and his partial understanding of them was already shown through the fact that gentle words and a compassionate voice could hush his passion. Children learn quickly from daily experience what influence other persons have upon them; it is not surprising then that they pay particular attention to other people to learn their disposition. So far he had expressed his displeasure in things only by crying and resisting, but had not yet employed his own strength in order to remove the object perforce. Now that he began to feel his powers, and could more clearly recognize the objects of his displeasure, perhaps also felt more keenly, he exhibited this antagonistic force plainly in the form of temper. To this was added the fact that he now had learned from experience how many unpleasant things were done to him by human agency, and could be altered by violent resistance, a matter of which he had previously had no idea. Children learn very quickly how others are impressed by their crying; at first they increase their crying only with increase of pain, but when they discover that the louder their complaint, the sooner will they be attended, then they cry merely for anger that they are not instantly given

their will. This I deem to be the first starting-point of temper—whereof one part is the great expenditure of energy in resisting the discomfort, coupled with keener appreciation of the latter; the other part, a desire to let others feel the wrong that has been done us, and to frighten them by awful sounds and contortions. This is why children, before they have learned that some of their discomforts are caused by other people, send forth only pitiable cries, but as soon as they have learned to hold others accountable utter embittered shrieks. So was it with this boy. If his weeping did not meet with immediate response, he broke into angry screams.

14. The more exactly the separate sensations are distinguished, the more vividly is each one perceived, and thus the degrees of sensitivity are augmented until they become transformed into emotions. Now the pleasant were given more and more expression, till the first outbursts of joy could be observed. The sight of light, especially in the evening, after a period of darkness, aroused unmistakable joy, where previously it had merely fascinated his attention. So far his expression of content had been a smile; now that the sensations had increased, it was replaced by loud laughter. Consequently variegated rapid motion of his own or another body, as for instance skipping and jumping, was met with hearty laughter. Also he showed the first signs of ticklishness, but this only at the belly, not at the soles of the feet; a proof that this sensation, too, requires comparison and the development of others before it can be appreciated intrinsically, and that the pleasant and the unpleasant cannot at first be felt distinctly and definitely. Now it was on the 10th of November the teeth began to push through the gum. The painful sensation which this caused in his mouth awakened and promoted the development of new ideas and faculties. Heretofore the hands had been employed but little because there was no special occasion to use them; if an object had perchance been seized upon, it was not long retained, since the mere act of grasping affords too little of occupation and amusement. The eyes, which supply the mind with the greatest variety of ever-changing images, were mainly employed. Now that the pain in the mouth craved constant assuaging, the fingers constantly sought the mouth, and not only these, but also anything that fell into his hands was carried thither in order to soothe and counteract the pain by biting. In this way the boy first learned to hold things, but this act was never of long duration; the object he had grasped was soon dropped again. This was, however, the fault of inexperience, not of boredom, for he was immediately ready to seize the thing again. His fingers were not yet under his control; they closed mechanically as yet, and in the same manner opened again although the object was supposed to be retained. Distant things, or such as were not immediately convenient to his hand, he did not attempt to reach; probably he knew not yet from experience that distant things may be fetched hither by the hand, in fact because he had no idea as yet of obtaining things with his hands. As long as children do not know how to bring things toward themselves with their hands, they try to approach the thing they want by bending the whole body forward and stretching forth their arms. This seems to take its origin in the primitive structure of human nature, for whenever there arises in us a

desire for something remote, we feel a tendency to bend the body forward, which entails the posture of holding out our hands. Therefore, when reflection forbids us to seize upon things, we cannot suppress at least that initial gesture.

15. On the 25th of the same month the boy already reached for things which lay directly before him, and began to play with them. The hands had gained more versatility, and he began to note that they, too, could be a source of occupation and of the acquisition of new ideas. At first children do not play with anything. Whatever they do not put into their mouths for purposes of biting or of gaining sensations of taste is immediately discarded; they exercise primarily vision and taste. But as soon as their more practiced vision and the closer integration of sight and touch perceptions reveal to them the fact that their hands are tools for carrying out new ideas—tools which can produce such pleasing motions and bring objects into the range of sight and taste—then they bring the hands into action, and begin to play with given objects. Even so they learn to seize distant objects with their hands, which at first will grasp only what they happen to find. Some of the commoner sensations were by this time fairly well distinguished and had become ideas; and now one could observe more and better examples of association. When held on [his mother's] lap, he would turn toward the breasts, howbeit they were covered; if he saw any one drinking, he would perform a motion with his mouth as though he, too, were tasting something. So it seems he could already recognize another's mouth as the seat of taste-sensations and the means of enjoying food. The sense of touch in his hands had given him the idea of his own mouth, and similarity caused the other idea, that another person's mouth served the same purpose. The first plausible signs of dreaming were now observed, for in his sleep he made sucking motions with his mouth. Probably some stimulus in the stomach or the mouth gave rise to a sense of hunger or thirst, and this in turn excited the sucking motion of the mouth, so that he dreamed he was nursing at the breast.

16. Increasing teething pains augmented his desire for all sorts of things that he might bite upon them; therefore he now began to long for distant things which he might bring to his mouth, as gradually his conceptions of distance evolved more and more, and experience taught him that even remote objects could be brought within his reach. Of course children have at first no idea that something distant can be brought near enough to them, or they approach near enough to it, that they may gratify their desire. The boy did not yet know distinctly that his hands were a means to this end, for he sought to catch distant things with his mouth, not to bring them to his mouth with the aid of his hands. This was on the 29th of November.

On the 30th he first heard piano music, and gave evidence of inordinate delight and happiness. Thus the tones themselves, without any knowledge of melody or of the emotions thereby conveyed, made a pleasant impression.

From that time until December 30th nothing of import was observed, but at that time he showed that he already thought to use his hands in self-preservation. If he was held in arms and then suddenly lowered from a considerable height, he strove to hold himself with his hands, to save himself from falling; and he did not like to be lifted very high. Since he could not possibly have had any conception of falling, his fear was unquestionably a purely mechanical sensation, such as older persons feel at a steep and unaccustomed height, something akin to dizziness. He turned away with evident displeasure from persons clothed in black; it appears, therefore, that black, being the color of darkness, must have an intrinsically disagreeable character, which is also illustrated by the fact that this color is generally donned in observance of untoward events. From habit we gradually become accustomed to this disagreeableness and finally persuade ourselves that it does not exist.

17. During this time the boy had learned the use of his hands to grasp and fetch things. Now he reached for everything, but he sorely lacked practice as yet. Instead of seizing his object immediately he had to extend his arms several times before he touched the correct spot, and having found this, he had to make more than one attempt to bring his fingers into such position that the article could be grasped. Partly were his fingers too unskilled in grasping, partly he knew not yet to make all movements with his hands, to produce at once the one appropriate to his purpose; and in part, also, was it that he had no clear conception of distance and position. Singing always commanded his attention now, and was accompanied with bouncing and waving of the arms as an expression of joy. Whistling, on the other hand, he did not notice, so it was only the tone itself that impressed him. The taste sensations were by this time fairly well differentiated; against a somewhat bitter medicine he rebelled with all his might, whereas he readily accepted wine and other edible things. Moreover, the original activity of the human soul, already somewhat developed, now manifested itself in its characteristic effect, namely, boredom. The absence of all attractive sensations made the boy restless and weepy; anything novel, some little variety or other, immediately satisfied him, even caused him often to forget a severe toothache. He also commenced to exercise the tools of speech by all sorts of sounds, without being incited to do so; but he attempted no imitation as yet, though the opportunity was offered him, probably because he had no clear idea as yet of the difference between sounds, especially between articulate ones, and had no conscious control over his speech-organs. Apparently children practice for a long time before they can produce simple inarticulate sounds and easy articulations, in order to gain a clear conception thereof before they attempt to repeat them [after their elders]; and the speech-organs, just like the hands, must be prepared by long rehearsal for the production of sounds previously imagined or exampled.

18. On December 31st it was observed that the boy, when hearing a sound, always turned his face in the direction whence it came; so he had already learned to tell what he heard through the right ear, and what through the left, had also accustomed himself to think of spaces in some

sort of relation to his body. This shows how the mind labors to discover even very fine distinctions, and such as are based almost entirely upon comparison.

19. His activity now visibly increased; as long as he was awake, his arms and legs were in constant motion; the mind also demanded perpetual entertainment, and he became restless as soon as this demand was not satisfied. He was now perfectly acquainted with the breast and showed signs of unmistakable joy at the sight of it. This was noted on January 16, 1782.

20. On January 26th his desire for knowledge was manifested even more clearly. Whenever the weather permitted, his nurse took him out upon the streets, which gave him inordinate pleasure and a great desire for this sort of diversion, despite the cold air. Therefore, he was loathe to leave his nurse, and even preferred her to his mother except when he was hungry. How quickly ideas become defined and associated, once these processes are begun, was plainly visible now. The boy had quickly observed that to have the nurse wrap his coat about him was a sign of going out; therefore he rejoiced whenever she put the coat upon him, even when he had just been in the act of crying. Also he had soon discovered that the door had to be opened in order to let him go out; so he strained toward the door whenever the nurse approached it, rejoiced when it was opened, and became impatient when it was closed again. Children generally at this age seek to be out of doors if they are well and happy, and hate all confinement, especially a long sojourn in one and the same room. This longing is produced by the pleasure of the open air, and doubtless even more by the variety and multiplicity of objects which afford the soul entertainment and increase of knowledge.

21. So far he had been completely indifferent as to what objects came into his hands. Without the least sign of displeasure he had let himself be deprived of anything that had just served him for a toy. Now, on the 7th of February, he seemed more attached to the things he had once obtained, that is, as long as he did not weary of them, and wept if any plaything was taken from him. Also he could already amuse himself a little while by playing. Heretofore things had only served him to look at, he had not been able to lend them any motion; now that he had learned the use of his hands, his toys served variously for his entertainment so he hated to be deprived of them.

22. On February 10th he showed the first signs of surprise and approval; so far his only expressions of pain, anger, impatience; and pleasure had been crying, writhing, laughing. Now, when he saw something new and delightful, he greeted it with the exclamation "ach!"—the natural sign of admiration. So he could clearly recognize what was new and had a distinct sensation of the novelty. At this time he also commenced to make use of his feet for walking. Whenever he was put upon his feet he gave evidence of joy.

23. Persons, too, he had learned to distinguish, and when he was hungry, sought among all those present to find his mother. Yet he had as yet no perfectly clear image of her, nor could he distinguish by people's

clothing the difference of sex. If a male person happened to hold him in arms when he was hungry, he sought the breast nevertheless. Differences of speaking tone, characteristic of different emotions, especially of disapproval and satisfaction, he had learned to comprehend, for he let himself be silenced by threats.

24. After all manner of exercise in the production of tones, and after the acquisition of some skill in using the speech-organs variously, he commenced, on the 14th of March, to articulate consciously and to repeat sounds. His mother said to him the syllable "Ma"; he gazed attentively at her mouth, and attempted to imitate the syllable. Furthermore, it was observed that when he heard a word easy of pronunciation, his lips would move as he softly repeated it to himself.

25. On April 27th he showed marked evidence of attachment to certain persons, and recognition of them, for the wept when his nurse or his mother was chastised. Also one could see him now perform the most difficult of all the associations of the ideas, that which animals rarely attain, and never of their impulse—the connection of an idea with its verbal symbol. When he was asked, where is this or that common and familiar object, he would point it out with his finger. So he had clear conceptions not only of such objects, but also of articulate sounds, and knew furthermore that these sounds designated those objects or images, i.e., he had associated these very diverse ideas. Therefore, one may safely assume that the higher mental faculties, judgment and comparison, had already commenced to function, and had distinguished ideas that were really very similar. In the case of articulation this power of comparison is particularly necessary. It is well known that the words of a foreign language seem to us at first to be all alike and in no wise distinguishable.

26. The association of ideas became more and more extensive, and gave rise to fairly composite feelings and desires. On the 28th of April, his mother teased him by taking a strange child to her breast; the boy became restless and tried to drag it away, although he had just been nursed. Thus he had not only connected the outward sight impression of nursing with the sensations of taste and the resulting pleasure so that he recognized from the position of the strange child what it was doing, but there was present coincidentally an unpleasant sense of being deprived of something, a feeling that it was his peculiar right to drink at this breast, which caused in him the impulse to remove the stranger and a sort of grudge. Hunger could not have been the motive thereof, as he had just been satisfied.

27. Visible signs of reflection and of the ability to differentiate appeared on May 13th. Whenever he met with anything novel or strange he would point his finger at it to call other people's attention to it, and employed the sound, "ha! ha!". That the pointing as well as the exclamation was addressed to others is apparent from the fact that he was satisfied as soon as people signified that they also had taken note. One may gather from this how deep in human nature lies the desire to reveal ourselves to others, and to feel their participation in anything that strikes our interest. At first reflection is stimulated mechanically through continuous

impressions, especially agreeable ones, to unite with after-sensations [Nachempfindung]; gradually this becomes merged with sensation. As soon as certain ideas have become familiar and associations have been established between them, then all things novel or strange are more quickly remarked, and now the act of awareness takes place even without enduring pleasurable sensations. That is why one cannot detect any trace of reflection in very young infants. Add to this the fact that with the extension of ideas the ambition hereto grows and the soul is ever expectant of new impressions. The boy gave evidence of such ready-made and current ideas in that he always recognized his mother, as also a few other persons, at first sight and at considerable distance.

28. Nothing further was noted until September 9th [1782]; on this day, however, he gave distinct signs of increased conceptions. Beholding a glass of water, he pointed to it, as also to his cradle, when he was weary. So he learned more and more to know those objects which served his physical needs; learned also to make use of his limbs in order to satisfy his wants. His motions, originally mechanical and merely accidental, had gradually left impressions; these united with sensations of his needs, and thus his hands as well as the rest of his body were now employed for the satisfaction of his desires. A few sounds he could already imitate recognizably, without, however, associating them at once with their proper ideas. Certain names of very familiar objects he understood perfectly, so that even in their absence he had the image of them in mind and looked around in order to point them out. Now he learned also to comprehend a few sentences; on the 14th he knew already what was meant by: "Make a bow," "Swat the fly," which he always accompanied by the appropriate motions.

29. Of the fact that bodies fall to earth from a height, and of full and empty spaces, he had as yet no conception. On the 14th of October he still attempted to leap from every elevation, and several times he dropped his rusk directly to the ground with the intention of dipping it. A higher degree of activity and autonomy of the human soul was clearly visible on the 9th of November. Whenever he had performed an action for the first time, given his toys a special motion or anything of the sort, he was distinctly pleased and took pleasure in repeating it. Children, in fact, are generally pleased whenever they can do for themselves what theretofore they had to let others do for them. That is why they are so eager to take their food with their own hands, and are unwilling to let themselves be dressed, washed, or in any way handled by others.

30. Sympathy and self-love had gradually developed into a sense of honor. On the 10th of November he wept when his hand, which he liked to give as a sign of affection, was declined; and showed distinct displeasure when he was given to understand that he had done something poorly. Self-love arises in children very early, even before one can see any signs thereof. The caresses and endearments of almost all people who approach them, especially of their mothers and nurses, teach them very early to value themselves, even before reflection upon their own acts, and the comparison of these with the acts of others, can give them a higher

opinion of themselves. A few words he pronounced clearly on November 27th, and knew also their meanings exactly; these were "Papa" and "Mama", though he did not use them to call persons, but merely by accident, without intending to say anything thereby. So it appears that words awakened in him their proper images and ideas, but not conversely, images of objects and desire of them, any concept of the corresponding word; presumably because children begin by learning words more for the sake of understanding the intention of others than in order to impart their own—just as adults, in learning a foreign language, will sooner translate the words thereof into their mother tongue than to give expression through the medium of the new language. Only a few simple sounds were significantly used by the boy, such as "ha! ha!" when something strange met his eyes, likewise a few expressions of displeasure and negation. The sound "ha!" seems indeed to be the natural expression of reflection and of surprise. It originates in a sudden expulsion of the breath which has been withheld, and the breath is stopped when by the sudden occurrence of some novelty the train of thought is hemmed and suddenly deflected into a new channel. Since the speech-organs were not yet sufficiently trained to produce all sorts of articulation, especially long and compound words, he usually denoted the corresponding objects by gestures. On November 29th one could observe a signification of this sort that indicated a certain amount of complexity in his ideas, and spoke of some amount of original composition on his part. He had been taught to reply to the question, "How big (*grand*) are you?", by lifting up his hands; now he was required to say the word "*grandmama*," and as the word "grand" was too difficult for him to pronounce, he lifted up his hands and at the same time said "mama." Now that he had learned a little more about external objects and about their relation to his satisfaction and amusement, his desire for certain objects became more acute; the least resistance, even by inanimate things, aroused violent anger. And these desires were persistent; he would not give in until he had realized his purpose.

31. The sense of sight was almost completely developed by December 8th [1782], and showed considerable practice in perspective vision. He liked to see pictures, and could distinguish a few familiar objects even in etchings, despite their small proportion. How much practice and private performance of comparisons this requires we know from Cheselden's blind man. Sympathy and self-love developed more and more; on December 26th he showed evident pleasure if any one laughed at his antics or praised them; indeed, he sought to invite laughter by all sorts of gestures and postures, as he could already walk without assistance. Now also he clearly showed an impulse to imitation, as he had his body and speech-organs fairly under control. Thus he imitated all sorts of sounds, the bell, for instance, when it rang. Also he learned to pronounce certain words significantly, especially "take, take," when he wanted to be picked up or taken from his chair. One could now discover distinct signs of memory, but only through present sensation, not through mere ideas. If he had been several times in a certain place and then beheld the scene from afar, he would point to it with his finger. As he still lacked verbal expression,

his ideas could as yet have no free course independent of sensations, and therefore the past could not return to his consciousness without sensuous assistance. Memory is always founded upon comparison, and there is ever an incomplete judgment concealed therein; so we have even here the first dawning of the autonomous power of thought, probably quite different from that which some animals exhibit, in whom memory seems to be merely the awakening of old associated tracks [Spuren] and movements without any trace of judgment. Only with the elephant a few experiences appear to prove something more, if they be otherwise correct and authentic.

32. His power of judgment was even more clearly evident on January 11, 1783, when he recognized his own image in the mirror, in which he liked to see himself, seeking to take all sorts of postures before it. Children are often held up to the mirror from earliest infancy, and thus they learn by repeated experience that the image is their own; which, indeed, requires much and frequent comparison, but could never be accomplished without the faculty of judgment. Herein, too, lies a special trait of egotism, that one likes to see one's own form rather than any other, and through reflection takes delight in the contemplation of one's self. For this reason, this form of enjoyment is totally absent in animals. A dog who sees for the first time his image in the mirror barks because he takes it to be another dog; if after repeated efforts the image does not reply, he is silent. It is not certain whether he has recognized the fraud or is merely tired of his unanswered barking, but never does one find that he takes any pleasure in the contemplation of his own form; perhaps because his power of reflection is not so far developed that he can enjoy himself and say, "That is myself; those features are my own." The boy's mania for imitation extended further and further. Besides a few sounds which he imitated, he attempted also to imitate conversations, to which end he produced a profusion of incomprehensible sounds. Imitation always begins with the most external aspect of things, because this most easily impresses the senses; also he had undoubtedly some conception of the purpose of speech, as he accompanied the senseless sounds with gestures that gave them meaning. If, for example, he wanted to be placed somewhere where he could not betake himself, he would point out the spot with his finger and accompany this with a string of half-articulated sounds.

33. He was very anxious to acquire new ideas with the greatest possible precision. On the 18th of January it was observed that whenever a new object came into his hands, he would regard and feel it from every angle, and turn it over and over; as soon as any part of it rattled, he sought to open the thing to see what it contained, because he had repeatedly seen that such articles could be opened. Furthermore, he understood a variety of phrases such as "fetch that," "leave that alone," "put it over there," and so forth; but he made no use of them as yet to demand anything of other people, partly because his speech-organs were not yet pliable and controlled enough, partly also because, although the transition from things to words was established through habit, the converse was not yet the case. His desire for praise and approval became more and more marked. If he had accomplished anything odd or novel in bodily attitudes or manipula-

tion of his toys, then he would laugh joyously and look about to receive the approbation of others. Moreover, he took great pleasure in seeing himself costumed or dressed in new clothes, presumably because he knew that others would praise and admire him. At this time a sister to him was born, and now he showed signs of jealousy. He wanted to strike her whenever she lay in her mother's lap or in his cradle, because he did not like to see himself bereft of something of which he had previously been the sole possessor. So far, his sympathy had been restricted almost entirely to a desire to impart his feelings to others; now he took part in another's feelings, and wept with his sister when she cried.

34. An example of broader judgment and more extended reflection was also seen. He had repeatedly been forbidden to touch anything edible that was not given explicitly to him, but he had never been frightened away from it. Now, unobserved, he had obtained a bit of sugar, and with this he retired to a corner where he could not been seen; his action was not understood, people sought him, and found him eating the sugar. Animals that have been whipped several times will run away with their prey, through mere association of ideas, because the punishment occurs to them. This was not the case with him, for he had never been chased away. It was pure calculation, that unseen he would be able to eat the sugar, which would be taken from him if it was remarked.

35. How pleasant is the sensation made by light was evident on February 7th, as the boy took special pleasure in watching the moon when it was shown to him, and thereafter, if one promised to show him the moon, he was always overjoyed. The same pleasant sensation was produced by the sunbeams that fell into his room. He now made considerable progress in talking; on the 8th of March, at the sight of an object, he would repeat its name if he had frequently heard it, but he still found it hard to pronounce words of several syllables. Of these he usually said only the end-syllables or the syllables that was chiefly accented, because this appealed most readily to his ear. The consonants z, sch, w, st, sp, as also the diphthongs, he could not well pronounce; p, t and k he found the easiest. The former consonants, by reason of their compoundness, require in part a greater pliability of the speech-organs and in part a more refined and practiced ear for their apprehension; the same is true of the double vowels. The progressive development of his autonomous activity now showed even more clearly in the fact that he liked to attempt things that involved difficulties: crawling through narrow passages, assuming dangerous positions, carrying heavy objects, etc. Ordinary and easy acts do not afford enough occupation, do not entertain enough; add to this the fact that superseded difficulties impart a sense of increased and extended power. Both of these principles are deeply rooted in human nature, not implanted by education or the spur of ambition, else they would not have awakened in the boy so early, nor by such purely internal impulsion; yes, what is more, they would have been promptly and easily suppressed, since parents and nurses try, and must try, to check the daredeviltry of children even by punishment because of the dire consequences.

36. On the 27th of March [1783] he could already pronounce words

of two syllables, and knew almost all the external parts of his body, which he pointed out correctly when their names were mentioned to him; also most of the objects in the room were known to him by name. Now began the purposive use of speech, and the words were linked directly with their meanings, so that the idea of a thing immediately suggested its name. If the boy desired anything, he would call it by its name, howbeit this was true of only a very few objects as yet. To combine several words in a sentence was still beyond his power. But even this he was secretly practicing, for on June 3rd he succeeded in saying short sentences, consisting of a noun and a verb, though without correct grammatical form. Instead of the imperative he always employed the infinitive, and used the nominative in place of all other cases; the article was omitted altogether. The nominative he had most frequently heard when things were named for him; the sense of the other case-endings was not clear to him as yet. Add to this the fact that these are often slurred over in pronunciation. The infinitive we use most frequently, since the other tenses are often expressed in our dialect by this form together with the permutation of other words; so he had been primarily impressed by it. Probably this incorrectness of speech has its source in the peculiarities of our language.

37. To train children in ways of cleanliness, especially to teach them not to soil themselves, is exceedingly difficult. Although the boy objected to uncleanliness on his fingers, also on his shirt, so that he would not don a shirt that was spotted, it had not been possible so far to make him keep himself entirely clean. After a naughty performance he knew very well to express it and demand a change of linen; also he was ashamed of his act. The reason is probably that children do not sufficiently feel the need of evacuation, and are apt to ignore it when engrossed by their play. Jealousy and love of praise developed more and more; if his little sister was petted, he came to be petted, too; when anything was given to her, he tried to take it away, and also tried to spank her in secret.

38. His faculty of memory had received considerable practice. On July 20th he came to a spot in the house where four weeks ago he had been punished for defiling the place; and immediately he said, without further incentive, that whoever dirtied the room would receive a spanking—not, indeed, in completely articulate words, but plainly enough to convey his meaning. So there were traces of ideas as old as this. However, if he was asked about an event which had passed but a few hours ago, he knew nothing about it any more; presumably because his memory was roused only by immediate sensation, not by the inward sequence of ideas. From this one may gather how much it takes so to control one's thoughts that various ideas may be recalled at will.

39. But in this also he soon made considerable headway, so that the series of associated ideas became longer and longer, and the transitions forward and backward became more facile. On July 24th he heard some ducks screaming without being able to see them, and at once he remarked, "Ducks," though he had rarely seen or heard them before. Here then the cry of the bird was already linked with the image thereof, and the image with the word. This presupposes not only association, but also reflection,

which determines that the two impressions of hearing and sight respectively are caused by the same object, and therefore must be conceived together. Ideas once associated became more and more surely linked, so that they would not separate even after several months. On the 26th of July he saw some potatoes, which he had not seen for several months, but had previously eaten with pleasure, and he immediately said, "Potatoes." By this and by the increase of his vocabulary his series of association now became more independent of external impressions and it became apparent that in his little brain several ideas were already spontaneously awakened and linked in sequences. The boy had heard people tell how a girl had been slain by lightning; the expression of the story tellers had impressed him deeply, so that upon a later occasion he tried with fragmentary words and gestures to reproduce the tale, though this could not be understood by any one save those who had been present at the previous telling.

40. On the 30th of July he finally succeeded in uttering complete, though short sentences, for example: *There he stands. There he lies.* His sister and a little dog, both heretofore indifferent objects, he gradually learned to love; on August 23rd he objected against having either of them suffer certain harm, for they both had begun to serve his pleasure in passing the time. Also he learned, for the sake of cleanliness, to demand attention when he felt the need of evacuation. And hereby he discovered a trick to realize entirely different purposes. His training-chair was high, so that from its seat he could easily overlook the table and usually reach whatever lay upon it; if now he noticed that edible things might be on the table, he always claimed the need of evacuation as a pretext to reach the table, for he knew that he had no other means of realizing his wish to be set upon the chair. Herein already we can see consideration, judgment, and the rudiments of reasoning, without which it were not possible to use certain means to certain ends, unless he were led to it through imitation. In this case imitation plays no part whatever, neither does instruction; only pure, spontaneous feeling. A few such examples are quoted concerning animals; but these are so rare, and are found in authors who repeat them only by hearsay, that we have reason to regard them as none too authentic. The boy used to say of his sister, whenever she failed to do his bidding, that she was stupid; so it appears his self-love had already taken the form of a comparison between himself and others.

41. A few vague conceptions of property were in evidence by August 26th. The boy did not approve of seeing his sister sitting in his chair or wearing his clothes; he called these things *his* things. The first source of the desire to have sole possession of a thing, and to debar others from the use of it, is undoubtedly a fear of being robbed of one's immediate enjoyment—a fear that is inspired by the mere sight of the situation. Therefore this fear may be found in very young infants and some animals, but is quickly allayed when their hunger is appeased. But that other desire, the real source of persistent property even beyond immediate use of the object, is based on the fear of losing some future pleasure or use; hence it presupposes some sort of prevision, of which animals are of course incapable. If certain animals lay up food against the coming winter, that cannot in

fairness be called prevision, since they do it even before they have experienced winter and its hardships. Although the boy would not let himself be deprived of his possessions, he readily deprived his sister of hers; the desire for more ownership did not let him see that the recognition he demanded for his personal property could be demanded by her for her things. Under the stress of strong desire we think only of ourselves; all further considerations disappear. Probably this is the reason why uncivilized nations are so ready to rob foreigners, though they have respect for property among themselves; for they regard foreigners as persons to whom they owe no such consideration, and who in no wise concern them, and furthermore, they have not learned to curb their desires.

42. With increasing practice in speaking and the acquisition of various words, his ideas were subjected more and more to the caprice and desires of his soul, so that more and longer series of them could be spontaneously aroused, and chains of thought be carried through. By this means the faculties which deal with and develop the ideas gained practice, especially the faculty of imagination. On the 29th of October the boy took several chopped-off stalks of white cabbage, and let them represent different persons who called upon each other. Thus without particular incentive, the images were here recalled of persons visiting each other, and these images were transferred to the cabbage stalks, so that the latter represented the former. So the first phase of imagination seems to be that familiar characters are transferred to unfamiliar objects. At the same time this entails a voluntary and autonomous association of ideas, the first source of all language, in fact, of any symbolic expression. Never has anything of the sort been observed on animals, never, amongst their images and ideas, any autonomous association of ideas; so the reason why animals have no speech does seem to lie deeper than in the mere lack of adroitness of the speech-organs.

43. Now, moreover, appeared the faculty of thought, and the search for a satisfactory reason. On the morning of the 13th of November the boy looked out of the window and saw a bright cloud in the sky; in this connection he remembered a rainbow he had seen several weeks before, and he immediately formed the judgment, "I see a rainbow." The relation of similarity is probably the first source of judgment, because similarity calls up absent images and thus stimulates comparison between present sensations and objects previously known. When he was told that this was not a rainbow, he promptly replied, "The rainbow is asleep just now." Very probably he wanted thereby to give himself some reason why this could not be the rainbow; thus his faculty of thought was already in search of reasons for his judgments. At the same time we can see herein a striking proof of the deep, ingrained human tendency to anthropomorphism, by reason of which one imagines all external objects as human-like, and all inanimate things as living. The former is certainly due to the fact that one always envisages an unknown thing through one that is known; an act which is indispensable to any limited mind, if it will not stand still at every step and interrupt its activity in an unpleasant fashion. To this is added the circumstance that old and familiar images fuse unconsciously

with our new ones through the self-propagating inner activity and association, thus causing the new impression always to be conceived under some previously accepted category. Now there is nothing nearer and more familiar to us than ourselves, wherefore images of our own reactions, our own way of doing things, are constantly mingled with our ideas of external objects; therefore, we conceive all things as being like to us, alive as ourselves, and acting by the same powers and motives as we do. This conception is due, furthermore, to the fact that inanimate things yield us too little entertainment, so that, in order to occupy ourselves therewith, we must bring the object nearer to ourselves and ascribe life to it. That is why children like so well to transform their lifeless toys into human beings, as we have just seen in the case of the cabbage stalks.

44. Another and similar example hereof was observed the same day. I held my watch to his ear; when he had listened for a while to its beat, he said that Fripon (a little dog in the house) was imprisoned therein. Thus he presupposed that the movement and sound must originate in a living creature, a proposition which almost all uncivilized races accept, and which is based on that same anthropomorphism which lets us conceive all moving objects as like to us or to the animals, that is to say, as endowed with life. This much is clear from these examples: that this opinion of untutored nations springs from the conceptions of an intellect not yet integrated nor led by experience. This is also borne out by a judgment the boy passed on April 2nd. In the evening, when he no longer saw the sun in the sky, he said, "The sun has gone to bed; tomorrow he will get up again, drink his tea and eat his bread and butter." All these opinions originated purely in his own deliberations; no one had told him this sort of thing before, so that he might have been adopting foreign notions. Also the variety of the occasions shows that nothing learned or repeated, but only the product of his own thinking was involved.

45. His self-estimation now began to develop more fully, and to grow into real desire for appreciation, so that the boy now took consideration of the praise and blame of others, without distinction. On February 14th, 1784, he said, when he thought he had acted very cleverly: "People will say, 'That is a nice little boy.'" If he was naughty and was told, "The neighbor sees you," he would desist at once.

46. This is as far as my observations go. Other business prevented me from their continuation. I greatly desire that others may make similar ones; it will then be possible to determine various things by comparison, and that important branch of psychology, too little exploited as yet, which studies the development of human faculties—the foundation of pedagogy—will make appreciable progress thereby.

4

JEAN MARC GASPARD ITARD (1775–1838)
First developments of the young savage of Aveyron (1801)

We return now to "abnormal" children. Following the tradition of the reports by Cheselden and Barrington, this selection presents a third type of exceptional case study in child psychology, a report of a "wild boy" or "feral man." Many reports of children believed to have lived in isolation from an early age or allegedly to have been reared with animals have appeared from medieval times onward. Most such reports are of doubtful authenticity, and in many cases convey little information.

The account of The Wild Boy of Aveyron, by Itard, exceeds all others in its documentation in respect to Victor's life before and after he was found, and in the persistent and brilliant attempts of Itard to educate him.

With regard to the life of Victor before his capture, and to Itard's attempts to train him, the account here presented speaks for itself, although it is considerably abridged.

The report from which this selection was taken was published in French in 1801. The subsequent account, presented in the selection which follows, was published in 1806. Victor was under the supervision of Itard from 1800 to 1806.

These accounts were translated into English by George and Muriel Humphrey and were published by Appleton-Century-Crofts in 1932. The excerpts contained in selections 4 and 5 are reprinted by permission of the publisher and the translators. A reprint edition (paperback) of The Wild Boy of Aveyron was published in 1962.

The information given in the following paragraph is taken largely from the introduction to The Wild Boy of Aveyron written by George Humphrey. Itard, a young physician, was appointed to a new institution for deaf-mutes when he was 25 years of age. Victor came under his care shortly thereafter. He believed that the cause of Victor's retardation was lack of experience, and that if given appropriate remedial experiences he would become normal. Itard set about to provide these experiences. While

Victor improved, in no respect did he become intellectually normal. The question remains unanswered as to whether Victor was biologically subnormal, due to heredity or injury, or whether the effects of early deprivation cound not be fully repaired at age eleven or later.

Following the events described in the 1806 report, Itard apparently gave up attempts at further training. It appears, although this is not clearly stated by Humphrey, that Victor remained in the institution for deaf-mutes, and died at about the age of 40.

Itard's ingenuity in respect to testing and training Victor is notable on the following two counts: (1) Testing him to see if he would use an object to obtain food which was too high to reach from the floor, a technique later used by Köhler with chimpanzees; (2) His use of inverted cups to test memory for hidden objects. This technique is now labeled "delayed reaction" and is used in several infant intelligence scales, including the 1960 edition of the Stanford-Binet. This test, however, was not original with Itard. It is an adaptation of the shell game employed immemorially by dishonest gamblers.

Many observations on allegedly isolated or animal-reared children have been summarized and interpreted in a book by J. A. L. Singh and Robert M. Zingg, Wolf-Children and Feral Man *(1939)*. Students may wish to consult also an article by the present editor, entitled "The Significance of Feral Man," published in the American Journal of Psychology 54 *(1941)*: 425–532. From time to time new accounts of wild children appear, usually in Sunday supplements of newspapers. When out of copy, some reporters invent a new wolf-boy. In several cases, we have written for further information. We have never received a reply.

A child of eleven or twelve, who some years before had been seen completely naked in the Caune Woods seeking acorns and roots to eat, was met in the same place toward the end of September 1799 by three sportsmen who seized him as he was climbing into a tree to escape from their pursuit. Conducted to a neighboring hamlet and placed in the care of a widow, he broke loose at the end of a week and returned to the mountains, where he wandered during the most rigorous winter weather, draped rather than covered with a tattered shirt. At night he retired to solitary places but during the day he approached the neighboring villages, where of his own accord he entered an inhabited house situated in the Canton of St. Sernin.

There he was retaken, watched and cared for during two or three days and transferred to the hospital of Saint-Afrique, then the Rodez, where he was kept for several months. During his sojourn in these different places he remained . . . wild and shy, impatient and restless, continually seeking to escape. He furnished material for most interesting observations, which were collected by credible witnesses whose accounts I shall not fail to report in this essay where they can be displayed to the best advantage. A minister of state with scientific interests believed that this event would throw some light upon the science of the mind. Orders were given that the child should be brought to Paris. He arrived there towards the end of September 1800 under the charge of a poor respectable old man....

The most brilliant and irrational expectations preceded the arrival of the Savage of Aveyron at Paris. A number of inquisitive people looked forward with delight to witnessing the boy's astonishment at the sights of the capital. On the other hand many people otherwise commendable for their insight, . . . believed that the education of this child would only be a question of some months, and that he would soon be able to give the most interesting information about his past life. In place of all this what do we see? A disgustingly dirty child affected with spasmodic movements and often convulsions who swayed back and forth ceaselessly like certain animals in the menagerie, who bit and scratched those who opposed him, who showed no sort of affection for those who attended him; and who was in short, indifferent to everything and attentive to nothing.

* * *

In the midst of . . . general indifference the administrators of the National Institute of the Deaf and Dumb and its celebrated director never forgot that society, in taking over this unfortunate youth, had contracted towards him binding obligations that must be fulfilled. Sharing then the hopes which I founded upon a course of medical treatment, they decided that this child should be confided to my care.

But before the details and results of this decision are presented I must begin with . . . a careful analysis of the description given of the boy, in a meeting to which I had the honor of being admitted, by a doctor whose genius for observation is as famous as his profound knowledge of mental diseases.

Proceeding first with an account of the sensory functions of the young savage, citizen Pinel showed that his senses were reduced to such a state of inertia that the unfortunate creature was, according to his report, quite inferior to some of our domestic animals. His eyes were unsteady, expressionless, wandering vaguely from one object to another without resting on anybody; they were so little experienced in other ways and so little trained by the sense of touch, that they never distinguished an object in relief from one in a picture. His organ of hearing was equally insensible to loudest noises and to the most touching music. His voice was reduced to a state of complete muteness and only a uniform guttural sound escaped him. His sense of smell was so uncultivated that he was equally indifferent to the odor of perfumes and to the fetid exhalation of the dirt with which his bed was filled. Finally, the organ of touch was restricted to the mechanical function of the grasping of objects. . . . He was destitute of memory, of judgment, of aptitude for imitation, and was so limited in his ideas, even those relative to his immediate needs, that he had never yet succeeded in opening a door or climbing upon a chair to get the food that had been raised out of reach of his hand. In short, he was destitute of all means of communication and attached neither expression nor intention to his gestures or to the movements of his body. He passed rapidly and without any apparent motive from apathetic melancholy to the most immoderate peals of laughter. He was insensible to every kind of moral influence. His perception was nothing but a computation prompted by gluttony, his pleasure an agreeable sensation of the organ of taste and his intelligence the ability to produce a few incoherent ideas relative to his wants. In a word, his whole life was a completely animal existence.

Later, reporting several cases collected at Bicêtre of children incurably affected with idiocy, citizen Pinel established very strict parallels between the condition of these unfortunate creatures and that of the child now under consideration, and convincingly established a complete and perfect identity between these young idiots and the Savage of Aveyron. This identity led to the inevitable conclusion that, attacked by a malady hitherto regarded as incurable, he was not capable of any kind of sociability or instruction. This was the conclusion which citizen Pinel drew but which, nevertheless, he accompanied by that philosophic doubt which pervades all his writings, and which accompanies the predictions of the man who estimates the science of prognosis at its true worth, seeing in it nothing but a more or less uncertain calculation of probabilities and conjectures.

I never shared this unfavorable opinion and in spite of the truth of the picture and the justice of the parallels I dared to conceive certain hopes. I founded them for my part upon the double consideration of the cause and the curability of this apparent idiocy. I cannot go further without dwelling a moment upon these two considerations. Moreover, they bear upon the present and depend upon a series of facts which I must relate, and to which I shall see myself obliged more than once to add my own reflections.

If it were proposed to solve the following problem of metaphysics: *to determine what would be the degree of intelligence and the nature of the ideas of an adolescent, who, deprived from his childhood of all education, had lived entirely separated from individuals of his own species,* unless I am greatly mistaken the solution of the problem would be found as follows. There should first be assigned to that individual nothing but an intelligence relative to the small number of his needs and one which was deprived, by abstraction, of all the simple and complex ideas we receive by education, which combine in our mind in so many ways solely by means of our knowledge of signs, or reading. Well, the mental picture of this adolescent would be that of the Wild Boy of Aveyron and the solution of the problem would consist in exhibiting the extent and the cause of his intellectual state.

But in order to justify still further my opinion of the existence of this cause, it is necessary to prove that it has operated for a number of years, and to reply to the objection that can be made and that has already been made to me, that the so-called savage was merely a poor imbecile whom his parents in disgust had recently abandoned at the entrance to some woods.

Those who lend themselves to such a supposition had not observed the child shortly after his arrival in Paris. They would have seen that all his habits bore the mark of a wandering and solitary life. He had an insurmountable aversion to society and to its customs, to our clothing, our furniture, to living in houses and to the preparation of our food. There was a profound indifference to the objects of our pleasures and of our fictitious needs; there was still in his present state, in spite of his new needs and dawning affections, so intense a passion for the freedom of the fields that during a short sojourn at Montmorency he would certainly have escaped into the forest had not the most rigid precautions been taken, and twice he did escape from the house of the Deaf and Dumb in spite of the supervision of his governess [Madame Guérin].

His locomotion was extraordinary, literally heavy after he wore shoes, but always remarkable because of his difficulty in adjusting himself to our sober and measured gait, and because of his constant tendency to trot and to gallop. He had an obstinate habit of smelling at anything that was given to him, even the things which we consider void of smell; his mastication was equally astonishing, executed as it was solely by the sudden action of the incisors, which because of its similarity to that of certain rodents was a sufficient indication that our savage, like these animals, most commonly lived on vegetable products. . . .

Other indications of an entirely isolated, precarious and wandering life are the nature and the number of scars with which the child's body is covered. To say nothing of the scar which is visible on his throat and which I shall mention elsewhere as having another origin and meriting particular attention, there could be counted four upon his face, six along his left arm, three at some distance from the right shoulder, four at the margin of the pubis, one upon the left buttock, three on one leg and two on the other which makes twenty-three altogether. Of these some appeared to be due to bites of animals and the others to scratches which were more or less large and deep, forming numerous and ineffaceable evidences of the long and total abandonment of this unfortunate creature. . . .

Let us add to all these facts derived from observation those not less authentic to which the inhabitants of the country near the woods in which he was found have testified. We shall find that in the first days following his entrance into society, his only nourishment was acorns, potatoes and raw chestnuts, that he made no sort of sound, that in spite of the most active supervision he succeeded several times in escaping, that he showed a great repugnance to sleeping in a bed, etc. We shall find above all that he had been seen more than five years before entirely naked and fleeing at the approach of men, which presupposes that he was already, at the time of his first appearance, habituated to this manner of life, which could only be the result of at least two years' sojourn in uninhabited places. Thus this child had lived in an absolute solitude from his seventh almost to his twelfth year, which is the age he may have been when he was taken in the Caune woods. It is then probable, and almost proved, that he had been abandoned at the age of four or five years, and that if, at this time, he already owed some ideas and some words to the beginning of an education, this would all have been effaced from his memory in consequence of his isolation.

* * *

If the progress of this child towards civilization and my success in developing his intelligence have hitherto been so slow and so difficult, I must attribute this more particularly to the innumerable obstacles I have met. . . . I have successively shown him toys of all kinds; more than once I have tried for whole hours to teach him how to use them and I have seen with sorrow that, far from attracting his attention, these various objects always ended by making him so impatient that he came to the point of hiding them or destroying them when the occasion offered itself. Thus, one day when he was alone in his room he took upon himself to throw into the fire a game of ninepins with which we had pestered him and which had been shut up for a long time in a night commode, and he was found gaily warming himself before his bonfire.

However, I succeeded sometimes in interesting him in amusements which had connection with his appetite for food. Here is one, for example, which I often arranged for him at the end of the meal when I took him to dine with me in town. I placed before him without any symmetrical order, and upside down, several little silver cups, under one of which was placed a chestnut. Quite sure of having attracted his attention, I raised them one after the other excepting that which covered the nut. After having thus shown him that they contained nothing, and having replaced them in the same order, I invited him by signs to seek in his turn. The first cup under which he searched was precisely the one under which I had hidden the little reward due to him. Thus far, there was only a feeble effort of memory. But I made the game insensibly more complicated. Thus after having by the same procedure hidden another chestnut, I changed the order of all the cups, slowly, however, so that in this general inversion he was able, although with difficulty, to follow with his eyes and with his attention the one which hid the precious object. I did more; I placed nuts under two or three of the cups and his attention, although divided between these three objects, still followed them none the less in their respective changes, and directed his first searches towards them. Moreover, I had a further aim in mind. This judgment was after all only a calculation of greediness. To render his attention in some measure less like an animal's, I took away from this amusement everything which had connection with his appetite, and put under the cups only such objects as could not be eaten. The result was almost as satisfactory and this exercise became no more than a simple game of cups, not without advantage in provoking attention, judgment, and steadiness in his gaze.

* * *

I have . . . done everything to awaken . . . [him] by means of the dainties most coveted by children and which I hoped to use as a new means of recompense, punishment, encouragement and instruction. But the aversion which he showed for all sweet substances and for our most delicate dishes was insurmountable. I then thought it advisable to try the use of seasoned dishes as being most suitable to arouse a sense necessarily dulled by rough foods. This was not any more successful and I offered him in vain, at such times when he was hungry and thirsty, strong liquors and spiced foods. Despairing at last of being able to inspire in him any new tastes, I cultivated the few to which he was limited by accompanying them with all accessories that could increase his pleasure in them.

. . . I often took him to dine with me in town. On such occasions there was on the table a complete collection of his favorite dishes. The first time that he found himself at such a feast there were transports of joy amounting almost to frenzy. Doubtless he thought that he would not do so well at supper time as he had just done at dinner, for on leaving the house that evening it was not his fault that he did not carry away with him a plate of lentils that he had pilfered from the kitchen. I congratulated myself on this first outcome. I had just procured him a pleasure; I had only to repeat it several times to make it a necessity. Which is what I actually did. I did more. I was careful to precede our expeditions by certain preparations which he would notice; these were to enter his home about four o'clock, my hat upon my head, his shirt folded in my hand. These preparations soon came to be for him the signal of departure. I scarcely appeared before I was understood; he dressed himself hurriedly and followed me with much evidence of satisfaction. I do not give this fact as proof of a superior intelligence and there is no one who will not object that the most ordinary dog will do at least as much. But in admitting this intellectual equality one is obliged to acknowledge a great change, and those who saw the Wild Boy of Aveyron at the time of his arrival in Paris, know that he was very inferior on the score of discernment to this most intelligent of our domestic animals.

It was impossible when I took him with me to go on foot. It would have been necessary for me to run with him or else use most tiring violence in order to make him walk in step with me. We were obliged, then, to go out only in a carriage, another new pleasure that he connected more and more with his frequent excursions. In a short time these days ceased to be merely holidays to which he gave himself up with liveliest pleasure, but were real necessities the privation of which, when there too long an interval between them, made him sad, restless and capricious.

How the pleasure was increased when these parties took place in the country! I took him not long ago to the country house of citizen Lachabeaussière in the valley of Montmorency. It was a most curious sight, and I venture to say one of the most touching, to see the joy that was pictured in his eyes at the sight of the little hills and woods of that laughing valley. It seemed as if the eagerness of his gaze could not be satisfied through the windows of the carriage. He leaned now towards the one, now towards the other, and showed the liveliest anxiety when the horses went more slowly or were about to stop. . . .

. . . I proposed to lead him to the use of speech *by inducing the exercise of imitation through the imperious law of necessity.* . . . I was convinced that a tardy functioning of the larynx must be expected and that I ought to accelerate its activity by coaxing it with something he wanted, I had reason to believe that the vowel "O," having been the first heard would be the first pronounced, and I found it very favorable to my plan that this simple pronunciation was, at least with respect to the sound, the sign of one of the most ordinary needs of the child. Nevertheless, I was unable to derive any advantage from this favorable coincidence. When his thirst was most intense, it was in vain that I held before him a glass of water, crying frequently *"eau," "eau"* [water]. Then I gave the glass to someone else who pronounced the same word beside him, asking for it back in the same way. But the unfortunate creature, tormented on all sides, waved his arms about the glass almost convulsively, producing a kind of hiss but not articulating any sound. It would have been inhuman to insist further. I changed the subject without, however, changing the method. It was upon the word *lait* [milk] that I carried out my next experiments.

On the fourth day of this next experiment I succeeded to my heart's content, and I heard Victor pronounce distinctly, though rather uncouthly it is true, the word *lait,* and he repeated it almost immediately. It was the first time that an articulate sound left his mouth and I did not hear it without the most intense satisfaction.

Nevertheless I made a reflection which in my eyes much diminished the advantage of this first success. It was not until the moment when, despairing of success, I came to pour the milk into the cup which he gave me, that the word *lait* escaped him with great demonstrations of pleasure; and it was only after I had poured it again as a reward that he pronounced it a second time. It can be seen why this result was far from fulfilling my intentions. The word pronounced instead of being the sign of his need was . . . merely an exclamation of pleasure. If this word had been uttered before the thing which he desired had been granted, success was ours, the real use of speech was grasped by Victor, a point of communication established between him and me, and the most rapid progress would spring from this first triumph. Instead of all this, I had just obtained a mere expression, insignificant to him and useless to us, of the pleasure which he felt. . . . It was useless to the needs of the individual and was swamped by a multitude of irrelevancies, like the ephemeral and variable sentiment for which it had become the sign. The subsequent results of this misuse of the word have been such as I feared.

It was generally only during the enjoyment of the beverage that the word *lait* was heard. Sometimes he happened to pronounce it before and at other times a little after but always without purpose. I attach no more importance to this spontaneous repetition than to his repetition of it even now during the night when he happens to wake. Following this result I have entirely given up the method by which I obtained it, awaiting the moment when circumstances will allow me to substitute another which I believe to be more efficacious.

* * *

The exclamation *"Oh Dieu!"* . . . he has taken from Madame Guérin, and . . . he lets escape frequently in moments of great happiness. He pronounces it by leaving out the *u* in *Dieu,* and laying stress on the *i* as if it were double and in such a way as to be heard to cry distinctly, *Oh Diie! Oh Diie!* The *o* found in this last combination of sounds was not new to him; I had succeeded some time previously in making him pronounce it.

This is our present position with reference to the vocal organs. It is seen that all the vowels with the exception of the *u*, already enter into the small number of sounds which he articulates and that only three consonants are found, *l, d,* and the liquid *l*. This progress is certainly very feeble if it is compared to that required for the complete development of the human voice; but it seems sufficient to guarantee the possibility of this development. . . .

Our young savage expresses his few wants otherwise than by speech. Each wish manifests itself by the most expressive signs which have in some measure, as have ours, their gradations and their equivalent values. If the time for his walk has come, he appears several times before the window and before the door of his room. If he then sees that his governess is not ready, he places before her all the objects necessary for her toilet and in his impatience even goes to help her dress. That done, he goes down first and himself pulls the check string of the door. Arriving at the Observatory, his first business is to demand some milk, which he does by presenting a wooden porringer which, on going out, he never forgets to put in his pocket, and with which he first provided himself the day after he had broken in the same house a china cup which had been used for the same purpose.

Then again, in order to complete the pleasure of his evenings he has for some time past kindly been given rides in a wheelbarrow. Since then, as soon as the inclination arises, if nobody comes to satisfy it, he returns to the house, takes someone by the arm, leads him to the garden and puts in his hands the handles of the wheelbarrow, into which he then climbs. If this first invitation is resisted he leaves his seat, turns to the handles of the wheelbarrow, rolls it for some turns, and places himself in it again; imagining doubtless, that if his desires are not fulfilled after all this, it is not because they are not clearly expressed. Where meals are concerned his intentions are even less doubtful. He himself lays the cloth and gives Madame Guérin the dishes, so that she may go down to the kitchen and get the food. If he is in town dining with me, all his requests are addressed to the person who does the honors of the table; it is always to her that he turns to be served. If she pretends not to hear him, he puts his plate at the side of the particular dish which he wants and, as it were, devours with his eyes. If that produces no result, he takes a fork and strikes two or three blows with it on the brim of his plate. If she persists in further delay, then he knows no bounds; he plunges a spoon or even his hand into the dish and in the twinkling of an eye he empties it entirely in his plate. He is scarcely less expressive in his way of showing his emotions, above all impatience and boredom. A number of people visiting him out of curiosity know how, with more natural frankness than politeness, he dismisses them when, fatigued by the length of their visits, he offers to each them, without mistake, cane, gloves and hat, pushes them gently towards the door, which he closes impetuously upon them.

JEAN MARC GASPARD ITARD (1775-1838)

A report made to his Excellency the Minister of Interior (1806)

This is a condensation of the second and final report on Victor. In this account the reader will note the presence of the commands or commissions tests, used by Binet in his 1905 scale, and still a part of the Stanford-Binet. The report contains, we believe, the first, and maybe the only, account of the behavior at puberty of a boy reared in almost complete sexual ignorance.

This selection also is reprinted from The Wild Boy of Aveyron *by the permission of Appleton-Century-Crofts.*

To speak of the *Wild Boy of Aveyron* is to revive a name which now no longer arouses any kind of interest; it is to recall a creature forgotten by those who merely saw him and disdained by those who have thought to pass judgment on him. As for me, who until now have limited myself to observing him and lavishing my care upon him, I am quite indifferent both to forgetfulness and to disdain. Supported by daily observations lasting for five years I now beg to make to your Excellency the report which you expect of me; to relate what I have seen and done; to reveal the present state of this young man, the long and difficult paths through which he has been led, and the obstacles which he has overcome as well as those which he has not been able to surmount. If, my Lord, all these details may appear scarcely worthy of your attention and the results much below your expectations, will your Excellency please believe as my excuse that without the formal command received from him, I might have enveloped in a profound silence and condemned to an eternal oblivion, certain labors of which the result shows the failure of the instructor, rather than the progress of the pupil. But, while judging myself impartially, I believe nevertheless that, without taking into consideration the aim which I had in view in this task which I have voluntarily imposed upon myself, and considering the enterprise from a general point of view, it will not be, my Lord, without a certain satisfaction that you will see in the diverse experiments which I have made and the numerous observations that I have gathered, a collection of facts qualified to throw light on the history of medical philosophy, on the study of uncivilized man, and on the direction of certain systems of private education.

In order to appreciate the present state of the *Wild Boy of Aveyron*, his past condition must be brought to mind. To be judged fairly, this young man must only be compared with himself. Put beside another adolescent of the same age he is only an ill-favored creature, an outcast of nature as he was of society. But if one limits oneself to the two terms of comparison offered by the past and present states of young Victor, one is astonished at the immense space which separates them; and one can question whether Victor is not more unlike the *Wild Boy of Aveyron* arriving at Paris, than he is unlike other individuals of his same age and species.

I will not recount in detail to you, Sir, the hideous picture of this man-animal as he was when he came out of his forests.

* * *

[I attempted to lead] the pupil to the point where he would designate the thing he wanted by means of letters arranged in such a way as to spell the name of the thing he desired. In my pamphlet upon this child I have given an account of the first step made in recognizing written signs. . . . But subsequent observations, by throwing light upon the nature of this result, soon came to weaken the hopes that I had conceived from it. I noticed that Victor did not use words which I had taught him for the purpose of asking for the objects, or of making known a wish or a need, but employed them at certain moments only, and always at the sight of the desired things. Thus for example, much as he wanted his milk it was only at the moment when he was accustomed to take it and at the actual instant when he saw that it was going to be given him that the word for this favorite food was expressed or rather formed in the proper way. In order to clear up the suspicion that this restricted employment of the words awoke in me I tried delaying the hour of his breakfast but waited in vain for the written expression of my pupil's needs although they had become very urgent. It was not until the cup appeared that the word *lait* (milk) was formed. I resorted to another test. In the middle of his lunch and without letting it appear in any way to be a punishment, I took away his cup of milk and shut it up in a cupboard. If the word *lait* had been for Victor the distinct sign of the thing and the expression of his want of it, there is no doubt that after this sudden privation, the need continuing to make itself felt, the word would have been immediately produced. It was not, and I concluded that the formation of this sign, instead of being for the pupil the expression of his desire, was merely a sort of preliminary exercise with which he mechanically preceded the satisfaction of his appetite. It was necessary then to retrace out steps and begin again.

I resigned myself courageously do do this, believing that if I had not been understood by my pupil it was my fault rather than his. Indeed, in reflecting upon the causes which might give rise to this defective reception of the written signs, I recognized that in these first examples of the expression of ideas I had not employed the extreme simplicity which I had introduced at the beginning of my other methods of instruction and which had insured their success. Thus although the word *lait* is for us only a simple sign, for Victor it might be a confused expression for the drink, the vessel which contained it, and the desire of which it was the object.

Several other signs with which I had familiarized him showed the same lack of precision in application. An even more considerable defect was inherent in the method of expression we had adopted. As I have already said, this consisted in placing metal letters on a line and in the proper order, in such a way as to form the name of each object. But the connection which existed between the thing and the word was not immediate enough for his complete apprehension. In order to do away with this difficulty, it was necessary to establish between each object and its sign a more direct connection and a sort of identity which fixed them simultaneously in his memory. The objects first submitted to a trial of this new method of expression had therefore to be reduced to the greatest simplicity, so that their signs could not on any way bear upon their accessories. Consequently I arranged on the shelves of a library several simple objects such as a pen, a key, a knife, a box, etc., each one on a card upon which its name was written. These names were not new to the pupil he already knew them and had learned to distinguish them from each other, according to the method of reading which I have already indicated.

The problem then was merely to familiarize his eyes with the respective display of each of these names under the object which it represented. This arrangement was soon grasped as I had proof when, displacing all the things and instantly replacing all the labels in another order, I saw the pupil carefully replace each object upon its name. I varied my tests, and the variation gave me the opportunity to make several observations relative to the degree of the impression which these written signs made upon the sensory apparatus of our savage. Thus, leaving all the things in one corner of the room and taking all the labels to another, I wished by showing them successively to Victor to make him fetch each thing for which I showed him the written word. On these occasions, in order for him to bring the thing it was necessary that he should not lose from sight for a single instant the characters which indicated it. If he was too far away to be able to read the label, or if after showing it to him thoroughly I covered it with my hand, from the moment the sight of the word escaped him he assumed an air of uneasiness and anxiety and seized at random the first object which chanced to his hand.

The result of this experiment was not very reassuring and would in fact have discouraged me completely if I had not noticed that after frequent repetitions the duration of the impression upon the brain of my pupil became by imperceptible degrees much longer. Soon he merely needed to glance quickly at the word I showed him, in order to go without haste or mistake to fetch the thing I asked for. After some time I was able to extend the experiment by sending him from my apartment into his own room to look in the same way for anything the name of which I showed him. At first the duration of the perception did not last nearly so long as that of the journey, but by an act of intelligence worthy of record, Victor sought and found in the agility of his legs a sure means of making the impressions persist longer than the time required for the journey. As soon as he had thoroughly read the word he set out like an arrow, coming back an instant later with the thing in his hand. More than once, nevertheless, the name escaped him on the way. Then I heard him stop in his tracks and come again towards my appartment, where he arrived with a timid and confused air. Sometimes it was enough for him to glance at the complete collection of names in order to recognize and retain the one which had escaped him. At other times the image of the word was so effaced from his memory that I was obliged to show it to him afresh. This necessity he indicated by taking my hand and making me pass my index finger over the whole series of names until I had shown him the forgotten one.

This exercise was followed by another which by offering his memory more work contributed more powerfully to develop it. Until then I had limited myself to asking for only one thing at a time. Then I asked for two, then three, and then four by showing a similar number of the labels to the pupil. He, feeling the difficulty of retaining them all, did not stop running over them with eager attention until I had entirely screened them from his eyes. Then there was no more delay or uncertainty. He set off hurriedly on the way to his room whence he brought the things requested. On his return his first care before giving them to me was to look hastily over the list, comparing it with the things of which he was the bearer. These he gave me only after he had reassured himself in this way that he had neither forgotten anything nor made a mistake. This last experiment gave at first very variable results but finally the difficulties which it offered were in their turn surmounted. The pupil, now sure of his memory, disdained the advantage which the agility of his legs gave him and applied himself quietly to this exercise. He often stopped in the corridor, put his face to the window which is at one end of it, greeted with sharp cries the sight of the country which unfolds magnificently in the distance, and then set off again for his room, got his little cargo, renewed his homage to the ever-regretted beauties of nature, and returned to me quite sure of the correctness of his errand.

In this way memory, reëstablished in all its functions, succeeded in retaining the symbols of thought while at the same time the intelligence fully grasped their importance. Such, at least, was the conclusion that I thought I could draw when I constantly saw Victor, wishing to ask for various things, either in our exercises or spontaneously, making use of the different words of which I had taught him the meaning by the device of showing or giving him the thing when we made him read the word, or by indicating the word when he was given the thing. Who could believe that this double proof was not more than sufficient to assure me that at last I had reached the point to gain which I had been obliged to retrace my steps and make so great a detour? But something happened at this juncture which made me believe for a moment that I was further from it than ever.

One day when I had taken Victor with me and sent him as usual to fetch from his room several objects which I had indicated upon his list of words, it came into my head to double-lock the door and unseen by him to take out the key. That done I returned to my study, where he was, and, unrolling his list, I asked him for some of the things on it, taking care to indicate none which were not also to be found in my room. He set out immediately, but finding the door locked and having searched on all sides for the key, he came beside me, took my hand and led me to the outer door as if to make me see that it would not open. I feigned surprise and sought for the key everywhere and even pretended to open the door by force. At last, giving up the vain attempt, I took Victor back into my study and showing him the same words again, invited him by signs to look about and see if there were not similar objects to be found there. The words designated were stick, bellows, brush, glass, knife. All these things were to be found scattered about my study in places where they could easily be seen. Victor looked at them but touched none of them. I had no better success in making him recognize them when they were brought together on a table and it was quite useless to ask for them one after the other by showing him successively their names. I tried another method. With scissors I cut out the names of the objects, thus converting them into single labels which were put into Victor's hands. By thus bringing him back to our original procedure, I hoped that he would put upon each thing the name which represented it. In vain. I had the inexpressible grief of seeing my pupil unable to recognize any of these objects or rather the connection which joined them to their signs. With a stupefied air which cannot be described he let his heedless glance wander over all these characters which had again become unintelligible. I felt myself sinking under a weight of impatience and discouragement.

* * *

Of all the phenomena observable during the first developments of a child perhaps the most astonishing is the facility with which he learns to speak. When one thinks that speech, which is without question the most marvelous act of imitation, is also its first result, admiration is redoubled for that Supreme Intelligence whose masterpiece is man, and Who, wishing to make speech the principal promoter of education, could not let imitation, like the other faculties, develop progressively, and therefore necessarily made it fruitful as well as active from its beginning. But this imitative faculty, the influence of which extends throughout the whole of life, varies in its application according to age. It is used in learning to speak only during earliest childhood. Later other functions come under its influence and it abandons, so to speak, the vocal instrument, so that a young child, even an adolescent, after leaving his native country, promptly loses its manners, etiquette and language, but never loses those intonations of voice which constitute what is called accent. It follows from this physiological truth that in awakening the faculty of imitation in this young savage, now an adolescent, I ought not to have expected to find any disposition in the vocal organ to profit by this development of the imitative faculties, even supposing that I had not found a second obstacle in the obstinate lethargy of the sense of hearing. With respect to hearing, Victor could be considered as a deaf mute although he was certainly much inferior to this class of unfortunates since they are essentially observers and imitators.

Nevertheless, I did not believe that I should allow this difference to bring me to a standstill or to let it deprive me of the hope of making him speak, with all the resulting advantages which I promised myself. I felt I should try a last resource, which was to lead him to the use of speech through the sense of sight, since it was out of the question to do so through the sense of hearing. Here the problem was to practise his eye in observing the mechanism of the articulation of sounds, and to practise his voice in the reproduction of the sounds by the use of a happy combination of attention and imitation. For more than a year all my work and all our exercises were directed towards this end. In order to follow the previous methods of insensible gradation, I preceded the study of the visible articulation of sounds by the slightly easier imitation of movements of the face muscles, beginning with those which were most easily seen. Thus we have instructor and pupil facing each other and grimacing their hardest; that is to say, putting the muscles of the eyes, forehead, mouth and jaw into all varieties of motion, little by little concentrating upon the muscles of the lips. Then after persisting for a long time with the movements of the fleshy part of the organ of speech, namely the tongue, we submitted it also to the same exercises, but varied them much more and continued them for a longer time.

Prepared in this way, it seemed to me that the organ of speech ought to lend itself without further trouble to the imitation of articulate sounds and I considered this result both near and inevitable. I was entirely mistaken. This long preparation resulted in nothing but the emission of unformed monosyllables sometimes shrill, sometimes deep and still far less clear than those which I had obtained in my first experiments.

* * *

In speaking of the intellectual faculties of our savage I have not concealed the obstacles which arrested the development of certain of them, and I have made it my duty to describe exactly the gaps in his intelligence. Following the same plan in my account of this young man's emotions, I will disclose the animal side of his nature with the same fidelity as I have described the civilized side. I will suppress nothing. Although he has become sensible to gratitude and friendship, although he appears to feel keenly the pleasure of usefulness, Victor remains essentially selfish. Full of alacrity and cordiality when the services required of him are found to be not opposed to his desires, he is a stranger to that courtesy which measures neither privation nor sacrifice; and the sweet sentiment of pity is yet to be born within him. If in his relations with his governess he has sometimes been seen to share her sadness, this is only an act of imitation, analogous to that which draws tears from a young child who sees his mother or nurse weep. In order to commiserate with other people's troubles, it is necessary to have known them, or at least be able to imagine them. This cannot be expected from a young child or from such a creature as Victor, foreign as all those pains and privations which are the basis of our emotional sufferings are to him.

But what appears still more astonishing in the emotional system of this young man, and beyond all explanation, is his indifference to women in the midst of the violent physical changes attendant upon a very pronounced puberty. Looking forward to this period as a source of new sensations for my pupil and of interesting observations for myself, watching carefully all phenomena that were forerunners of this mental crisis, I waited each day until some breath of that universal sentiment which moves all creatures and causes them to multiply should come and animate Victor and enlarge his mental life. I have seen this eagerly awaited puberty arrive or rather burst forth, and our young savage consumed by desires of an extreme violence and of a startling constancy and this without any presentiment of its purpose or the slightest feeling of preference for any woman. Instead of that expansive impulse which precipitates one sex towards the other, I have observed in him only a sort of blind and slightly pronounced instinct which, as a matter of fact, does make him prefer the society of women to that of men without in any way involving his heart. Thus I have seen him in a company of women attempting to relieve his uneasiness by sitting beside one of them and gently taking hold of her hand, her arms and her knees until, feeling his restless desires increased instead of calmed by these odd caresses, and seeing no relief from his painful emotions in sight, he suddenly changed his attitude and petulantly pushed away the woman whom he had sought with a kind of eagerness. Then he addressed himself without interruption to another woman with whom he behaved in the same way. One day, nevertheless, he became a little more enterprising. After first employing the same caresses, he took the lady by her hands and drew her, without violence however, into the depths of an alcove. There, very much out of countenance, and showing in his manners and in his extraordinary facial expression an indescribable mixture of gaiety and sadness, of boldness and uncertainty, he several times solicited the lady's caresses by offering her his cheeks, and walked slowly round her with a meditative air, finally flinging his arms about her shoulders and holding her closely by the neck. This was all, and these amorous demonstrations ended, as did all the others, with a movement of annoyance which made him repulse the object of his transitory inclinations.

Since this time although the unhappy young man has been no less tormented by this natural ebullition, nevertheless he no longer seeks to relieve his restless desires by fruitless caresses. But instead of alleviating his situation this resignation has served only to exasperate him and has led the unfortunate creature to find nothing but a cause for despair in an imperious need which he has given up hope of satisfying. When this storm of the senses breaks forth anew in spite of the help of baths, of a soothing diet and violent exercise, there follows a complete change in the naturally sweet character of this young man. Passing suddenly from sadness to anxiety, and from anxiety to fury, he takes a dislike to all his keenest enjoyments; he sighs, sheds tears, utters shilll cries, tears his clothes and sometimes goes as far as to scratch or bite his governess. But even when he yields to a blind fury which he is not able to overcome, he gives evidence of a real repentance and asks to kiss the arm or hand which he has just bitten. In this state his pulse is raised and his face apoplectic. Sometimes blood flows from his nose and ears. This puts an end to the transport, and further postpones a recurrence of the outburst, especially if the hemorrhage is abundant. Starting from this observation I have been obliged, in order to remedy this state and because I could not or dared not do better, to attempt the use of bleeding, not, however, without many misgivings because I am persuaded that true education should cool and not extinguish this vital ebullition. But I ought to say that if I have obtained a measure of calm by this means and many others which it would be quite useless to enumerate here, this effect has only been transitory; and the result of this continual desire, as violent as it is indeterminate, has been an habitual state of restlessness and suffering which has continually impeded the progress of this laborious education.

Such has been the critical period which promised so much and which would, without doubt, have fulfilled all the hopes which we had entertained for it, if, instead of concentrating all its activity upon the senses it had also animated the moral system with the same fire and carried the torch of love into this benumbed heart. Nevertheless, on serious reflection, I will not conceal the fact that when I counted on this mode of development of the phenomena of puberty, I was not justified in comparing my pupil, mentally, to an ordinary adolescent in whom the love of women very often precedes, or at least always accompanies the excitement of the reproductive organs. This agreement between need and inclination could not occur in a creature whose education had not taught him to distinguish between a man and a woman, and who was indebted solely to the promptings of instinct for his glimpse of this difference without being able to apply it to his present situation. Also I did not doubt that if I had dared to reveal to this young man the secret of his restlessness and the aim of his desires, an incalculable benefit would have accrued. But, on the other hand, suppose I had been permitted to try such an experiment, would I not have been afraid to make known to our savage a need which he would have sought to satisfy as publicly as his other wants and which would have led him to acts of revolting indecency. Intimidated by the possibility of such a result, I was obliged to restrain myself and once more to see with resignation these hopes, like so many others, vanish before an unforeseen obstacle. . . .

✻   ✻   ✻

Thus, bringing together those facts which are scattered [through this account] one cannot help concluding: first, that by reason of the almost complete apathy of the organs of hearing and speech, the education of this young man is still incomplete and must always remain so; secondly, that by reason of their long inaction the intellectual faculties are developing slowly and painfully, and that this development, which in children growing up in civilized surroundings is the natural fruit of time and circumstances, is here the slow and laborious result of a very active education in which the most powerful methods are used to obtain most insignificant results; thirdly, that the emotional faculties, equally slow in emerging from their long torpor, are subordinated to an utter selfishness and that his puberty, which was very strongly marked and which usually sets up a great emotional expansion, seems only to prove that if there exists in human beings a relation between the needs of the senses and the affections of the heart, this sympathetic agreement is, like the majority of great and generous emotions, the happy fruit of education. . . .

JAMES WARDROP (1782–1869)

History of James Mitchell, a boy born blind and deaf with the account of an operation performed for recovery of his sight (1813)

James Mitchell differs from Cheselden's case in that he was deaf, as well as being almost completely blind. Because he was deaf as well as blind no effort was made to teach him any language other than gestures. The idea of a tactile language for the deaf-blind was then non-existant.

The voracious "stimulus-hunger" of this boy deprived of hearing and of seeing will be noted.

Wardrop seems to imply that vibrating objects applied to the teeth were heard. It is possible that only vibratory sensations, not auditory sensations, were what were being perceived.

The operation on this boy, as in the case of Cheselden's, was performed before the discovery of anesthetics. In this case the difficulty of restraining the patient is fully described.

Wardrop was an eminent British surgeon. His report was published as a monograph in London and Edinburgh. The case of James Mitchell received the attention of several British philosophers.

The following history of a Boy, born Blind and Deaf, affords a most interesting, though lamentable, example of a defect in the organization of the human frame, which, as far as I know, has not yet been described; and lays open a field of curious and valuable philosophical investigation, which has not hitherto been much explored.

The boy, when brought to London, and put under my care, had passed the fourteenth year of his age. He was accompanied by his father, a respectable clergyman in the north of Scotland, and by his sister; from whom, and from the observations I was enabled to make, the subsequent history has been collected.

He had the usual appearances of strength and good health, and his countenance was extremely pleasing, and indicated a considerable deal of intelligence.

On examining the state of his eyes, the pupil of each was observed to be obscured by a Cataract.

In the right eye the cataract was of a white colour and pearly lustre, and appeared to pervade the whole of the crystalline lens. The pupil, however, readily dilated or contracted, according to the different degrees of light to which it was exposed. The cataract in the left eye was not equally opake; about one-third of it being dim and clouded, arising, as it appeared, from very thin dusky webs crossing it in various directions, the rest being an opake white colour. The pupil of this eye did not, however, seem so susceptible of impressions from the varieties in the intensity of light, as that of the other eye, nor did he employ this eye, so often as the other, to gratify his fondness for light.

I could discover no defect in the organization of his Ears.

Soon after his birth, his parents observed the cataracts in both eyes, and they also discovered, at a very early age, that he was Deaf, as no sounds appeared to excite his attention, and no noise seemed to awake him during sleep.

About the time of life when he was attempting to walk, he began to be attracted by bright and dazzling colours, and to derive pleasure from striking his teeth with sonorous bodies. He also appeared anxious to smell and feel those substances which had become known to him through the medium of his other senses.

As he advanced in years, various circumstances concurred to prove, that neither the retina nor the auditory nerve were entirely insensible to the impressions of light and sound; and that, though he derived little information from these organs, he received from them a considerable degree of gratification.

He used to hold between his eye and luminous objects, such bodies as he had found to increase the quantity of light; and it was one of his chief amusements to concentrate the sun's rays, by means of pieces of glass, transparent pebbles, or similar substances which he held between his eye and the light, and turned about in various directions. There were other modes by which he was often in the habit of gratifying his desire of light. He would go to any outhouse or room within his reach, shut the windows and doors, and remain there for a considerable time, with his eyes fixed on some small hole or chink which admitted the sun's rays, eagerly catching them. He would also, during the winter nights, frequently retire to a corner of a dark room, and kindle a light for his amusement. Such, indeed, seemed to be the degree of pleasure, which he received from feasting his eyes with light, that he would often occupy himself, in this manner, for several hours, without interruption. In this, as well as in the gratification of the other senses, his countenance and gestures displayed a most interesting avidity and curiosity.

It was difficult, if not impossible, to ascertain with precision, the degree of Sight which he enjoyed; but from the preternatural acuteness which his senses of Touch and Smell had acquired, in consequence of having been habitually employed to collect that information for which the Sight is peculiarly adapted; it may be with confidence presumed, that he derived little, if any, assistance from his eyes, as organs of vision. Besides, the appearances of the disease in the eyes were such, as to render it extremely probable, that they enabled him merely to distinguish some colours and differences in the intensity of light.

The organs of Hearing seemed equally unfit for receiving the impressions of ordinary sounds, as his eyes were those of objects of sight.

Many circumstances, at the same time, seemed to prove, that he was not altogether insensible to *sound*. It has been already observed, that he often amused himself by striking hard substances against his teeth, from which he appeared to derive as much gratification, as he did from receiving the impression of light on his eyes. In his childhood, one of the most remarkable circumstances relating to him, was this eager desire to strike any hard substance against his teeth. He was particularly gratified when it was a key, or any instrument which produced a sharp sound; and he struck it always upon his front teeth. When a ring of keys was given to him, he seized them with great avidity, and tried each separately by suspending it loosely between two of his fingers, so as to allow it to vibrate freely; and after tingling them amongst his teeth, in this manner, he generally selected one from the others, the sound of which seemed to please him most. This, indeed, was one of his most favorite amusements, and it was surprising how long it would arrest his attention, and with what eagerness he would, on all occasions, renew it. A gentleman observing this circumstance, brought to him a musical snuff-box (a French trinket containing a small musical instrument, which played airs by means of a spring), and placed it between his teeth. This seemed not only to excite his wonder, but to afford him exquisite delight; and his father and sister, who were present, remarked, that they had never seen him so much interested on any former occasion. Whilst the instrument continued to play, he kept it closely between his teeth, and even when the notes were ended, he continued to hold the box to his mouth, and to examine it minutely with his fingers, his lips, and the point of his tongue, expressing by his gestures and by his countenance, extreme curiosity.

Besides the musical snuff-box, I procured for him a common *musical key*. When it was first applied to his tooth, he exhibited expressions of fear mixed with surprise. However, he soon perceived that it was attended with no harm, so that he not only allowed it to be renewed, but he soon acquired the habit of striking it on his own hand, so as to make it sound, and then touching his teeth with it. One day his father observed him place it upon the external ear. He has also, on some occasions, been observed to take notice of, and to appear uneasy with very loud sounds. Though, therefore, the teeth, besides being organs of mastication, and also serving as organs of touch in examining the food in the mouth, so that the hard and indigestible part may be rejected, in this boy they seemed to be the best channel of communicating sound to the auditory nerve.

His organs of Touch, of Smell, and of Taste had all acquired a preternatural degree of acuteness, and appeared to have supplied, in an astonishing manner, the deficiencies in the senses of Seeing and Hearing. By those of Touch, and Smell in particular, he was in the habit of examining every thing within his reach. Large objects, such as the furniture of a room, he felt over with his fingers, whilst those which were more minute, and which excited more of his interest, he applied to his teeth, or touched with the point of his tongue. In exercising the sense of Touch, it was interesting to notice the delicate and precise manner by which he applied the extremities of his fingers, and with what ease and flexibility he would insinuate the point of his tongue into all the inequalities of the body under his examination.

But there were many substances which he not only touched, but smelled during his examination.

To the sense of Smell, he seemed chiefly indebted for his knowledge of different persons, He appeared to know his relations and intimate friends, by smelling them very slightly, and he at once detected strangers. It was difficult, however, to ascertain at what distance he could distinguish people by this sense; but, from what I was able to observe, he appeared to be able to do so at a considerable distance from the object. This was particularly striking when a person entered the room, as he seemed to be aware of this before he could derive information from any other sense, than that of smell.

In selecting his food, he was always guided by his sense of smell; for he never took any thing into his mouth, without previously smelling it attentively.

His Taste was extremely delicate, and he showed a great predeliction for some kinds of food, whilst there were others of which he never partook. He had on no occcasion tasted butter, cheese, or any of the pulpy fruits; but he was fond of milk, plain dressed animal food, apples, peas, and other simple nutriment. He never took food from any one, but his parents or sister.

But the imperfections which have been noticed in his organs of sight and of hearing, were by no means accompanied with such defects in the *powers of his mind,* as might be suspected. He seemed to possess the faculties of the understanding in a considerable degree, and when we reflect that his channels of communication with the external world must have afforded very slow means of acquiring information, it is rather surprising how much knowledge he had obtained.

Impressions transmitted to the human soul through the medium of *one* sense might call into being some of the most important operations of intellect. Facts have been given to prove, that this boy possessed both recollection and judgment. We are ignorant of the qualities of bodies which influenced his determinations and his affections. On all occasions, however, it was clear, that he made his experiments on the objects which he examined, with all the accuracy and caution that his circumscribed means of gaining intelligence could admit. The senses he enjoyed being thus disciplined, acquired a preternatural degree of acuteness, and must have furnished him with information respecting the qualities of many bodies, which we either overlook, or are in the habit of obtaining through other channels.

Perhaps the most striking feature of the Boy's mind, was his avidity and curiosity to become acquainted with the different objects around him. When a person came into the room where he was, the moment he knew of his presence, he fearlessly went up to him, and touched him all over and smelled him with eagerness. He showed the same inquisitiveness, in becoming acquainted with every thing within the sphere of his observation, and was daily in the habit of exploring the objects around his father's abode. He had become familiar with all the most minute parts of the house and furniture, the out-houses, and several of the adjacent fields, and the various farming utensils.

He showed great partiality to some animals, particularly to horses, and nothing seemed to give him more delight than to be put on one of their backs. When his father went out to ride, he was always the first to watch his return; and it was astonishing how he became warned of this, from remarking a variety of little incidents. His father putting on his boots, and such like occurrences, were all accurately observed by the boy, and led him to conclude how his father was to be employed. In the remote situation where he resided, male visitors were most frequent, and therefore the first thing he generally did, was to examine whether or not the stranger wore boots; if he did, he immediately quitted him, went to the lobby, found out, and accurately examined the whip, then proceeded to the stable and handled his horse, with great care, and the utmost attention. It occasionally happened, that visitors arrived in a carriage. He never failed to go to the place where the carriage stood, examined the whole of it with much anxiety, and amused himself with the elasticity of the springs.

The locks of doors attracted much of his notice, and he seemed to derive great pleasure from turning the keys.

He was very docile and obedient to his father and to his sister, who accompanied him to London, and reposed in them every confidence for his safety, and for the means of his subsistence.

It has been already noticed, that he never took food from any one, but the branches of his own family. I several times offered him an apple, of which I knew he was extremely fond, but he always refused it with signs of mistrust, though the same apple, afterwards given him by his sister, was accepted greedily.

It was difficult to ascertain the manner in which his mind was guided in the judgment he formed of strangers, as there were some people whom he never permitted to approach him, whilst others at once excited his interest and attention.

The opinions which he formed of individuals and the means he employed to study their character, were extremely interesting. In doing this, he appeared to be chiefly influenced by the impressions communicated to him by his sense of Smell. When a stranger approached him, he eagerly began to touch some part of his body, commonly taking hold of the arm, which he held near his nose, and after two or three strong inspirations, through the nostrils, he appeared to form a decided opinion regarding him. If this was favourable, he showed a disposition to become more intimate, examined more minutely his dress, and expressed by his countenance more or less satisfaction: but if it happened to be unfavorable, he suddenly went off to a distance, with expressions of carelessness or of disgust.

When he was first brought to my house, to have his eyes examined, he both touched and smelled several parts of my body, and the following day, whenever he found me near him, he grasped my arm, then smelled it, and immediately recognized me; which he signified to his father, by touching his eye-lids with the fingers of both hands, and imitating the examination of his eyes, which I had formerly made. I was very much struck with his behaviour during this examination. He held his head, and allowed his eyes to be touched, with an apparent interest and anxiety, as if he had been aware of the object of my occupation. On expressing to his father my surprise, at the apparent consciousness of the Boy of what was to be done, he said that he had frequently, during the voyage from Scotland, signified his expectation and his desire that some operation should be performed on his eyes. About two years before this period, he had been brought up to London by sea, with the hope of getting an attempt made to improve his sight and his hearing. The membrane of tympanum, of both ears, was punctured by Mr. Astley Cooper, with no benefit; and several medical gentlemen examined his eyes, and endeavoured to perform some operations on them. In this, however, they completely failed, from the powerful resistance which he made to all their efforts to secure him, and hold the eye quiet. The lively remembrance, which he seemed to have, of these events, and the recurrence of the same circumstances attending his coming here at this time, made him very naturally conceive, that his parents had again brought him from home, with the same view as formerly. During the first examination, and on several future ones, when I purposely handled the eye roughly, I was surprised to find him submit to every thing that was done with fortitude, and complete resignation; as if he was persuaded that he had an organ imperfectly developed, and an imperfection to be remedied by the assistance of his fellow-creatures.

Many little incidents in his life have displayed a good deal of reasoning and observation. On one occasion, a pair of shoes were given to him, which he found too small, and his mother put them aside into a closet. Some time afterwards, young Mitchell found means to get the key of the closet, opened the door, and taking out the shoes, put them on a young man, his attendant, whom they fitted exactly.

On another occasion, finding his sister's shoes very wet, he appeared very uneasy until she changed them.

From his father having had farm servants, he attempted to imitate them in some of their employments, and was particularly fond of assisting them in cleaning the stable.

At one time, when his brothers were employed making basket-work, he attempted to imitate them; but he did not seem to have patience to overcome the difficulties he had to surmount.

In many of his actions, he displayed a retentive memory, and in no one was this more remarkable, than on his second voyage to London. Indeed, as the objects of his attention must have been very limited, it is not to be wondered at, that those few should be well remembered.

He seemed to select and show a preference to particular *forms, smells,* and other *qualities* of bodies. He has often been observed to break substances with his teeth, or by other means, so as to give them a form which seemed to please him. He also preferred to touch those substances which were smooth, and which had a rounded form; and he has been known to employ many hours in selecting from the channel of a river, which was near his father's house, small stones of a rounded shape, nearly of the same weight, and having smooth surfaces. These too he would arrange in a circular form on the bank of the river, and place himself in the center of the circle. He also seemed to be much pleased with some Smells, and equally disgusted with others, and this latter he expressed by squeezing his nostrils, and turning his head from whence the smell came. He showed an equal nicety in the selection of his food.

He sometimes showed a good deal of *drollery* and *cunning,* particularly in his amusements with his constant companion and friend, his sister. He took great pleasure in locking people up in a room or closet, and would sometimes conceal things about his person, or otherwise, which he knew not to be his own property; and when he was detected doing so, he would laugh heartily.

That he was endowed with affection and kindness to his own family cannot be doubted. The meeting with his mother, after his return from London (to be afterwards noticed) showed this very strongly. On one occasion, finding his mother unwell, he was observed to weep; and on another, when his attendant happened to have a sore foot, he went up to a garret room to find a particular stool for his foot to rest upon, which he himself had made use of, on a similar occasion, long before. He seemed fond too of young children, and was often in the habit of taking them up in his arms.

His disposition and temper were generally placid, and when kind means were employed, he was obedient and docile. But if he was teazed or interrupted in any of his amusements, he became irascible and sometimes got into violent paroxysms of rage. At no other time did he ever make use of his voice, with which he produced most harsh and loud screams.

It is not one of the least curious parts of his history, that he seemed to have *a love of finery.* He early showed a great partiality to new clothes, and when the tailor used to come to make clothes at his father's house (a practice common in that part of the country), it seemed to afford him great pleasure to sit down beside him whilst he was at work, and he never left him until his own suit was finished. He expressed much disappointment and anger, when any of his brothers got new clothes, and none were given to him. Immediately before he came to London, each of his brothers got a new hat, his father considering his old one good enough for the sea voyage. Such, however, was his disappointment and rage, that he secretly went to one of the out-houses, and tore the old hat to pieces.

Indeed, his fondness for any new clothes afforded a means of rewarding him when he merited approbation, and his parents knew no mode more severe of punishing him than by obliging him to wear old ones.

With respect to the means which were employed to communicate to him information, and which he employed to communicate his desires and feelings to others, these were very ingenious and simple. His sister, under whose management he chiefly was, had contrived signs addressing his organs of Touch, by which she could control him, and regulate his conduct. On the other hand he, by his gestures, could express his wishes and desires. His sister employed various modes of holding his arm, and patting him on the head and shoulders, to express consent and different degrees of approbation. She signified *time* by shutting his eye-lids and putting down his head; which done once, meant one night. He expressed his wish to go to-bed by reclining his head, distinguished me by touching his eyes, and many workmen by imitating their different employments. When he wished for food he pointed to his mouth, or to the place where provisions were usually kept.

Operation

In the hope of restoring this Boy's sight, my attention was solely directed to the removal of the cataract of the right eye. Having thought it preferable *to extract* the lens of that eye, and conceiving this might be accomplished by having him properly secured, I placed him on a table in a room lighted from the roof: and having secured him with skilful assistants, I attempted to introduce the cornea knife; but the resistance which he made was such as to render it impracticable to use that instrument. He seemed to know that something was to be done to his eye, and he at first readily yielded, and allowed himself to be placed and held on the table. The uneasiness, however, which the pressure necessary to keep the eye-ball steady and the eye-lids open, seemed to overcome his resolution, and his exertions became so violent that it was quite impossible to secure even his head.

A second attempt was made the day following, having previously taken more precautions in order to secure him; but so violent were his exertions and cries, and so irascible did he become, that all present were glad to relinquish their posts, and I was impressed with the conviction, that nothing but a powerful piece of machinery calculated to grasp every joint of his body, would be at all sufficient to enable any operation to be performed. Some days having elapsed without the hope of being able to get the operation performed, I at last thought of a machine which completely answered the wished-for purpose, and which I may describe, as on a future occasion, under similar circumstances, it may be found useful. It consisted of a kind of box, long enough to contain all his body except the head. The sides were fixed on hinges, so that they might be folded in upon the body; it had no top part, and the bottom was made long enough to reach sufficiently far beyond the sides at one extremity, so that a perpendicular plane of wood was fixed on it, in which there was a niche of such a size as accurately to contain the head. The machine being placed erect, and lined with a blanket, to prevent any risk of his being injured, he was easily secured in it by folding the sides on his body, and fixing them with circular ropes; and in this manner, notwithstanding a most powerful resistance and many harassing screams, he was placed on a table and kept quite steady. I had now given up all hopes of extracting the cataract, and determined to try *couching,* an operation which, though not generally so successful, was preferable in this case, as there was not so much danger of doing any essential injury to the eye, even if it did not succeed. Much difficulty was found in holding open the eye-lids, and keeping the globe of the eye steady; but this was ultimately accomplished by Mr. Ware, who was kind enough on this occasion to lend me his able assistance. As soon as the couching needle touched the eye he remained quite steady, and his dreadful screaming ceased. I made use of the needle recommended by Mr. Cheselden, and with its sharp edge cut through the anterior portion of the crystalline capsule, and with its point dragged the lens from the sphere of the pupil. On depressing the point of the needle the lens remained out of view, except a small portion of its inferior edge, so that I then withdrew the instrument. A small quantity of blood was effused in the anterior chamber. The operation being finished, he was liberated from the machine in which he was fixed. He then expressed great satisfaction, gazed around him, and appeared as if he could distinguish objects. This, however, could not be ascertained in a manner quite satisfactory, as it would have been prejudicial to his recovery to make any experiments; but it might be perceived from the change in the expression of his countenance. The eye, accordingly, being bound up, he was carried home, and put to bed in a dark room; after which he was bled in the arm.

On the *second day* after the operation the eye was slightly inflamed. The bandage was continued, and he remained in the darkened room. He had been restless and impatient during the night, his skin dry and hot, and his pulse quicker than natural.

On the *third day* all febrile symptoms were gone, and he had slept well. His eye too appeared less inflamed, though easily irritated by exposure to light.

On the *fourth day* I examined the eye accurately, and observed the state of his vision. I found that the crystalline lens had altered its situation since the operation, and could again be distinguished, covering about one fourth of the upper edge of the pupil. The other part of the pupil was quite transparent, and all the blood which had been effused into the anterior chamber during the operation was now absorbed. On making trial if he could distinguish any object, he readily discerned a book placed on the coverlet of his bed, and many of his attempts to touch it seemed to judge pretty accurately of its distance.

On the *fifth day* he got out of bed, and was brought into a room having an equal and moderate light. Before either touching or *seeming* to smell me he recognized me, which he expressed by the fear of something to be done to his eyes. He went about the room readily, and the appearance of his countenance was much altered, having acquired that look which indicated the enjoyment of vision. Indeed, before the operation he always walked with much freedom, and I had observed, that even on a very rugged and unequal road he did not stumble, or suffer the least from jolting.

He appeared well acquainted with the furniture of the room, having lived in it several days previous to the operation; and though, from placing things before him, he evidently distinguished and attempted to touch them, judging their distances with tolerable accuracy, yet he seemed to trust little to the information given by the eye, and always turned away his head, while he carefully examined his sense of Touch, the whole surfaces of the bodies presented to him.

On the *sixth day* he appeared stronger, amused himself a good deal with looking out at the window, and seemed to observe the carts and carriages which were passing in the street. On putting a shilling on the middle of a table he instantly touched it.

On the *seventh day* the inflammation was nearly gone, and he observed a piece of white paper of the size of half a sixpence put upon the table. I took him into the street, and he appeared much interested in the busy scene around him, though at times he seemed frightened. A post supporting a scaffold at the distance of two or three yards chiefly attracted his notice, and he timorously approached it, groping, and stretching out his hand cautiously until he touched it.

He was at this time removed from his lodging to an uncle's house, who being a taylor, had a room full of various coloured cloths, which afforded young Mitchell an unceasing source of pleasure and amusement.

He expressed a great desire for a suit of new clothes, and it was signified to him, that his wishes would be complied with; and being allowed to make a choice, he selected from among the variety of colours a light yellow for his breeches, and a green colour for his coat and waistcoat. Accordingly, these were made, and as I solicited his father not to allow them to be put on until I was present, it was signified to him, that he should have permission to wear them in two days. The mode by which he received this communication was by closing his eye-lids, and bending down his head twice, thereby expressing that he must first have two sleeps. One day after the clothes were finished, I called, and requested that he should be dressed in them. This was intimated to him by his uncle, touching his coat, and giving him a ring of keys, one of which opened the door of the room where the clothes were kept. He gladly grasped the keys, and in an instant pitched on the one he wanted, opened the door, and brought a bundle containing his new suit into the room where his father, uncle, sister, another gentleman and myself were sitting. With a joyful smile he loosened the bundle, and took out of the coat-pocket a pair of new white stockings, a pair of yellow gloves, and a pair of new shoes. The succeeding scene was, perhaps, one of the most extraordinary displays of sensual gratification which can well be conceived. He began by first trying his new shoes after throwing away the old ones with great scorn, and then with a smiling countenance went to his father and to his sister, holding up to each of them and to me his feet in succession, that we might admire his treasure.

He next put on the yellow gloves and in like manner shewing them to his father and sister, they expressed their admiration by patting him on the head and shoulders. He afterwards sat down opposite to a window, stretched out on each knee an expanded hand, and seemed to contemplate the beauty of his gloves with a degree of gratification scarcely to be imagined. At one time I attempted to deceive him, by putting a yellow glove, very little soiled, in place of one of his new ones. But this he instantly detected *as a trick,* and smiled, throwing away the old glove and demanding his new one. This occupation lasted a considerable time, after which he and his sister retired to another room, where he was dressed completely in his new suit. The expression of his countenance, on returning into the room in his gaudy uniform excited universal laughter, and every means were taken to flatter his vanity and increase his delight!

Though the garments continued to occasion much delight, yet there were additional sources of enjoyment now laid open to him from his newly acquired powers of vision. One day I gave him a pair of green glasses to wear in order to lessen the influence of the bright sunshine on his eye, which remained still irritable. He looked through them at a number of objects in succession, and so great was his surprise, and so excessive his pleasure, that he burst into a loud fit of laughter. He continued to keep possession of the glasses, wearing which became one of his favourite amusements.

He, in general, seemed much pleased with objects which were of a *white,* and still more particularly those of a *red* colour. I observed him one day take from his pocket a piece of red sealing-wax, which he appeared to have preserved for the beauty of its colour. A white waistcoat or white stockings pleased him exceedingly, and he always gave a marked preference to yellow gloves.

Young Mitchell left London towards the beginning of September, 1810, and returned home by sea. Soon after, I received from his father the following account of his son. "James seemed much amused with the shipping in the river, and until we passed Yarmouth Roads. During the rest of the passage we were so far out at sea that there was little to attract his notice, except the objects around him on deck. He appeared to feel no anxiety till we reached this coast, and observed land and a boat coming along side of the vessel to carry some of the passengers on shore. He seemed then to express both anxiety and joy, and we had no sooner got into the river which led to the landing place than he observed, from the side of the boat, the sandy bottom, and was desirous to get out. When we got to land he appeared happy, and felt impatient to proceed homewards. On our arrival that evening, after a journey of seventeen or eighteen miles, he expressed great pleasure on meeting with his mother and the rest of the family. He made signs that his eye had been *operated* upon, that he also *saw* with it, and at the same time signified that he was fixed in a particular posture, alluding to the machine in which he had been secured during the operation. He has now learnt to feed himself, and to put on his own clothes. No particular object has yet attracted his attention in the way of amusement."

A considerable time elapsed before any further accounts of young Mitchell reached me. I then learnt that his sight, instead of improving, as I had been led to hope, was impaired, from the opake crystalline lens not having been absorbed, and again covering the pupil; an accident by no means unusual after *couching* the cataract.

Since that time, however, I have been informed that his sight has begun to improve, the fragments of the lens, and opake portion of its capsule are undergoing a gradual absorption, and enabling him to distinguish objects which are not very minute, and of a bright colour. From this sense therefore, he is not yet enabled to acquire much additional information, and it still seems only to afford him the enjoyment of feasting his eyes with light, and with various colours.

As he has advanced in life, his temper has become more irascible, he is less tractable; and he has all the signs of puberty. No circumstance in his history seems to show that has any notion of difference in sex.

The picture which I have attempted to delineate of this Boy's lamentable situation, whilst it must excite our sympathy, cannot fail at the same time to give rise to much philosophical speculation on one of the most interesting subjects which can engage the human understanding. It is a most wonderful and instructive experiment instituted by *Nature* herself to illustrate the progress of the human intellect, to mark the influence of the different organs of perception in the development of its various faculties; thereby realizing what many philosophers have contemplated in imagination, but never before witnessed.

The Boy is now in Scotland, and Professor Dugald Stewart, to whom I have communicated every circumstance of his case, is taking a lively interest in procuring some suitable provision, which might enable the Boy to be placed where an attempt could be made to educate him, and perhaps also to improve his sight by another operation. If this plan be executed under the immediate care and management of Mr. Stewart, everything will be done which can promote the happiness of this interesting youth, whilst science will reap the benefit of the observations of one of the most ingenious and most profound philosophers of the present day.

7

SAMUEL GRIDLEY HOWE (1801–1876)

The education of Laura Bridgman (Published 1837 and later)

This selection deals primarily with the lives of two people, Laura Bridgman, who became deaf and blind at an early age, and Samuel Gridley Howe, M. D., who taught her, a deaf-blind person, a tactile language as a substitute for the usual auditory and visual language. Without this tactile language Laura would have remained as incommunicado as James Mitchell. In her case there was no possibility of restoration of sight. Laura Bridgman was born to Daniel and Harmony Bridgman in Hanover, New Hampshire on December 21, 1829. The Bridgmans were successful and well-established farmers.

During infancy Laura was not strong and was given to "fits" whose nature cannot now be determined. Although ill earlier, she is reported to have been quite well between 20 and 24 months of age. At two years, she had a severe case of scarlet fever which destroyed her sense of sight and hearing, and blunted her sense of smell. She was kept in bed in a darkened room for five months and was feeble for two years following her illness.

Dr. Howe was a man whose entire life was devoted to philanthropy, not through money but through service. After graduation from Harvard Medical School, he went to Greece to participate in the Greeks' attempt to free their country from Turkish domination. He returned to the United States after spending six years in the Greek war, and soon left his country again, this time to help the Poles in their struggle against Germany. Upon returning to the United States in 1832 he became interested in aiding the blind, and established the Perkins Institution for the Blind. Laura Bridgman became his most prominent pupil.

Dr. Howe kept records of his methods of education and of Laura's progress. For many years a report on Laura was a part of the annual report of the Perkins Institution. A compilation of all of these reports appeared as an appendix in the report for 1889.

The brief record of Laura Bridgman's learning a language presented here consists of excerpts from Dr. Howe's accounts which are contained in the book Laura Bridgman *by Maud Howe and Florence Howe Hall, Dr. Howe's two daughters, published by Little, Brown and Co. in 1903.*

It will be noted that in the present set of readings Dr. Howe is the first American author and Laura Bridgman is the first American subject.

Laura Bridgman became adapted to life in the Perkins Institution, which was the only place where there were others who were proficient in her tactile English. She tried living elsewhere for short periods but each time returned to Perkins Institution. She died at the Institution at age 60.

Laura Bridgman was not highly gifted, but few deaf-blind persons since her time have been able to learn a tactile language as she did.

The first knowledge I had of Laura's existence was from reading an account of her case written by Dr. Mussey, then resident at Hanover. It struck me at once that here was an opportunity of assisting an unfortunate child, and, moreover, of deciding the question so often asked, whether a blind-mute could be taught to use an arbitrary language. I had concluded, after closely watching Julia Brace, the well-known blind-mute in the American Asylum at Hartford, that the trial should not be abandoned, though it had failed in her case, as well as in all that had been recorded before.

It was rather a discouragement . . . to find that Laura had no sense of smell; or, to be more precise, only the latent capacity for using it; the organ of that sense not having been destroyed by the disease, as had those of sight and hearing. . . . I determined, however, to make an attempt to reach her mind through the one remaining sense, especially as there was something about her which seemed to give promise of her aiding the attempt as much as she could.

The loss of the eye-balls of course occasioned some deformity, but otherwise she was a comely child. She had a good form and regular features; but what was of vastly more importance, there were marks of fineness in her organization; and the nervous temperament predominated. This gave sensibility, activity, and, of course, capacity.

I found that she had become familiar with much in the world about her. She knew the form, weight, density, and temperature of things in the house. She used to follow her mother about, clinging to her dress, and feeling her arms and hands when she was doing any work. The faculty of imitation of course led her to strive to do whatever she perceived others doing, whether she could understand it or not.

She knew every one of the household, and seemed to be fond of them. She loved to be noticed and caressed; but, as she grew up out of infancy into childhood, the necessity of greater means of mental intercourse with others began to be painfully apparent. Endearments and caresses suffice only for infants. As the brain and other parts of the nervous system were developed, there arose a necessity for the development of the mental and moral capacities. Her mind and spirits were as cruelly cramped by her isolation as the foot of a Chinese girl is cramped by an iron shoe. Growth would go on; and without room to grow naturally deformity must follow. The child began to have a will of her own. The means of communicating with her were so limited that she could only understand the pleasure and displeasure of others. Patting her head signified approval, rubbing her hand disapproval; pushing her one way meant to go, and drawing her another to come.

* * *

Her parents, who were intelligent and most worthy persons, yielded to my earnest solicitations, and Laura was brought to the Institution for the Blind, in October, 1837, being then seven years old.

She seemed quite bewildered at first, but soon grew contented, and began to explore her new dwelling. Her little hands were continually stretched out, and her tiny fingers in constant motion, like the feelers of an insect.

She was left for several days to form acquaintance with the little blind girls, and to become familiar with her new home. Then the attempt was made, systematically, to give her a knowledge of language, by which, and by which only, she could ever attain to any considerable development of intellect, or of affections.

One of two ways was to be adopted. The first and easiest was to go on and build up a system of signs upon the basis of the natural language, which she had already begun to construct for herself. Every deaf mute does this. He makes signs for the things which he sees, and he addresses these signs to the sense which he has in common with you, that is, to your sight. He lifts his fingers to his mouth, and makes the motion of putting something into it, to show you that he is hungry or thirsty; or, he holds up one, two, or five fingers, when he wants to express his notion of number. Hence, in old English "to five," was to count; because, among unlettered people, counting was done by five fingers. You see children using their fingers to aid them in counting; and many grown people have to use audible sounds, or to *count out loud,* in order to aid the mental process, which cannot go on without a sign.

Laura could not address any sign to the sight, because she had no idea of visual appearances of things. She could, however, make a sign for being hungry, another for being thirsty. She had several signs of her own for several persons and things. It would have been easy to go on and enlarge this list, and make it include all tangible objects. But, of course, this plan would have required a sign for every object; one for a pin, another for a needle, another for an apple, and so on. She would, in this way, need as many hundreds or thousands of signs as she had objects or thoughts to express by them. Such a language could be taught easily, because she had acquired its rudiments; but it would have been very rude and imperfect. It could hardly go beyond material existences and tangible qualities. When it came to be applied to abstract matters and moral qualities, it would have been utterly at fault.

The other plan was to teach her a system of purely arbitrary signs, by combination of which she could give names to anything and everything, that is, the letters of the alphabet. For this she would only have to learn twenty-six signs, but, having learned them, she could express countless modifications of thought by combining them in countless ways.

The obvious difficulty in the way of this plan was to take the first step. There was no such difficulty in the plan of a natural language, for in this the first step was already taken. For instance, her father's whiskers made his face different from her mother's; the sign therefore of drawing her hand down each of her cheeks would express that she was thinking of her father, and, by a natural mental process, it would be made to signify men in general, as distinguished from women. So a motion of her fingers like scratching with claws, would signify a cat; a motion of her two first fingers like cutting with scissors, would signify her thought of that instrument, and the like, because there was, so to speak, in all these a *tangible* likeness. There was some analogy between the thing and its sign; hence such signs were the rudiments of a natural language.

Words, however, though many of them may have originated in a supposed resemblance between the thing and its name (as clang, bang, and the like), have no such analogy. They are purely arbitrary. But Laura could not hear the spoken word, or name of a thing, and she could not see the visible sign of it, or the written word, and learn as deaf-mutes learn; consequently the only way was to make the word sign tangible.

... The first experiments were made by pasting upon several common articles, such as keys, spoons, knives, and the like, little paper labels on which the name of the article had been printed in raised letters. The child sat down with her teachers and was easily led to feel these labels, and examine them curiously. So keen was the sense of touch in her tiny fingers that she immediately perceived that the crooked lines in the word *key*, differed as much in form from the crooked lines in the word *spoon* as one article differed from the other.

Next, similar labels, on detached pieces of paper, were put into her hands, and she now observed that the raised letters on these labels resembled those pasted upon the articles. She showed her perception of this resemblance by placing the label with the word *key* upon the key, and the label *spoon* upon the spoon. A gentle pat of approval upon her head was reward enough; and she showed a desire to continue the exercise, though utterly unconscious of its purpose.

The same process was then repeated with a variety of articles in common use, and she learned to match the label attached to each one by a similar label selected from several on the table.

After continuing this exercise several days, with care not to weary her, a new step was taken. Articles were placed upon the table without having a label upon them, as a book, a knife, etc. The loose printed labels, *book, knife,* etc., were placed upon the article until she had felt them sufficiently, when they were taken off, and mingled in a heap. She norrowly watched the process by feeling her teacher's hands, and soon learned to imitate it by finding out the label for *book,* and placing it upon the volume; the same with the *knife,* etc.

This apparently was all done by mere memory and imitation, but probably the natural tendency of the mind to associate things that are proximate in space and time, was leading her to think of the label *book* as a sign for the volume. Let it be borne in mind that the four letters were to her, not as four separate signs, but the whole was as one complex sign, made up of crooked lines.

The next step was to give a knowledge of the component parts of the complex sign, *book,* for instance. This was done by cutting up the label into four parts, each part having one letter upon it. These were first arranged in order, b-o-o-k, until she had learned it, then mingled up together, then re-arranged, she feeling her teacher's hand all the time, and eager to begin and try to solve a new step in this strange puzzle.

Slowly and patiently, day after day, and week after week, exercises like these went on, as much time being spent at them as the child could give without fatigue. Hitherto there had been nothing very encouraging; not much more success than in teaching a very intelligent dog a variety of tricks. But we were approaching the moment when the thought would flash upon her that all these were efforts to establish a means of communication between her thoughts and ours.

The poor child had sat in mute amazement, and patiently imitated everything her teacher did; but now the truth began to flash upon her, her intellect began to work, she perceived that here was a way by which she could herself make up a sign of anything that was in her own mind, and show it to another mind, and at once her countenance lighted up with a human expression; it was no longer a dog or parrot,—it was an immortal spirit, eagerly seizing upon a new link of union with other spirits! I could almost fix upon the moment when this truth dawned upon her mind, and spread its light to her countenance; I saw that the great obstacle was overcome, and that henceforward nothing but patient and persevering, plain and straightforward efforts were to be used.

In order to facilitate her progress . . . a set of types was procured, with the letters in high relief upon their ends. Then a metal frame was cast, and the surface perforated with square holes, into which the types could be set, in such a way as to be in rows, and to have only the letters upon their end felt above the surface. With this machine she could arrange the letters which "spelt out" the names of any article; she could have many rows of those names; she could correct any mistake in the spelling, and could pursue her exercise until she wished to take out the types and put in new ones.

Many weeks were passed in this exercise, when the attempt was made to substitute her own fingers and hand for the cumbrous apparatus of the types and metal board. The attempt was successful, and the success was easily gained, because her mind had become very active, and she made constant efforts to aid her teacher.

Acting still upon her disposition to associate things that were placed in apposition, the teacher took a type which she had learned to use, and of which she knew the form, though she could not know that it was called A, and, holding it in one hand, made with the fingers of the other hand the sign used in the deaf-mute language to express the letter A. This was repeated over and over so often that the child associated the sign upon the fingers with the sign upon the end of the type; and the one became a sign or name for the other.

Next, another letter was taken, say B, and the same process gone over and over. Soon the child caught the idea that there were new signs for things. When she had learned these on four types, these were put together, and she was taught that four different positions of the fingers, standing for four signs on the ends of the types, would express *apple,* in the same way she had been doing it by the types.

The process was continued until she had learned all the letters of the alphabet, and then of course she had the key to our language, and every language whose written signs are Roman letters.

It will help the reader in understanding this rather obscure description of a novel process, if he will bear in mind that it is not by any means an essential way, perhaps not even the best way, to teach common children their letters in alphabetical order,—a, b, c, d, and so on.

Afterwards she learned the names of the ten numerals or digits, of the punctuation and exclamation and interrogation points, some forty-six in all. With these she could express the name of everything, of every thought, of every feeling, and all the numberless shades thereof. She had thus got the *"open sesame"* to the whole treasury of the English language. She seemed aware of the importance of the process; and worked at it eagerly and incessantly, taking up various articles, and inquiring by gestures and looks what signs upon her fingers were to be put together in order to express their names. At times she was too radiant with delight to be able to conceal her emotions.

8

THE PEDAGOGICAL SOCIETY OF BERLIN

The contents of children's minds on entering school at the age of six years (1870)

All the selections presented up to this point have been case studies, and most child studies conducted before 1870 were case studies. The weakness of case studies is obvious. A study of one person cannot reveal whether the person studied is unique or typical. It shows only that there was such a person.

As child psychology progressed, studies based upon many cases began to appear. But historically there is no sharp dividing line between studies of single individuals and studies of many individuals.

We have chosen to include the present selection as the first quantitative survey. Earlier ones can be found, but in general, they are more badly done than this one, although this one is bad enough. In terms of numbers, the Berlin study is big. It is the first one published on the contents of children's minds on entering school. A few earlier studies of this topic were conducted but not published. The present study may be called the first published study in educational psychology. It was stimulated by a course of lectures given to Berlin teachers by Professor O. Willmann, and by a book of lectures published by him. This led to the participation on the part of many teachers in a report which was published in the yearbook of the city of Berlin for 1870.

A letter giving instructions on how to conduct the investigation was submitted to the Pedagogical Society by its president, K. Schobert, in October, 1869. The statistical report of the results was prepared by Professor Bartholomai who was a member of the statistical bureau of Berlin.

The instructions and report were translated into English and published in the first annual report of the U. S. Commissioner of Education in 1900–1901, Volume 1, pages 709–729.

It is not feasible to republish the entire study here. The following *excerpts will indicate its character. The first paragraph consists of extracts from a letter sent to all elementary school principals in Berlin.*

Gentlemen: During the August session of the Pedagogical Society, a discussion of Dr. Willmann's book, entitled "Pedagogical lectures on elevating the intellectual activity through instruction," led to the resolution to propound certain pedagogical questions, the solution of which will essentially contribute to the development of the schools, if the questions be framed with especial regard to the urban conditions characteristic of Berlin.

Since it has been admitted by educators of the most varied views that education and formative instruction are out of the question so long as the knowledge of the pupil is not known, we propose, as a first task, to ascertain the knowledge of the little boys and girls just entering the lowest grade of our Berlin elementary schools, so far as it rests upon the ideas they have acquired of their environments.

It is an undeniable fact that the average knowledge of the child in a metropolis, hence also in Berlin, is a different one, in consequence of the influence of his surroundings, from that of a child living in a rural district or in a small town. It is also a fact that the conditions of the various parts of the city exercise different influences upon the knowledge of children, in consequence of which the mental receptivity of children of different wards shows a noticeable inequality. It is not at all impossible to investigate the causes—at least partly—to which this dissimilarity in the pupils on the one hand and similarity on the other may be traced.

The selection of the questions to be submitted to the children was not easy. To many they may seem strange, especially the questions concerning natural objects; for instance, it may sound odd to ask, "How many of you children have seen a rabbit running free in the country?" The first group of questions is intended to ascertain whether the supposition is correct that the child of a metropolis notices things moving in nature, while his ideas or concepts of things in repose remain indistinct or blurred, sometimes till the end of his school life; hence that his interest, in many cases, can not be easily awakened in things in repose. If this should prove true, many intellectual phenomena in the life of the people of Berlin might be explained, and from the facts ascertained a suitable method in instruction and training in school may be devised to counteract these critical currents in the life of the people.

A similar purpose is aimed at by such questions as "How many children have an idea of a birch, oak, or pine tree standing in the woods?" Experience speaks for the supposition that the Berlin child, if indeed it has observed the woods frequently, comprehends with especial interest quite different ideas of the woods than the country child, hence that the totality of the idea of woods is an entirely different one in the city child from that in the country child.

That the investigation proposed for the purpose of a statistical summary will lead to surprising results, is seen from some preliminary inquiries made to test the questions prepared. Thus, for instance, the children of an upper grade in a girl's school were asked what mountains or hills they had seen. All, without exception, mentioned the Pepperhill, a beer garden situated on the point of a little knoll in the neighborhood of the school. Some also mentioned the Kreuzberg and the Windmuhlenberg as having been seen. A few questions revealed the fact that all these children thought a place of refreshment, or a beer garden, a characteristic quality of the idea hill or mountain. How this association of ideas, easily explained by local circumstances, will make it difficult for these children to comprehend song texts, selections for reading, lessons in geography, etc., in school is obvious. In another classroom, in a school near the Rosenthaler Gate, 80 per cent of the pupils between 11 and 13 years had never seen the Friedrichshain (a well-known grove-like park). Fifty per cent had no idea of a forest, a park, a meadow, etc., other than that which they had acquired on a visit to the zoological garden made in the company of their teachers. These children are lacking, almost up to the time they leave school, a large number of those concepts which must be presupposed in the instruction in geography, nature study, singing, and language, ideas upon which the teacher has to base his instruction.

Now, if similar results be discovered in the majority of schools in Berlin, there will arise the necessity of special tasks for primary language and object lessons, and for lessons in reading and writing; also for a utilization of the walks to the zoological garden and the museums customary with our schools; for a preparation of local and foreign geography, the selection and treatment of song texts, reading matter, the study of natural objects and laws, and the proper acquisition of appliances for these branches.

We are fully aware of the difficulties and obstacles which have to be overcome in getting replies to our questions, but we are convinced that you gentlemen will gladly undertake the arduous task in view of the supreme value which such pedagogical statistics will have in future for each separate school and the whole system of city schools of Berlin.

The questions proposed to be submitted to the children refer to the existence or nonexistence in their minds of the following concepts:

1. Rabbit running free, squirrel on a tree, grazing flock of sheep.
2. Stork on its nest, floating swan, hen and its chicks, call of a cuckoo, song of a lark in liberty.
3. Hopping frog in liberty, fish swimming in river.
4. Beehive, butterfly on a flower, snail creeping in garden or field.
5. Birch, pine, and oak tree in the woods, willow on the edge of the water.
6. Toadstool and moss in the woods, wild flowers.
7. Hazel and huckleberry bush in the woods, reeds on the banks of a pond.
8. Sand pit, turf or peat pit.
9. Thunderstorm, dew.

10. Moving clouds, hail, sleet.
11. Rainbow, evening and morning red.
12. Starry sky, phases of the moon, sunrise and sunset.
13. Dwelling place (address), the Lustgarten, Unter-den-Linden, Wilhelmsplatz, Alexanderplatz, Gensdarmenmarkt, Brandenburgerthor, the King's castle and the palace, museum, arsenal, city hall, place of refreshment, Friedrichshain, Thiergarten, zoological garden, botanical garden, Kreuzberg, Hasenhaide, Invalidenpark.
14. Suburbs of Berlin, such as Treptow, Stralau, Rummelsburg, and Tegel.
15. Ride in a boat, on a railroad, range of mountains, ocean.
16. Mount or hill, forest, meadow, lake, river, grain field, potato field, snow-covered landscape.
17. Village, plowing, harvesting, windmill.
18. Triangle, square, circle, cube, sphere.
19. The numbers 2, 3, 4, etc.
20. God, Christ, biblical stories, prayers, hymns, church service.
21. Name and profession or occupation of father.
22. King, coins, monuments of the Great Elector, Frederick the Great, the Victory column.
23. Fairy stories of Snow-White, Red Riding Hood, Sleeping Beauty, Cinderella.
24. How many can pronounce correctly words told them?
25. How many can recite a memorized poem?
26. How many can sing a song?
27. How many can repeat a musical tone sung?
28. How many have attended a concert?

From [Table 1] we see that by far the greater number of ideas, nearly 75 per cent, were found more frequently in boys than in girls. It is plain, therefore, that the school must assume an attitude with reference to boys different from that assumed toward girls. Many of the ideas in question may have been familiar to children who professed not to have them, they never having connected such ideas with the names by which they are expressed; or, perchance, there may have been neglect to call the children's attention to them.

From our findings we derived another table [Table 2] for purposes of comparison:

The relations of children to their homes and families are so intimate and so frequently renewed after brief intervals spent in school or on the street that one can not but expect them to know family and home. But in this the more introspective life of the girls is revealed, in contrast to the life of boys, which is directed, even in early childhood, toward the outside world. This tendency of boys to look at things outside is so noticeable that the girls come to school richer than the boys in only three groups of ideas, to wit: In ideas of home and family, and in geometrical and in meteorological ideas. The fact that with girls the ideas of space, with boys the ideas of number, should predominate is certainly worthy of notice. That

Table I

No.	Concepts inquired after	Number of each 10,000 children having the concept	Excess of Boys over girls	Excess of Girls over boys
1	Dwelling address	9,026	215	
2	Occupation of father	8,945		672
3	Name of father	8,517		871
4	Starry sky	8,145	542	
5	Thunderstorm at day	7,873		596
6	Rainbow	7,770		143
7	Sphere	7,623	136	
8	Two	7,435	98	
9	Three	7,399	180	
10	Four	7,265	32	
11	Hail	7,015		938
12	Cube	6,957	31	
13	Potato field	6,323		132
14	Moon	6,215		425
15	Swan	6,175	1,385	
16	Butterfly	6,028	2,522	
17	Clouds	5,925	379	
18	Fish	5,853	2,307	
19	Unter den Linden	5,590	1,219	
20	Thiergarten	5,496	1,071	
21	Square	5,474		113
22	Evening red	5,384	419	
23	Hasenhaide	5,121	1,522	
24	Frog	5,085	1,069	
25	Circle	4,991		562
26	Snail	4,750	292	
27	Sunset	4,625	688	
28	Meadow	4,607	908	
29	Alexanderplatz	4,366		645
30	Triangle	4,182	235	
31	Field of grain	4,062	596	
32	Zoological garden	4,057	661	
33	Friedrichshain	3,887		658
34	Flock of sheep	3,870	310	
35	Lustgarten	3,861	367	
36	Forest	3,646	894	
37	City hall	3,615	202	
38	Morning red	3,592		218
39	Squirrel	3,579	705	
40	Brandenburger Thor	3,467	917	
41	Kreuzberg	3,454	1,661	
42	Schloss (castle)	3,423	98	
43	Village	3,374	683	
44	Thunderstorm at night	3,347		321
45	Mountain	3,248	352	
46	Museum	3,222	523	
47	Cuckoo	3,137	935	
48	Treptow	3,065	299	
49	Sunrise	3,052	820	
50	Gensdarmanmarkt	2,909	1,229	
51	Stork	2,887	745	
52	Palace of the king	2,886	672	
53	Toadstool	2,855	799	

Table I (Continued)

No.	Concepts inquired after	Number of each 10,000 children having the concept	Excess of Boys over girls	Excess of Girls over boys
54	Oak	2,641		36
55	Ploughing	2,636	1,483	
56	Sleet	2,493	810	
57	Moss	2,484	467	
58	Rabbit	2,466	36	
59	Stranlau	2,453	885	
60	Harvesting	2,368	911	
61	Dew	2,364		64
62	Wilhelmsplatz	2,158	1,232	
63	Lake	2,078	865	
64	Arsenal	1,957	476	
65	Pine	1,828	864	
66	Lark	1,796	971	
67	Reed	1,702	315	
68	Willow	1,667	1,123	
69	Huckleberry bush	1,640	349	
70	Birch	1,318	487	
71	Rummelsburg	1,242	496	
72	Invalidenpark	1,135	379	
73	River	1,122	11	
74	Hazel bush	907	348	
75	Botanical garden	527		172

Table II

Ideas	Number of children having the idea in every 10,000	Excels Among boys	Excels Among girls
Concerning family and home	8,829		458
Arithmetical	7,367	104	
Geometrical	5,846		58
Thunderstorm	5,610		480
Atmospherical phenomena	5,582	20	
Astronomical	5,509	414	
Cold-blooded vertebrates	5,469	1,678	
Mollusks	5,389	1,407	
Precipitations	4,449	49	
Agricultural	3,772	633	
Locations	3,725	719	
Birds	3,499	995	
Landscapes	3,382	640	
Mammals	3,023	360	
Buildings	3,021	395	
Geographical	2,940	607	
Cryptogamous plants	2,670	633	
Suburbs	2,253	560	
Phanerogamous plants	1,671	493	

the concepts of thunderstorm and its attendant phenomena should be more lasting in girls than in boys shows that the girls have a greater disposition to fear and apprehension. A boy is not generally moved by thunder, lightning, and pouring rain any more than by other phenomena; they appear to him not more important than others. The same disposition in girls to apprehension may also give rise to their observing hail and dew on the grass, things less often observed by boys.

From the foregoing it is seen that the children are the more ignorant of things the farther away the things are from home, a fact which might have been foreseen. Number of house, street of parents' dwelling, and occupation of the father, likewise simple mathematical concepts, can be acquired by a child without crossing the threshold of his home, and without being taken out into the open air into parks or into the country. In all classes of ideas, with exception of those concerning home and family, the girls' knowledge is less than that of the boys.

The general conclusion, then, is that occasional instruction in families, in replies to questions such as: What is this? What is it called? is much neglected. The child comes to school comparatively poor in concepts, and school is forced either to operate with mere words or to substitute in place of observation of living or actual objects lifeless representation on charts, or, thirdly, go back to actual observation of natural objects.

9

CHARLES DARWIN (1809-1882)

The expression of the emotions in man and animals (1872)

Darwin is known by most people only for the theory of evolution, but he was in fact a "scientist at large" who investigated many things in which he became interested. One of these was behavior, including the expression of emotions in man and animals.

Although his book on this topic appeared in 1872, thirteen years after The Origin of Species, *the observations reported in the present book began in 1838, long before his theory of evolution was published or even well formulated in his own mind.*

In this selection, we have chosen for reproduction chiefly his observations on emotional expression in children, mostly on his own children. His writing is remarkable for its direct observational quality and also for the role which he attributed to experience.

Darwin wrote an often-cited baby biography of his son, which was kept in 1840 but not published until 1877. In the editor's opinion the observations contained in the present selection constitute a greater contribution of child psychology than does his diary of his son's development.

WEEPING

Infants, when suffering even slight pain, moderate hunger, or discomfort, utter violent and prolonged screams. Whilst thus screaming their eyes are firmly closed, so that the skin round them is wrinkled, and the forehead contracted into a frown. The mouth is widely opened with the lips retracted in a peculiar manner, which causes it to assume a squarish form; the gums or teeth being more or less exposed. The breath is inhaled almost spasmodically. It is easy to observe infants whilst screaming; but I have found photographs made by the instantaneous process the best means for observation, as allowing more deliberation. I have collected twelve, most of them made purposely for me; and they all exhibit the same general characteristics. . . .

The firm closing of the eyelids and consequent compression of the eyeball,—and this is a most important element in various expressions—serves to protect the eyes from becoming too much gorged with blood. . . .

The action of . . . opposed muscles, above and below, tends to give to the mouth an oblong, almost squarish outline. . . . An excellent observer, in describing a baby crying whilst being fed, says, "it made its mouth like a square, and let the porridge run out at all four corners." I believe . . . that the depressor muscles of the angles of the mouth are less under the separate control of the will than the adjoining muscles; so that if a young child is only doubtfully inclined to cry, this muscle is generally the first to contract, and is the last to cease contracting. When older children commence crying, the muscles which run to the upper lip are often the first to contract; and this may perhaps be due to older children not having so strong a tendency to scream loudly, and consequently to keep their mouths widely open; so that the above-mentioned depressor muscles are not brought into such strong action.

With one of my own infants, from his eighth day and for some time afterwards, I often observed that the first sign of a screaming-fit, when it could be observed coming on gradually, was a little frown, . . . the capillaries of the naked head and face becoming at the same time reddened with blood. As soon as the screaming-fit actually began, all the muscles round the eyes were strongly contracted, and the mouth widely opened . . . so that at this early period the features assumed the same form as at a more advanced age.

Infants whilst young do not shed tears or weep, as is well known to nurses and medical men. This circumstance is not exclusively due to the lacrymal glands being as yet incapable of secreting tears. I first noticed this fact from having accidentally brushed with the cuff of my coat the open eye of one of my infants, when seventy-seven days old, causing this eye to water freely; and though the child screamed violently, the other eye remained dry, or was only slightly suffused with tears. A similar slight effusion occurred ten days previously in both eyes during a screaming-fit. The tears did not run over the eyelids and roll down the cheeks of this child, whilst screaming badly, when 122 days old. This first happened 17 days later, at the age of 139 days. A few other children have been observed for me, and the period of free weeping appears to be very variable. In one case, the eyes became slightly suffused at the age of only 20 days; in another, at 62 days. With two other children, the tears did *not* run down the face at the ages of 84 and 110 days: but in a third child they did run down at the age of 104 days. In one instance, as I was positively assured, tears ran down at the unusually early age of 42 days. It would appear as if the lacrymal glands required some practice in the individual before they are easily excited into action.

The fact of tears not being shed at a very early age from pain or any mental emotion is remarkable, as later in life, no expression is more general or more strongly marked than weeping. When the habit has once been acquired by an infant, it expresses in the clearest manner suffering of all kinds, both bodily pain and mental distress, even though accompanied by other emotions, such as fear or rage. . . .

With adults, especially of the male sex, weeping soon ceases to be caused by, or to express, bodily pain. This may be accounted for by its being thought weak and unmanly by men, both of civilized and barbarous races, to exhibit bodily pain by any outward sign. . . .

With one of my infants, when seventy-seven days old, the inspirations were so rapid and strong that they approached in character to sobbing; when 138 days old I first noticed distinct sobbing, which subsequently followed every bad crying-fit. The respiratory movements are partly voluntary and partly involuntary, and I apprehend that sobbing is at least in part due to children having some power to command after early infancy their vocal organs and to stop their screams, but from having less power over their respiratory muscles, these continue for a time to act in an involuntary or spasmodic manner, after having been brought into violent action. Sobbing seems to be peculiar to the human species; for the keepers in the Zoological Gardens assure me that they have never heard a sob from any kind of monkey. . . .

I may remark that if, during an early period of life, when habits of all kinds are readily established, our infants, when pleased, had been accustomed to utter loud peals of laughter (during which the vessels of their eyes are distended) as often and as continuously as they have yielded when distressed to screaming-fits, then it is probable that in after life tears would have been as copiously and as regularly secreted under the one state of mind as under the other. Gentle laughter, or a smile, or even a pleasing thought, would have sufficed to cause a moderate secretion of tears. There does indeed exist an evident tendency in this direction. . . .

So again if our infants, during many generations, and each of them during several years, had almost daily suffered and prolonged choking-fits, during which the vessels of the eye are distended and tears copiously secreted, then it is probable, such is the force of associated habit, that during after life the mere thought of a choke, without any distress of mind, would have suffered to bring tears into our eyes.

To sum up this chapter, weeping is probably the result of some such chain of events as follows. Children, when wanting food or suffering in any way, cry out loudly, like the young of most other animals, partly as a call to their parents for aid, and partly from any great exertion serving as a relief. Prolonged screaming inevitably leads to the gorging of the blood-vessels of the eye; and this will have led, at first consciously and at last habitually, to the contraction of the muscles round the eyes in order to protect them. At the same time the spasmodic pressure on the surface of the eye, and the distension of the vessels within the eye, without necessarily entailing any conscious sensation, will have affected, through reflex action, the lacrymal glands. . . . Finally, it has come to pass that suffering readily causes the secretion of tears, without being necessarily accompanied by any other action.

Although in accordance with this view we must look at weeping as an incidental result, as purposeless as the secretion of tears from a blow outside the eye, or as a sneeze from the retina being affected by a bright light, yet this does not present any difficulty in our understanding how the secretion of tears serves as a relief to suffering. And by as much as the weeping is more violent or hysterical, by so much will the relief be greater, —on the same principle that the writhing of the whole body, the grinding of the teeth, and the uttering of piercing shrieks, all give relief under any agony of pain.

LAUGHTER

Laughter seems primarily to be the expression of mere joy or happiness. We clearly see this in children at play, who are almost incessantly laughing. With young persons past childhood, when they are in high spirits, there is always much meaningless laughter. The laughter of the gods is described by Homer as "the exuberance of their celestial joy after their daily banquet." A man smiles—and smiling, as we shall see, graduates into laughter—at meeting an old friend in the street, as he does at any trifling pleasure, such as smelling a sweet perfume. Laura Bridgman, from her blindness and deafness, could not have acquired any expression through imitation, yet when a letter from a beloved friend was communicated to her by gesture-language, she "laughed and clapped her hands, and the colour mounted to her cheeks." On other occasions she has been seen to stamp for joy. . . .

With grown-up persons laughter is excited by causes considerably different from those which suffice during childhood; but this remark hardly applies to smiling. Laughter in this respect is analogous with weeping, which with adults is most confined to mental distress, whilst with children it is excited by bodily pain or any suffering, as well as by fear or rage. . . .

The imagination is sometimes said to be tickled by a ludicrous idea; and this so-called tickling of the mind is curiously analagous with that of the body. Every one knows how immoderately children laugh, and how their whole bodies are convulsed when they are tickled. . . . I touched with a bit of paper the sole of the foot of one of my infants, when only seven days old, and it was suddenly jerked away and the toes curled about, as in an older child. Such movements, as well as laughter from being tickled, are manifestly reflex actions; and this is likewise shown by the minute unstriped muscles, which serve to erect the separate hairs on the body, contracting near a tickled surface. Yet laughter from a ludicrous idea, though involuntary, cannot be called a strictly reflex action. In this case, and in that of laughter from being tickled, the mind must be in a pleasurable condition; a young child, if tickled by a strange man, would scream from fear. . . .

Whether we look at laughter as the full development of a smile, or, as is more probable, at a gentle smile as the last trace of a habit, firmly fixed during many generations, of laughing whenever we are joyful, we can follow in our infants the gradual passage of the one into the other.

It is well known to those who have the charge of young infants, that it is difficult to feel sure when certain movements about their mouths are really expressive; that is, when they really smile. Hence I carefully watched my own infants. One of them at the age of forty-five days, and being at the time in a happy frame of mind, smiled; that is, the corners of the mouth were retracted, and simultaneously the eyes became decidedly bright. I observed the same thing on the following day, but on the third day the child was not quite well and there was no trace of a smile, and this renders it probable that the previous smiles were real. Eight days subsequently and during the next succeeding week, it was remarkable how his eyes brightened whenever he smiled, and his nose became at the same time transversely wrinkled. This was now accompanied by a little bleating noise, which perhaps represents a laugh. At the age of 113 days these little noises, which were always made during expiration, assumed a slightly different character, and were more broken or interrupted, as in sobbing; and this was certainly incipient laughter. The change in tone seemed to me at the time to be connected with the greater lateral extension of the mouth as the smiles became broader.

In a second infant the first real smile was observed at about the same age, viz. forty-five days; and in a third, at a somewhat earlier age. The second infant, when sixty-five days old, smiled much more broadly and plainly than did the one first mentioned at the same age; and even at this early age uttered noises very like laughter. In this gradual acquirement, by infants, of the habit of laughing, we have a cast in some degree analogous to that of weeping. As practice is requisite with the ordinary movements of the body, such a walking, so it seems to be with laughing and weeping. The art of screaming, on the other hand, from being of service to infants, has become finely developed from the earliest days.

10

FRANCIS GALTON (1822–1911)

The history of twins, as a criterion of the relative power of nature and nurture (1876)

Galton was a phenomenal man. An English gentleman of private means, he was an explorer, an inventor, a meteorologist, an anthropologist, a student of heredity, and the originator of fingerprint identification. In addition he had some time for psychology. Among his contributions to psychology is the present article in which he describes the importance of twins in the study of nature and nurture. The article reports the first study in this direction. This was done before chromosomes and genes were known and before the biological difference between monozygotic and dizygotic twins was fully understood. This article, here reprinted in full, appeared in the Journal of the Royal Anthropological Institute, *5 (1876): 391–406. In a preliminary form it appeared in* Fraser's Magazine *in 1875. In a modified but less complete form it was a section of Galton's book* Inquiries into Human Faculty and Its Development *(1883).*

The exceedingly close resemblance attributed to twins has been the subject of many novels and plays, and most persons have felt a desire to know upon what basis of truth those works of fiction may rest. But twins have many other claims to attention, one of which will be discussed in the present memoir. It is, that their history affords means of distinguishing between the effects of tendencies received at birth, and of those that were imposed by the circumstances of their after lives; in other words, between the effects of nature and of nurture. This is a subject of especial importance in its bearings on investigations into mental heredity, and I, for my part, have keenly felt the difficulty of drawing the necessary distinction whenever I tried to estimate the degree in which mental ability was, on the average, inherited. The objection to statistical evidence in proof of its inheritance has always been: "The persons whom you compare may have lived under similar social conditions and have had similar advantages of education, but such prominent conditions are only a small part of those that determine the future of each man's life. It is to trifling accidental circumstances that the bent of his disposition and his success are mainly due, and these you leave wholly out of account—in fact, they do not admit of being tabulated, and therefore your statistics, however plausible at first sight, are really of very little use." No method of inquiry which I have been able to carry out—and I have tried many methods—is wholly free from this objection. I have therefore attacked the problem from the opposite side, seeking for some new methods by which it would be possible to weigh in just scales the respective effects of nature and nurture, and to ascertain their several shares in framing the disposition and intellectual ability of men. The life history of twins supplies what I wanted. We might begin by inquiring about twins who were closely alike in boyhood and youth, and who were educated together for many years, and learn whether they subsequently grew unlike, and, if so, what the main causes were which, in the opinion of the family, produced the dissimilarity. In this way we may obtain direct evidence of the kind we want. Again, we may obtain yet more valuable evidence by a converse method. We might inquire into the history of twins who were exceedingly unlike in childhood, and learn how far their characters became assimilated under the influence of identical nurtures, inasmuch as they had the same home, the same teachers, the same associates, and in every other respect the same surroundings.

My materials were obtained by sending circulars of inquiry to persons who were either twins themselves or the near relations of twins. The printed questions were in thirteen groups; the last of them asked for the addresses of other twins known to the recipient, who might be likely to respond if I wrote to them. This happily led to a continually widening circle of correspondence, which I pursued until enough material was accumulated for a general reconnaissance of the subject.

There is a large literature relating to twins in their purely surgical and physiological aspect. The reader interested in this should consult *Die Lehre von den Zwillingen,* von L. Kleinwächter, Prag. 1871. It is full of references, but is is also unhappily disfigured by a number of numerical misprints, especially in page 26. I have not found any book that treats of twins from my present point of view.

The reader will easily understand that the word "twins" is a vague expression, which covers two very dissimilar events—the one corresponding to the progeny of animals that have usually more than one young at a birth, each of which is derived from a separate ovum, while the other is due to the development of two germinal spots in the same ovum. In the latter case, they are enveloped in the same membrane, and all such twins are found invariably to be of the same sex. The consequence of this is, that I find a curious discontinuity in my results. One would have expected that twins would commonly be found to possess a certain average likeness to one another; that a few would greatly exceed that degree of likeness, and a few would greatly fall short of it. But this is not at all the case. Extreme similarity and extreme dissimilarity between twins of the same sex, are nearly as common as moderate resemblance. When the twins are a boy and a girl, they are never closely alike; in fact, their origin is never due to the development of two germinal spots in the same ovum.

I have received about eighty returns of cases of close similarity, thirty-five of which entered into many instructive details. In a few of these not a single point of difference could be specified. In the remainder, the colour of the hair and eyes were almost always identical; the height, weight, and strength were generally nearly so. Nevertheless, I have a few cases of a notable difference in these, although the resemblance was otherwise very near. The manner and address of the thirty-five pairs of twins is usually described as very similar, though there often exists a difference of expression, familiar to near relatives, but unperceived by strangers. The intonation of the voice when speaking is commonly the same, but it frequently happens that the twins sing in different keys. Most singularly the one point in which similarity is rare, is the handwriting. I can with difficulty account for this, considering how strongly handwriting runs in families, but I am sure of the fact. I have only one case in which nobody, not even the twins themselves, could distinguish their own notes of lectures, &c.; barely two or three in which the handwriting was undistinguishable by others, and only a few in which it was described as closely alike. On the other hand, I have many in which it is stated to be unlike, and some in which it is alluded to as the only point of difference. It would appear that the handwriting is a very delicate test of difference in organisation—a conclusion which I commend to the notice of enthusiasts in the art of discovering character by the handwriting.

One of my inquiries was for ancedotes as regards the mistakes made by near relatives, between the twins. The replies are numerous, but not very varied in character. When the twins are children, they have commonly to be distinguished by ribbons tied round their wrist or neck; nevertheless the one is sometimes fed, physicked, and whipped by mistake for the other, and the description of these little domestic catastrophes is usually given to me by the mother, in a phraseology that is somewhat touching by reason of its seriousness. I have one case in which a doubt remains whether the children were not changed in their bath, and the presumed A is not really B, and *vice versa*. In another case, an artist was engaged on the portraits of twins who were between three and four years of age; he had to lay aside his work for three weeks, and, on resuming it, could not tell to which child the respective likenesses he had in hand belonged. The mistakes are less numerous on the part of the mother during the boyhood and girlhood of the twins, but almost as frequent on the part of strangers. I have many instances of tutors being unable to distinguish their twin pupils. Two girls used regularly to impose on their music teacher when one of them wanted a whole holiday; they had their lessons at separate hours, and the one girl sacrificed herself to receive two lessons on the same day, while the other one enjoyed herself. Here is a brief and comprehensive account: "Exactly alike in all, their schoolmasters never could tell them apart; at dancing parties they constantly changed partners without discovery; their close resemblance is scarcely diminished by age." The following is a typical schoolboy ancedote: "Two twins were fond of playing tricks, and complaints were frequently made; but the boys would never own which was the guilty one, and the complainants were never certain which of the two he was. One head master used to say he would never flog the innocent for the guilty, and another used to flog both." No less than nine ancedotes have reached me of a twin seeing his or her reflection in a looking-glass, and addressing it, in the belief it was the other twin in person. I have many ancedotes of mistakes when the twins were nearly grown up. Thus: "Amusing scenes occurred at college when one twin came to visit the other; the porter on one occasion refusing to let the visitor out of the college gates, for, though they stood side by side, he professed ignorance as to which he ought to allow to depart."

Children are usually quick in distinguishing between their parent and his or her twin; but I have two cases to the contrary. Thus, the daughter of a twin says: "Such was the marvellous similarity of their features, voice, manner, &c., that I remember, as a child, being very much puzzled, and I think, had my aunt lived much with us, I should have ended by thinking I had two mothers." In the other case, a father who was a twin, remarks of himself and his brother: "We were extremely alike, and are so at this moment, so much so that our children up to five and six years old did not know us apart."

I have four or five instances of doubt during an engagement of marriage. Thus: "A married first, but both twins met the lady together for the first time, and fell in love with her there and then. A managed to see her home and to gain her affection, though B went sometimes courting in his place, and neither the lady nor her parents could tell which was which." I have also a German letter, written in quaint terms, about twin brothers who married sisters, but could not easily be distinguished by them. In the well-known novel by Mr. Wilkie Collins of "Poor Miss Finch," the blind girl distinguishes the twin she loves by the touch of his hand, which gives her a thrill that the touch of the other brother does not. Philosophers have not, I believe, as yet investigated the conditions of such thrills; but I have a case in which Miss Finch's test would have failed. Two persons, both friends of a certain twin lady, told me that she had frequently remarked to them that "kissing her twin sister was not like kissing her other sisters, but like kissing herself—her own hand for example."

It would be an interesting experiment for twins who were closely alike, to try how far dogs could distinguish between them by scent.

I have a few ancedotes of strange mistakes made between twins in adult life. Thus, an officer writes: "On one occasion when I returned from foreign service my father turned to me and said, 'I thought you were in London,' thinking I was my brother—yet he had not seen me for nearly four years—our resemblance was so great."

The next and last ancedote I shall give is, perhaps, the most remarkable of those I have; it was sent me by the brother of the twins, who were in middle life at the time of its occurrence: "A was again coming home from India, on leave; the ship did not arrive for some days after it was due; the twin brother B had come up from his quarters to receive A, and their old mother was very nervous. One morning A rushed in, saying, 'Oh, mother, how are you?' Her answer was, 'No, B, it's a bad joke; you know how anxious I am!' and it was a little time before A could persuade her that he was the real man."

Enough has been said to prove that an extremely close personal resemblance frequently exits between twins of the same sex; and that, although the resemblance usually diminishes as they grow into manhood and womanhood, some cases occur in which the resemblance is lessened in a hardly perceptible degree. It must be borne in mind that the divergence of development, when it occurs, needs not be ascribed to the effect of different nurtures, but it is quite possible that it may be due to the appearance of qualities inherited at birth, though dormant, like gout, in early life. To this I shall recur.

There is a curious feature in the character of the resemblance between twins, which has been alluded to by a few correspondents; it is well illustrated by the following quotations. A mother of twins says: "There seemed to be a sort of interchangeable likeness in expression, that often gave to each the effect of being more like his brother than himself." Again, two twin brothers, writing to me, after analysing their points of resemblance, which are close and numerous, and pointing out certain shades of difference, add "These seem to have marked us through life, though for a while, when we were first separated, the one to go to business, and the other to college, our respective characters were inverted; we both think that at that time we each ran into the character of the other. The proof of this consists in our own recollections, in our correspondence by letter, and in the views which we then took of matters in which we were interested." In explanation of this apparent interchangeableness, we must recollect that no character is simple, and that in twins who strongly resemble each other, every expression in the one may be matched by a corresponding expression in the other, but it does not follow that the same expression should be the dominant one in both cases. Now it is by their dominant expressions that we should distinguish between the twins; consequently when one twin has temporarily the expression which is the dominant one in his brother, he is apt to be mistaken for him. There are also cases where the development of the two twins is not strictly *pari passu;* they reach the same goal at the same time, but not by identical stages. Thus: A is born the larger, then B overtakes and surpasses A, and is in his turn overtaken by A, the end being that the twins become closely alike. This process would aid in giving an interchangeable likeness at certain periods of their growth, and is undoubtedly due to nature more frequently than to nurture.

Among my thirty-five detailed cases of close similarity, there are no less than seven in which both twins suffered from some special ailment or had some exceptional peculiarity. One twin writes that she and her sister "have both the defect of not being able to come downstairs quickly, which, however, was not born with them, but came on at the age of twenty." Three pairs of twins have peculiarities in their fingers; in one case it consists in a slight congenital flexure of one of the joints of the little finger; it was inherited from a grandmother, but neither parents, nor brothers, nor sisters show the least trace of it. In another case the twins have a peculiar way of bending the fingers, and there was a faint tendency to the same peculiarity in the mother, but in her alone of all the family. In a third case, about which I made a few inquiries, which is given by Mr. Darwin, but not included in my returns, there was no known family tendency to the peculiarity in the twins of a crooked little finger. In another pair of twins, one was born ruptured, and the other became so at six months old. Two twins at the age of twenty-three were attacked by toothache, and the same tooth had to be extracted in each case. There are curious and close correspondences mentioned in the falling off of the hair. Two cases are mentioned of death from the same disease; one of which is very affecting. The outline of the story was the twins were closely alike and singularly attached, and had identical tastes; they both obtained Government clerkships, and kept house together, when one sickened and died of Bright's disease, and the other also sickened of the same disease and died seven months later.

In no less than nine of the thirty-five cases does it appear that both twins are apt to sicken at the same time. This implies so intimate a constitutional resemblance, that it is proper to give some quotations in evidence. Either the illnesses were non-contagious in the instances to which I refer, or if contagious, they caught them simultaneously; they did not catch them the one from the other. Thus, the father of two twins says: "Their general health is closely alike; whenever one of them has an illness, the other invariably has the same within a day or two, and they usually recover in the same order. Such has been the case with whooping-cough, chicken-pox, and measles; also with slight bilious attacks, which they have successively. Latterly, they had a feverish attack at the same time." Another parent of twins says: "If anything ails one of them, identical symptoms *nearly always* appear in the other; this has been singularly visible in two instances during the last two months. Thus, when in London, one fell ill with a violent attack of dysentery, and within twenty-four hours the other had precisely the same symptoms." A medical man writes of twins with whom he is well acquainted: "Whilst I knew them, for a period of two years, there was not the slightest tendency towards a difference in body or mind; external influences seemed powerless to produce any dissimilarity." The mother of two other twins, after describing how they were ill simultaneously up to the age of fifteen, adds, that they shed their first milk teeth within a few hours of each other.

Trousseau has a very remarkable case (in the chapter on Asthma) in his important work "Clinique Médicale." (In the edition of 1873, it is in vol. ii. p. 473). It was quoted at length in the original French, in Mr. Darwin's "Variations under Domestication," vol. ii. p. 252. The following is a translation:

"I attended twin brothers so extraordinarily alike, that it was impossible for me to tell which was which, without seeing them side by side. But their physical likeness extended still deeper, for they had, so to speak, a yet more remarkable pathological resemblance. Thus, one of them, whom I saw at the Néothermes at Paris, suffering from rheumatic ophthalmia, said to me, 'At this instant my brother must be having an ophthalmia like mine;' and, as I had exclaimed against such an assertion, he showed me a few days afterwards a letter just received by him from his brother, who was at that time at Vienna, and who expressed himself in these words 'I have my ophthalmia; you must be having yours.' However singular this story may appear, the fact is none the less exact; it has not been told to me by others, but I have seen it myself; and I have seen other analogous cases in my practice. These twins were also asthmatic, and asthmatic to a frightful degree. Though born in Marseilles, they were never able to stay in that town, where their business affairs required them to go, without having an attack. Still more strange, it was sufficient for them to get away only as far as Toulon in order to be cured of the attack caught at Marseilles. They travelled continually, and in all countries, on business affairs, and they remarked that certain localities were extremely hurtful to them, and that in others they were free from all asthmatic symptoms."

I do not like to pass over here a most dramatic tale in the "Psychologie Morbide" of Dr. J. Moreau (de Tours), Médecin de l'Hospice de Bicêtre. Paris, 1859, p. 172. He speaks "of two twin brothers who had been confined, on account of monomania, at Bicêtre. . . . Physically the two young men are so nearly alike that the one is easily mistaken for the other. Morally, their resemblance is no less complete, and is most remarkable in its details. Thus, their dominant ideas are absolutely the same. They both consider themselves subject to imaginary persecutions; the same enemies have sworn their destruction, and employ the same means to effect it. Both have hallucinations of hearing. They are both of them melancholy and morose; they never address a word to anybody, and will hardly answer the questions that others address to them. They always keep apart, and never communicate with one another. An extremely curious fact which has been frequently noted by the superintendents of their section of the hospital, and by myself, is this: From time to time, at very irregular intervals of two, three, and many months, without appreciable cause, and by the purely spontaneous effects of their illness, a very marked change takes place in the condition of the two brothers. Both of them, at the same time, and often on the same day, rouse themselves from their habitual stupor and prostration; they make the same complaints, and they come of their own accord to the physician, with an urgent request to be liberated. I have seen this strange thing occur, even when they were some miles apart, the one being at Bicêtre, and the other living at Saint-Anne." Dr. Moreau ranked as a very considerable medical authority, but I cannot wholly accept this strange story without fuller information. Dr. Moreau writes it in too off-hand a way to carry the conviction that he had investigated the circumstances with the sceptic spirit and scrupulous exactness which so strange a phenomenon would have required. If full and precise notes of the case exist, they certainly ought to be published at length. I sent a copy of this passage to the principal authorities among the physicians to the insane in England, asking if they had ever witnessed any similar case. In reply, I have received three noteworthy instances, but none to be compared in their exact parallelism with that just given. The details of these three cases are painful, and it is not necessary to my general purpose that I should further allude to them.

There is another curious French case of insanity in twins, which was pointed out to me by Professor Paget, described by Dr. Baume in the "Annales Médico-Psychologiques," 4 série, vol. i. 1863, p. 312, of which the following is an abstract. The original contains a few more details, but is too long to quote: François and Martin, fifty years of age, worked as railroad contractors between Quimper and Châteaulin. Martin had twice had slight attacks of insanity. On January 15 a box in which the twins deposited their savings was robbed. On the night of January 23-4 both François (who lodged at Quimper) and Martin (who lived with his wife and children at St. Lorette, two leagues from Quimper) had the same dream at the same hour, three a.m., and both awoke with a violent start, calling out, "I have caught the thief! I have caught the thief! they are doing mischief to my brother!" They were both of them extremely agitated, and gave way to similar extravagances, dancing and leaping. Martin sprang on his grandchild, declaring that he was the thief, and would have strangled him if he had not been prevented; he then became worse, complained of violent pains in his head, went out of doors on some excuse, and tried to drown himself in the River Steir, but was forcibly stopped by his son, who had watched and followed him. He was then taken to an asylum by gendarmes, where he died in three hours. François, on his part, calmed down on the morning of the 24th, and employed the day in inquiring about the robbery. By a strange chance, he crossed his brother's path at the moment when the latter was struggling with the gendarmes; then he himself became maddened, giving way to extravagant gestures and using incoherent language (similar to that of his brother). He then asked to be bled, which was done, and afterwards, declaring himself to be better, went out on the pretext of executing some commission, but really to drown himself in the River Steir, which he actually did, at the very spot where Martin had attempted to do the same thing a few hours previously.

The next point which I shall mention, in illustration of the extremely close resemblance between certain twins, is the similarity in the association of their ideas. No less than eleven out of the thirty-five cases testify to this. They make the same remarks on the same occasion, begin singing the same song at the same moment, and so on; or one would commence a sentence, and the other would finish it. An observant friend graphically described to me the effect produced on her by two such twins whom she had met casually. She said: "Their teeth grew alike, they spoke alike and together, and said the same things, and seemed just like one person." One of the most curious anecdotes that I have received concerning this similarity of ideas was that one twin, A, who happened to be at a town in Scotland, bought a set of champagne glasses which caught his attention, as a surprise for his brother B; while, at the same time, B, being in England, bought a similar set of precisely the same pattern as a surprise for A. Other anecdotes of a like kind have reached me about these twins.

The last point to which I shall allude regards the tastes and dispositions of the thirty-five pairs of twins. In sixteen cases—that is, in nearly one-half of them—these were described as closely similar; in the remaining nineteen they were much alike, but subject to certain named differences. These differences belonged almost wholly to such groups of qualities as these: The one was the more vigorous, fearless, energetic; the other was gentle, clinging, and timid: or again, the one was more ardent, the other more calm and gentle: or again, the one was the more independent, original, and self-contained; the other the more generous, hasty, and vivacious. In short, the difference was that of intensity or energy in one or other of its protean forms; it did not extend more deeply into the structure of the characters. The more vivacious might be subdued by ill health, until he assumed the character of the other; or the latter might be raised by excellent health to that of the former. The difference was in the key-note, not in the melody.

It follows from what has been said concerning the similar dispositions of the twins, the similarity in the associations of their ideas, of their special ailments, and of their illnesses generally, that the resemblances are not superficial, but extremely intimate. I have only two cases altogether of a strong bodily resemblance being accompanied by mental diversity, and one case only of the converse kind. It must be remembered that the conditions which govern extreme likeness between twins are not the same as those between ordinary brothers and sisters (I have spoken of this in my memoir on the "Theory of Heredity," "Journal Anthropological Institute," December, 1875, p. 829); and that it would be wholly incorrect to generalise from what has just been said about the twins, that mental and bodily likeness are invariably co-ordinate, such being by no means the case.

We are now in a position to understand that the phrase "close similarity" is no exaggeration, and to realise the value of the evidence about to be adduced. Here are thirty-five cases of twins who were "closely alike" in body and mind when they were young, and who have been reared exactly alike up to their early manhood and womanhood. Since then the conditions of their lives have changed; what change of conditions has produced the most variation?

It was with no little interest that I searched the records of the thirty-five cases for an answer; and they gave an answer that was not altogether direct, but it was very distinct, and not at all what I had expected. They showed me that in some cases the resemblance of body and mind had continued unaltered up to old age, notwithstanding very different conditions of life; and they showed in the other cases that the parents ascribed such dissimilarity as there was wholly, or almost wholly to some form of illness. In four cases it was scarlet fever; in one case, typhus; in one, a slight effect was ascribed to a nervous fever; then I find effects from an Indian climate; from an illness (unnamed) of nine months' duration; from varicose veins; from a bad fracture of the leg, which prevented all active exercise afterwards; and there were three other cases of ill health. It will be sufficient to quote one of the returns; in this the father writes: "At birth they were *exactly* alike, except that one was born with a bad varicose affection, the effect of which had been to prevent any violent exercise, such as dancing or running, and, as she has grown older, to make her more serious and thoughtful. Had it not been for this infirmity, I think the two would have been as exactly alike as it is possible for two women to be, both mentally and physically; even now they are constantly mistaken for one another."

In only a very few cases is there some allusion to the dissimilarity being partly due to the combined action of many small influences, and in none of the 35 cases is it largely, much less wholly, ascribed to that cause. In not a single instance have I met with a word about the growing dissimilarity being due to the action of the firm freewill of one or both of the twins, which had triumphed over natural tendencies; and yet a large proportion of my correspondents happen to be clergymen whose bent of mind is opposed, as I feel assured from the tone of their letters, to a necessitarian view of life.

It has been remarked that a growing diversity between twins may be ascribed to the tardy development of naturally diverse qualities; but we have a right, upon the evidence I have received, to go further than this. We have seen that a few twins retain their close resemblance through life; in other words, instances do exist of an apparently thorough similarity of nature, in which external circumstances do not create dissimilarity. Positive evidence, such as this, cannot be outweighed by any amount of negative evidence. Therefore, in those cases where there is a growing diversity, and where no external cause can be assigned either by the twins themselves or by their family for it, we may feel sure that it must be chiefly or altogether due to a want of thorough similarity in their nature. Nay, further, in some cases it is distinctly affirmed that the growing dissimilarity can be accounted for in no other way. We may therefore broadly conclude that the only circumstance, within the range of those by which persons of similar conditions of life are affected, capable of producing a marked effect on the character of adults, is illness or some accident which causes physical infirmity. The twins who closely resembled each other in childhood and early youth, and were reared under not very dissimilar conditions, either grow unlike through the development of natural characteristics which had lain dormant at first, or else they continue their lives, keeping time like two watches, hardly to be thrown out of accord except by some physical jar. Nature is far stronger than nurture within the limited range that I have been careful to assign to the latter.

The effect of illness, as shown by these replies, is great, and well deserves further consideration. It appears that the constitution of youth is not so elastic as we are apt to think, but that an attack, say of scarlet fever, leaves a permanent mark, easily to be measured by the present method of comparison. This recalls an impression made strongly of my mind several years ago, by the sight of some curves drawn by a mathematical friend. He took monthly measurements of the circumference of his children's heads during the first few years of their lives, and he laid down the successive measurements on the successive lines of a piece of ruled paper, by taking the edge of the paper as a base. He then joined the free ends of the lines, and so obtained a curve of growth. These curves had, on the whole, that regularity of sweep that might have been expected, but each of them showed occasional halts, like the landing places on a long flight of stairs. The development had been arrested by something, and was not made up for by after growth. Now, on the same piece of paper my friend had also registered the various infantine illnesses of the children, and corresponding to each illness was one of these halts. There remained no doubt in my mind that, if these illnesses had been warded off, the development of the children would have been increased by almost the precise amount lost in these halts. In other words, the disease had drawn largely upon the capital, and not only on the income, of their constitutions. I hope these remarks may induce some men of science to repeat similar experiments on their children of the future. They may compress two years of a child's history on one side of a ruled half-sheet of foolscap paper, if they cause each successive line to stand for a successive month, beginning from the birth of the child; and if they mark off the measurements by laying, not the 0-inch division of the tape against the edge of the pages, but, say, the 10-inch division—in order to economise space.

The steady and pitiless march of the hidden weaknesses in our constitutions, through illness to death, is painfully revealed by these histories of twins. We are too apt to look upon illness and death as capricious events, and there are some who ascribe them to the direct effect of supernatural interference, whereas the fact of the maladies of two twins being continually alike, shows that illness and death are necessary incidents in a regular sequence of constitutional changes, beginning at birth, upon which external circumstances have, on the whole, very small effect. In cases where the maladies of the twins are continually alike, the clocks of their two lives move regularly on, and at the same rate, governed by their internal mechanism. When the hands approach the hour mark, there are sudden clicks, followed by a whirring of wheels; the moment that they touch it, the strokes fall. Necessitarians may derive new arguments from the life histories of twins.

We will now consider the converse side of our subject, which appears to me even the more important of the two, though I had little suspected it would be so, when I first began the inquiry. Hitherto we have investigated cases where the similarity at first was close, but afterwards became less; now we will examine those in which there was great dissimilarity at first, and will see how far an identity of nurture in childhood and youth tended to assimilate them. As has been already mentioned, there is a large proportion of cases of sharply contrasted characteristics, both of body and mind, among twins. I have twenty such cases, given with much detail. It a fact that extreme dissimilarity, such as existed between Esau and Jacob, is a no less marked peculiarity in twins of the same sex, than extreme similarity. On this curious point, and on much else in the history of twins, I have many remarks to make, but this is not the place to make them.

The evidence given by the twenty cases above mentioned is absolutely accordant, so that the character of the whole may be exactly conveyed by two or three quotations. One parent says: "They have had *exactly the same nurture* from their birth up to the present time; they are both perfectly healthy and strong, yet they are otherwise as dissimilar as two boys could be, physically, mentally, and in their emotional nature." Here is another case: "I can answer decidedly that the twins have been perfectly dissimilar in character, habits, and likeness from the moment of their birth to the present time, though they were nursed by the same woman, went to school together, and were never separated till the age of fifteen." Here again is one more, in which the father remarks: "They were curiously different in body and mind from their birth." The surviving twin (a senior wrangler of Cambridge) adds: "A fact struck all our school contemporaries, that my brother and I were complementary, so to speak, in point of ability and disposition. He was contemplative, poetical, and literary to a remarkable degree, showing great power in that line. I was practical, mathematical, and linguistic. Between us we should have made a very decent sort of a man." I could quote others just as strong as these, in some of which the word "complementary" again appears, while I have not a single case in which my correspondents speak of originally dissimilar characters having become assimilated through identity of nurture. The impression that all this evidence leaves on the mind is one of some wonder whether nurture can do anything at all, beyond giving instruction and professional training. It emphatically corroborates and goes far beyond the conclusions to which we had already been driven by the cases of similarity. In these, the causes of divergence began to act about the period of adult life, when the characters had become somewhat fixed; but here the causes conducive to assimilation began to act from the earliest moment of the existence of the twins, when the disposition was most pliant, and they were continuous until the period of adult life. There is no escape from the conclusion that nature prevails enormously over nurture when the differences of nurture do not exceed what is commonly to be found among persons of the same rank of society and in the same country. My only fear is, that my evidence seems to prove too much, and may be discredited on that account, as it seems contrary to all experience that nurture should go for so little. But experience is often fallacious in ascribing great effects to trifling circumstances. Many a person has amused himself with throwing bits of stick into a tiny brook and watching their progress; how they are arrested, first by one chance obstacle, then by another; and again, how their onward course is facilitated by a combination of circumstances. He might ascribe much importance to each of these events, and think how largely the destiny of the stick has been governed by a series of trifling accidents. Nevertheless all the sticks succeed in passing down the current, and they travel, in the long run, at nearly the same rate. So it is with life, in respect to the several accidents which seem to have had a great effect upon our careers. The one element, which varies in different individuals, but is constant in each of them, is the natural tendency; it corresponds to the current in the stream, and inevitably asserts itself.

Much stress is laid on the persistence of moral impressions made in childhood, and the conclusion is drawn, that the effects of early teaching generally, must be important in a corresponding degree. I acknowledge the fact, but doubt the deduction. The child is usually taught by its parents, and their teachings are of an exceptional character, for the following reason. There is commonly a strong resemblance, owing to inheritance, between the dispositions of the child and its parents. They are able to understand the ways of one another more intimately than is possible to persons not of the same blood, and the child instinctively assimilate the habits and ways of thought of its parents. Its dispositions is "educated" by them, in the true sense of the word; that is to say, it is evoked earlier than it would otherwise have been. On these grounds, I ascribe the persistence of habits that date from the early periods of home education, to the peculiarities of the instructors, rather than to the period when the instruction was given. The marks left on the memory by the instructions of a foster-mother are soon spunged clean away. Consider the history of the cuckoo, which is reared exclusively by foster-mothers. It is probable that nearly every young cuckoo, during a series of many hundred generations, has been brought up in a family whose language is a chirp and a twitter. But the cuckoo cannot or will not adopt that language, or any other of the habits of its foster-parents. It leaves its birthplace as soon as it is able, and finds out its own kith and kin, and identifies itself henceforth with them. So completely is its change of life carried out, and so utterly are its earliest instructions in an alien bird-language neglected, that the note of the cuckoo tribe is singularly correct. Mr. Romanes tells me that he has compared the cuckoo's note with a tuning-fork, at home and abroad, and has found it to be identically the same in both cases.

Much might finally be said in qualification of the broad conclusions to which we have arrived, as to certain points in which education appears to create a permanent effect, partly by training the intellect, and partly by subjecting the boy to a higher or lower tone of public opinion; but this is foreign to my immediate object. The latter has been to show broadly, and, I trust, convincingly, that statistical estimation of natural gifts by a comparison of successes in life, is not open to the objection stated at the beginning of this memoir. We have only to take reasonable care in selecting our statistics, and then we may safely ignore the many small differences in nurture which are sure to have characterised each individual case.

11

FRANCIS GALTON (1822–1911)

Psychometric experiments (1879)

By 1879, the date of this selection, philosophers had been writing about the association of ideas for two centuries, but not a single empirical study had been conducted. Galton's was the first. Ebbinghaus' study of association appeared six years after Galton's was published.

Freud's use of the "free association" method, according to Ernest Jones in the Life and Work of Sigmund Freud, Volume 1, page 242, *"evolved very gradually between 1892 and 1895," thirteen to sixteen years after Galton published his paper.*

Galton studied only his own associations, but he placed the origin of many of them where Freud did, in childhood.

The article appeared in Brain, 2 *(1879): 148–159. It was later reprinted as a part of Galton's* Inquiries into Human Faculty and its Development, 1883.

Psychometry, it is hardly necessary to say, means the art of imposing measurement and number upon operations of the mind, as in the practice of determining the reaction-time of different persons. I propose in this memoir to give a new instance of psychometry, and a few of its results. They may not be of any very great novelty or importance, but they are at least definite, and admit of verification; therefore I trust it requires no apology for offering them to the readers of this Journal, who will be prepared to agree in the view, that until the phenomena of any branch of knowledge have been subjected to measurement and number, it cannot assume the status and dignity of a science.

The processes of thought fall into two main categories: in the first of these, ideas present themselves by association either with some object newly perceived by the senses or with previous ideas; in the second process, such of the associated ideas are fixed and vivified by the attention, as happened to be germane to the topic on which the mind is set. In this memoir I do not deal with the second process at all, so I need not speak more in detail concerning it, but I address myself wholly to the first. It is an automatic one; the ideas arise of their own accord, and we cannot, except in indirect and imperfect ways, compel them to come.

My object is to show how the whole of these associated ideas, though they are for the most part exceedingly fleeting and obscure, and barely cross the threshold of our consciousness, may be seized, dragged into daylight, and recorded. I shall then treat the records of some experiments statistically, and will make out what I can from them.

* * *

When we attempt to trace the first steps in each operation of our minds, we are usually baulked by the difficulty of keeping watch, without embarrassing the freedom of its action. The difficulty is much more than the common and well-known one of attending to two things at once. It is especially due to the fact that the elementary operations of the mind are exceedingly faint and evanescent, and that it requires the utmost painstaking to watch them properly. It would seem impossible to give the required attention to the processes of thought and yet to think as freely as if the mind had been in no way preoccupied. The peculiarity of the experiments I am about to describe is that I have succeeded in evading this difficulty. My method consists in allowing the mind to play freely for a very brief period, until a couple or so of ideas have passed through it, while the traces or echoes of those ideas are still lingering in the brain, to turn the attention upon them with a sudden and complete awakening; to arrest, to scrutinise them, and to record their exact appearance. Afterwards I collate the records at leisure, and discuss them and draw conclusions. It must be understood that the second of the two ideas was never derived from the first, but always directly from the original object. This was ensured by absolutely withstanding all temptation to reverie. I do not mean that the first idea was of necessity a simple elementary thought: sometimes it was a glance down a familiar line of associations, sometimes it was a well-remembered mental attitude or mode of feeling, but I mean that it was never so far indulged in as to displace the object that had suggested it, from being the primary topic of attention.

I must add, that I found the experiments to be extremely trying and irksome, and that it required much resolution to go through with them, using the scrupulous care they demanded. Nevertheless, the results well repaid the trouble. They gave me an interesting and unexpected view of the number of the operations of the mind, and of the obscure depths in which they took place, of which I had been little conscious before. The general impression they have left upon me is like that which many of us have experienced when the basement of our house happens to be under thorough sanitary repairs, and we realise for the first time the complex system of drains and gas- and water-pipes, flues, bell-wires, and so forth, upon which our comfort depends, but which are usually hidden out of sight, and of whose existence, so long as they acted well, we had never troubled ourselves.

The first experiments I made were imperfect, but sufficient to inspire me with keen interest in the matter, and suggested the form of procedure that I have already partly described. My first experiments were these. On several occasions, but notably on one when I felt myself unusually capable of the kind of effort required, I walked leisurely along Pall Mall, a distance of 450 yards, during which time I scrutinised with attention every successive object that caught my eyes, and I allowed my attention to rest on it until one or two thoughts had arisen through direct association with that object; then I took very brief mental note of them, and passed on to the next object. I never allowed my mind to ramble. The number of objects viewed was, I think, about 300, for I have subsequently repeated the same walk under similar conditions and endeavouring to estimate their number, with that result. It was impossible for me to recall in other than the vaguest way the numerous ideas that had passed through my mind; but of this, at least, I was sure, that samples of my whole life had passed before me, that many bygone incidents, which I never suspected to have formed part of my stock of thoughts, had been glanced at as objects too familiar to awaken the attention. I saw at once that the brain was vastly more active than I had previously believed it to be, and I was perfectly amazed at the unexpected width of the field of its everyday operations. After an interval of some days, during which I kept my mind from dwelling on my first experiences, in order that it might retain as much freshness as possible for a second experiment, I repeated the walk, and was struck just as much as before by the variety of the ideas that presented themselves, and the number of events to which they referred, about which I had never consciously occupied myself of late years. But my admiration at the activity of the mind was seriously diminished by another observation which I then made, namely that there had been a very great deal of repetition of thought. The actors in my mental stage were indeed very numerous, but by no means so numerous as I had imagined. They now seemed to be something like the actors in theatres where large processions are represented, who march off one side of the stage, and, going round by the back, come on again at the other. I accordingly cast about for means of laying hold of these fleeting thoughts, and, submitting them to statistical analysis, to find out more about their tendency to repetition and other matters, and the method I finally adopted was the one already mentioned. I selected a list of suitable words and wrote them on different small sheets of paper. Taking care to dismiss them from my thoughts when not engaged upon them, and allowing some days to elapse before I began to use them, I laid one of these sheets with all due precautions under a book, but not wholly covered by it, so that when I leant forward I could see one of the words, being previously quite ignorant of what the word would be. Also I held a small chronograph, which I started by pressing a spring the moment the word caught my eye, and which stopped of itself the instant I released the spring; and this I did so soon as about a couple of ideas in direct association with the word had arisen in my mind. I found that I could not manage to recollect more than two ideas with the needed precision, at least not in a general way; but sometimes several ideas occurred so nearly together that I was able to record three or even four of them, while sometimes I only managed one. The second ideas were, as I have already said, never derived from the first, but always direct from the word itself, for I kept my attention firmly fixed on the word, and the associated ideas were seen only by a half glance. When the two ideas had occurred, I stopped the chronograph and wrote them down, and the time they occupied. I soon got into the way of doing all this in a very methodical and automatic manner, keeping the mind perfectly calm and neutral, but intent and, as it were, at full cock and on hair trigger, before displaying the word. There was no disturbance occasioned by thinking of the imminent revulsion of the mind when the chronograph was stopped. My feeling before stopping is was simply that I had delayed long enough, and this in no way interfered with the free action of the mind. I found no trouble in ensuring the complete fairness of the experiment, by using a number of little precautions, hardly necessary to describe, that practice quickly suggested, but it was a most repugnant and laborious work, and it was only by strong self-control that I went through my schedule according to programme. The list of words that I finally secured was 75 in number, though I began with more. I went through them on four separate occasions, under very different circumstances, in England and abroad, and at intervals of about a month. In no case were the associations governed to any degree worth recording, by remembering what had occurred to me on previous occasions, for I found that the process itself had great influence in discharging the memory of what it had just been engaged in, and I of course took care between the experiments never to let my thoughts revert to the words. The results seem to me to be as trustworthy as any other statistical series that has been collected with equal care.

On throwing these results into a common statistical hotch-pot, I first examined into the rate at which these associated ideas were formed. It took a total time of 660 seconds to form the 505 ideas; that is at about the rate of 50 in a minute or 3000 in an hour. This would be miserably slow work in reverie, or wherever the thought follows the lead of each association that successively presents itself. In the present case, much time was lost in mentally taking the word in, owing to the quiet unobtrusive way in which I found it necessary to bring it into view, so as not to distract the thoughts. Moreover, a substantive standing by itself is usually the equivalent of too abstract an idea for us to conceive it properly without delay. Thus it is very difficult to get a quick conception of the word "carriage," because there are so many different kinds—two-wheeled, four-wheeled, open and closed, and all of them in so many different possible positions, that the mind possibly hesitates amid an obscure sense of many alternatives that cannot blend together. But limit the idea to, say, a landau, and the mental association declares itself more quickly. Say a landau coming down the street to opposite the door, and an image of many blended landaus that have done so, forms itself without the least hesitation.

Next, I found that my list of 75 words gone over 4 times, had given rise to 505 ideas and 13 cases of puzzle, in which nothing sufficiently definite to note occurred within the brief maximum period of about 4 seconds, that I allowed myself for any single trial. Of these 505, only 289 were different. The precise proportions in which the 505 were distributed in quadruplets, triplets, doublets or singles, is shown in the uppermost lines of Table I. The same facts are given under another form in the lower lines of the table, which show how the 289 different ideas were distributed in cases of fourfold, treble, double, or single occurrences.

Table I. Recurrent associations

Total number of associations		Occurring in		
	quadruplets	triplets	doublets	singles
505	116	108	114	167
per cent 100	23	21	23	33

Total number of different associations		Occurring		
	four times	three times	twice	once
289	29	36	57	167
per cent 100	10	12	20	58

I was fully prepared to find much iteration in my ideas, but had little expected that out of every hundred words twenty-three would give rise to exactly the same association in every one of the four trials; twenty-one, to the same association in three out of the four, and so on, the experiments having been purposely conducted under very different conditions of time and local circumstances. This shows much less variety in the mental stock of ideas than I had expected, and makes us feel that the roadways of our minds are worn into very deep ruts. I conclude from the proved number of faint and barely conscious thoughts, and from the proved iteration of them, that the mind is perpetually travelling over familiar ways without our memory retaining any impression of its excursions. Its footsteps are so light and fleeting, that it is only by such experiments as I have described that we can learn anything about them. It is apparently always engaged in mumbling over its old stores, and if any one of these is wholly neglected for a while, it is apt to be forgotten, perhaps irrecoverably. It is by no means keen interest and attention when first observing an object, that fixes it in the recollection. We pore over the pages of a "Bradshaw," and study the trains for some particular journey with the greatest interest; but the event passes by, and the hours and other facts which we once so eagerly considered become absolutely forgotten. So in games of whist, and in a large number of similar instances. As I understand it, the subject must have a continued living interest in order to retain an abiding-place in the memory. The mind must refer to it frequently, but whether it does so consciously or unconsciously, is not perhaps a matter of much importance. Otherwise, as a general rule, the recollection sinks, and appears to be utterly drowned in the waters of Lethe.

The instances, according to my personal experience, are very rare, and even those are not very satisfactory, in which some event recalls a memory that had lain *absolutely* dormant for many years. In this very series of experiments, a recollection which I thought had entirely lapsed appeared under no less than three different aspects on different occasions. It was this: when I was a boy, my father, who was anxious that I should learn something of physical science, which was then never taught at school, arranged with the owner of a large chemist's shop to let me dabble at chemistry for a few days in his laboratory. I had not thought of this fact, so far as I was aware, for many years; but in scrutinising the fleeting associations called up by the various words, I traced two mental visual images (an alembic and a particular arrangement of tables and light), and one mental sense of smell (chlorine gas) to that very laboratory. I recognised that these images appeared familiar to me, but I had not thought of their origin. No doubt if some strange conjunction of circumstances had suddenly recalled those three associations at the same time, with perhaps two or three other collateral matters which may still be living in my memory, but which I do not as yet identify, a mental perception of startling vividness would be the result, and I should have falsely imagined that it had supernaturally, as it were, started into life from an entire oblivion extending over many years. Probably many persons would have registered such a case as evidence that things once perceived can never wholly vanish from the recollection, but that in the hour of death, or under some excitement, every event of a past life may reappear. To this view I entirely dissent. Forgetfulness appears absolute in the vast majority of cases, and our supposed recollections of a past life are, I believe, no more than that of a large number of episodes in it, to be reckoned in hundreds or thousands, certainly not in tens of hundreds of thousands, which have escaped oblivion. Every one of the fleeting, half-conscious thought which were the subject of my experiments admitted of being vivified by keen attention, or by some appropriate association; but I strongly suspect that ideas which have long since ceased to fleet through the brain, owing to the absence of current associations to call them up, disappear wholly. A comparison of old memories with a newly-met friend of one's boyhood, about the events we then witnessed together, shows how much we had each of us forgotten. Our recollections do not tally. Actors and incidents that seem to have been of primary importance in those events to the one, have been utterly forgotten by the other. The recollection of our earlier years are, in truth, very scanty, as any one will find who tries to enumerate them.

My associated ideas were for the most part due to my own unshared experiences, and the list of them would necessarily differ widely from that which another person would draw up who might repeat my experiments. Therefore one sees clearly, and I may say, one can see *measurably,* how impossible it is in a general way for two grown-up persons to lay their minds side by side together in perfect accord. The same sentence cannot produce precisely the same effect on both, and the first quick impressions that any given word in it may convey, will differ widely in the two minds.

I took pains to determine as far as feasible the dates of my life at which each of the associated ideas was first attached to the word. There were 124 cases in which identification was satisfactory, they were distributed as in Table II.

Table II. Relative number of associations formed at different periods of life

Total number of different associations	four times	Occurring three times	twice	once	Whose first formation was in
48 (39)*	12 (10)	11 (9)	9 (7)	16 (13)	boyhood and youth
57 (46)	10 (8)	8 (7)	6 (5)	33 (26)	subsequent manhood
19 (15)		4 (3)	1 (1)	14 (11)	quite recent events
124 (100)	22 (18)	23 (19)	16 (13)	63 (50)	*Totals*

*Numbers in parentheses are percentages.

It will be seen from the table that out of the 48 earliest associations no less than 12, or one quarter of them occurred in each of the four trials; of the 57 associations first formed in manhood, 10, or about one-sixth of them had a similar recurrence, but as to the 19 other associations first formed in quite recent times, not one of them occurred in the whole of the four trials. Hence we may see the greater fixity of the earlier associations, and might measurably determine the decrease of fixity as the date of their first formation becomes less remote.

The largeness of the number 33 in the fourth column, which disconcerts the run of the series, is wholly due to a visual memory of places seen in manhood. I will not speak about this now, as I shall have to refer to it further on. Neglecting, for the moment, this unique class of occurrences, it will be seen that one-half of the associations date from the period of life before leaving college; and it may easily be imagined that many of these refer to common events in an English education. Nay further, on looking through the list of all the associations it was easy to see how they are pervaded by purely English ideas, and especially such as are prevalent in that stratum of English society in which I was born and bred, and have subsequently lived. In illustration of this, I may mention an ancedote of a matter which greatly impressed me at the time. I was staying in a country house with a very pleasant party of young and old, including persons whose education and versatility were certainly not below the social average. One evening we played at a round game, which consisted in each of us drawing as absurd a scrawl as he or she could, representing some historical event; the pictures were then shuffled and passed successively from hand to hand, every one writing down independently their interpretation of the picture, as to what the historical event was that the artist intended to depict by the scrawl. I was astonished at the sameness of our ideas. Cases like Canute and the waves, the Babes in the Tower, and the like, were drawn by two and even three persons at the same time, quite independently of one another, showing how narrowly we are bound by the fetters of our early education. If the figures in the above table may be accepted as fairly correct for the world generally, it shows, still in a measurable degree, the large effect of early education in fixing our associations. It will of course be understood that I make no absurd profession of being able by these very few experiments to lay down statistical constants of universal application, but that my principal object is to show that a large class of mental phenomena, that have hitherto been too vague to lay hold of, admit of being caught by the firm grip of genuine statistical inquiry.

* * *

It would be very instructive to print the actual records at length, made by many experimenters, if the records could be clubbed together and thrown into a statistical form; but it would be too absurd to print one's own singly. They lay bare the foundations of a man's thoughts with curious distinctness, and exhibit his mental anatomy with more vividness and truth than he would probably care to publish to the world.

It remains to summarise what has been said in the foregoing memoir. I have desired to show how whole strata of mental operations that have lapsed out of ordinary consciousness, admit of being dragged into light, recorded and treated statistically, and how the obscurity that attends the initial steps of our thoughts can thus be pierced and dissipated. I then showed measurably the rate at which associations sprung up, their character, the date of their first formation, their tendency to recurrence, and their relative precedence. Also I gave an instance showing how the phenomenon of a long-forgotten scene, suddenly starting into consciousness, admitted in many cases of being explained. Perhaps the strongest of the impressions left by these experiments regards the multifariousness of the work done by the mind in a state of half-unconsciousness, and the valid reason they afford for believing in the existence of still deeper strata of mental operations, sunk wholly below the level of consciousness, which may account for such mental phenomena as cannot otherwise be explained. We gain an insight by these experiments in to the marvellous number of nimbleness of our mental associations, and we also learn that they are very far indeed from being infinite in their variety. We find that our working stock of ideas is narrowly limited, but that the mind continually recurs to them in conducting its operations, therefore its tracks necessarily become more defined and its flexibility diminished as age advances.

12

MELVILLE BALLARD (1839–1912)

Recollections of a deaf mute (1881)

It is implicit in the preceding selections that psychology is concerned with general human nature, and that many aspects of human behavior require the study of childhood.

A persistent question in psychology has been whether or not thinking is possible without language. Many philosophers, who are very verbal, have said no, and have argued at great length. But science requires an empirical, not an armchair approach.

One empirical approach consists of obtaining data on thinking from a person who has learned to understand and use language only when he was several years of age. Some subjects suitable for such a study are congenital deaf-mutes who have learned to communicate when they were beyond the usual age of language acquisition.

All deaf-mutes invent or learn gestures and hence to some degree they communicate. But many ideas canot be expressed to, or by, persons who know only gestures.

The present report is a case in point. Melville Ballard, an American boy, became deaf at 17 months as a result of an injury. At this time his comprehension and use of speech must have been minimal. He was about eleven years old when he entered an institution for the deaf in which he was taught to read and write.

A professor of philosophy, Samuel Porter (1810–1901), was interested in the question, "Is thought possible without language?" and prevailed upon Mr. Ballard, who was then an instructor in a school for the deaf, now Gallaudet College, to write his recollections of his ideas prior to his learning of language. Mr. Ballard did so, and his manuscript was published in an article by Professor Porter, under the title cited above, in the Princeton Review, 57 *(1881)*: 104–120. Since Ballard, not Porter, wrote what is quoted here we have put this selection under Ballard's name. Apparently Porter published, in quotation marks, all of Ballard's manuscript.

William James reprinted approximately two-thirds of Ballard's recollections in his Principles of Psychology, *1890, volume I, pages 266–269.*

Many other writers have used this material, including Piaget, for whom this was grist for his mill, in his Child's Conception of the World (1929).

William James published the memoirs of a similar case (Thomas d'Estrella) in the Philosopical Review, 1 (1892): 613–624. This too has been used by Piaget, because he uncovered in it ideas similar to those of normal children.

In consequence of the loss of my hearing in infancy, I was debarred from enjoying the advantages which children in the full possession of their senses derive from the exercises of the common primary school, from the everyday talk of their school-fellows and playmates, and from the conversation of their parents and other grown-up persons.

I could convey my thoughts and feelings to my parents and brothers by natural signs or pantomine, and I could understand what they said to me by the same medium; our intercourse being, however, confined to the daily routine of home affairs and hardly going beyond the circle of my own observation.

My mother made the attempt to teach me to articulate by speaking loud close to my ear, and also by making me look at her lips and try to repeat what she had uttered. There was many a word of encouragement from the mother and many an expression of discouragement on the part of the child; and she persevered, hoping against hope, in this labor of love, until I was five years old, when she gave it up as a hopeless task. She, however, renewed the attempt occasionally at different periods afterwards.

There was one thing to which she ever adhered, in our relations as mother and child. That was her endeavor for the molding of my character. She did not indulge me in anything on account of my privation. She did not suffer my misfortune to lead her to surrender her judgment to the fondness of her affection. She taught me to treat my brothers and sisters just as they were to treat me, and especially to respect their property in the playthings which belonged to them. An uncle of mine remonstrated with her in my behalf, saying that my brothers would be willing to gratify my humor. She answered him that she did not wish to have me grow up in the belief that I was a person different from others, having claims superior to theirs.

My father adopted a course which he thought would in some measure, compensate me for the loss of my hearing. It was that of taking me with him, when business required him to ride abroad; and he took me more frequently than he did my brothers; giving, as the reason for his apparent partiality, that they could acquire information through the ear, while I depended solely upon my eye for acquaintance with affairs of the outside world. He believed that observation would help to develop my faculties, and he also wished to see me deriving pleasure from some source.

I have a vivid recollection of the delight I felt in watching the different scenes we passed through, observing the various phases of nature, both animate and inanimate; tho we did not, owing to my infirmity, engage in conversation. It was during those delightful rides, some two or three years before my initiation into the rudiments of written language, that I began to ask myself the question: *How came the world into being?* When this question occurred to my mind, I set myself to thinking it over a long time. My curiosity was awakened as to what was the origin of human life in its first appearance upon the earth, and of vegetable life as well, and also the cause of the existence of the earth, sun, moon, and stars.

I remember at one time when my eye fell upon a very large old stump which we happened to pass in one of our rides, I asked myself, "Is it possible that the first man that ever came into the world rose out of that stump? But that stump is only a remnant of a once noble magnificent tree, and how came that tree? Why, it came only by beginning to grow out of the ground just like those little trees now coming up." And I dismissed from my mind, as an absurd idea, the connection between the origin of man and a decaying old stump.

For my knowledge of the motives of my parents in their treatment of me during my childhood, I am indebted to a long recital, given by my mother about five years ago, of incidents of my early life and the details connected therewith.

I have no recollection of what it was that first suggested to me the question as to the origin of things. I had before this time gained ideas of the descent from parent to child, of the propagation of animals, and of the production of plants from seeds. The question that occurred to my mind was: whence came the first man, the first animal, and the first plant, at the remotest distance of time, before which there was no man, no animal, no plant; since I knew they all had a beginning and an end.

It is impossible to state the exact order in which these different questions arose, *i.e.*, about men, animals, plants, the earth, sun, moon, &c. The lower animals did not receive so much thought as was bestowed upon man and the earth; perhaps because I put man and beast in the same class, since I believed that man would be annihilated and there was no resurrection beyond the grave,—tho I am now told by my mother that, in answer to my question, in the case of a deceased uncle who looked to me like a person in sleep, she had tried to make me understand that he would awake in the far future. It was my belief that man and beast derived their being from the same source, and were to be laid down in the dust in a state of annihilation. Considering the brute animal as of secondary importance, and allied to man on a lower level, man and the earth were the two things on which my mind dwelled most.

I think I was five years old, when I began to understand the descent from parent to child and the propagation of animals. I was nearly eleven years old, when I entered the Institution where I was educated; and I remember distinctly that it was at least two years before this time that I began to ask myself the question as to the origin of the universe. My age was then about eight, not over nine years.

Of the form of the earth, I had no idea in my childhood, except that, from a look at a map of the hemispheres, I inferred there were two immense discs of matter lying near each other. I also believed the sun and moon to be two round, flat plates of illuminating matter; and for those luminaries I entertained a sort of reverence on account of their power of lighting and heating the earth. I thought from their coming up and going down, traveling across the sky in so regular a manner, that there must be a certain something having power to govern their course. I believed the sun went into a hole at the west and came out of another at the east, traveling through a great tube in the earth, describing the same curve as it seemed to describe in the sky. The stars seemed to me to be tiny lights studded in the sky.

The source from which the universe came was the question about which my mind revolved in a vain struggle to grasp it, or rather to fight the way up to attain to a satisfactory answer. When I had occupied myself with this subject a considerable time, I perceived that it was a matter much greater than my mind could comprehend; and I remember well that I became so appalled at its mystery and so bewildered at my inability to grapple with it that I laid the subject aside and out of my mind, glad to escape being, as it were, drawn into a vortex of inextricable confusion. Tho I felt relieved at this escape, yet I could not resist the desire to know the truth; and I returned to the subject; but as before, I left it, after thinking it over for some time. In this state of preplexity, I hoped all the time to get at the truth, still believing that, the more I gave thought to the subject, the more my mind would penetrate the mystery. Thus, I was tossed like a shuttlecock, returning to the subject and recoiling from it, till I came to school.

I remember that my mother once told me about a being up above, pointing her finger towards the sky and with a solemn look on her countenance. I do not recall the circumstance which led to this communication. When she mentioned the mysterious being up in the sky, I was eager to take hold of the subject, and plied her with questions concerning the form and appearance of this unknown being, asking if it was the sun, moon, or one of the stars. I knew she meant that there was a living one somewhere up in the sky; but when I realized that she could not answer my questions, I gave it up in despair, feeling sorrowful that I could not obtain a definite idea of the mysterious living one up in the sky.

One day, while we were haying in a field, there was a series of heavy thunder-claps. I asked one of my brothers where they came from. He pointed to the sky and made a zigzag motion with his finger, signifying lightning. I imagined there was a great man somewhere in the blue vault, who made a loud noise with his voice out of it; and each time I heard a thunder-clap I was frightened, and looked up at the sky, fearing he was speaking a threatening word.

In the year after my admission into the school for deaf-mutes, at Hartford, Conn., I learned a few sentences every Sunday, such as "God is great," "God is wise," "God is strong," "God is kind," etc., and tho I studied those simple words, I never acquired any idea of God as the Creator. I attended the chapel services, but they were almost unintelligible, owing to my imperfect knowledge of the sign-language as employed in the Institution. The second year I had a small catechism containing a series of questions and answers. The first question was, "Who made this watch?" Answer: "A man made it. "Second question: "Who made that house?" Answer: "Some men built it." Third question: "Who made the sun?" Answer: "God created the sun, moon and stars." Fourth question: "Who made the earth?" Answer: "God created the earth, sea, trees, grass and vegetables."

This method of proceeding from the lower stages of intelligent construction to the act of creation began to clear away, in my mind, the mystery of the origin of the universe. I was now able to understand well the sign-language used by my instructors in their explanations. While the creation of the heavens and the earth was being related to us, the Creator was described as a great invisible spirit, seeing and knowing all things, and at whose creative word the world sprang into existence. As this truth was dawning on my mind, I felt a sensation of awe at the magnitude of the work done by the one ruling mind. From the uncertain preplexing round of speculation in which I had been groping back and back through the dark depths of time, seeking to discover the origin of the universe, I found myself translated into a world of light, wherein my mind was set at rest on this great question; and I felt as tho I had become a new being. This revelation of the truth seemed to give a new dignity to everything, as deriving its existence from an almighty and wise Creator; and it seemed to elevate the world to a higher and more honorable place.

It may be said, and perhaps to my reproach, that my inquiring disposition ought to have been satisfied. It was not so; for when I had learned of the creation of the universe by the one great ruling spirit, I began to ask myself whence came the Creator, and set myself to inquiring after his nature and origin. While I revolve this question, I ask myself, "Shall we ever know the nature of God and comprehend his infinity after we enter his kingdom?" And would it not be better for us to say with the patriarch of old, "Canst thou by searching find out God?"

13

WILHELM PREYER (1842–1897)

The mind of the child (1882)

Wilhelm Preyer was a German physiologist and biologist who undertook to study the development of the mind as well as of the body. As an outcome of this interest he wrote the first full empirical treatise on child development. It was published in two volumes, entitled The Mind of the Child *(1882).*

By this date many baby biographies had been published. Many of them were fragmentary, and many were devoted to special topics. Preyer made use of them, but in addition used data from careful and continuous observations of his son.

In the present selection, his day-by-day observations have not been included, because his observations while more complete than others, were not new. Rather we have chosen his extensive studies of the development of color identification by his son, which show that the experimental approach can be used longitudinally. Few children have had to make as many color decisions as did Preyer's son.

While Preyer does not explicitly say so, it seems almost certain that parental reinforcements, by language and by pats on the head, were used to obtain such continued performance. B. F. Skinner could not have elicited a greater number of responses than did Preyer.

I proposed to myself a number of years ago, the task of studying the child, both before birth and in the period immediately following, from the physiological point of view, with the object of arriving at an explanation of the origin of the separate vital processes. It was soon apparent to me that a division of the work would be advantageous to its prosecution. For life in the embryo is so essentially different a thing from life beyond it, that a separation must make it easier both for the investigator to do his work and for the reader to follow the exposition of its results. I have, therefore, discussed by itself, life before birth, the "Physiology of the Embryo." The vital phenomena of the human being in the earliest period of his independent existence in the world are, again, so complicated and so various in kind, that here too a division soon appeared expedient. I separated the physical development of the newly-born and the very young child from his mental development, and have endeavored to describe the latter in the present book; at least, I hope that, by means of personal observations carried on for several years, I have furnished facts that may serve as material for a future description.

A forerunner of the work is a lecture, "Psychogenesis" (the Genesis of Mind), given before a scientific association at Berlin on the 3d of January, 1880, and soon after made public in my book, "Naturwissenschaftliche Thatsachen und Probleme" ("Facts and Problems of Natural Science") Berlin, 1880.

This sketch has given manifold incitement to fresh observations. But great as is the number of occasional observations in regard to many children, I do not thus far know of diaries regularly kept concerning the mental development of individual children. Now precisely this chronological investigation of mental progress in the first and second years of life presents great difficulties, because it requires the daily registering of experiences that can be had only in the nursery. I have, notwithstanding, kept a complete diary from the birth of my son to the end of his third year. Occupying myself with the child at least three times a day—at morning, noon, and evening—and almost every day, with two trifling interruptions, and guarding him, as far as possible, against such training as children usually receive, I found nearly every day some fact of mental genesis to record. The substance of that diary has passed into this book.

No doubt the development of one child is rapid and that of another is slow; very great individual differences appear in children of the same parents even, but the differences are much more of time and degree than of the order in which the steps are taken, and these steps are the same in all individuals; that is the important matter. Desirable as it is to collect statistics concerning the mental development of *many* infants—the activity of their senses, their movements, especially their acquirement of speech—yet the accurate, daily repeated observation of *one* child—a child sound in health, having no brothers or sisters, and whose development was neither remarkably rapid nor remarkably slow—seemed at least quite as much to be desired. I have, however, taken notice, as far as possible, of the experiences of others in regard to other normal children in the first years of life, and have even compared many of these where opportunity offered.

Discrimination of colors

At what age the child is capable of distinguishing colors, at least red, yellow, green, and blue, it is hard to determine. In the first days, it is certain that only the difference of light and dark is perceived, and this imperfectly.

The first object that made an impression on account of its color, upon my boy, was probably a rose-colored curtain which hung, brightly by the sun but not dazzlingly bright, about a foot before the child's face. This was on the twenty-third day. The child laughed and uttered sounds of satisfaction.

As the smooth, motionless, bright-colored surface alone occupied the whole field of vision, it must have been on account either of its brightness or of its color that it was the source of pleasure. In the evening of the same day, the flame of the candle, at the distance of one metre, caused quite similar expressions of pleasure when it was placed before the eyes, which had been gazing into empty space; and so did, on the forty-second day, the sight of colored tassels in motion, but in this case the movement also was a source of pleasure.

In the eighty-fifth week, when I undertook the first systematic tests, with counters alike in form but unlike in color, no trace of discrimination in color was as yet to be discerned, although without doubt it already existed. Different as were the impressions of sound made by the words "red," "yellow," "green," "blue" (these were certainly distinguished from one another), and well as the child knew the meaning of "give," he was not able to give the counters of the right color, even when only "red" and "green" were called for. We are not to infer from this, however, an inability of the eye to distinguish one color from another, for here it is essential to consider the difficulty of associating the sound of the word "red" or "green" with the proper color-sensation, even when the sensation is present.

At this time, before the age of twenty-one months, there must have been recognition not only of the varying intensity of light (white, gray, black), but also of the quality of some colors, for the delight in striking colors was manifest. Yet in the case of little children, even after they have begun to speak, it can not be determined without searching tests what colors they distinguish and rightly name.

In order, then, to ascertain how the separate colors are related to one another in this respect, I have made several hundred color-tests with my child, beginning at the end of his second year. These I used to apply every day in the early morning, for a week; then, after an interval of a week, again almost every day, but in a different manner—as will be shown directly.

In all these tests I made use of the colored ovals which Dr. H. Magnus, of Breslau, gives in his . . . "Chart for the Training of the Color-Sense" (1879).

After the names "red" and "green" had been repeatedly pronounced while the corresponding colors were presented, then these two colors were simply presented and the questions, "Where is red?" and "Where is green?" were put, always in alternation. The trials were absolutely without result in the eighty-sixth and eighty-seventh weeks. After an interval of twenty-two weeks, on the seven hundred fifty-eighth day, I received eleven times a right answer, six times a wrong answer. On the following day the answers were right seven times, wrong five times; on the day after that, nine times right, five times wrong. From this it seemed probable, already, that the two colors were distinguished, either on account of their quality or on account of their brightness, and that the right names were often associated with them. To my surprise, however, on the seven hundred sixty-third day the answers were right fifteen time and wrong only once, and on the following day ten times right and not once wrong. The child had therefore firmly grasped the connection of the sound-impressions "red" and "green" with two different light-impressions. For such proportions as those of the above numbers exclude the possibility of chance.

I carried the test further. To red and green I added yellow, and when the three colors were lying near one another, each one was rightly pointed out in answer to the question where it was. Then came a disinclination on the part of the child to continue, such as often makes color-tests impossible in children so young. When the trial was repeated, he was inattentive, and he confounded the three colors with one another. On the following day, the seven hundred sixty-fifth, green especially was confounded with yellow. The answers on five days of the one hundred tenth week were:

	Right	Wrong
Red	26	10
Green	24	7
Yellow	23	5
Total	73	22

Blue was now added as a fourth color. The answers in eight trials, during the time from the end of the one hundred tenth to the beginning of the one hunded twelfth week, were:

	Right	Wrong
Red	32	14
Green	31	8
Yellow	34	2
Blue	27	12
Total	124	36

Often, especially on being asked "Where is blue?" the child would consider long, observe the four colors attentively before deciding, and then give me the color quickly. It appears evident that yellow is recognized more surely than are the other colors. Yellow seems to be the easiest to distinguish, and hence the easiest also to retain in memory. I made other tests of the same sort, which showed the superiority of yellow. Then violet was added as the fifth color, called "lila," as easier to speak, and a different way of conducting the experiment was adopted.

I laid each color separately before the child and asked, "What is that?" He answered, *rroot* [Eng. pronunciation *wrote*] (for *roth*, red), *delp, depp, gelp* (for *gelb*, yellow), *rihn, ihn* [Eng. pr. *reen, een*] (for *grün*, green), *balau* (for *blau*, blue), and *lilla* (for *lila*, violet).

In the one hundred twelfth week [2-0 years] the answers in four trials were:

	Right	Wrong
Red	10	2
Yellow	9	0
Green	9	1
Blue	5	7
Violet	11	1
Total	44	11

Here, too, yellow is foremost; it was named correctly nine times, not once wrongly named. Blue comes last. It was confounded especially with green and violet. If the child's attention failed, I broke off.

Afterward the tests were continued in both ways combined; but these proved to the great consumers of time. It often happens that the child takes no interest in the colors. Sometimes, from roguishness, he *will* not name the color he knows, and will not point out or give me the one I ask for. At other times he himself brings the box that holds the color-ovals, and says *wawa* = "Farbe" (color), in expectation of a lesson. The trials in which the attention is undivided are, however, not numerous.

Gray is added. In the one hundred twelfth and one hundred thirteenth weeks five tests yielded the following answers:

	Right	Wrong
Red	16	3
Yellow	22	1
Green	14	5
Blue	10	15
Violet	18	1
Gray	10	2
Total	90	27

Yellow maintains the first place, being rightly named in twenty-two instances, and wrongly only once. The judgment in regard to blue is the worst; fifteen wrong judgments to ten right ones. It is noteworthy that in this series, as in the preceding, violet is rightly named oftener than green.

I now bade the child, repeatedly, to place together the ovals of the same color. After much moving hither and thither, he succeeded with yellow, red, rose, green, and violet, but very incompletely. The expressions "light" and "dark," before the names of the colors, were beyond the child's understanding. So the saturated and the less saturated colors, the light and the dark, were, as before, indicated by the common name of the quality alone. Four trials with the colors mixed, during the time from the one hundred fourteenth to the one hundred sixteenth week, resulted as follows:

	Right	Wrong
Red	15	1
Yellow	13	0
Green	4	7
Blue	3	10
Violet	11	2
Gray	6	0
Brown	4	0
Rose	1	2
Black	2	0
Total	59	22

Blue was especially confounded with violet, also with green. All very pale colors were confounded with gray, all dark ones with black. The order in which the colors were recognized, i.e., rightly named, is now the following: Yellow best of all, then red, violet, green; and worst of all, blue.

On other days I laid before the child, as I had done previously, a single color, with the question, what it was, and marked the answer wrong if it were not given right immediately. The colors are now called by the child *rott, delp, drün, blau, lila, grau, swarz, rosa, braun.*

Four trials in the one hundred fourteenth and one hundred fifteenth weeks yielded the answers:

	Right	*Wrong*
Red	13	0
Yellow	11	0
Green	7	9
Blue	5	13
Violet	10	3
Gray	1	3
Brown	4	1
Rose	3	3
Black	4	0
Total	58	32

For the first five colors this trial gives the same order of succession as above. Blue and green are very uncertain; blue is called *drün* (meant for grün) and *lila* (violet), green is called gray; and, oftener still, neither blue nor green is named at all; while yellow, and red, and black, are given correctly and quickly.

I now let the child take out of the box of colored ovals one after another of them, at pleasure, name it, and give it to me. At the first trial he seized at random; at the second he sought his favorite color, yellow.

Two trials in the one hundred fifteenth week:

	Right	*Wrong*
Red	6	0
Yellow	8	0
Green	1	2
Blue	0	5
Violet	4	1
Gray	1	5
Brown	0	1
Rose	3	2
Black	2	0
Total	25	16

The result is the same as above. Red, yellow, and black are the only colors that are surely recognized.

I now made no more trials for two months. The child spent the larger part of the day in the open air, with me, on a journey; the greater part of the time was spent in the neighborhood of Lake Garda.

In the one hundred twenty-first week, an occasional examination showed a greater uncertainty than before. Blue was scarcely once named rightly, in spite of the most urgent cautions. When the trials were resumed, after our return, the result was bad. I took the colored counters in my hand and put questions. At the very first questioning, yellow was indeed named rightly three times, and not wrongly at all; but red was twice wrongly and not once rightly named.

I got the following answers in the one hundred twenty-fourth week, in the first four trials with all the colors after the interval:

	Right	*Wrong*
Red	17	0
Yellow	22	0
Green	0	18
Blue	0	13
Violet	9	4
Gray	0	5
Brown	4	3
Rose	3	4
Black	3	0
Orange	0	2
Total	58	49

Here it is still more evident than before that red and yellow are more surely recognized and more correctly named than green and blue. On the eight hundred sixty-sixth day the child, without being constrained, took colors out of the box and gave them to me, naming them as he did so. The colors that were mistaken for one another were rose, gray, and pale green; brown and gray; green and black; finally, blue and violet.

In the following experiments, also, the child every time took the colors out of the box and gave them to me, telling the names at the same time, without the least direction. Five trials out of the one hundred twenty-fourth and one hundred twenty-fifth weeks gave:

	Right	*Wrong*
Red	29	1
Yellow	16	0
Green	0	4
Blue	0	6
Violet	14	0
Gray	0	8
Rose	14	5
Brown	7	2
Black	0	2
Orange	0	6
Total	80	34

Red and yellow are eagerly sought and almost always rightly named; blue and green avoided and always named wrongly (e.g., as *lila, swarz*). I now removed all the red and yellow colors from the collection, and let the child give to me, and name as many of the remaining ones as he could. Now that red and yellow are wanting, however, he shows from the first a less degree of interest, and in the case of green he says "Papa tell!" In all other cases he had a name for the color he took. If that was wrong, it was always corrected by me, often by the child himself; but it was always entered in the record as wrong, if the first answer was wrong. In the one hundred twenty-fifth and one hundred twenty-sixth weeks six trials were made in which this method was strictly observed and the following judgments were registered:

	Right	Wrong
Green	2	19
Blue	6	20
Violet	20	3
Gray	0	6
Rose	19	6
Brown	15	0
Black	7	2
Orange	11	7
Total	80	63

The brighter colors were at first selected. The child confuses orange (*oroos,* as he calls it) with yellow, blue with violet, green with gray, black with brown.

I tried repeatedly to induce the child to place together the colors that seemed to him alike, but it was a total failure. Then I asked for single colors by their names, but the results of this procedure were likewise poor. (This on the eight hundred seventy-ninth day.) Finally, I took a single color at a time and asked, "What is that?" In four trials in the one hundred twenty-sixth, one hundred twenty-seventh, and one hundred twenty-eighth weeks, the answers were:

	Right	Wrong
Red	11	(1)
Yellow	11	0
Green	1	14
Blue	1	11
Violet	12	1
Gray	6	1
Rose	11	2
Brown	10	0
Black	6	1
Orange	6	2 and (1)
Total	75	34

For green and blue—which are confounded with gray when they are light, and with black when they are dark—there is probably a less degree of sensibility, certainly a less interest. Blue is still called *lila*. Besides, it is very difficult to direct the attention persistently to the colors. The child, although tested only in the early hours of morning, seeks now other means of entertaining himself. Now and then he makes a mistake in speaking. (Errors of this kind are indicated by parentheses). But on the eight hundred ninety-eighth day every color was rightly named—green and blue, to be sure, only after some guessing. In six trials in the one hundred twenty-ninth, one hundred thirty-fifth, one hundred thirty-sixth, one hundred thirty-seventh, and one hundred thirty-eighth weeks the child took the colors and gave them to me, naming them. The answers were:

	Right	Wrong
Red	27	1
Yellow	27	0
Green	2	14
Blue	2	13
Violet	15	2
Gray	5	1
Rose	10	3
Brown	14	0
Black	5	1
Orange	12	3
Total	119	38

There is confounding of colors as before. The only thing new is the designation *garnix* (for *gar nichts*, "nothing at all") for green and blue. Unknown colors are now often named green—e.g., blue. In a bouquet of yellow roses these were designated as yellow, but the leaves were obstinately called *garnix*, and so likewise were very whitish colors, whose quality is, however, recognizable at once, in a moderate light, by adults acquainted with colors.

On the nine hundred thirty-fourth day there was this remarkable utterance when green and blue were placed before the child: *grin blau kann e nicht, grosse mann kann grin blau,* which meant (as appeared from similar utterances), "I can't give green and blue rightly; a grown person can." Green was mostly called gray; very rarely (inquiringly) it was called red; blue was named *lila*. In the one hundred thirty-first and one hundred thirty-fourth weeks I made three trials, asking for colors which I laid out; in the one hundred thirty-eighth and one hundred thirty-ninth weeks, in three trials, sometimes the child took the colors himself, sometimes I put them before him. The answers were:

	Right	Wrong
Red	14	1
Yellow	24	0
Green	4	13
Blue	0	15
Violet	9	5
Gray	5	0
Rose	9	2
Brown	11	1
Black	7	1
Orange	10	1
Total	93	39

Here begins at last the right naming of green, while blue is not yet so often correctly designated. The child took the colors of his own accord and named them in three trials, in the one hundred thirty-ninth, one hundred forty-first, and one hundred forty-sixth weeks, as follows:

The mind of the child 115

	Right	Wrong
Red	19	2
Yellow	12	0
Green	2	2
Blue	2	11
Violet	6	1
Gray	1	2
Rose	3	0
Brown	10	0
Black	3	0
Orange	8	1
Total	66	19

The red twice misnamed was dark. The word "green" was now rightly applied continually to leaves and to meadows, and, before the completion of the third year, blue also was almost invariably designated correctly, if the attention was not diverted.

With regard to the order in which the colors were rightly named up to the thirty-fourth month, the total result is as follows:

	Judgments		Per Cent	
	Right	Wrong	Right	Wrong
Yellow	232	8	96.7	3.3
Brown	79	8	90.8	9.2
Red	235	36	86.7	13.3
Violet	139	24	85.3	14.7
Black	39	7	84.8	15.2
Rose	76	29	72.4	27.6
Orange	47	23	67.1	32.9
Gray	35	33	51.5	48.5
Green	101	123	45.0	55.0
Blue	61	151	28.8	71.2
Total	1,044	442	70.3	29.7

Thus, of the four principal colors, yellow and red are *named rightly much sooner* than are green and blue; and yellow first—brown is (dull) yellow—then red. That the color-sensations, green, blue, and violet, exist in very different proportions, is probably not a peculiarity of the individual. Violet, which was much oftener named rightly than were green and blue, contains the already well-known red, and may appear to the child as a dirty red, or as dark red. For it is in fact probable that blue and greenish-blue were perceived in the earliest period, not as blue and greenish-blue, but as gray and black. That green of every sort is not named rightly till very late, may be owing, in part, to a stronger absorption of light, by means of the blood of the vessels of the retina. Although the place of the clearest vision, in the back part of the eye, is free from blood-vessels, yet the other colors which, like yellow, orange, red, and brown, reach the retina undimmed, in great extension, have, on that account, an advantage over green and blue, which are most easily confounded with gray.

Even in the fourth year, blue was still often called gray in the dusk of morning, when it appeared to me distinctly blue. The child would wonder that his light-blue stockings had become gray in the night. This I observed on three days.

Gray is, without doubt, along with white and black, rightly known long before the first discrimination of colors, but is often wrongly named, for the reason that green and blue are probably perceived as gray. The right naming of it became the rule before the end of the third year, whereas yellow was rightly named, almost invariably, nearly a year earlier. To this color the pigment of the yellow spot is most helpful. Red may also have an advantage, in the fact that in bright daylight, when the eyes are shut, especially when snow is on the ground, that is the only color in the field of vision [i.e., the eyelids are translucent, and we perceive red]; as black is the only one before we fall asleep in the dark.

On the whole we must, accordingly, declare the child to be still somewhat lacking in sensibility to the cold colors in the second year and the first half of the third year; a conclusion with which occasional observations concerning other children harmonize. At any rate, by very many children, yellow is first rightly named and blue last.

The incapacity of the two-year-old child to name blue and green correctly can not be attributed solely to his possible inability to associate firmly the names "blue" and "green" (which he has heard and which he uses fluently) with his possibly distinct sensations; for "yellow" and "red" have already been used correctly many months before. If green and blue were as distinct as yellow and red in his sensation, then there would not be the least occasion for his giving them wrong names, and preferring red and yellow to them in all circumstances. The child does not yet *know* what green and blue signify, although he is already acquainted with yellow and red. Neither does he yet know what "green" means when, in the one hundred ninth and one hundred twelfth weeks of his life, he apparently distinguishes "red" and "green" correctly. Green is at this time, for him, merely something that is not red.

WILHELM PREYER (1842–1897)

Observations on a newborn acephalic child (1884)

Preyer's treatise included many things. As appendices to the second edition in 1884 it included Cheselden's case and several other congenital cataract cases upon whom operations had been performed. Also reprinted in it were several short baby biographies. In it Preyer also reported the following original observations of a child born without a cerebrum which indicate that the newborn's behavior is largely subcortical.

The data we have concerning the behavior of children born, living, without head or without brain, and of microcephalous children, as well as of idiots and cretins more advanced in age, are of great interest, as helping us to a knowledge of the dependence of the first physical processes upon the development of the brain, especially of the cerebral cortex. Unfortunately, these data are scanty and scattered.

Very important, too, for psychogenesis, are reports concerning the physiological condition and activity of children whose mental development has seemed to be stopped for months, or to be made considerably slower, or to be unusually hastened.

Scanty as are the notes I have met with on this matter, after much search, yet I collect and present some of them, in the hope that they will incite to more abundant and more careful observation in the future than has been made up to this time.

A good many data concerning the behavior of cretin children are to be found in the very painstaking book . . . *New Investigations concerning Cretinism, or Human Deterioration, in its Various Forms and Degrees,* by Maffei and Rösch. But, in order that these data should be of value, the observed anomalies and defects of the cerebral functions ought to be capable of being referred to careful morphological investigations of the cretin brain. As the authors give no results of *post-mortem* examinations, I simply refer to their work here.

I once had the opportunity myself of seeing a hemicephalus, living, who was brought to the clinic of my respected colleague, Prof. B. Schultze, in Jena. The child was of the male sex, and was born on the 1st of July, 1883, at noon, along with a perfectly normal twin sister. The parents are of sound condition. I saw the child for the first time on the 3d of July, at two o'clock. I found all the parts of the body, except the head, like those of ordinary children born at the right time. The head had on it a great red lump like a tumor, and came to an end directly over the eyes, going down abruptly behind; but, even if the tumor were supposed to be covered with skin, there would by no means be the natural arched formation of the cranium of a newly-born child. The face, too, absolutely without forehead, was smaller in comparison than the rest of the body. I found now, in the case of this child, already two days old, a remarkably regular breathing, a very cool skin—in the forenoon a specific warmth of 32° C. had been found—and slight mobility. The eyes remained closed. When I opened them, without violence, the pupil was seen to be immobile. It did not react in the least upon the direct light of the sun on either side. The left eye did not move at all, the right made rare, convulsive, lateral movements. The conjunctiva was very much reddened. The child did not react in the least to pricks of a dull needle tried on all parts of the body, and reacted only very feebly to pinches; not at all to sound-stimuli, but regularly to stronger, prolonged cutaneous stimuli; in particular, the child moved its arms after a slap on the back, just like normal new-born children, and uttered very harsh, feeble tones when its back was rubbed. When I put my fingers in its mouth vigorous sucking movements began, which induced me to offer the bottle—this had not yet been done. Some cubic centimetres of milk were vigorously swallowed, and soon afterward the breast of a nurse was taken. While this was going on I could feel quite distinctly with my finger, under the chin, the movements of swallowing. It was easy to establish the further fact that my finger, which I laid in the hollow of the child's hand, was frequently clasped firmly by the little fingers, which had well-developed nails. Not unfrequently, sometimes without previous contact, sometimes after it, the tip of the tongue, and even a larger part of the tongue, was thrust out between the lips, and once, when I held the child erect, he plainly gave a prolonged yawn. Finally, the fact seemed to me very noteworthy that, after being taken and held erect, sometimes also without any assignable outward occasion, the child inclined its head forward and turned it vigorously both to the right and to the left. When the child had sucked lustily a few times, it opened both eyes about two millimetres wide, and went on with its nursing. An assistant physician saw the child sneeze.

These observations upon a human child, two days old, unquestionably acephalous, i.e., absolutely without cerebrum, but as to the rest of its body not in the least abnormal, prove what I have already advanced, that the cerebrum takes no part at all in the first movements of the newly-born. In this respect the extremely rare case of an acephalous child, living for some days, supplies the place of an experiment of vivisection. Unfortunately, the child died so early that I could not carry on further observations and experiments.

15

G. STANLEY HALL (1846–1924)

The contents of children's minds (1883)

G. Stanley Hall was a man of many talents. He was a psychologist, an educator, and the president of an important university. He was the father of the American Psychological Association and its first and thirty-third president. The leader of the child study movement in America, he directed more dissertations in child psychology than any other man of his era.

In Hall's day Clark University granted degrees in psychology to Bryan, Leuba, Goddard, Gesell, and Terman as well as to many less renowned men. No set of readings in child psychology would be complete without him. But if one asks what permanent substantive contribution he made, the question is hard to answer.

Of Hall's own work in child psychology perhaps the best is the study reprinted here much abridged. It was modeled after, but greatly improved upon, the Berlin study of 1870. It appeared in the Princeton Review *1883: 249–272.*

Hall is the first American psychologist to appear in this book. He took his degree with William James at Harvard at age 32 and then proceeded to Europe for further study. The present study was done after his return. In it there appear many adumbrations of the later work of other child psychologists.

In October, 1869, the Pedagogical Society of Berlin issued a circular requesting the masters of the eighty-four established schools of that city to ascertain how many of the children who entered the primary classes that fall had seen and could name certain common animals, insects, and plants, had taken certain walks, visited specified parks, museums, etc. It is more common in that country than in our own to connect songs, poems, reading exercises, and object lessons with the locality with which the child is most familiar, so that not only does the matter of elementary instruction vary considerably with the geographical, zoological, and botanical character of the different towns, and often even with the surroundings of different schools in the same city, but much importance is attached to stated holiday and half-holiday walks which teachers are expected to conduct with their pupils for educational purposes. To "determine the knowledge of the children so far as conditioned by the concepts arising from their immediate environment," for statistical uses, was the express purpose of the questions proposed. It was expected that this "entrance examination" scheme, as it was humorously called, would show in a more definite form than ever before the psychic peculiarities of the different school districts of Berlin, upon which, from preliminary tests, locality seemed to exert a surprising influence. Besides a score or so of topographical questions, however—such as the public buildings, squares, chief streets, suburban resorts, etc.—others pertaining to the home, the farm, objects in natural history, and the aspects of the heavens were added, and finally the children were asked if they had any notion of God, Christ, could tell a Bible story, say a hymn or prayer, or had ever heard either of four of the best known of Grimm's tales. At first many of the children were questioned in classes, till, on account of intimidation in the presence of others, and other errors arising from a desire to appear wiser or not more ignorant than their mates, etc., it was found that more truthful results were obtained by questioning them in sections of eight or ten, altho this method nearly doubled he average ignorance displayed and quadrupled the work, which with one hundred and thirty-eight questions was no small addition to that already required of the subordinate teachers to whom it was mainly entrusted. Of a little over two thousand children to whom these questions were put reliable results were thought to be obtained from about one-half, while some teachers expressed the opinion that even they had no value owing to the haste and not unfrequently the unwillingness with which the work was undertaken.

It was with the advantages of many suggestions and not a few warnings from this attempt that the writer undertook, soon after the opening of the Boston schools in September last, to make out a list of questions suitable for obtaining an inventory of the contents of the mind of children of average intelligence on entering the primary schools of that city. All the local and many of the German questions were for various reasons not suitable to children here, and the task of selecting those that should be so, tho perhaps not involving quite as many preplexing considerations as choosing an equally long list of normal words, was by no means easy. They must not be too familiar nor too hard and remote, but must give free and easy play to reason and memory. But especially, to yield most practical results, they must lie within the range of what children are commonly supposed or at least desired, by teachers and by those who write primary text-books and prescribe courses of instruction, to know. Many preliminary half-days of questioning small groups of children and receiving suggestions from many sources and the use of many primers, object-lesson courses, etc., now in use in this country were necessary before the first provisional list of one hundred and thirty-four questions was printed. The problem first in mind was strictly practical; viz., what may city children be assumed to know and have seen by their teachers when they enter school; altho other purposes more psychological shaped many other questions used later.

The difficulties and sources of possible error in the use of such questions are many. Not only are children prone to imitate others in their answers without stopping to think and give an independent answer of their own, but they often love to seem wise, and, to make themselves interesting, state what seems to interest us without reference to truth, divining the lines of our interest with a subtlety we do not suspect; if absurdities are doubted they are sometimes only the more protested, the faculties of some are benumbed and perhaps their tongues tied by bashfulness, while others are careless, listless, inattentive, and answer at random. Again, many questions are brusque, lacking in sympathy or tact, or real interest or patience in the work, or perhaps regard it as trivial or fruitless. These and many other difficulties seemed best mnnimized by the following method which was finally settled upon and, with the co-operation of Mr. E. P. Seaver, superintendent of the Boston schools, put into operation. Four of the best trained and experienced kindergarten teachers were employed by the hour to question three children at a time in the dressing-room of the school by themselves alone, so as not to interrupt the school-work. No constraint was used, and, as several hours were necessary to finish each set, changes and rests were often needful, while by frequent correspondence and by meetings with the writer to discuss details and compare results uniformity of method was sought. The most honest and unembarrassed child's first answer to a direct question, e.g., whether it has seen a cow, sheep, etc., must rarely or never be taken without careful cross-questioning, a stated method of which was developed respecting many objects. If the child says it has seen a cow, but when asked its size points to its own finger-nail or hand and says, so big, as not unfrequently occurs, the inference is that it has at most only seen a picture of a cow, and thinks its size reproduced therein, and accordingly he is set down as deficient on that question. If, however, he is correct in size, but calls the color blue, does not know it as the source of milk, or that it has horns or hoofs,—several errors of the latter order have been generally allowed. A worm may be said to swim on the ground, butchers to kill only the bad animals, etc.; but when hams are said to grow on trees or in the ground, or a hill is described as a lump of dirt, or wool as growing on hens, as often occurs, deficiency is obvious. So many other visual and other notions that seem to adults so simple that they must be present to the mind with some completeness or not at all, are in the process of gradual acquisition element by element in the mind of a child, so that there must sometimes be confessedly a certain degree of arbitariness in saying, as, except in cases of peculiar uncertainty, the questioners attempted to do, that the child has the concept or does not have it. Men's first names seem to have designated single striking qualities, but once applied they become general or specific names according to circumstances. Again, very few children knew that a tree had bark, leaves, trunk, and roots; but very few indeed had not noticed a tree enough for our "pass." Without specifying further details it may suffice here to say that the child was given the benefit of every doubt and credited with knowledge wherever its ignorance was not so radical as to make a chaos of what instruction and most primary text-books are wont to assume. It is important also to add that the questioners were requested to report manifest gaps in the child's knowledge in its own words, reproducing its syntax, pronunciation, etc.

About sixty teachers besides the above four have made returns from three or more children each. Many returns, however, are incomplete, careless, or show internal contradictions, and can be used only indirectly to control results from the other sources. From more than twice that number two hundred of the Boston children were selected as the basis of the following table. For certain questions and for many statistical purposes this number is much too small to yield very valuable results, but where, as in the majority of cases, the averages of these children taken by fifties have varied less than ten per cent it is safe to infer that the figures have considerable representative worth and far more than they could have if the percentages were small. The precautions that were taken to avoid schools where the children come from homes representing extremes of either culture or ignorance, or to balance deviations from a conjectured average in one direction by like deviations in the other, and also to select from each school-room with the teacher's aid only children of average capacity and to dismiss each child found unresponsive or not acquainted with the English language, give to the percentages, it is believed, a worth which without these and other precautions to this end only far larger numbers could yield.

The following table shows the general results for a number of those questions which admit of categorical answers, only negative results being recorded; the italicized question in the "miscellaneous" class being based on only from forty to seventy-five children, the rest on two hundred, or in a few cases two hundred and fifty:

The high rate of ignorance here indicated may surprise most who will be likely to read this report, because the childhood they know will be much above the average of intelligence here sought, as it may all, because the few memories of childhood which survive in adult life necessarily bear such slight traces of its imperfections and are from many causes so illusory. Skeins and spools of thread were said to grow on the sheep's back or on bushes, stockings on trees, butter to come from buttercups, flour to be made of beans, oats to grow on oaks, bread to be swelled yeast, trees to be stuck in the ground by God and rootless, meat to be dug from the ground, and potatoes to be picked from trees. Cheese is squeezed butter, the cow says "bow-wow," the pig purrs or burrows, worms are not distinguished from snakes, moss from the "toad's umbrella," bricks from stones, nor beans from trees. An oak may be known only as an acorn-tree or a button-tree, a pine only as a needle-tree, a bird's nest only as its bed, etc. So that while no one child has all these misconceptions none are free from them, and thus the liabilities are great that, in this chaos of half-

Table I

No.	Name of the object or concept	Per cent of children ignorant of it	No.	Name of the object or concept	Per cent of children ignorant of it
1	Beehive	80	19	Growing potatoes	61
2	Crow	77	20	Growing buttercup	55.5
3	Bluebird	72.5	21	Growing rose	54
3	Ant	65.5	22	Growing grapes	53
5	Squirrel	63	23	Growing dandelion	52
6	Snail	62	24	Growing cherries	46
7	Robin	60.5	25	Growing pears	32
8	Sparrow	57.5	26	Growing apples	21
9	Sheep	54			
10	Bee	52	1	Where are the child's ribs	90.5
11	Frog	50	2	Where are the child's lungs	81
12	Pig	47.5	3	Where is the child's heart	80
13	Chicken	33.5	4	Where are the child's wrists	70.5
14	Worm	22	5	Where are the ankles	65.5
15	Butterfly	20.5	6	Where is the waist	52.5
16	Hen	19	7	Where are the hips	45
17	Cow	18.5	8	Where are the knuckles	36
			9	Where are the elbows	25
1	Dew	78	10	Know right and left hand	21.5
2	What season it is	75.5	11	Know cheek	18
3	Seen hail	73	12	Know forehead	15
4	Seen rainbow	65	13	Know throat	13.5
5	Seen sunrise	56.5	14	Know knee	7
6	Seen sunset	53.5	15	Know stomach	6
7	Seen clouds	35			
8	Seen stars	14	1	Concept of a triangle	92
9	Seen moon	7	2	Concept of a square	56
			3	Concept of a circle	35
1	Concept of an Island	87.5	4	The number five	28.5
2	Concept of a Beach	55.5	5	The number four	17
3	Concept of a Woods	53.5	6	The number three	8
4	Concept of a River	58			
5	Concept of a Pond	40	1	Seen watchmaker at work	68
6	Concept of a Hill	28	2	Seen file	65
7	Concept of a Brook	15	3	Seen plough	64.5
			4	Seen spade	62
1	Growing wheat	92.5	5	Seen hoe	61
2	Elm tree	91.5	6	Seen bricklayer at work	44.5
3	Poplar tree	89	7	Seen shoemaker at work	25
4	Willow	89	8	Seen axe	12
5	Growing oats	87.5			
6	Oak tree	87	1	Know green by name	15
7	Pine	87	2	Know blue by name	14
8	Maple	83	3	Know yellow by name	13.5
9	Growing moss	84.5	4	Know red by name	9
10	Growing strawberries	78.5			
11	Growing clover	74			
12	Growing beans	71.5			
13	Growing blueberries	67.5			
14	Growing blackberries	66			
15	Growing corn	65.5			
16	Chestnut tree	64			
17	Planted a seed	63			
18	Peaches on a tree	61			

Table I (Continued)

No.	Name of the object or concept	Per cent of children ignorant of it	No.	Name of the object or concept	Per cent of children ignorant of it
	Miscellaneous		12	Not know wooden things are from trees	55
1	That leathern things come from animals	93.4	13	Origin of butter	50.5
2	Maxim or proverb	91.5	14	Origin of meat from animals	48
3	Origin of cotton things	90	15	Cannot sew	47.5
4	What flour is made of	89	16	Cannot strike a given musical note	40
5	Ability to knit	88	17	Cannot beat time regularly	39
6	What bricks are made of	81.1	18	Have never saved cents at home	36
7	Shape of the world	70.3	19	Never been in the country	35.5
8	Origin of woolen things	69	20	Can repeat no verse	28
9	Never attended Kindergarten	67.5	21	Source of milk	20.5
10	Never been in bathing	64.5			
11	Can tell no rudiment of a story	58			

assimilated impressions, half right, half wrong, some lost link may make utter nonsense or mere verbal cram of the most careful instruction, as in the cases of children referred to above who knew much by rote about a cow, its milk, horns, leather, meat, etc., but yet were sure from the picture-book that it was no bigger than a small mouse.

For 86 per cent of the above questions the average intelligence of thirty-six country children who were tested ranks higher than that of the city children of the table, and in many items very greatly. The subject-matter of primers for the latter is in great part still traditionally of country life; hence the danger of unwarranted presupposition is considerable. As our methods of teaching grow natural we realize that city life is unnatural, and that those who grow up without knowing the country are defrauded of that without which childhood can never be complete or normal. On the whole the material of the city is no doubt inferior in pedagogic value to country experience. A few days in the country at this age has raised the level of many a city child's intelligence more than a term or two of school training could do without it. It is there, too, that the foundations of a love of natural science are best laid. We cannot accept without many careful qualifications the evolutionary dictum that the child's mental development should repeat that of the race. Unlike primitive man the child's body is feeble and he is ever influenced by a higher culture about him. Yet from the primeval intimacy with the qualities and habits of plants, with the instincts of animals—so like those of children—with which hawking and trapping, the riding on instead of some distance behind horses, etc., made men familiar; from primitive industries and tools as first freshly suggested, if we believe Geiger, from the normal activities of the human organism, especially the tool of tools, the hand; from primitive shelter, cooking, and clothing, with which anthropological researches make us familiar, it is certain that not a few educational elements of great value can be selected and systematized for children, an increasing number of them in fact being already in use for juvenile games and recreations and for the vacation pastimes of adults. A country barn, a forest with its gloom and awe, its vague fears and indefinite sounds, is a great school at this age. The making of butter, which some teachers, after hearing so often that it grew inside eggs or on ice, or was made from buttermilk, think it worth while to make a thimbleful of it in a toy churn at school as an object-lesson; more acquaintance with birds, which, as having the most perfect senses, most constant motion in several elements, even Leopardi could panegyrize as the only real things of joy in the universe, and which the strange power of flight makes ideal beings with children, and whose nests were often said to grow on trees; more knowledge of kitchen-chemistry, of foods, their preparation and origin; wide prospects for the eyes—this is more pedagogic industrial training for young children, because more free and play-like, than sewing, or cooking, or whittling, or special trade-schools can be, as well as more hygienic. Many children locate all that is good and imperfectly known in the country, and nearly a dozen volunteered the statement that good people when they die go to the country—even here from Boston. It is things that live and, as it were, detach themselves from their background by moving that catch the eye and with it the attention, and the subjects which occupy and interest the city child are mainly in motion and therefore transient, while the country child has more solitude, and is likely to develop more independently and is less likely to be prematurely caught up into the absorbing activities and throbbing passions of manhood, and becomes more familiar with the experiences of primitive man. The city child knows a little of many more things and so is more liable to superficiality and has a wider field for error. At the same time it has two great advantages over the country child, in knowing more of human nature and in entering school with a much better developed sense of rhythm and all its important implications. On the whole, however, additional force seems thus given to the argument for excursions, by rail or otherwise, regularly provided for the poorer children who are causing the race to degenerate in the great centres of population, unfavorable enough for those with good homes or even for adults.

Words, in connection with rhyme, rhythm, alliteration, cadence, etc., or even without these simply as sound-pictures, often absorb the attention of children and yield them a really aesthetic pleasure either quite independently of their meaning or to the utter bewilderment of it. They hear fancied words in noises and sounds of nature and animals, and are persistent punners. As butterflies make butter to eat it or give it by squeezing, so grasshoppers give grass, bees give beads and beans, kittens grow on the pussy-willow, and all honey is from honeysuckles, and even a poplin dress is made of poplar-trees. When the cow lows it somehow blows its own horn; crows and scarecrows are confounded; ant has some subtle relationship to aunt; angleworm suggests angle or triangle or ankle; Martie eats "tomarties;" a holiday is a day to "holler" on; Harry O'Neil is nicknamed Harry Oatmeal; isoceles is somehow related to sausages; October suggests knocked over: "I never saw a hawk, but I can haw and spit too;" "I will not sing do re mi, but do re you;" "Miss Eaton will eat us"—these and many more from the questioners' notes, and the story of the child who, puzzled by the unfamiliar reflexive use of the verb, came to associate "now I lay me," etc., with a lama, or of another who was for years stultified as against a dead blank wall whenever the phrase "answer sought" occurred, suggest to us how, more or less consciously and more or less seriously, a child may be led, in the absence of corrective experience, to the most fantastic and otherwise unaccountable distortions of facts by shadowy word-spectres or husks. In many of the expressions quoted the child seems playing with relations once seriously held, and its "fun" to be jolly over but lately broken mental fetters. Some at least of the not infrequently quite unintelligible statements or answers may perhaps be thus accounted for. Again, the child more than the adult thinks in pictures, gestures, and inarticulate sounds. The distinction between real and verbal knowledge has been carefully and constantly kept in mind by the questioners. Yet except a very few objects in the above table, as e.g. triangle and sparrow, a child may be said to know almost nothing of them, at least for school purposes, if he has no generally recognized name for them. The far greater danger is the converse, that only the name and not the thing itself will be known. To test for this was, with the exceptions presently to be noted, our constant aim, as it is that of true education to obviate it. The danger, however, is after all quite limited here, for the linguistic imperfections of children are far more often shown in combining words than in naming the concrete things they know or do not know. To name an object is a passion with them, for it is to put their own mark upon it, to appropriate it. From the talk which most children hear and use to book language is again an immense step. Words live only in the ear and mouth, and are pale and corpse-like when addressed to the eye. What we want, and indeed are likely soon to have, are carefully arranged child vocabularies and dictionaries of both verbal forms and meanings, to show teachers just the phonic elements and vocal combinations children have most trouble with, the words they most readily and surely acquire, their number and order in each thought-sphere—and the attributes and connotations most liable to confuse them. To that work it is believed the method here employed has already furnished valuable material in protocol soon to be augmented and digested.

To specify a few items more fully, the four color-questions were designed to test not color-blindness but the power to use color-names. The Holmgren worsteds were used, from which the child was asked to pick out, not colors like others to which its attention is directed without naming them, but the color named, to which he has no clue but the name. It did not seem safe to complicate the objects of the latter educational test with the former, so that some of those marked defective in the table may or may not have been color-blind. Excluding colored and Jewish children, both of whom seem to show exceptional percentages, and averaging the sexes, both Magnus and Jeffries found a little over two per cent of many thousand children color-blind. The children they tested, however, were much older than these, and two or three hundred is far too small a number to warrant us, were it otherwise allowable, in simply subtracting two per cent and inferring that the remainder were deficient only in knowledge of the color-word. Our figures, then do not bear upon the question whether the color-sense itself is fully developed before the age of five or six or not. Again number cannot be developed to any practical extent without knowledge of the number-name. As Wundt's careful experiments show, the eye can apprehend but three of the smallest and simplest objects, unless they are arranged in some geometrical order, without taking considerable additional time to count. As the chromatic scale grades musical intervals or the names we count by graduate the vague sense of more or less, and later, as visible notes change all musical ideas and possibilities, so figures or number-signs almost create arithmetic. A child who seriously says a cat has three or five legs will pick out its own, e.g. fourth, seat in the fifth row in an empty school-room almost every time by happy guessing, and hold up "so many" fingers or blocks, when, if the number-name five or six were called for and nothing shown, it would be quite confused. In our tests the number-name was sought because it is that which is mainly serviceable for educational purposes. As to the physiological and geographical questions little need be said. Joint, flesh, and vein are often unknown terms, or joint is where the bone is broken, and there are stones in the knee. Within the skin is blood and something hard, perhaps wood. Physical self-consciousness, which is in little danger of becoming morbid at this age, begins with recognition of the hand, then of the foot, because these are the most mobile parts, but has not often reached the face at this age, and blushing is rare; while psychic self-consciousness is commonly only of pain, either internal, as of stomach-ache, or peripheral, of cuts, bruises, etc. The world is square, straight, or flat, and if the other side has been thought of it is all woods or water or ice, or where saved people or Protestants or anything much heard of but little seen are; if we go to the edge of the world we come to water or may fall off, or it may be like a house and we live on the top. The first notion of a hill may be of some particular pile of sand, perhaps on the moulding-board, three inches high, or a rubbish-heap in the back yard, or a slant where a shed will run along; but a comprehensive idea of hill with opposite sides, tho simpler and easier than most geographical categories, is by no means to be assumed.

If children are pressed to answer questions somewhat beyond their ken they often reply confusedly and at random, while if others beside them are questioned they can answer well; some are bolder and invent things on the spot if they seem to interest the questioner, while others catch quick and subtle suggestions from the form of the question, accent, gesture, feature, etc., so that what seems originality is really mind-reading, giving back our every thought and sometimes only a direct reproduction, with but little distortion because little apprehension, of what parents or teachers have lately told them. But there are certain elements which every tactful and experienced friend of children learns to distinguish from each of these with considerable accuracy—elements which, from whatever source, take or spring from deep roots in the childish heart, as distinct from all these as are Grimm's tales from those of some of our weakly juvenile weeklies. These are generally not easily accessible. I could not persuade an old nurse to repeat to me a nonsensical song I had half overheard that delighted a two-year-old child, and the brothers Grimm experienced a similar difficulty in making their collections. As many working men nail a horseshoe over their door for luck and many people really prefer to begin nothing important on Friday who will not confess to a trace of superstition in either case, so children cling to their "old credulities to nature dear," refusing every attempt to gain their full confidence or explore secret tracts in their minds, as a well-developed system of insane illusions may escape the scrutiny of the most skilful alienist. As a reasoning electric light might honestly doubt the existence of such things as shadows because, however near or numerous, they are always hidden from it, so the most intelligent adults quite commonly fail to recognize sides of their own children's souls which can be seen only by strategy. A boy and girl often play under my window as I write, and when either is quite alone unconscious words often reveal what is passing in their own minds, and it is often very absurd or else meaningless, but they run away with shame and even blushes if they chance to look up suddenly and catch me listening. Yet who of us has not secret regions of soul to which no friend is ever admitted, and which we ourselves shrink from full consciousness of? Many children half believe the doll feels cold or blows, that it pains flowers to tear or burn them, or that in summer when the tree is alive it makes it ache to pound or chop it. Of 48 children questioned 20 believed sun, moon, or stars to live, 15 thought a doll and 16 thought flowers would suffer pain if burned. Children who are accounted dull in school-work are more apt to be imaginative and animistic.

The chief field for such fond and often secret childish fancies is the sky. About three fourth of all questioned thought the world a plain, and many described it as round like a dollar, while the sky is like a flattened bowl turned over it. The sky is often thin, one mighty easily break through; half the moon may be seen through it, while the other half is this side; it may be made of snow, but is so large that there is much floor-sweeping to be done in heaven. Some thought the sun went down at night into the ground or just behind certain houses, and went across on or under the ground to go up out of or off the water in the morning, but 48 per cent of all thought that at night it goes or rolls or flies, is blown or walks, or God pulls it up higher out of sight. He takes it into heaven, and perhaps put it to bed, and even takes off its clothes and puts them on in the morning, or again it lies under the trees where the angels mind it, or goes through and shines on the upper side of the sky, or goes into or behind the moon, as the moon is behind it in the day. It may stay where it is, only we cannot see it, for it is dark, or the dark rains down so, and it comes out when it gets light so it can see. More than half the children questioned conceived the sun as never more than 40 degrees from the zenith, and, naturally enough, city children knew little of the horizon. So the moon comes around when it is a bright night and people want to walk, or forget to light some lamps; it follows us about and has nose and eyes, while it calls the stars into, under, or behind it at night, and they may be made of bits of it. Sometimes the moon is round a month or two, then it is a rim, or a piece is cut off, or it is half struck or half buttoned into the sky. The stars may be sparks from fire-engines or houses, or, with higher intelligence, they are silver, or God lights them with matches and blows them out or opens the door and calls them in in the morning. Only in a single case were any of the heavenly bodies conceived as openings in the sky to let light or glory through, or as eyes of supernatural beings—a fancy so often ascribed to children and so often found in juvenile literature. Thunder, which anthropologists tell us, is or represents the highest God to most savage races, was apperceived as God groaning or kicking, or rolling barrels about, or turning a big handle, or grinding snow, walking loud, breaking something, throwing logs, having coal run in, pounding about with a big hammer, rattling houses, hitting the clouds, or clouds bumping or clapping together or bursting, or else it was merely ice sliding off lots of houses or cannon in the city or sky, hard rain down the chimney, or big rocks pounding, or piles of boards falling down, or very hard rain, hail, or wind. Lightning is God putting out his finger or opening a door, or turning on gas quick, or (very common) striking many matches at once, throwing stones and iron for sparks, setting paper afire, or it is light going outside and inside the sky, or stars falling. God keeps rain in heaven in a big sink, rows of buckets, a big tub or barrels, and they run over or he lets it down with a water hose through a seive, a dipper with holes, or sprinkles or tips it down or turns a faucet. God makes it in heaven out of nothing or out of water, or it gets up by splashing up, or he dips it up off the roof, or it rains up off the ground when we don't see it. The clouds are close to the sky; they move because the earth moves and makes them. They are dirty, muddy things, or blankets, or doors of heaven, and are made of fog, of steam that makes the sun go, of smoke, of white wool or feathers and birds, or lace or cloth. In their changing forms very many children, whose very life is fancy, think they see veritable men, or more commonly, because they have so many more forms, animals, faces, and very often God, Santa Claus, angels, etc., are also seen. Closely connected with the above are the religious concepts so common with children. God is a big, perhaps blue man, very often seen in the sky on or in clouds, in the church, or even street. He came in our gate, comes to see us sometimes. He lives in a big place or a big brick or stone house on the sky. He makes lamps, babies, dogs, trees, money, etc., and the angels work for him. He looks like the priest, Frobel, papa, etc., and they like to look at him, and a few would like to be God. He lights the stars so he can see to go on the sidewalk or into the church. Birds, children, Santa Claus, live with him, and most but not all like him better than they do the latter. When people die they just go, or are put in a hole, or a box or a black wagon that goes to heaven, or they fly up or are drawn or slung up into the sky where God catches them. They never can get out of the hole, and yet all good people somehow get where God is. He lifts them up, they go up on a ladder or rope, or they carry them up, but keep their eyes shut so they do not know the way, or they are shoved up through a hole. When children get there they have candy, rocking-horses, guns, and everything in the toy-shop or picture-book, play marbles, top, ball, cards, hookey, hear brass bands, have nice clothes, gold watches, and pets, ice-cream and soda-water, and no school. There are men there who died in the war made into angels, and dolls with broken heads go there. Some think they must go through the church to get there, a few thought the horse-cars run here, and one said that the birds that grow on apple-trees are drawn up there by the moon. The bad place is like an oven or a police-station, where it burns, yet is all dark, and folks want to get back, and God kills people or beats them with a cane. God makes babies in heaven, tho the holy mother and even Santa Claus makes some. He lets them down or drops them, and the women or doctors catch them, or he leaves them on the sidewalk, or brings them down a wooden ladder backwards and pulls it up again, or mamma or the doctor or the nurse go up and fetch them sometimes in a balloon, or they fly down and lose off their wings in some place or other and forget it, or jump down to Jesus, who gives them around. They were also often said to be found in flour-barrels, and the flour sticks ever so long, you know, or they grow in cabbages, or God puts them in water, perhaps in the sewer, and the doctor gets them out and takes them to sick folks that want them, or the milkman brings them early in the morning, they are dug out of the ground, or bought at the baby-store. Sometimes God puts on a few things or else sends them along if he don't forget it; this shows that no one since Basedow believes in telling children the truth in all things.

Now a few children have or can be made to disclose no such ideas as the above, and indeed they seem to be generally already on the ebb at this age, and are sometimes timidly introduced by, as if, some say it is like, or I used to think. Clear and confident notions on the above topics are the exception and not the rule, yet most have some of them, while some are common to many, indeed most, children. They represent a drift of consentient infantile philosophy about the universe not without systematic coherence, altho intimdated and broken through at every point by fragmentary truths, often only verbal indeed, without insight or realization of a higher order, so that the most diametrical contradictions often subsist peacefully side by side, and yet they are ever forming again at lower levels of age and intelligence. In all that is remote the real and ideal fade into each other like clouds and mountains in the horizon, or as poetry which keeps alive the standpoints of an earlier culture co-exists with science. Children are often hardly conscious of them at all, and the very questions that bring them to mind and invite them to words at the same time often abash the child to the first disquieting self-consciousness of the absurdity of his fond fancies that have felt not only life but character into natural objects. Between the products of childish spontaneity, where the unmistakable child's mark is seen, and those of really happy suggestion by parents, etc., the distinction is as hard as anywhere along the line between heredity and tradition. It is enough that these fancies are like Galton's composite portraits, resultants in form and shading of the manifold deepest impression which what is within and what is without have together made upon the child's soul in these spheres of ideas. Those indicated above represent many strata of intelligence up through which the mind is passing very rapidly and with quite radical transformations. Each stratum was once with but a little elaboration, or is now somewhere, the highest culture, relegated to and arrested in an earlier and earlier stage as civilization and educational methods advance. Belief in the false is as necessary as it is inevitable, for the proper balance of head and heart, and happy the child who has believed or loved only healthy, unaffected, platonic lies like the above, which will be shed with its milk-teeth when more solid mental pabulum can be digested. It is possible that the present shall be so attractive and preoccupying that the child never once sends his thoughts to the remote in time and place, and that these baby-fancies— ever ready to form at a touch, and which made the impartation of truth, however carefully put, on these themes impossible before its time; which, when long forgotten, yet often reverberate, if their old chords be struck, in adults to the intensity of fanaticism or even delusion—shall be quite repressed. If so, one of the best elements of education which comes from long experience in laying aside a lower for a higher phase of culture of doubting opportunely, judiciously, and temperately, is lost.

De Quincey's pseudopia is thought by Dr. E. H. Clarks (*Visions*, p. 212) to be common with children; but altho about 40 were asked to describe what they saw with their eyes shut, it is impossible to judge whether they visualize in any such distinctive sense as Mr. Galton has described or only imagine and remember, often with Homeric circumstance, but with less than picturesque vividness. Childish thought is very largely in visual terms, hence the need of object (*anschauungs*) lessons, and hence, too, it comes that most of the above questions address the eye without any such intent. If phonic symbols could be made pictorial as they were originally, and as illustrated primers make them in a third and still remoter sense, the irrational elements in learning to read would be largely obviated. Again, out of 53 children 21 described the tones of certain instruments as colored. The colors, or *photisms*, thus suggested, tho so far as tested constant from week to week in the same child, had no agreement for different instruments, a drum, e.g., suggesting yellow (the favorite color of children) to one child and black or red to another, and the tone of a fife being described as pale or bright, light or dark colored, intensity and saturated varying greatly with different children. For this and other forms of association or analogies of sensation of a large and not yet explored class so common in children, many data for future study were gathered. This is also the case with their powers of time and tone reproduction, and their common errors in articulation, which have suggested other and more detailed researches, some of which are already in progress.

Each child was asked to name three things right and three things wrong to do, and nearly half could do so. In no case were the two confused, indicating not necessarily intuitive perception, but a general consensus in what is allowed and forbidden at home, and how much better and more surely they learn to do than to know. Wrong things were specified much more readily and by more children than right things, and also in much greater variety. In about 450 answers 53 wrong acts are specified, while in over 350 answers only 34 different good acts are named. The more frequent answers are to mind and be good, or to disobey, be naughty, lie, and say bad words; but the answers of the girls differ from the boys in two marked ways, they more often name specific acts and nearly twice as often conventional ones, the former difference being most common in naming right, the latter in naming wrong things. Boys say it is wrong to steal, fight, kick, break windows, get drunk, stick pins into others, or to "sass," "cuss," shoot them, while girls are more apt to say it is wrong to not comb the hair, to get butter on the dress, climb trees, unfold the hands, cry, catch flies, etc. The right things seem, it must be confessed, comparatively very tame and unattractive, and while the genius of an Aristotle could hardly extract categories or infer intuitions by classification from either list, it is very manifest that the lower strata of conscience are dislike of dirt and fear. Pure intuitionalists may like to know that over a dozen children were found who convinced their questioners that they thought they ought not to say bad words if no one heard them, or lie if not found out, etc., or who felt sick at the stomach when they had been bad, but the soap and water or sand with which their mouths are sometimes washed after bad words in kindergartens, or the red pepper administered at home after lies, may possibly have something to do with the latter phenomenon.

For several hundred drawings, with the name given them by the child written by the teacher, the chief difference inferred is in concentration. Some make faint, hasty lines representing all the furniture of a room, or sky and stars, or all the objects they can think of, while others concentrate upon a single object. It is a girl with buttons, a house with a keyhole or steps, a man with a pipe or heels or ring grotesquely prominent. The development of observation and sense of form is best seen in the pictures of men. The earliest and simplest representation is a round head, two eyes and legs. Later comes mouth, then nose, then hair, then ears. Arms like legs at first grow directly from the head, rarely from the legs, and are seldom fingerless, tho sometimes it is doubtful whether several arms or fingers from head and legs without arms are meant. Of 44 human heads only 9 are in profile. This is one of the many analogies which the rock and cave drawings of primitive man, and suggests how Catlin came to nearly lose his life by "leaving out the other half" in drawing a profile portrait of an Indian chief. Last, as least mobile and thus attracting least attention, comes the body; first round like the head, then elongated, sometimes prodigiously, and sometimes articulated into several compartments, and in three cases divided, the upper part of the figure being in one place and the lower in another. The mind and not the eye alone is addressed, for the body is drawn and then the clothes are drawn on it (as the child dresses), diaphanous and only in outline. Most draw living objects except the kindergarten children, who draw their patterns. More than two thirds of all objects are decidedly in action, and under 18 per cent word-pictures or scribbles called the name of the objects are made to imitate writing or letters, as sounds to imitate talking. The very earliest pencillings, commonly of three-year-old children, are mere marks to and fro, often nearly in the same line. Of 13 of these most were nearly in the angle described by Javal as corresponding to the earliest combination of finger and fore-arm movements and not far from the regulation slant of 52° taught in school penmanship.

Each child was asked to tell a verse or story to be recorded verbatim, and nearly half could do so. Children of this age are no longer interested in mere animal noises or rhymes or nonsense-words of the "Mother Goose" order, but everything to interest them deeply must have a cat, dog, bird, baby, another child, or possibly parent or teacher in it, must be dramatic and full of action, appeal to the eye as a "chalk-talk" or an object-lesson, and be copious of details, which need be varied but slightly to make the story as good as new for the twentieth time. A long gradation of abstractions culminates here. First, it is a great lesson for the child to eliminate touch and recognize objects by the eye alone. The first pictures are felt of, turned over with much confusion to find the surface smooth. To abstract from visual terms to words is still harder. Eyes and tongue must work together a long time before the former can be eliminated and stories told of objects first absent, then remote, then before unknown. Children must be far beyond this before they can be interested in e.g., fairy tales, and stories told interest them far more than if read to them no matter how apt the language. They are reproduced about as imperfectly as objects are drawn, only a few salient and disconnected points being seized at first, and sentence and sequence coming very slowly after many repetitions. Their own little faults may be woven in or ascribed to animals or even plants in a remote way which they themselves will feel at each stage, and the selfish birdie or the runaway squirrel or flowers as kind words may be referred to in case of need as a reserve moral capital. Why do we never teach maxims and proverbs which, when carefully selected, are found so effective at this age and teach the best morality embodied in the briefest and most impressive way?

Of the 36 per cent or 72 children of the table who never saved their pennies, 52 spend them for candy, which growing children need, but the adulterations of which are often noxious. Of toys, big things please them best. A recent writer in Austria fears that school savings-banks tend to call attention too early to money matters, and to cause its value to be dangerously overrated; but to pass the candy by and drop the cents where they are beyond their control for a year is much less pedagogic than to save them till a larger and more costly toy can be bought.

There are but 11 questions on which any comparison between the intelligence of the Boston and Berlin children can be made. On all of these except elementary number, where the average is nearly 20 per cent in favor of the Boston children, the figures vary surprisingly little despite local differences and another mode of questioning.

Table I is based upon about equal number of boys and girls, and children of Irish and American parentage greatly predominate; there are 21 Germans, and 19 are divided between eight other nationalities. 14 per cent of all examined did not know their age; 6 per cent were four, 37 per cent were five, 25 per cent were six, 12 percent were 7, and 2 per cent were eight years old. The returns were carefully tabulated to determine the influence of age, which seems surprisingly unpronounced, indicating, so far as the small numbers go, a slight value of age per se as an index of ripeness for school.

In Table II columns 2 and 3 are based upon larger numbers and upon less carefully restricted selections from the aggregate returns. In 34 representative questions out of 49 the boys surpass the girls, as the German boys did in 75 per cent of the quite different Berlin questions. The girls excel in knowledge of the parts of the body, home and family life, thunder, rainbows, in knowledge of square, circle, and triangle, but not in that of cube, sphere, and pyramid, which is harder and later. Their stories are more imaginative, while their knowledge of things outward and remote, their power to sing and articulate correctly from dictation, their acquaintance with number and animals, is distinctly less than that of the boys. The Berlin report indicates that girls knew the four best of Grimm's tales nearly twice as frequently as the boys, but that in the concepts of God, Christ, and Bible stories the relation was exactly reversed, and proceeds to infer that the more common, near, or easy a notion is the more likely are the girls to excel the boys, and vice versa. Save possibly in the knowledge of the parts of the body, our returns do not particularly indicate this. Boys do seem, however, more likely than girls to be ignorant of common things right about them, where knowledge is wont to be assumed. Column 5 shows that the Irish children tested were behind others on nearly all topics. The Irish girls decidedly outrank the Irish boys, the advantage to the sex being outweighed by the wider knowledge of the boys of other nationalities. Whether, however, the five- and six-year-old Irish boys are not after all so constituted as to surpass their precocious American playmates later in school or adult life, as since Sigismund may think "slow" children generally do, is one of the most serious questions for the philosophical educator. Column 6 shows the advantage of the kindergarten children, without regard to nationality, over all others in a striking way. Most of the latter tested were from the charity kindergartens, so that superior intelligence of home surroundings can hardly be assumed. Many of them had attended kindergarten but a short time, and the questions were so ordered that the questioners who had a special interest in the kindergarten should not know till near the end of their tests whether or not they had ever attended it. On the other hand, a somewhat larger proportion of the children from the kindergarten had been in the country. Yet on the whole we seem to have here an illustration of the law that we really see not what is near or impress the retina, but what the attention is called

Table II

Name of the object or concept	Per cent of ignorance in 150 girls	Per cent of ignorance in 150 boys	Per cent of ignorance in 50 Irish children	Per cent of ignorance in 50 American children	Per cent of ignorance in 64 kindergarten children
Beehive	81	75	86	70	61
Ant	59	60	74	38	26
Squirrel	69	50	66	42	43
Snail	69	73	92	72	62
Robin	69	44	64	36	29
Sheep	67	47	62	40	40
Bee	46	32	52	32	26
Frog	53	38	54	35	35
Pig	45	27	38	26	22
Chicken	35	21	32	16	22
Worm	21	17	26	16	9
Butterfly	14	16	26	8	9
Hen	15	14	18	2	14
Cow	18	12	20	6	10
Growing clover	59	68	84	42	29
Growing corn	58	50	60	68	32
Growing potatoes	55	54	62	44	34
Growing buttercup	50	51	66	40	31
Growing rose	48	48	60	42	33
Growing dandelion	44	42	62	34	31
Growing apples	16	16	18	12	5
Ribs	88	92	98	82	68
Ankles	58	52	62	40	38
Waist	53	52	64	32	36
Hips	50	47	72	31	24
Knuckles	27	27	34	12	23
Elbow	19	32	36	16	12
Right from left hand	20	8	14	20	4
Wrist	21	34	44	9	19
Cheek	10	12	14	14	4
Forehead	10	11	12	10	7
Throat	10	18	14	16	14
Knee	4	5	2	10	2
Dew	64	63	92	52	57
What season it is	59	50	68	48	41
Hail	75	61	84	52	53
Rainbow	59	61	70	38	38
Sunrise	71	53	70	36	53
Sunset	47	49	52	32	29
Stars	15	10	12	4	7
Island	74	78	84	64	55
Beach	82	49	60	34	32
Woods	46	36	46	32	27
River	38	44	62	12	13
Pond	31	34	42	24	28
Hill	23	22	30	12	19
The number five	26	16	22	24	12
The number four	15	10	16	14	7
The number three	7	6	12	8	0

and held to, and what interests are awakened and words found for. Of nearly thirty primary teachers questioned as to the difference between children from kindergartens and others, four saw no difference, and all the rest thought them better fitted for school-work, instancing superior use of language, skill with the hand and slate, quickness, power of observation, singing, number, love of work, neatness, politeness, freedom from the benumbing school-bashfulness, or power to draw from dictation. Many thought them at first more restless and talkative generally—a trifling and transient fault.

There are many other details and more or less probable inferences, but the above are the chief. The work is laborious, involving about fifty thousand items in all; and as but few of the Berlin methods or results except statistical tables have been published, these results are it is believed to be in some degree the first opening of a new field, which should be specialized and single concept-groups subjected to more detailed study with larger numbers of children. It should also be applied to older children and youth, as the writer is already attempting to do. The difficulty is to get essential points to test for. If these are not characteristic and typical, all such work is worthless. We believe that not only practical educational conclusions of great scope and importance may be based on or illustrated by such results, but, who deeply sensible of many sources of inaccuracy which may limit their value, that they are of great importance for anthropology and psychology. It is characteristic of an educated man, says Aristotle in substance, not to require a degree of scientific exactness on any subject more than that which the subject admits. As scientific methods advance not only are increasingly complex matters subjected to them, but probabilities (which guide nearly all our acts) more and more remote from mathematical certainty are valued.

Steinthal tells an opposite story of six German gentlemen riding socially in a coupe all day, and as they approached the station where they were to separate one proposed to tell the vocation of each of the others, who were strangers to him, if they would write without hesitation an answer to the question "What destroys its own offspring?" One wrote, Vital force. "You," said the questioner, "are a biologist." Another wrote, War. "You," he said, "are a soldier." Another wrote, Kronos, and was correctly pronounced a philologist; while the publicist revealed himself by writing Revolution, and the farmer by writing Shebear. This fable teaches the law of appreception. As Don Quixote saw an army in a flock of sheep and a giant in a windmill, as some see all things in the light of politics, others in that of religion, education, etc., so the Aryan races apperceived the clouds as cows and the rain as their milk, the sun as a horse, the lightning as an arrow, and so the children apperceive rain as God pouring down water; thunder as barrels, boards falling, or cannon; heaven as a well-appointed nursery, &c., &c. They bring more or less developed apperceiving organs with them into school, each older and more familiar concepts gaining more apperceptive power over the newer concepts and percepts by use. The older impressions are on the lurch, as it were, for the new ones, and mental freedom and all-sidedness depends on the number and strength of these appropriating concepts. If there are very few, as with children, teaching is, as some one has well said, like pouring water from a big tub into a small narrow-necked bottle. A teacher who acts upon the now-everywhere-admitted fallacy that knowledge of the subject is all that is needed in teaching children pours at random on to more than into the children, talking to rather than with them, and gauging what he gives rather than what they receive. All now agree that the mind can learn only what is related to other things learned before, and that we must start from the knowledge that the children really have and develop this as germs, otherwise we are showing objects that require close scrutiny only to indirect vision, or talking to the blind of color. Alas for the teacher who does not learn more from his children then he can ever hope to teach them! Just in proportion as teachers do this they cease to be merely mechanical and acquire interest, perhaps enthusiasm, and surely an all-compensating sense of growth in their work and life.

From the above tables it seems not too much also to infer:

1. That there is next to nothing of pedagogic value the knowledge of which it is safe to assume at the outset of school-life. Hence the need of objects and the danger of books and word-cram. Hence many of the best primary teachers in Germany spend from two to four or even six months talking of objects and drawing them before any beginning of what we till lately have regarded as primary-school work.

2. The best preparation parents can give their children for good school-training is to make them acquainted with natural objects, especially with the sights and sounds of the country and talk about them, and send them to good and hygienic as distinct from most fashionable kindergartens.

3. Every normal-school pupil should be required, as an essential part of his training, and every teacher on starting with a new class or in a new locality, to make sure that his efforts along some lines are not utterly lost, should undertake to explore carefully section by section children's minds with all the tact and ingenuity he can command and acquire, to determine exactly what is already known.

4. The concepts which are most common in the children of a given locality are the earliest to be acquired, while the rarer ones are later. This order may generally be assumed in teaching as a natural one, e.g. apples first and wheat last (Cf. Table I.). This order, however, varies very greatly with every change of environment, so that the results of exploration of children's minds in one place cannot be assumed to be valid for those of another save within comparatively few concept-spheres.

16

JOSEPH JASTROW (1863–1944)

The dreams of the blind (1888)

A topic of perennial interest to psychologists and others, is the permanence of the effects of early experiences. One approach to this question is to determine whether or not visual imagery developed in childhood is preserved after a later onset of blindness. Jastrow refers to a study of this topic by Dr. G. Heerman published as early as 1838. Unfortunately no English translation is available, but Jastrow in the article here reproduced with some abridgment, summarizes Heerman's findings.

The reader will note that the concept of a critical period, now fashionable was employed by Jastrow as well as by Itard.

Some biographical data about Jastrow are presented later in the introduction to selection 19. His autobiography is in Volume I of History of Psychology in Autobiography.

The present selection was published in the New Princeton Review *5 (1888): 18–34.*

Though as a race we are eye-minded, individually we differ much with regard to the role that sight plays in our psychic life. Under one aspect a good index of its importance is to be found in the perfection of the visualizing faculty of which Mr. Galton has given an interesting account. Mr. [Francis] Galton . . . asked various persons to describe, amongst other things, the vividness of their mental picture when calling to mind the morning's breakfast-table. To some the mental scene was as clear and as natural as reality, lacking none of the details of form or color; to others the resulting mental image was tolerably distinct, with the prevailing features well brought out, but the rest dim and vague; while a third group could only piece together a very vague, fragmentary, and unreliable series of images, with no distince or constant picture.

Similar differences can be observed with regard to memories, some persons firmly retaining what they read, while the memory-forte of others is in what they hear: and pathology supports this subdivision of the sense-memories by showing, for example, that all remembrance for seen objects may be lost while that for sounds remains intact.

* * *

The function of vision in dreams is doubtless subject to similar individual variations, though probably to a less extent. . . . Seeing is, with rare exceptions, the typical operation in dreams.

With regard to the blind much of what has been said above is entirely irrelevant. However intimately we appreciate the function of sight in our own mental development, it is almost impossible to imagine how different our life would have been, had we never seen. But here, at the outset, a fundamental distinction must be drawn between those blind from birth or early infancy and those who lose their sight in youth or adult life. "It is better to have seen and lost one's sight than never to have seen at all," is quite as true as the sentiment which this form of statement parodies. Expressed physiologically, his means that to have begun the general brain-building process with the aid of the eye insures some further self-development of the visual centre, and thus makes possible a kind of mental possession of which those born blind are inevitably deprived.

A fact of prime importance regarding the development of the sight-centre is the age at which its education is sufficiently completed to enable it to continue its function without further object-lessons on the part of the retina. If we accept as the test of the independent existence of the sight-centre its automatic excitation in dreams, he question can be answered by determining the age of the onset of blindness which divides those who still retain in their dreams the images derived from the world of sight, from those who do not. The data that enable me to answer this question were gathered at the Institutions for the Blind in Philadelphia and Baltimore; and I desire to express my gratitude to the authorities and teachers of these Institutions for the courtesy and privileges extended to me in my research. Nearly 200 persons of both sexes were personally examined, and their answers to quite a long series of questions recorded. All dates and ages were verified by the register of the institution, and the degree of sight was tested.

Beginning with cases of total blindness . . . I find on my list fifty-eight such cases. Of these, thirty-two became blind before completing their fifth year, and *not one* of these thirty-two sees in dreams. Six became blind between the fifth and the seventh year; of these, four have dreams of seeing, but two of them do so seldom and with some vagueness, while two never dream of seeing at all. Of twenty persons who became blind after their seventh year *all* have "dream-vision"— as I shall term the faculty of seeing in dreams. *The period from the fifth to the seventh year is thus marked out as the critical one.* Before this age the visual centre is undergoing its elementary education; its life is closely dependent upon the constant food-supply of sensations, and when these are cut off by blindness it degenerates and decays. If blindness occurs between the fifth and the seventh years, the preservation of the visualizing power depends on the degree of development of the individual. If the faculty is retained, it is neither stable nor pronounced. If sight is lost after the seventh year, the sight-centre can, in spite of the loss, maintain its function, and the dreams of such an individual are hardly distinguishable from those of a seeing person.

I had already entered upon this research when I discovered that I had a predecessor. So long ago as 1838 Dr. G. Heermann studied the dreams of the blind with the view of determining this same question, the physiological significance of which, however, was not then clearly understood. He records the answers of fourteen totally blind persons who lost their sight previously to their fifth year, and *none* of these have dream-vision. Of four who lost their sight between the fifth and the seventh year one has dream-vision, one has it dim and rare, and two do not definitely know. Of thirty-five who became blind after their seventh year *all* have dream-vision. The two independent researches thus yield the very same conclusion. Doctor Heermann includes in his list many aged persons, and from their answers is able to conclude that, generally speaking, those who become blind in mature life retain the power of dream-vision longer than those who become blind nearer the critical age of five to seven years. He records twelve cases where dream-vision still continues after a blindness of from ten to fifteen years, four of from fifteen to twenty years, four of from twenty to twenty-five years, and one of thirty-five years. In one case dream-vision was maintained for fifty-two, and in another for fifty-four years, but then faded out.

With regard to the partially blind, the question most analogous to the persistence of dream-vision after total blindness is whether or not the dream-vision is brighter and clearer than that of waking life; whether the sight-centre maintains the full normal power to which it was educated, or whether the partial loss of sight has essentially altered and replaced it. To this rather difficult question I have fewer and less satisfactory answers than to the former inquiry, but the evidence is perfectly in accord with my previous conclusions. Of twenty-three who describe their dream-vision as *only as clear* as waking sight, *all* became blind *not later than* the close of their *fifth year;* while of twenty-four whose dream-vision is more or less markedly clearer than their partial sight, *all* lost their full sight *not earlier* than their *sixth year*. The age that marks off those to whom total blindness carries with it the loss of dream-vision from those whose dream-vision continues, is thus the age at which the sight-centre has reached a sufficient stage of development to enable it to maintain its full function when partially or totally deprived of retinal stimulation. The same age is also assigned by some authorities as the limiting age at which deafness will cause muteness (unless special pains be taken to prevent it), while later the vocal organs, though trained to action by the ear, can perform their duties without the teacher's aid. This, too, is assigned as the earliest age at which we have a remembrance of ourselves. This last statement I can directly test by one hundred answers which I have to the question, "What is your earliest remembrance of yourself?" The average age to which these memories go back is 5.2 years, seventy-nine instances being included between the third and the sixth years. At this period of child development—the centre of which is at about the close of the fifth year—there seems to be a general "declaration of independence" of the sense-centres from their food-supply of sensations.

* * *

What is true of the visual is doubtless equally true of the other perceptive centres. The dreams of the deaf-mute offer an attractive and untouched field for study. . . . Cripples dream of their lost limbs for many years after their loss, though here stimulation of the cut nerves may in some cases be the suggestive cause of such dreams. A man of forty, who lost his right arm seventeen years ago, dreams of having the arm. The earliest age of losing and dreaming about a lost limb, of which I can find a record, is of a boy of thirteen years who lost a leg at the age of ten; this boy still dreams of walking on his feet. Those who are born cripples must necessarily have these defects represented in their dream consciousness. Heermann cites the case of a man born without hands, forearms, feet, or lower legs. He always dreams of walking on his knees, and all the peculiarities of his movements are present in dream-life.

I have had the opportunity of questioning a blind deaf-mute, whose life-history . . . illustrates with all the force of an experimental demonstration the critical educational importance of the early years of life. The young man in question is now twenty-three years of age, earns a comfortable living as a broom-maker, has an active interest in the affairs of the world, and dislikes to be considered peculiar. His eyesight began to fail him in early childhood, and in his fifth year the sight of one eye was entirely lost, while that of the other was very poor. After a less gradual loss of hearing, he became completely deaf in his ninth year. At the age of twelve, when admitted to the institution for the blind at Baltimore, he was (practically) totally blind, deaf, and nearly mute. The small remnant of articulating power has been cultivated, and those who are accustomed to it can understand his spoken language. . . . He remembers the world of sight and hearing perfectly, and in a little sketch of his life which he wrote for me, vividly describes the sights and sounds of his play-days. He usually dreams of seeing and hearing, though the experiences of his present existence also enter into his dreams. Some of his dreams relate to flowers which he smelled and saw; he dreamt of being upset in a boat; shortly after his confirmation he dreamt of seeing God. When he dreams of making brooms his dream is entirely in terms of motion and feeling, not of sight.

* * *

Whether there is a difference in the vividness, or any other characteristics which sight would lend, in the dreams of events before and after blindness, is a question to which I could obtain few intelligent and satisfactory answers; but, as far as they go, the tendency of these replies is to show that when blindness ensues close upon the critical period of five to seven years of age, the power of vivid dream-vision is more exclusively limited to the events of the years of full sight, and, as Heermann pointed out, this power is often subject to a comparatively early decay. Similarly, I find that those who lose their sight near the critical age are not nearly so apt to retain color in their dream-vision as those who become blind later on. The average age of "blinding" of twenty-four persons who have colored dream-vision, is 16.6 years, including one case in which blindness set in as early as the seventh year. (All who see enough to see color, have colored dream-vision.)

I also asked those who became blind in youth, or later, whether they were in the habit of giving imaginary faces to the persons they met after their blindness, and whether they ever saw such in their dreams. Some answered in very vague terms, but several undoubtedly make good use of this power, probably somewhat on the same basis as we imagine the appearance of eminent men of whom we have read or heard, but whose features we have never seen. When we remember how erroneous such impressions often are, we can understand how it often misleads the blind. Such imaginary faces and scenes also enter into their dreams, but to a less extent than into those of the sighted. Doctor Kitto quotes a letter from a musician who lost his sight when eighteen years old, but who retains a very strong visualizing power both in working life and in dreams. The mention of a famous man, of a friend, or of a scene, always carries with it a visual picture, complete and vivid. Moreover, these images of his friends change as the friends grow old; and he feels himself intellectually in no way different from the seeing.

Let me, finally, give some examples from the collection of dreams and parts of dreams which these blind people have put at my command. Many are such as we ourselves commonly experience, and many exhibit the peculiarities which have been noticed above. A boy with more than usual imagination dreamed that he was in a battle in which Alexander the Great put the Gauls to flight; he heard the thunder of the cannons, but saw no flash. A very musical young man dreamed that his mother was dead; this he knew by the cold touch of her body. He next heard the chanting of the Mass at her funeral. (This young man at times improvises airs in his dreams.) A partially sighted girl dreams repeatedly of a wide river, and is afraid of being dashed across it, while anxious to secure the flowers on the opposite bank, which she dimly sees. A boy dreamed of being picked up by some mysterious agency, and then suddenly allowed to fall from a tremendous height. Here he awoke, and found his head at the foot of the bed. Another dreamed of the Judgment Day, mainly in terms of hearing. He was drawn to heaven by a rope, clinging to a pole used for exercising; he heard the trumpets sounding, and the voices singing, and so on. . . .

* * *

The "critical period," revealed by the above research, must not be understood as marking the point at which the visual centre begins its life; this occurs at a much earlier age, and this centre is continually increasing in complexity and stability. Nor was the statement made that there was no difference here relevant, between a child losing its sight at two years of age and one losing it at four years. The latter has doubtless a considerable advantage—to some extent indicated by the influence of the age of "blinding" on the future development of noted blind persons, as well as by other considerations. Similarly, after the "critical period," the same processes of growth and assimilation continue, as is evidenced by the vague character and comparatively early decay of the dream-vision of those becoming blind close upon the end of the seventh year. The more time spent in gathering in the provisions, the longer do they hold out. The significance of the "critical period" lies in its demonstrating a point in the growth of the higher sense-centres, at which a divorce from sense-impression is no longer followed by a loss of their physical meaning; a point at which imagination and abstraction find a sufficiently extended and firmly knit collection of experiences to enable them to build up and keep alive their important functions. . . .

The indication of such a period in the development of the human mind brings clearly into view the dependence of the higher mental processes upon the basis furnished them by the experiences of sensation.

17

JOSEPH JACOBS (1854–1916)

Experiments on "prehension" (1887)

In the 1880's the idea that intellectual performances improve with age throughout childhood and that the rate of improvement provides a significant indicator of differences in intelligence among children was gradually emerging. The present study was among the first to present evidence of an increase in proficiency in a specific function with age, and to show that proficiency is related to class standing. The suggestion is made by Jacobs that what was later called "span of apprehension" is a test of mental capacity. It was later called digit span.

The digit span test was used in the first Binet-Simon test of 1905, and is retained in the 1960 Stanford-Binet Scale.

Joseph Jacobs was an Englishman of wide interests who worked for a while with Galton. The present short article no doubt resulted from that contact. So far as we can determine, he made no other contribution to psychology. Jacobs came to the United States in 1900 and remained in this country devoting himself largely to the study of the folklore of several ethnic groups and to Jewish philanthropy. The present article was published in the British journal Mind, *12 (1887): 75–79 and is here reprinted in full.*

It is obvious that there is a limit to the power of reproducing sounds accurately. Anyone can say Bo after once hearing it: few could catch the name of the Green statesman M. Papamichalopoulos without the need of a repetition. It is here attempted to ascertain the normal limits of such reproduction in various circumstances and under varying conditions. At first experiments were made with nonsense-syllables like cral-forg-mul-tal-nop, as suggested by Ebbinghaus's experiments. It was found, however, that the syllables used varied greatly in relative difficulty of pronunciation and in relative facility of rhythm. After a few trials they were abandoned for letters (omitting "double U") and numerals (omitting "seven" as dissyllabic). It was found on the whole that the facility of reproducing the different kinds of sounds, after once hearing them, went together in a tolerably constant ratio. Thus a number of school-girls who could repeat on an average 6.1 nonsense-syllables could repeat 7.3 letters and 9.3 numerals. The explanation for this order of difficulty is not far to seek. The syllables, as contrasted with numerals and letters, are new to the hearer, have to be learnt, and absorb more energy; then, again, their grotesqueness would distract the attention more. The comparative difficulty of reproducing letters as compared with numerals is not so obvious. Reading accustoms us to take letters in groups having a phonetic value, and collocations of consonants like bsvlrtm strike us in a minor degree with the same sense of incongruity which prevents our minds from easily assimilating a conjunction like dak-mil-tak-bin-roz. Numerals on the other hand, have few, if any, associations of contiguity, and we are accustomed to find them in haphazard order. Finally, our expectant attention has only to search among nine numerals, whereas it has to be ready to select from twenty-five letters. School-habits however might modify these conditions, and the cases were not infrequent in which the limit for letters was higher than for numerals: thus in one set of schoolboys no less than 14 boys out of 88 could repeat more letters than they could numerals, while 33 of the remainder had the same limit for both.

Numerals have the further advantage that school-children are accustomed to take them down from dictation, and this leads us to deal with the modus operandi adopted in obtaining our results. It was necessary, in the first place, to adopt some uniform rate at which the dictation should be given, as the power of apprehension varied with the rate of utterance. A sound every half-second was found to be a convenient rate, and a little practice with a metronome beating twice a second gives the experimenter a sense of the proper interval. The repetition was in the first experiments oral, but afterwards was taken in written form. If possible, two sets of the series of sounds should be given, and the highest number correctly reproduced is to be regarded as the limit which we wish to find, and which we term here the *span*. The reading should be in a monotonous tone, so as not to give any perceptible accent or rhythm, either of which, it appears, assists the power of repetition in a considerable degree. The papers, when handed in, were marked with the names of the "subjects," to which it was found useful to add their ages and, if possible, their places in form.

Early in the inquiry it became evident that the power of reproducing a number of sounds increased steadily with age. Our materials enable us to draw up the following Table, which clearly shows the increasing power of school-girls in mastering nonsense-syllables as they grow older:

Age	11	12	13	13	17	18	19	20
Number of Subjects	3	7	11	9	12	13	6	2
Average of Syllables	5.3	5.3	5.7	5.2	5.7	6.1	7.2	7.0

Here there is a distinct rise from 11 to 13, and from 17 to 19, and a marked progress in the whole series from 5.3 at 11 to 7.0 at 20. The same gradual increase of span is also shown in the following results for boys and girls of various ages in reproducing numerals and letters:

	Boys			Girls			
Age	11	12	13	13	17	18	19	20
Number of Subjects	70	57	47	60	32	28	4	3
Av. of Numerals	6.5	6.8	8.8	8.3	9.1	9.9	9.4	9.9
Av. of Letters	5.5	5.7	6.9	7.3	8.7	8.9	8.1	8.0

Steady advance is shown on the average throughout this table except in the highest ages of the girls, where, however, the numbers are too small to allow us to draw any definite conclusions. The progress must, however, stop at some time, and the familiar fact of minds getting "stale" after a certain age suggests the possibility that the increase in the span ceases with the increase in the bodily growth. The most noteworthy result of the table is the sudden leap of two syllables in the cyphering powers of the boys between the ages of 12 and 13. This may be due to greater practice in arithmetic. At any rate it raises them above the average for the girls of the same age, though they hold the reverse position as regards letters. No conclusions can be drawn as to the relative spans of the two sexes at the age of 13, as the subjects were drawn from two entirely different grades of society. . . .

If, then, the span increases normally with age up to a certain point, it follows that in any class of the population, and in the population generally, below that age there will be a fixed number of syllables, letters and numbers which can on the average be seized after once hearing by persons of each age. This number can be determined by the means referred to above, and might easily form an addition to the usual items of anthropometric inquiries. If this were done we should obtain a standard span for the various ages and conditions just as we do for height, weight, etc., a standard relative and not absolute, but still enabling us to ascertain whether a boy or girl were above or below the average, and even the rate of growth in this particular. Another fact came out with equal clearness as our materials accumulated. This was that, as a rule, high span went with high place in form. Thus, selecting 30 boys of 12 years old out of a class and taking the average of their span as regards numerals, this was found to be 9.1 for the first ten, 8.3 for the next ten, and 7.9 in the remainder. In another class, also of 30 boys of the same age, the average of the three sets of ten were in order 7.6, 7.1 and 6.3 respectively. Eight girls of the same age, taken in their order in class, gave for the first four an average of 8.2 for numerals against 8.0 for the last four, while the span for letters remained constant. With 12 girls of 13 years of age the first six had an average span of 8.3 against 7.8 for the last six in the case of numerals, while for letters the two sets were again equal. But the generality of the relation comes out clearly in the following Table, giving the averages for the first and second halves of the various classes at the North London Collegiate School for Girls:

Experiments on "prehension" 147

	Numerals		*Letters*	
Form	1st half	2d half	1st half	2d half
VI	10.5	9.1	9	8.1
Up.V	9.8	9.1	8.8	8.2
V	7.9	8.6	8.1	7.8
L.V.R.	8.2	8.1	8	8.1
Low V	8.5	9	8.2	8
Up.IV.R	8.4	8	8.4	7.5
Up.IV	8.4	7.8	7.4	6.5
IV.R.	8.6	7.6	7.2	6.9
IV	8	6.6	7	6.5
L.IV.R.	8	6.7	7.1	7.5
L.IV.	7.5	7.5	7	6.3
Up.III	7.4	6.4	6.4	5.4
III	7.8	8.5	6.7	6.4
II	6.8	4.9	6.5	6
I	7.4	7.1	6.8	7

This notable concomitance of high span and high place in form, though at first sight surprising, is perhaps nothing more than a corollary of the one previously shown. If the span rises with age, and is thus seemingly a measure of a pupil's relation to the standard of his or her age, it should not be surprising that a pupil with a span higher than the normal should take rank above those of the same age. At any rate, whatever be the cause, the above facts are too consistent and widespread to leave much doubt as to there being a definite connexion between high span and high place in form. And, so far as high place in form can be said to measure ability, the span may serve as some indication of ability.

This at once raises the question as to what is the exact power of the mind which is involved in reproducing these sounds. In our experiments we have simply tested the power of temporarily retaining sounds long enough to reproduce them correctly. . . . We propose to call this power *Prehension* from the analogy of Apprehension and Comprehension, to both of which it is clearly related as a similar process. It may be described as the mind's power of taking on certain material: in this case auditory sensations. Now, of course, this power of taking on need not necessarily go with that of taking in, but, on the other hand, we clearly cannot take in without taking on, and the mental operation we have been testing thus seems a necessary preliminary to all obtaining of mental material, i.e., through auditory presentations. Under these circumstances we might expect that "span of prehension" should be an important factor in determining mental grasp, and its determination one of the tests of mental capacity. The results given above, as far as they go, seem to confirm in no slight degree the theoretical probability.

18

LOUIS ROBINSON (1857–1925)

Darwinism in the nursery (1891)

The recapitulation theory of child development was very prominent in the fourth quarter of the nineteenth century. It held that the individual, in his development, repeats the course of evolution. This principle, it was claimed, accounts for the fact that the human embryo in its early stages has body hair and a tail which disappears before its birth. G. Stanley Hall was a proponent of the evolutionary theory and extended it to explain postnatal psychological development to and beyond adolescence.

This theory plays almost no part in the present book because there is little evidence to support it, and because it led to little productive research.

The present selection is an exception. The evolutionary theory led Dr. Robinson, an English physician, to observe the grasp reflex which had received little attention, although Tiedemann had mentioned it in 1787. Later the grasp reflex was described by John B. Watson without credit to Tiedemann or Robinson. It will appear again in the selection by Myrtle McGraw.

Robinson's article, under the title repeated above, appeared in the journal The Nineteenth Century, 30 (1891): 831–842. Here it is greatly abridged.

At present there is a gap between embryology and anthropology which has never been filled up; and, oddly enough, with one or two exceptions, there have been hitherto no attempts to make use of the abundant material close at hand for the purpose of filling it. In this essay I propose to bring forward a few results of researches that have been carried out during several years under rather unusually favourable circumstances, in the hope that in some humble degree I may contribute to this end.

Some of the results obtained have been extraordinary, and the hesitation with which they have been received by some of my friends well versed in physiology and anthropology shows that hitherto the facts have escaped attention. They are, however, easily verified, and in several instances a single experiment performed in presence of a sceptic has cut short the controversy in a satisfactory manner. Many of the inferences drawn are no doubt much more open to question, and they are here put forward chiefly with the purpose of drawing the attention of those much better able to judge of the value and bearing of the facts than the present writer.

It is curious how little has been written on the natural history of the human infant in its normal state. We have of course an abundant medical literature on the ailments and care of young children, but the many eminent physicians who have written on the subject have confined their attention almost entirely to abnormal or diseased conditions.

* * *

It has been well said that the development of the individual from the single germ cell to maturity, is an epitome of the infinitely longer development of the race from the simplest form of life to its present condition. No branch of science, not even paleontology, has thrown so much light on the evolution theory as the study of the structure and progress of the embryo up to the time of birth. There seems, however, no reason why embryology should stop here. An animal until independent of parental care, and even beyond that point, until the bodily structure and functions are those of an adult, is still, strictly speaking, an embryo; and we may learn much of its racial history by observing the peculiarities of its anatomy and habits of life.

* * *

In the case of our own race it has often been observed that schoolboys present many points of resemblance to savages both in their methods of thinking—especially about abstract subjects—and in their actions. Younger children without a doubt also reflect some of the traits of their remote progenitors. If, as in the case of the calf and the foal, we look for traces of habits of self-preservation that for incalculably long periods were most necessary for the safety of the individual (and therefore for the preservation of the race), we shall find that such habits exist, and are impossible to explain on any other hypothesis than that they were once of essential service.

Take, for instance, the shyness of very young children and their evident terror and distress at the approach of a stranger. At first sight it seems quite unaccountable that an infant a few months old, who has experienced nothing but the utmost kindness and tender care from every human being that it has seen, should cling to its nurse and show every sign of alarm when some person new to it approaches. Infants vary much in this respect, and the habit is not by any means universal, though it is far more often present than absent. This would suggest that, whatever its origin, it was not for any very long period (in the evolutionary sense) absolutely necessary to preserve the species from extinction. Darwin merely alludes to the shyness of children as probably a remnant of a habit common to all wild creatures. We need not, however, go back to any remote ancestral form to find a state of affairs in which it might prove of the greatest service. We know that the cave-dwellers of the Dordogne Valley were cannibals, and that much later, when the races that piled together the Danish "kitchen middens" lived on the shores of the Baltic and German Oceans, they were very much such savages as the present inhabitants of Tierra del Fuego, and lived after the same fashion. Like the Fuegians, they were probably divided into small clans, each of a few families, and these, from conflicting interests and other causes, would be constantly at war. The earlier paleolithic savages, living in caves and rock shelters, would be even more isolated and uncompromising in their treatment of strangers, for the game of any given district would only be sufficient to support a few.

* * *

Under such circumstances the child who ran to its mother, or fled into the dark recesses of the cave, upon first spying an intruder, would be more likely to survive than another of a more confiding disposition. Often, during the absence of the men on a hunting expedition, a raid would be made, and all the women and children that could be caught carried away or killed. The returning warriors would find their homes desolate, and only those members of their families surviving who, by chance or their own action, had escaped the eyes of the spoilers. On the approach of an enemy—and "stranger" would be synonymous—the child which first ran or crawled to its mother, so that she could catch it up and dash out of the wigwam and seek the cover of the woods, might be the only one of all the family to survive and leave offspring. Naturally the instinct which caused the child to turn from the stranger to the mother would be perpetuated; and from the frequency of the habit at the present day it seems probable that many of our ancestors were so saved from destruction. We must remember that the state of society in which such occurrences would be frequent lasted many thousand years, and that probably scarcely a generation was exempt from this particular and unpleasant form of influence.

When we bear in mind that the play of young animals is almost always mimic war, it is well worthy of note how very early young children will take to the game of "hide and seek". I have seen a child of a year old who, with scarcely any teaching, would hide behind the curtains and pretend to be in great alarm when discovered. Probably the readiness with which infants play at "bo-peep," and peer round the edge of a cradle curtain, and then suddenly draw back into hiding, is traceable to a much earlier ancestor. Here we see the remains of a habit common to nearly all arboreal animals, and the cradle curtain, or chair, or what not, is merely a substitute for a part of the trunk of a tree behind which the body is supposed to be hidden, while the eyes, and as little else as possible, are exposed for a moment to scrutinise a possible enemy and then quickly withdrawn.

* * *

Among all arboreal apes the ability firmly to hold on to the branches is of course extremely important, and in consequence they have developed a strong power of grip in the hands. The late Frank Buckland compares the hands of an anthropoid ape to grapnels, from their evident adaptation to this end. Nor does this power exist only among adults, for although most apes, when at rest, nurse their young on one arm, just as does a mother of our own species, when, as often happens, they are fleeing from an enemy, such as a leopard or some other tree-climbing carnivorous animal, the mother would need all her hands to pass from branch to branch with sufficient celerity to escape. Under such circumstances the infant ape must cling on to its mother as best it can; and naturalists who have repeatedly seen a troop of monkeys in full flight state that the young ones as a rule hang beneath the necks and breasts of the mothers, holding on by the long hair of their shoulders and sides. This was the case with a young Rhœsus monkey born in the Zoological Gardens. Wallace, in his *Malay Archipelago,* gives an account of a very young orang which he secured after shooting the mother. He states that the baby orang was in most points as helpless as a human infant, and lay on its back, quite unable to sit upright. It had, however, an extraordinary power of grip, and when it had once secured a hold of his beard he was not able to free himself without help. On his taking it home to his house in Sarawak he found that it was very unhappy unless it could seize and hold on to something, and would lie on its back and sprawl about with its limbs until this could be accomplished. He first gave it some bars of wood to hold on to, but finding it preferred something hairy he rolled up a buffalo skin, and for a while the little creature was content to cling to this, until, by trying to make it perform other maternal duties and fill an empty stomach, the poor orphan nearly choked itself with mouthfuls of hair and had to be deprived of its comforter.

* * *

This power to hold on to the parent in any emergency . . . is the one chief means of self-preservation adopted by the young of the arboreal quadrumana. During long epochs, impossible to measure by years, it would constantly be exercised; and it is plain that every infant ape that failed to exercise it, or which was physically unable from any cause to cling to its mother, when pursued by an agile foe, would either fall to the ground or be devoured among the branches.

* * *

This being so, it occurred to me to investigate the powers of grip in young infants; for if no such power were present, or if the grasp of the hands proved only to be equally proportionate to any other exhibition of muscular strength in those feeble folk, it would either indicate that our connection with quadrumana was of the slightest and most remote description, or that man had some other origin than the Darwinian philosophy maintains.

In *The Luck of Roaring Camp* everyone will remember the expression of one of Bret Harte's mining ruffians after he had passed through the shanty containing the newly born "Luck" and the corpse of the wretched mother. "He wrastled with my finger," said Mr. Kentuck, regarding that member with curiosity, and characteristically adding some adjectives more emphatic than to the point. On reading the story aloud in company several years ago a discussion arose as to whether the novelist was as correct an observer of infant human nature as he doubtless was of the vagaries of the pious cut-throats and chaste courtesans of the Pacific slope in the golden days of '49, and considerable doubt was thrown on the statement of Mr. Kentuck, since it did not seem probable that so gelatinous and flabby a creature as a new-born babe could "wrastle" (and prevail) even with a finger. . . .

Finding myself placed in a position in which material was abundant, and available for reasonable experiment, I commenced a series of systematic observations with the purpose of finding out what proportion of young infants had a noticeable power of grip, and what was the extent of the power. I have now records of upwards of sixty cases in which the children were under a month old, and in at least half of these experiment was tried within a hour of birth. The results as given below are, as I have already indicated, both curious and unexpected.

In every instance, with only two exceptions, the child was able to hang on to the finger or a small stick three-quarters of an inch in diameter by its hands, like an acrobat from a horizontal bar, and *sustain the whole weight of its body* for at least ten seconds. In twelve cases, in infants under an hour old, half a minute passed before the grasp relaxed, and in three of four nearly a minute. When about four days old I found that the strength had increased, and that nearly all, when tried at this age, could sustain their weight for half a minute. At about a fortnight or three weeks after birth the faculty appeared to have attained its maximum, for several at this period succeeded in hanging for over a minute and a half, two for just over two minutes, and one infant of three weeks old for *two minutes thirty-five seconds*! As, however, in a well-nourished child there is usually a rapid accumulation of fat after the first fortnight, the apparently diminished strength subsequently may result partly from the increased disproportion of the weight of the body and the muscular strength of the arms, and partly from neglect to cultivate this curious endowment. In one instance, in which the performer had less than one hour's experience of life, he hung by both hands to my forefingers for ten seconds, and then deliberately let go with his right hand (as if to seek a better hold) and maintained his position for five seconds more by the left, hand only. A curious point is, that in many cases no sign of distress is evinced, and no cry uttered, until the grasp begins to give way. In order to satisfy some sceptical friends I had a series of photographs taken of infants clinging to a finger or to a walking-stick, and these show the position adopted excellently. Invariably the thighs are bent nearly at right angles to the body, and in no case did the lower limbs hang down and take the attitude of the erect position. This attitude, and the disproportionately large development of the arms compared with the legs, give the photographs a striking resemblance to a well-known picture of the celebrated chimpanzee "Sally" at the Zoological Gardens. . . .

I think it will be acknowledged that the remarkable strength shown in the flexor muscles of the fore-arm in these young infants, especially when compared with the flaccid and feeble state of the muscular system generally, is a sufficiently striking phenomenon to provoke inquiry as to its cause and origin. The fact that a three-weeks-old baby can perform a feat of muscular strength that would tax the powers of many a healthy adult—if any of my readers doubt this let them try hanging by their hands from a horizontal bar for three minutes—is enough to set one wondering.

So noteworthy and so exceptional a measure of strength in this set of muscles, and at the same time one so constantly present in all individuals, must either be of some great utility now, or must in the past have proved of material aid in the battle for existence. Now it is evident that to human infants this gift of grip is of no use at all.

* * *

It seems plain that this faculty of sustaining the whole weight by the strength of the grasp of the fingers is totally unnecessary, and serves no purpose whatever in the newly born offspring of savage or civilised man. It follows therefore that, as is the case with many vestigial structures and useless habits, we must look back into the remote past to account for its initiation and subsequent confirmation; and whatever views we may hold as to man's origin, we find among the arboreal quadrumana, and among these only, a condition of affairs in which not only could the faculty have originated, but in which the need of it was imperative, since its absence meant certain and speedy death.

19

JOSEPH JASTROW (1863–1944)

Psychological notes on Helen Keller (1894)

As we have noted earlier, studies of individual cases have had great impact upon psychological thinking. For example, that a person both deaf and blind could learn to read and write was beyond comprehension until it was demonstrated by Dr. Howe and Laura Bridgman. However, Laura Bridgman's accomplishments, while phenomenal for one deaf and blind, were within the realm of mediocrity when compared with those of persons with normal sensory equipment.

It remained for Helen Keller (1880–1968) to show that a deaf-blind person can be brilliant in intellectual accomplishments. She graduated from Radcliffe at 24 and wrote her first book, The Story of My Life, in the same year. She subsequently wrote several other books, all of which increased her fame. Her last book was Teacher, published shortly before her death in 1968. There may never be among the deaf-blind another person as accomplished as Helen Keller, but her life shows that one person so handicapped led a very remarkable life.

The present study by Jastrow, conducted when Helen Keller was only 14 years of age, is of interest in showing her psychological traits at that time. Her span of apprehension for letters and words was unusual.

Jastrow has appeared before in this book as the author of selection 17, "The dreams of the blind." He was not specifically a child psychologist, but rather a "general" psychologist whose researches were not restricted to any field.

Jastrow was a Jew born in Warsaw, Poland, who emigrated to the United States and received his professional training at the University of Pennsylvania. His Ph.D. degree was received at Johns Hopkins in 1886, and he was the chairman of the department of psychology at the University of Wisconsin for many years. He was one of the founders of the American Psychological Association and was its president in 1900 when he was 37. His autobiography will be found in Murchison's History of Psychology in Autobiography, Volume I, pages 135–162 (1930).

The article here reprinted was published in the Psychological Review *1 (1894): 356–362.*

During the past summer I had the opportunity of making a few tests and observations upon Helen Keller, the blind and deaf girl whose life and education, in many respects, offer a still more interesting and attractive subject than the remarkable career of Laura Bridgeman. These notes are altogether meagre and fragmentary and offer nothing more than indications of the special development of her faculties. I am urged to print them simply because no more thorough study has as yet been undertaken. The tests were made for the most part in the Psychological Laboratory in the Anthropological Building at the World's Fair, Chicago. . . .

My first tests related to her powers of touch and movement. For the pressure sense two series of weights, the first increasing by $\frac{1}{15}$, the second by $\frac{1}{30}$, beginning with a standard weight of 300 grammes, were to be arranged in order. Both sets were correctly arranged, and in rather a brief time. As these weights were raised by the hand the main sense involved was the muscle sense; about one third of all persons tested with these weights were able to arrange both sets correctly. The test accordingly indicates nothing more than a muscle sensibility at least normally delicate. Accurate tests would have required more time than was at my disposal.

An aesthesiometer [an instrument for measuring skin sensitivity] applied to the tip of the forefinger of the left hand indicated that with a distance of 1.5 mm between the points they were clearly felt as double, while points separated by 1 mm felt like one broad point. The sensibility was not finer than this on the tip of her tougue. On the palm of the hand points 3 and 4 mm apart were felt as distinct. The normal sensibility for these parts of the skin is differently given by various writers; but if I may trust to the averages obtained from experiments upon a general public, Helen's finger-tips and the palm of her hand (a region interesting because it is here that the impressions of the manual finger-alphabet which she "reads" are in part received) are decidedly more acute than in the average individual.

In the next test two series of five graded surfaces were presented to her forefinger (right hand), and by passing the finger across the wires she was to obtain a notion of their relative roughness or coarseness, and indicate their order in this respect. The surfaces were produced by tightly wrapping brass wires of various grades around an iron form. In the first series the wires increased in diameter by $\frac{1}{4}$, beginning with a wire .051 inches in diameter, and in the second series they increased by $\frac{1}{8}$. Helen arranged both series in order correctly and with considerable confidence in her judgment. Less than one fourth of all persons tested succeeded in doing this, and there was rarely any confidence in the correctness of the result.

I attempted a more accurate test of the delicacy of the "form-sense" of her finger-tips by means of a very serviceable touch-apparatus which has been devised by Prof. Münsterberg. In this instrument small wire forms of several sizes and shapes are applied to the skin in order to determine to what extent the form can be distinguished. The best evidences of acute sensibility that I obtained were as follows: a right angle 10 mm on each side was correctly called such and distinguished from an angle of 60°; a set of 8 points set upon a wire circle 10 mm in diameter was at first called 10 points and then 8, set in a "round"; a series of 10 points set 3 mm apart, with the two central ones separated by 5 mm, was called "nearly ten," some "not the same distance apart." A few tests with raised types were made, but with no noteworthy result; the statement of her teacher, Miss Sullivan, that Helen is not a rapid reader is interesting in this respect.

Furthermore a few observations with tuning-forks were extremely suggestive. The vibrations of a tuning-fork with a pitch of 1024 were distinctly, almost painfully, perceived when the finger-tip was placed lightly on the prong; and the same is true of one with a pitch of 1365, while the vibrations of a fork of about 5000 were not perceived. With the one of 1024, particularly, the vibrations could be felt by the finger when $\frac{1}{2}$ or $\frac{3}{4}$ of an inch away from the fork. This suggests a sensitiveness to the vibrations-sense or sense of jar which has frequently been noted by the deaf. . . . Further experiments in this direction are desirable. Helen's motor faculties seem not unusually well developed and are doubtless far surpassed by many blind persons. Miss Sullivan has observed that she is not skilful in finding her way about nor in knowing where things are in a familiar room. In the apparatus for testing the accuracy of the perception of lengths by finger-movements, the task is to arrange in order two series of five lengths, the one advancing by $\frac{2}{15}$, the other by $\frac{1}{15}$, from a standard of 150 mm. The first series was correctly arranged, in the second there was one error, and in both there was considerable hesitation and uncertainty. I next arranged a board about 2 ft. square, ruled off in inch squares. A needle was set in a convenient wooden handle, and a thumb-tack was placed at various points upon the board. Helen's finger was first guided to the tack, then taken away, whereupon she attempted to place the needle upon the tack. She was seated with the centre of the board opposite to the centre of the body and moved the needle on an average through a distance of 12 to 15 inches. Her errors in four trials were 35, 15, 15, and 25 mm, a degree of accuracy which may well be equalled by a seeing person with his eyes closed.

The rapidity of her movement seems also below normal. A single test indicated a maximum finger-movement of about 2.5 per second, where the normal (for adults) is about 5 per second. Helen is right-handed, and the attempt to move the two hands simultaneously to an equal extent, away from the centre of the body, indicates the same fact. For left-hand excursions of 133, 138, 169, and 99 mm the right-hand equivalents were 210, 168, 253, and 162 mm. The attempt to draw lines of equal length, or mark off equal distances by making a series of dots on a strip of paper, showed about a normal degree of error.

Tested with Prof. Cattell's pain-tester she declared a just-perceptible degree of pain when a pressure of 3.75 kilogrammes was brought to bear upon the tip of the forefinger of her left hand (average of three trials.) The usual result for adult women is about 5 kilogrammes, but the variation is large owing to the subjective difficulty of indicating the pain limit.

I attempted a few tests of the quickness and scope of more complex processes. Beginning with a simple reaction-time, I touched her left hand and required her to respond by touching a key with her right hand. The times, in hundredths of a second, measured by a D'Arsonval chronoscope, were 36, 17, 16, 34, 16, 14, 15, 25. When the functions of the right and left hand were reversed the times were 28, 32, 16, 16, 20, 22. In the first series the two long reactions were clearly due to an awkward manner of closing the key. Omitting these, the first series gives an average time of 17 hundredths of a second which for a child of 14 years is probably a quick reaction. In the next series, if I touched her right shoulder she was to press a key with her right hand, if I touched the left shoulder the left-hand key with her left hand, thus involving a distinction of the location of contact and a choice of movements. The times in hundredths of a second were 18, 20, 25, 22, 16, 36, 29, 24, 22, 26, 32, 29, or an average of 25, making a difference of 8 hundredths of a second for the combined distinction and choice. Compared with the average record of persons unused to reacting this is a decidedly creditable record.

My final notes deal with various memory tests, which were performed with the aid of Miss Sullivan, who spelled upon Helen's hand the letters, numbers, or words which I dictated, whereupon Helen would speak vocally the letters, numbers, or words as she remembered them. It should be mentioned that Helen is so entirely accustomed to vocal utterances that this mode of speech seems to have taken the place in her mental habits of her more primitive mode of answering in the finger alphabet. This was shown by her very strong tendency to murmur the words or letters as she interpreted the movements of Miss Sullivan's fingers. Such motor innervations clearly offered an aid to the memory, and it was with difficulty that she succeeded in repressing this tendency when I requested her to do so. It should be added that her control of the finger alphabet is remarkable. She accepted with great glee my challenge to speak with her fingers Longfellow's "Psalm of Life" as rapidly as possible, and succeeded in forming nearly seven letters in a second throughout the recitation. This is a rapidity sufficient to test the utmost capacity of a sign-reader to keep up with it. Helen had not at the time a set of single signs for the numerals; to convey to her 1, it was necessary to spell o-n-e. She at once learned a set of signs for use in my tests, but the newness of the acquisition clearly acted to the disadvantage of her memory. I shall therefore omit the tests with numerals, which showed about a normal memory-span.

158 Joseph Jastrow

Beginning with letters I have the following, in which the columns O are the original series and R the recalled series.

O.	R.	O.	R.	O.	R.	O.	R.	O.	R.
b	b	c	c	k	k	c	c	h	h
m	m	z	z	l	l	l	l	a	a
o	o	l	l	r	r	o	o	y	y
s	s	t	t	p	p	f	f	z	
i		v	v	o	o	k	b	r	r
k	k	w	u	t	t	b	r	p	p
r	r	k	k	i	i	r	k	k	l
y	y	s	s	p	p	y	y	c	
b	b	c	c	a	a	a	b	f	y
c	c	b	b	y		c	a	y	f
v	v	o	o	c		u	o	g	g
				f			u		
				w	w				

With less than ten letters in a set there were rarely any errors, the series being correctly reproduced in *order*. With the above series of 11, 12, and 13 letters there were a few errors. It is interesting to note that the tendency to recall the first members of the series and the last is as marked in this variety of tactual motor memory as in the auditory or visual.

I also tried nonsense syllables, but these seemed very confusing, six syllables being as many as she could repeat. With monosyllabic words, such as the following, *gate, bell, moon, foot, nest, kite, meal, chair, nail, toy,* she several times succeeded in repeating thirteen words correctly and in order; while with ten or eleven one could count upon a faultless reproduction. A few of these memory-tests were made in the evening; in the morning of the following day Helen was still able to repeat correctly the series of thirteen words she had learned the evening before, but had repeated them to herself a few times during the interval between the two trials. I have collected comparable data for a few hundred individuals, but they have not yet been finally computed. However, upon the basis of a preliminary survey of my material I have no hesitation in pronouncing Helen's verbal memory decidedly above the normal, and particularly when the correctness of the order is taken into account. How far this may be due to the concentration of her attention upon one sense, and to her acquiring through verbal means what to us is visible or audible, is an open question. The account of her mental habits given by Miss Sullivan (*Helen Keller:* The Volta Bureau, Washington, 1892) amply corroborates the extraordinary powers of her literary memory.

I cannot conclude these notes without commenting upon the remarkable alertness and receptivity of mind displayed by her in visiting the exhibits at the World's Fair. By the courtesy of the officials the universal admonition "Do not touch" was disregarded in her case; and it certainly was most interesting to observe the rapidly-varying expressions of her animated features, and listen to her comments, as one specimen after another from the ethnological collections was placed in her hands with some brief description of its character communicated to her through Miss Sullivan. The acuteness of intellect, breadth of interest, wholesomeness of emotional sensibility, along with such confined avenues of intercourse with the outer world, could not but impress the psychological observer as an admirable illustration of the relative functions of the senses, and the faculties that interpret and assimilate the facts of sensation in the economy of the mental life.

My obligations are due not only to Helen Keller herself for her cheerful compliance with my somewhat arduous demands, but to her able teacher Miss Sullivan, and to the distinguished scientist who has so generously espoused her cause, Dr. Alexander Graham Bell.

20

MILLICENT SHINN (1859–1940)

The biography of a baby (1900)

This is the last baby biography and the last case history which will be presented in this book. It is included in preference to other possibilities in large part because Miss Shinn was so perceptive and wrote so well.

Primarily an editor and writer, she was a spinster who, under the spell of the child study movement, studied the development of her niece. As a result she published four thick monographs of observations, which few people will ever read, and a popular book from which the excerpts reproduced here were chosen.

In the interest of unity the sections which have been reproduced are primarily those devoted to visual perception and visual-motor coordination. Since nearly all babies develop in much the same manner, a skilled observer of a baby describes visual-perceptual-motor development in the same manner whether he is Miss Shinn, Tiedemann, Preyer, Gesell, or Piaget. Many of the descriptions in this section are clear forerunners of later "scientific" work.

Miss Shinn's book, published by Houghton, Mifflin and Co. in 1900, has long been out of print.

Most studies of children deal with later childhood, the school years; and these are almost always statistical in their method, taking the individual child very little into account. My own study has been of babyhood, and its method has been biographical.

I am often asked if the results one gets in this way are not misleading, since each child might differ greatly from others. One must, of course, use great caution in drawing general conclusions from a single child, but in many things all babies are alike, and one learns to perceive pretty well which are the things. Babyhood is mainly taken up with the development of the large, general racial powers; individual differences are less important than in later childhood. And the biographical method of

160

child study has the inestimable advantage of showing the process of evolution going on, the actual unfolding of one stage out of another, and the steps by which the changes come about. No amount of comparative statistics could give this. If I should find out that a thousand babies learned to stand at an average age of forty-six weeks and two days, I should not know as much that is important about standing as I should after watching a single baby carefully through the whole process of achieving balance on his little soles.

* * *

Perhaps I should say a word here as to the way in which I came to make a baby biography, for I am often asked how one should go to work at it. It was not done in my case for any scientific purpose, for I did not feel competent to make observations of scientific value. But I had for years desired an opportunity to see the wonderful unfolding of human powers out of the limp helplessness of the new-born baby; to watch this fascinating drama . . . daily, minutely, and with an effort to understand it as far as I could, for my own pleasure and information. I scarcely know whence the suggestion had come; probably almost by inheritance, for my mother and grandmother had both been in somewhat notable degree observers of the development of babies' minds. But, unlike them, I had the notebook habit from college and editorial days, and jotted things down as I watched, till quite unexpectedly I found myself in possession of a large mass of data.

* * *

There are several actions that come ready-made to the baby at birth, before he can possibly have had any chance to learn them, or any idea of what they are for. Babies sneeze, swallow, and cry on the first day; they shut their eyes at a bright light, or at a touch. On the first day, moreover, they have been seen to start at a sound or a jar; Preyer observed hiccoughing, choking, coughing, and spreading the toes when the soles were tickled; and Darwin saw yawning and stretching within the first week, though I do not know that any one has seen it on the first day.

These movements are all of the class called reflex movements, that is, in which the bodily mechanism is set off by some outside action on the senses, as a gun is set off by a touch on the trigger. Thus, when a tickling affects the mucous membrane, a sneeze executes itself without any will of ours. . . .

Mothers do not like to think that the baby is at first an automaton; and they would be quite right in objecting if that meant that he was a mere machine. He is an automaton in the sense that he has practically neither thought, wish, nor will; but he is a living, conscious automaton, and that makes all the difference in the world. And it would be a bold psychologist who should try to say what *germ* of thought and will lies enfolded in his helplessness.

* * *

Here is the conception I gathered of the dim life on which the little creature entered at birth. She took in with a dull comfort the gentle light that fell on her eyes, seeing without any sort of attention or comprehension the moving blurs of darkness that varied it. She felt motions and changes; she felt the action of her own muscles; and, after the first three or four days, disagreeable shocks of sound now and then broke through the silence, or perhaps through an unnoticed jumble of faint noises. She felt touches on her body from time to time, but without the least sense of the place of the touch (this became evident enough later, as I shall relate in its order); and steady slight sensations of touch from her clothes, from arms that held her, from cushions on which she lay, poured in on her.

From time to time sensations of hunger, thirst, and once or twice of pain, made themselves felt through all the others, and mounted till they became distressing; from time to time a feeling of heightened comfort flowed over her, as hunger and thirst were satisfied, or release from clothes, and the effect of the bath and rubbing on her circulation, increased the net sense of well-being. She felt slight and unlocated discomforts from fatigue in one position, quickly relieved by the watchful nurse. For the rest, she lay empty-minded, neither consciously comfortable nor uncomfortable, yet on the whole pervaded with a dull sense of wellbeing. Of the people about her, of her mother's face, of her own existence, of desire or fear, she knew nothing.

* * *

On the twenty-fifth day, toward evening, the baby was lying on her grandmother's knee by the fire, in a condition of high well-being and content, gazing at her grandmother's face with an expression of attention. I came and sat down close by, leaning over the baby, so that my face must have come within the indirect range of her vision. At that she turned her eyes to my face and gazed at it with the same appearance of attention, and even of some effort, shown by a slight tension of brows and lips, then turned her eyes back to her grandmother's face, and again to mine, and so several times. . . . I watched now for what Preyer's record had led me to expect as the next development in vision—the ability to follow a moving object with the eyes; that is, to hold the fovea fixed on the object as it moved, moving the eyeball in time with it in order to do so. I used my hand to move to and fro before the baby, and could not satisfy myself that she followed it, though she sometimes seemed to; but the day after she was a month old I tried a candle, and her eyes followed it unmistakably; she even threw her head back to follow it farther. . . .

The baby's increased interest in seeing centered especially on the faces about her, at which she gazed with rapt interest. Even during the period of mere staring, faces had oftenest held her eyes, probably because they were oftener brought within the range of her clearest seeing than other light surfaces. The large, light, moving patch of the human face coming and going in the field of vision, and oftener chancing to hover at the point of clearest seeing than any other object, embellished with a play of high lights on cheeks, teeth, and eyes, is calculated to excite the highest degree of attention a baby is capable of at a month old. . . .

And now the baby had come to six weeks old, and could hold up her head perfectly for a quarter of a minute at a time, and liked greatly to be held erect or in sitting position. Apparently all this was for the sake of seeing better, for her joys still centered in her eyes. She had made no advance in visual power, however, except that within a few days she could follow with her eyes the motion of a person passing near her.

Human faces were still the most entertaining of all objects. She gazed at them with her utmost look of intentness, making movements with her hands, and panting in short, audible breaths. Nothing else had ever excited her so, except once a spot of sunlight on her white bed.

At seven weeks she opened her mouth for the nipple on being laid in the proper position. The food association group was enlarging; but sight did not yet enter into it: the look of the breast did not seem to bring the faintest suggestion of satisfied hunger, and the baby would lie and cry with her lips an inch from it. . . .

During the last days of the second month the baby was possessed by the most insatiate impulse to be up where she could see. It was hard to think that her fretting and even wailing when forced to lie down could mean only a formless discontent, and not a clear idea of what she wanted. Still, it is not common, when an instinct is thwarted, to feel a dim distress that makes us perfectly wretched without knowing why. As soon as she was held erect, or propped up sitting amid cushions, she was content; but the first time that she was allowed to be up thus most of the day, she slept afterward nine unbroken hours, recuperating, probably, quite as much from the looking and the taking in that the little brain and eyes had been doing as from any muscular fatigue there may have been in the position.

* * *

During the whole third month the baby had insisted on a sitting position, and had wailed as vigorously over being left flat on her back as over being left hungry. She had soon tried to take the matter into her own hands, and made efforts to lift herself, sometimes by pulling on our fingers when we had laid them in her hands, sometimes by sheer strain of the abdominal muscles. She never succeeded in raising more than her head and shoulders till the last week of the month: then she did once lift herself, and in the following days tried with the utmost zeal to repeat the success. She would strive and strain, with a grave and earnest face, her whole baby soul evidently centered on the achievement. She would tug at our fingers till her little face was crimson; she would lift her head and shoulders and strain to rise higher, fall back and try it again, till she was tired out. The day she was three months old, she tried twenty-five times, with scarcely a pause, and even then, though she was beginning to fret pitifully with disappointment, she did not stop of her own accord.

* * *

In the fourth month the baby was looking about her silently, studying her world. She would inspect the familiar room carefully for many minutes, looking fixedly at object after object till the whole field of vision was reviewed, then she would turn her head eagerly and examine another section; and when she had seen all she could from one place, she would fret till she was carried to another, and there begin anew her inspection of the room in its changed aspect—always with the look of surprise and eagerness, eyes wide and brows raised.

We can only guess what was going on in the baby mind all this time; but I cannot resist the thought that I was looking on at that very process which must have taken place somewhere about this time—the learning to see things clear and separate, by running the eyes over their surfaces and about their edges.

* * *

Did she, then, see the world as a world of *things*—solid objects, visible and tangible? Probably not. Her whole behavior showed that she never blended the feel of a thing and the look of a thing into the perception of the thing itself. If her body was touched anywhere, she never looked toward the place to see what touched her. When she groped on her tray, she seemed to be merely repeating motions that had formerly brought sensations, not seeking for things that she supposed were there; she never looked for them, nor even looked at them as she held them; she seemed to have no suspicion that the feeling in her hand was due to a visible object there.

Nor could she well have had any idea of an object, even as one may get it from touch alone, without sight; for she did not feel over the things she held—she was conscious only of the part that touched her. If she laid hold of her rattle one day by one part, and another day by another, she could not have known it was the same object, except as she learned a little about it in fumbling for a better hold. I short, the things she touched and held can hardly have been to her definite objects, but only disjointed touch and weight sensations.

Just at the end of the third month the baby had once gazed at her rattle as she held it in her hand; but it was not till the second week of the fourth month that she seemed really to learn that when she felt the familiar touch in her hand, she could see something by looking. Then her eyes began to rest on things while she picked them up; but in a blank and passive way—the eyes looking on like outsiders, while the awkward little hands funmbled just as they would have done in the dark. The baby seemed to have no idea that what she saw was the same thing as what she felt.

There was about a fortnight of this. Then, on one great day, when three weeks of the month had passed, the baby looked at her mother's hand, held up before her, and made fumbling motions toward it; keeping her eyes on it, till her hand struck it; then took hold of it. She had formed an association between the sight of an object and the groping movement of her hand toward it.

* * *

The discovery of the new quality of tangibility in the visible world must have been gradual, however, and her new power of grasping hardly more at first than a blind use of association. In the next fortnight she grasped doubtfully, depending only partly on sight for guidance. She would put out her hand uncertainly, with fingers spread, not ready to grasp, and it was only when they touched the object that her movement became confident. Sometimes both hands were brought cautiously down on either side of the thing she wished to get hold of.

In this fortnight she grasped better with the mouth than with the hands, and was more disposed to use it. She brought her mouth to the nipple easily by sight. She dived at me with her head to get the loose folds of my bodice into her mouth. In our arms, she would attack our faces with a sudden dive of her head and a funny doubling up movement of her body, and would mouth them over with satisfaction.

* * *

From the middle of the fourth month she followed us constantly with her eyes as we moved about. Her eyes were thus drawn to greater distances, and her range of vision increased; before this she had hardly noticed anything across the room. In the latter part of the month she looked with especial curiosity at people's faces on the other side of the room, and I guessed that it was because they looked so much smaller to her—as they would to us if we had not learned to allow for the distance. A face fifteen feet away can be completely hidden by a fifty cent piece held out at arm's length; our friends shrink to small dolls in our eyes every time they cross the room, but we bring them up to their real size by trained imagination. The baby, who had not yet the trained imagination, must have seen strange shrinkings and swellings as people moved from her or toward her, and as she was carried about the room.

She saw a complete change of appearance, too, each time any one turned around, and each time she was carried from one side to another of a person, or of a piece of furniture. We have become so used to this that we do not notice it; but to the baby each side of an object must have looked like an entirely new thing. I think it was some time before she learned to associate together the different sides and the different sizes of each object—all the aspects one chair could take, for instance, gathering into one group in her mind, and all the aspects a table or a person could take, into another; but she was learning. . . .

The changes that people went through, as they moved about, were much more complicated than those of the furniture; but that only made them the more interesting. No wonder that as soon as the baby knew she could touch and feel what she saw, it was our faces she dived for with especial zeal, to explore their surfaces with her mouth; and a fortunate thing it is for the baby's progress in knowledge that mothers do not mind having great and moist liberties taken with their faces. Our baby learned, too, at this time, with the connivance of her grandfather, and afterward her father, to fix her fingers in their beards and tug. This was doubtless educational, and it brought still another interest into the number that gathered about the faces of her fellow beings: but it led to trouble later, as her hands grew quicker and stronger in clutching.

* * *

When the baby had passed ten days of her fifth month, she was still grasping half mechanically. On the eleventh day, lying on her back, she held her rattle above her and looked at it carefully. Her attention had turned to the things that she grasped. She had come before to the perception of a world of objects, but apparently only now to the realization of it. And thereupon, that very day, I saw that she was no longer using eyes and hands merely as means of getting mouth sensations; she was holding objects, looking at them, and pulling them about, for some moments, before they went to her mouth.

* * *

In a few hours the baby was reaching for everything near her, and in three days more her desire to lay hold on things was the dominant motive of her life. Her grasping was still oftener with both hands than one, and was somewhat slow, but always accurate. Some babies learn to grasp more suddenly than she did, and often miss their aim; but with her cautious method of bringing down her hands toward an object from either side, penning it in between, she could hardly make errors. The thing once corralled, she would pull it around, perhaps a minute, then put it to her mouth.

* * *

In these first days of the passion for grasping at things, the baby reached for flat figures as readily as for solid objects; but she learned to discriminate with surprising ease, and after the first week I have only three or four notes of her trying to pick up such things as pictures on a page, roses on a quilt, shadows in the sun. Yet I do not think this was because she gained quickly any such sense of the difference between plane and solid form as we have, but rather that she learned quickly to associate a certain look about an object with the experience of being able to get hold of it.

The reason that I think so is that even weeks later, when she was six months old, she showed signs of having no real ability to judge form by the eye. At that age she turned a round cracker round and round at her lips, trying to find the corner to bite, as she was used to doing with square ones. And the only time she was ever taken in by a flat figure afterward was when (at nine months old) she tried a long time to capture the swaying shadow of a rope end on the deck of a yacht; things that moved could always be taken hold of in her experience, and she went solely by experience, not by any general ideas of form.

21

EDWARD L. THORNDIKE (1874-1949)

Some data concerning the value of Latin as a secondary school subject (1900)

Thorndike was a pioneer investigator in educational psychology. Beginning his career with studies of learning in sub-human animals, he soon shifted to studies of learning in children. He challenged many dicta in education, and attempted to test them by research, and he was persistent in this attempt. The following selection is one of his early studies and gives the flavor of Thorndike's work.

In 1900 Latin was a required subject in many American high schools where pupils probably did not speak or write good English. They may not today, but they are no longer required to write bad Latin, thanks in part to Thorndike. He spent his life, beginning at about age 23, in the empirical investigation of what has been called the human mind and the ways in which it learns.

Thorndike's article was published in the Journal of Pedagogy 13 *(1900): 27–38.*

Thorndike's autobiography, with many others, is in History of Psychology in Autobiography, *Volume III, Clark University Press, 1936. A selection of his papers, chosen by Thorndike, has been published in Selected Writings from a Connectionist's Psychology,* Appleton-Century-Crofts, 1949.

We really know very little about the values of different school studies. In spite of the wide experience and pronounced acumen of many of those who have theorized about the matter, it seems that we really do not know what different courses do actually do for the scholars who complete them. We do not know with surety the total effects of any study on the average scholar and so we cannot estimate the study's value, nor estimate more than roughly even its relative value. If the men of school experience and good insight agreed about these questions, we might well forego any actual demonstration of the effects of studies and consequently of their values and, as all thought alike, be content without actual knowledge. But as a matter of sad fact no such agreement exists. One man thinks, for example, that Latin disciplines the mind; another that it does not; and between the two men there is no way of choosing. One declares that the study of Latin helps the power of expression in English, and another declares that on the contrary it weakens and debauches one's English style.

Theorizing and discussion would seem to have gone as far as they could, and yet they have not succeeded in constructing anything like a science of educational values. It would seem, therefore, worth while to attempt some careful observational and inductive work along the lines of these problems. The value of a study depends, of course, upon some real change which happens in the pupil on account of having studied it. This change may lie in the way of changed powers, habits, interests, information or ideals. Now all such changes are real events in a real world; can be observed and described and in a certain way measured. In short, they are amenable to scientific treatment. Their importance would seem to justify an attempt at such treatment even against great practical difficulties.

The present investigation was undertaken in the hope of gaining some data of value on one particular question and also of testing, though to only a slight extent, the applicability of certain methods to the solution of such problems. Possibilities and difficulties alike might be expected to be clearer after an attempt, no matter how trivial, at an inductive investigation of the value of studies.

The question chosen concerned the value of the study of Latin in our high schools as a means of giving information about and interest in the life and civilization of the Romans and their influence on modern life and civilization. Almost any other of the quarrels of the theorists would have done as well but the importance of a right estimate of Latin in reconstructing our high school courses and the weight which has been attached to this element of the general influence of classical study by Dr. Harris, Prof. N. M. Butler and others, suggested this as a fit problem. It surely is as complex and subtle as any, so that if work of the sort I have advocated contributes anything of value here, it may hopefully be undertaken elsewhere.

The study, a report of which follows, consisted of three distinct parts: (1) the collection under scientific conditions of data about the knowledge of Roman life and civilization gained by pupils from three or four years' study of Latin; (2) the collection of data about the knowledge (and interest as well) of a similar sort gained by men, at present teachers of history, from the four years' course in Latin which they took in the high school, and (3) the comparison of the results of (1) and (2) with the opinions of a number of teachers of Latin about the general subject.

The means for getting data for (1) were papers written by high school students and college freshmen in answer to the following four questions: (1) Was Cicero courageous? (2) Which were the Romans best at, making laws, writing books, or building beautiful buildings? (3) Which were the Romans most like, the English or the Americans? Why? (4) Is there any other reason for reading Cæsar besides the wish to learn the Latin language?

The answers were written in class, with no assistance by teacher or other pupils before or during the test. Ten or fifteen minutes' time was given in which to write the answers. The need of having a very short test in order not to infringe on ordinary school work is the reason for the extremely narrow scope of these questions. Aside from this they would seem to be legitimate enough. The present writer did not, of course, intend to use questions which would weigh the dice in favor of any theory. And he at least cannot see that they do. The first is intended of course to test definitely the culture value of a Latin text. The second and third aim to get some notion of the general feeling for Roman civilization given by the prolonged study of Latin, while the last question serves to present certain opinions (sincere or conventional) of the student about our general topic. These opinions, of course, have no direct value for our purpose but are indirectly of some interest in connection with it as we shall later on see.

These questions were answered by: (*a*) forty-seven first-year students in college, all girls; (*b*) twenty-six third-year students in a high school; (*c*) nineteen third-year students in another high school; (*d*) twenty fourth-year students in this last school; (*e*) thirty-three third-year students in another high school; (*f*) fourteen fourth-year students in this last school; (*g*) fifteen fourth-year students in a private preparatory school.

Eighty-five per cent of these students had studied ancient history about three hours a week for one term on the average. All the schools represented are schools paying their Latin teachers from $600 to $2000, and bearing the repute of doing excellent work. The tests were given in February and March, 1899. The numbers are so small that the only useful judgments that can be made on the basis of the results are judgments concerning the one hundred and seventy-four students as a whole. These may fairly be taken to represent an average lot of the better grade of students from the better class of high schools. They ought to show traces of the culture due to reading Latin texts, if such culture results to high-school pupils in general.

Of the one hundred and seventy-four pupils, one hundred and thirty-eight gave a decisive answer to the first question; sixteen of the failures to answer decisively were due to general ignorance about Cicero, being all found in class *c* above (the class that had not read Cicero for at least half a year). The others were due to either lack of any decided opinion or to ambiguous expression. Of the one hundred and thirty-eight answering decidedly, one hundred and thirteen, or about eighty-two per cent, thought Cicero was courageous. It would prolong this article over much and would, considering the short time allowed for answering the test, be unfair to present statistics of the reasons for the decisions. The majority of them are extremely superficial and show a simple-minded way of looking at historical data which shows far more strongly than the bare figures . . . the inability of the average high-school student to get historical information from such a text. But even from the bare percentage of yeas and nays, it seems fairly sure that the average high-school student is more likely to be misinformed than instructed about Roman history by his year's reading of Cicero. He gets at only a superficial stratum of fact and may be utterly mistaken in his interpretation of it. The text seems to have failed signally to arouse any useful interest in the man Cicero or the times. Few of the students seem to have been led to think intelligently about either or even to have read the historical introductions in the text-books. A naive acceptance of some few statements made by Cicero about himself, and shot directly at the reader as it were out of a gun, is about all that the reading of the text produces.

The second question (Which were the Romans best at, making laws, writing books or building beautiful buildings?) was chosen because the correct answer to it depended upon the commonest bit of knowledge about Roman civilization that I could think of. One hundred and fifty-three pupils answered it, one hundred and two saying that the Romans were best at making laws, thirty-seven and one-half at building fine buildings, and thirteen and one-half at writing books.*

If we leave out of account the college freshmen, we have one hundred and six pupils, of whom sixty-five favored "laws," twenty-seven and one-half "buildings," and thirteen and one-half "books."

One hundred and forty-eight pupils answered the third question, ninety-five and one-half thinking that the Romans were most like the English, fifty-two and one-half that they were most like the Americans. If we leave out the college freshmen, we have sixty-four and one-half (sixty-one per cent) favoring the English, and forty and one-half the Americans.

To make these results at all decisive it would be necessary to get more answers from students who have had courses in ancient history but none in Latin. It is quite possible that the appreciation (if such it may be called) for Roman civilization shown in these answers may be due to general reading and historical study apart from Latin courses. In the case of a very few people whom I have had an opportunity of asking about this matter, I find in general denials that their courses in the Latin language were in no way the source of their information on these two simple points. But even if we do not make the probable discount due to outside sources, there still seems to be no great virtue in the study of Latin as a producer of a valuable appreciation of Roman civilization. Our answers show little appreciation that is of value. The incorrect answers and the extremely superficial nature of the majority of the reasons for all the answers make it seem almost comical to speak of these young people as realizing Roman civilization, much less its influence. To the writer, as he read through

* The fractions refer to pupils who thought the Romans equally good at two of the three.

paper after paper among these, it grew increasingly absurd to suppose that the union of some hundreds of pages of Cæsar, Cicero and Virgil with these immature minds should beget any such appreciation.

It is noteworthy that no pupil in answering either of these questions ever quoted any passage in any of the texts read or even referred to them in any way whatever. On the other hand we have apparent evidence of the beneficial influence of direct instruction by the teacher or some English source. Thus in one school, out of ten scholars who declare the Romans to have been best at making laws, nine give as their reason the fact that their architect and literature were borrowed from the Greeks.

The last question was put to the classes for several reasons. It seemed worth while, for general pedagogical reasons, to try to ascertain scholars' thoughts about the purpose of the work, to compare their thoughts about what it was for with what they actually gained from it, with what they actually did with it in their own studying. It was also expected that the results might furnish data about a certain general aspect of human thinking which is rather important for teachers to know about, namely the habit of making judgments conventionally, of saying, "Yea! Yea!" with our lips when our real mental conduct is inconsistent with our answer. Children for instance will say that they would prefer to live in New Orleans rather than Boston because New Orleans "is the greatest gulf port," or because "it exports more cotton than any other port in the United States,"—reasons which, of course, would play no real part in the child's preferences. It was also desirable to find out how far one could in other investigations rely on the student's own statements; how far, for instance, we could accept as valid students' answers to such questions as, "Has reading Cæsar made you become interested in Roman history?" "What have you learned about Cæsar's character from reading the Galic War?" etc.

All the pupils who seemed to have understood the question replied in the affirmative. Three or four may, however, have really meant to deny to the reading of Cæsar any other usefulness than its usefulness as a drill book on the language. Knowledge of the life of the Romans, or Roman history, of Roman methods of warfare, lead among the reasons. Knowledge of Gallic tribes, Cæsar's character, his style of writing, are often mentioned. Mental training is mentioned by a big majority of one class, though rarely referred to among any of the others. Very instructive is the answer of one honest child who, after puzzling to think of something that Cæsar had taught her, wrote that *"we learn from reading Caesar how the Romans built bridges."* Verily the modern teachers of Latin forget the claims of culture when they skip that knotty passage! Even more instructive is the opinion of another youth that we read Cæsar to get certain knowledge about the Romans *"for nobody would read Caesar, even in English, if they didn't have to in school."* In general the reasons of these students are the same reasons as those high in authority would give. Just as the talk of little girls with their dolls conventionally imitates the talk of mothers, so the children in school adopt the notions of their parents and teachers and text-books about what their studies amount to.

The chief lesson of these answers is that scholars whom Cicero's orations have taught nothing of value about Cicero may yet have advanced ideas about the culture to be gained from a Latin text. One wonders whether this may not be true of teachers as well; whether there may not be many who say grand things about the aims they have in teaching Cæsar or geometry or what not, but whose real teachings is the same old matter of grammar and dictionary that we know so well.

It is unfortunate that we haven't answers from these same pupils to questions about the character of Cæsar, the life of the Roman soldier, the history of the campaigns in Gaul, etc. One fancies from the answers to questions (1) that the comparison would be enlightening, that the real meaning to the student of his year's work in Cæsar and the conventional opinion of the student about that work would make a pretty contrast.

It should be remembered that the data which have suggested all the reflections so far presented are very slight, that a thorough-going study of the facts in the case might well revoke some of these reflections and modify others. The present writer, at least, does not regard his inferences as anything more than probabilities at most. At the same time it should also be remembered that though these facts are slight, nothing but other facts is fitted to oppose them. Until other facts are on the road, these should have the right of way. Opinion and rhetoric should for the present be side-tracked.

The last paragraph may serve not only as a supplement to what went before but also as a preface to our next discussion. For although the historians who replied to our question are probably representative of their class, and although their answers are undoubtedly honest, presumably accurate within fairly narrow limits and in most cases unprejudiced, yet the number is so small that one should not regard their evidence as final.

The following question was sent to thirty-nine teachers or advanced students of history: "How much information about and interest in the character, life, institutions and influence on modern civilization of the Romans do you think that you gained from the course in Latin (excluding Roman history) which you took in preparatory school? Please estimate in terms of the number of hours of direct instruction about Roman civilization, etc., which you think would have been required to produce an equal effect (*e.g.*, two hours per week for a year) and send such estimate on the annexed card. Your reply is desired as a partial means to more accurate knowledge of the value of Latin as a secondary school subject."

Twenty-four sent no reply (save an excuse on account of absence in one case). Two were unable to give such an estimate. One gentleman apparently reckoned the value of Latin for these purposes as infinite. He writes, "My study of Latin in preparation for college laid the necessary foundation for all that I know about the character, life, institutions and influence of the Romans. No number of hours of direct instruction about Roman civilization, etc., could have produced an equal effect." One said, "Not even of slight value." The remaining estimates are definite and are as follows: Three, three, two, one and one-half, one, one, one-half, one-half, one-half, and either one or four (it was not clear whether the writer meant one hour for a year or for four years, but apparently the latter.) Calling the last four, we have an average estimate of one and seven-elevenths per hours per week for a year of direct instruction as the equivalent of the instruction the Latin course of four years gives.

Before remarking upon the conclusions suggested by these data, it is necessary to discuss briefly the possibility that the men who answered were not representative, that the very fact that only sixteen out of thirty-nine replied shows that the sixteen had some especial prejudice which interested them in the question. How we can decide this I do not know. My own opinion, which possibly may be worth mentioning on account of its basis in a feeling of the general tone of the replies, is that no marked prejudice either way can be rightly attributed to these gentlemen, that they replied out of courtesy. The thirty-nine to whom the question was sent were chosen at random. It is, however, interesting to notice that three of those placing the lowest valuation upon their study of Latin are teachers at Harvard University. The recent thorough-going discussion of entrance subjects in the Harvard faculty may have been influential in these cases. Whether it worked to stir up antagonism to Latin among the teachers of history or to cause a more thoughtful and accurate answer to our question I cannot pretend to decide, though in view of the nature of the persons concerned I should myself be convinced that the latter would be the truer hypothesis.

If we provisionally accept these answers as approximately accurate statements of the influence of Latin upon these men when students, we are led to conclude that the study of Latin authors in the original in high schools has little to do with presenting Roman civilization to students. The tastes and abilities of these men would probably have been such as would seize upon and make the most of anything in this line which their Latin courses offered. They should have been the most favored cases for the exertion of the influence under discussion. Yet if we except one enthusiast they rate it as very slight. If further testimony should accord with theirs, it would seem to justify considerable distrust of Dr. Harris's theory. The truth may be in accord with the following opinion, which deserves quotation:

> Dear Sir:—In my three years of preparation in Latin I learned practically nothing of the history and civilization of Rome—certainly less than might be learned in a half-hour a day for a year. The eternal grind in grammar left no time or strength for the study of civilization. Though some improvement can be made, I am convinced that the reading and interpretation of Latin authors can not alone give a good knowledge of Roman history. The knowledge thus gained is of the dictionary type—it is disconnected and gives no idea of development or of the unity of a national life, the essential elements of history. This applies to the college and the graduate school as well as to the academy. The candidate for the Ph.D. in the classics usually knows less Roman history than he could learn in a single two-hour course running through a year.

The replies of the teachers of Latin show a somewhat higher estimate of the value of Latin as a culture study. The question was as follows: "How much information about and interest in the character, life, institutions and influence on modern civilization of the Romans do you think your students gain from their four-year study of Latin (excluding Roman history)? Please estimate in terms of hours of direct instruction about Roman civilization, influence, etc., which you think would produce an equal effect, (e.g., two hours per week for a year,) and send such estimate on the annexed card. Your reply is desired as a partial means to more accurate knowledge of the influence of the study of Latin on general culture."

Thirty-four copies of the question were sent out. Seventeen of the teachers failed to reply (one of these was absent in Europe), five said that they could give no estimate of the sort required; one said "nearly zero," another "small," and ten gave definite estimates, as follows: Four, three and one-half, three, two, two, two, two, one, one, one-half. The average estimate is two and two-tenths hours, but if we estimate the "nearly zero" and "small" as one-half hour each, the average becomes one and eleven-twelfth hours.

These results serve to confirm our opinion that the testimony of the teachers of history could be depended upon, and to deepen the impression made by the other facts presented. It is even possible that the average student gets less Roman civilization out of his Latin course than the historians did from theirs and that the teachers of Latin are led to an overestimate by their natural and laudable enthusiasm for Latin. On the whole it seems fair to say that this investigation puts the burden of proof upon the advocates of the study of Latin as a means to an appreciation of Roman and through it modern civilization. Latin *may* do a great deal of this but this but it doesn't *seem* to, and until it is actually shown to, we ought to limit ourselves to other factors in our arguments for Latin as a high-school study.

Probably many a patient reader will now say, "Yes, certainly; but any one could see that translations could do all that better than Latin texts. I knew and could have told you beforehand that you wouldn't find any such knowledge coming from the Latin texts read." Truly so. And any one else could have flatly maintained that we would. And several long articles could have been written and all parties could have hardened their hearts in whatever belief they had before. The fact is that the patient reader did not *know* but only *thought beforehand* and whereas knowledge begets more knowledge of the same kind, opinion usually begets other opinions directly opposite.

It seems best to close this paper with an apology and a request. The apology is, of course, for the slight and fragmentary nature of the data presented. It was hard to get even those, but their collector laments more than any one else probably will, that his attempt to present a sample of a scientific study of one of the problems of educational values should be so trivial a one. It may, by its very weakness, be the cause of other and better ones.

It is published more for that reason than for its own sake. The request I have to make is that any teachers or superintendents who feel that possibly by such inquiries as this, though more adequate because more detailed and extensive, worthy facts about the real effects of certain studies may be brought to light, and who are willing to give an hour or two of their classes' time to such inquiries, will signify their willingness to me and let me propose certain tests. Problems are at hand in connection with every study.

22

ALFRED BINET (1857-1911) AND
THEOPHILE SIMON (1873-1961)

The development of the Binet-Simon scale (1905-1908)

Binet, one of the leading French psychologists of his time, worked in many fields, including child psychology. The public schools of France had found that often a year or more was required by teachers to detect seriously retarded children and refer them for proper grade placement. Binet was asked to develop a method for the identification and reassignment of retarded pupils which would reduce the waste of both theirs and the teachers' time. After much exploratory work, Binet and Simon, a young physician, produced the first intelligence test in 1905.

The development of the Binet-Simon test was an event of prime importance in modern psychology. Binet worked on its improvement and extension until his death in 1911.

The material here reprinted is chosen from two of Binet and Simon's articles, one dated 1905 and one 1908, which were translated by Elizabeth S. Fite and published in 1916 by the Training School at Vineland, New Jersey under the title The Development of Intelligence in Children. *They are reprinted with the permission of the American Institute of Mental Studies, Training School Unit.*

NEW METHODS FOR THE DIAGNOSIS OF THE INTELLECTUAL LEVEL OF SUBNORMALS

Our purpose is to be able to measure the intellectual capacity of a child who is brought to us in order to know whether he is normal or retarded. We should therefore, study his condition at the time and that only. We have nothing to do either with his past history or with his future; consequently we shall neglect his etiology, and we shall make no attempt to distinguish between acquired and congenital idiocy; for a stronger reason

177

we shall set aside all consideration of pathological anatomy which might explain his intellectual deficiency. So much for his past. As to that which concerns his future, we shall exercise the same abstinence; we do not attempt to establish or prepare a prognosis and we leave unanswered the question of whether this retardation is curable, or even improvable. We shall limit ourselves to ascertaining the truth in regard to his present mental state.

Furthermore, in the definition of this state, we should make some restrictions. Most subnormal children, especially those in the schools, are habitually grouped in two categories, those of backward intelligence, and those who are unstable. This latter class, which certain alienists call moral imbeciles, do not necessarily manifest inferiority of intelligence; they are turbulent, vicious, rebellious to all discipline; they lack sequence of ideas, and probably power of attention. It is a matter of great delicacy to make the distinction between children who are unstable, and those who have rebellious dispositions. Elsewhere we have insisted upon the necessity of instructors not treating as unstable, that is as pathological cases, those children whose character is not sympathetic with their own. It would necessitate a long study, and probably a very difficult one, to establish the distinctive signs which separate the unstable from the undisciplined. For the present we shall not take up this study. We shall set the unstable aside, and shall consider only that which bears upon those who are backward in intelligence.

This is not, however, to be the only limitation of our subject because backward states of intelligence present several different types. There is the insane type—or the type of intellectual decay—which consists in a progressive loss of former acquired intelligence. Many epileptics, who suffer from frequent attacks, progress toward insanity. It would be possible and probably very important, to be able to make the distinction between those with decaying intelligence on the one hand, and those of inferior intelligence on the other. But as we have determined to limit on the side also, the domain of our study, we shall rigorously exclude all forms of insanity and decay. Moreover we believe that these are rarely present in the schools, and need not be taken into consideration in the operation of new classes for subnormals.

Another distinction is made between those of inferior intelligence and degenerates. The latter are subjects in whom occur clearly defined, episodical phenomena, such as impulsions, obsessions, deliriums. We shall eliminate the degenerates as well as the insane.

Lastly, we should say a word upon our manner of studying those whom alienists call idiots but whom we here call of inferior intelligence. The exact nature of this inferiority is not known; and today without other proof, one very prudently refuses to liken this state to that of an arrest of normal development. It certainly seems that the intelligence of these beings has undergone a certain arrest; but it does not follow that the disproportion between the degree of intelligence and the age is the only characteristic of their condition. There is also in many cases, most probably a deviation in the development, a perversion. The idiot of fifteen years, who, like a baby of three, is making his first verbal attempts, can not be completely likened to a three-year old child, because the latter is normal, but the idiot is not. There exists therefore between them, necessarily, differences either apparent or hidden. The careful study of idiots shows, among some of them at least, that whereas certain faculties are almost wanting, others are better developed. They have therefore certain aptitudes. Some have a good auditory or musical memory, and a whole repertoire of songs; others have mechanical ability. If all were carefully examined, many examples of these partial aptitudes would probably be found.

Our purpose is in no wise to study, analyze, or set forth the aptitudes of those of inferior intelligence. That will be the object of a later work. Here we shall limit ourselves to the measuring of their general intelligence. We shall determine their intellectual level, and, in order the better to appreciate this level, we shall compare it with that of normal children of the same age or of an analogous level. The reservations previously made as to the true conception of arrested development, will not prevent our finding great advantage in a methodical companion between those of inferior and those of normal intelligence.

To what method should we have recourse in making our diagnosis of the intellectual level? No one method exists, but there are a number of different ones which should be used cumulatively, because the question is a very difficult one to solve, and demands rather a collaboration of methods. It is important that the practitioner be equipped in such a manner that he shall use, only as accessory, the information given by the parents of the child, so that he may always be able to verify this information, or, when necessary, dispense with it. In actual practice quite the opposite occurs. When the child is taken to the clinic the physician listens a great deal to the parents and questions the child very little, in fact scarcely looks at him, allowing himself to be influenced by a very strong presumption that the child is intellectually inferior. If, by a chance not likely to occur, but which would be most interesting some time to bring about, the physician were submitted to the test of selecting the sub-normals from a mixed group of children, he would certainly find himself in the midst of grave difficulties, and would commit many errors especially in cases of slight defect.

The organization of methods is especially important because, as soon as the schools for subnormals are in operation, one must be on his guard against the attitude of the parents. Their sincerity will be worth very little when it is in conflict with their interests. If the parents wish the child to remain in the regular school, they will not be silent concerning his intelligence. "My child understands everything," they will say, and they will be very careful not to give any significant information in regard to him. If, on the contrary, they wish him to be admitted into an institution where gratuitous board and lodging are furnished, they will change completely. They will be capable even of teaching him how to simulate mental debility. One should, therefore, be on his guard against all possible frauds.

In order to recognize the inferior states of intelligence we believe that three different methods should be employed. We have arrived at this synthetic view only after many years of research, but we are now certain that each of these methods renders some service. These methods are:

1. *The medical method,* which aims to appreciate the anatomical, physiological, and pathological signs of inferior intelligence.
2. *The pedagogical method,* which aims to judge of the intelligence according to the sum of acquired knowledge.
3. *The psychological method,* which makes direct observations and measurements of the degree of intelligence.

From what has gone before it is easy to see the value of each of these methods. The medical method is indirect because it conjectures the mental from the physical. The pedagogical method is more direct; but the psychological is the most direct of all because it aims to measure the state of the intelligence as it is at the present moment. It does this by experiments which oblige the subject to make an effort which shows his capability in the way of comprehension, judgment, reasoning, and invention.

The psychological method

The fundamental idea of this method is the establishment of what we shall call a measuring scale of intelligence. This scale is composed of a series of tests of increasing difficulty, starting from the lowest intellectual level that can be observed, and ending with that of average normal intelligence. Each group in the series corresponds to a different mental level.

This scale properly speaking does not permit the measure of the intelligence, because intellectual qualities are not superposable, and therefore cannot be measured as linear surfaces are measured, but are on the contrary, a classification, a hierarchy among diverse intelligences; and for the necessities of practice this classification is equivalent to a measure. We shall therefore be able to know, after studying two individuals, if one rises above the other and to how many degrees, if one rises above the average level of other individuals considered as normal, or if he remains below. Understanding the normal progress of intellectual development among normals, we shall be able to determine how many years such an individual is advanced or retarded. In a word we shall be able to determine to what degrees of the scale idiocy, imbecility, and moronity correspond.

The scale that we shall describe is not a theoretical work; it is the result of long investigations, first at the Saltpetriere, and afterwards in the primary schools of Paris, with both normal and subnormal children. These short psychological questions have been given the name of tests. The use of tests is today very common, and there are even contemporary authors who have made a specialty of organizing new tests according to theoretical views, but who have made no effort to patiently try them out in the schools. Theirs is an amusing occupation, comparable to a person's making a colonizing expedition into Algeria, advancing always only upon the map, without taking off his dressing gown. We place but slight confidence in the tests invented by these authors and we have borrowed nothing from them. All the tests which we propose have been repeatedly tried, and have been retained from among many, which after trial have been discarded. We can certify that those which are here presented have proved themselves valuable.

We have aimed to make all our tests simple, rapid, convenient, precise, heterogeneous, holding the subject in continued contact with the experimenter, and bearing principally upon the faculty of judgment. Rapidity is necessary for this sort of examination. It is impossible to prolong it beyond twenty minutes without fatiguing the subject. During this maximum of twenty minutes, it must be turned and turned about in every sense, and at least ten tests must be executed, so that not more than about two minutes can be given to each. In spite of their interest, we were obliged to proscribe long exercises. For example, it would be very instructive to know how a subject learns by heart a series of sentences. We have often tested the advantage of leaving a person by himself with a lesson of prose or verse after having said to him "Try to learn as much as you can of this in five minutes." Five minutes is too long for our test, because during that time the subject escapes us; it may be that he becomes distracted or thinks of other things; the test loses its clinical character and becomes too scholastic. We have therefore reluctantly been obliged to renounce testing the rapidity and extent of the memory by this method. Several other equivalent examples of elimination could be cited. In order to cover rapidly a wide field of observation, it goes without saying that the tests should be heterogeneous.

Another consideration. Our purpose is to evaluate a level of intelligence. It is understood that we here separate natural intelligence and instruction. It is the intelligence alone that we seek to measure, by disregarding in so far as possible, the degree of instruction which the subject possesses. He should, indeed, be considered by the examiner as a complete ignoramus knowing neither how to read nor write. This necessity forces us to forego a great many exercises having a verbal, literary or scholastic character. These belong to a pedagogical examination. We believe that we have succeeded in completely disregarding the acquired information of the subject. We give him nothing to read, nothing to write, and submit him to no test in which he might succeed by means of rote learning. In fact we do not even notice his inability to read if a case occurs. It is simply the level of his natural intelligence that is taken into account.

But here we must come to an understanding of what meaning to give to that word so vague and so comprehensive, "the intelligence." Nearly all the phenomena with which psychology concerns itself are phenomena of intelligence; sensation, perception, are intellectual manifestations as much as reasoning. Should we therefore bring into our examination the measure of sensation after the manner of the psycho-physicists? Should we put to the test all of his psychological processes? A slight reflection has shown us that this would indeed be wasted time.

It seems to us that in intelligence there is a fundamental faculty, the alteration or the lack of which, is of the utmost importance for practical life. This faculty is judgment, otherwise called good sense, practical sense, initiative, the faculty of adapting one's self to circumstances. To judge well, to comprehend well, to reason well, these are the essential activities of intelligence. A person may be a moron or an imbecile if he is lacking in judgment; but with good judgment he can never be either. Indeed the rest of the intellectual faculties seem of little importance in comparison with judgment. What does it matter, for example, whether the organs of sense function normally? Of what import that certain ones are hyperesthetic, or that others are anesthetic or are weakened? Laura Bridgman, Helen Keller and their fellow-unfortunates were blind as well as deaf, but this did not prevent them from being very intelligent. Certainly this is demonstrative proof that the total or even partial integrity of the senses does not form a mental factor equal to judgment. We may measure the acuteness of the sensibility of subjects; nothing could be easier. But we should do this, not so much to find out the state of their sensibility as to learn the exactitude of their judgment.

The same remark holds good for the study of the memory. At first glance, memory being a psychological phenomenon of capital importance, one would be tempted to give it a very conspicuous part of an examination of intelligence. But memory is distinct from and independent of judgment. One may have good sense and lack memory. The reverse is also common. Just at the present time we are observing a backward girl who is developing before our astonished eyes a memory very much greater than our own. We have measured that memory and we are not deceived regarding it. Nevertheless that girl presents a most beautifully classic type of imbecility.

As a result of all this investigation, in the scale which we present we accord the first place to judgment; that which is of importance to us is not certain errors which the subject commits, but absurd errors, which prove that he lacks judgment. We have even made special provision to encourage people to make absurd replies. In spite of the accuracy of this directing idea, it will be easily understood that it has been impossible to permit of its regulating exclusively our examinations. For example, one can not make tests of judgment on children of less than two years when one begins to watch their first gleams of intelligence. Much is gained when one can discern in them traces of coordination, the first delineation of attention and memory. We shall therefore bring out in our lists some tests of memory; but so far as we are able, we shall give these tests such a turn as to invite the subject to make absurd replies, and thus under cover of a test of memory, we shall have an appreciation of their judgment.

Measuring scale of intelligence

General recommendations. The examination should take place in a quiet room, quite isolated, and the child should be called in alone without other children. It is important that when a child sees the experimenter for the first time, he should be reassured by the presence of someone he knows, a relative, an attendant, or a school superintendent. The witness should be instructed to remain passive and mute, and not to intervene in the examination either by word or gesture.

The experimenter should receive each child with a friendly familiarity to dispel the timidity of early years. Greet him the moment he enters, shake hands with him and seat him comfortably. If he is intelligent enough to understand certain words, awaken his curiosity, his pride. If he refuses to reply to a test, pass to the next one, or perhaps offer him a piece of candy; if his silence continues, send him away until another time. These are little incidents that frequently occur in an examination of the mental state, because in its last analysis, an examination of this kind is based upon the good will of the subject.

We here give the technique of each question. It will not suffice simply to read what we have written in order to be able to conduct examinations. A good experimenter can be produced only by example and imitation, and nothing equals the lesson gained from the thing itself. Every person who wishes to familiarize himself with our method of examination should come to our school. Theoretical instruction is valuable only when it merges into practical experience. Having made these reservations, let us point out the principal errors likely to be committed by inexperienced persons. There are two: the first consists in recording the gross results without making psychological observations, without noticing such little facts as permit one to give to the gross results their true value. The second error, equally frequent, is that of making suggestions. An inexperienced examiner has no idea of the influence of words; he talks too much, he aids his subject, he puts him on the track, unconscious of the help he is thus giving. He plays the part of the pedagogue, when he should remain psychologist. Thus his examination is vitiated. It is a difficult art to be able to encourage a subject, to hold his attention, to make him do his best without giving aid in any form by an unskilled suggestion.

The development of intelligence in the child

"The Measurement of Intelligence" is, perhaps, the most oft repeated expression in psychology during these last few years. Some psychologists affirm that intelligence can be measured; others declare that it is impossible to measure intelligence. But there are still others, better informed, who ignore these theoretical discussions and apply themselves to the actual solving of the problem. The readers of *L'Année* know that for some time we have been trying approximations, but they were not so well thought out as are those which we now present.

We have constantly kept in mind the point of view of pedagogy, normal as well as pathological. For several years we have tried to gather all the data and material capable of shedding light upon the intellectual and moral character of children. This is by no means the minor part of pedagagy, the least important, nor the least difficult. We set for ourselves the following program: first, to determine the law of the intellectual development of children and to devise a method of measuring their intelligence; and second, to study the diversity of their intellectual aptitudes.

We hope that we shall be able to keep faithfully to this rather extensive program, and especially that we shall have the time and the strength to realize it, but already we see that the subject is far richer than we at first imagined. Our minds always tend to simplify nature. It had seemed to us sufficient to learn how to measure the child's intelligence. This measurement we now set forth, which if not complete is at least established upon correct lines, and already usable.

This measurement is taken by means of a series of tests, the gradation of which constitutes what we call a "Measuring Scale of Intelligence." It is important, above all, to set forth these tests with sufficient precision to enable any one to repeat them correctly who will take the trouble to assimilate them.

Classification of the tests according to age. We here give the series of tests ranged according to the ages at which the majority of children succeed in them. This constitutes our measuring scale of intelligence. (Descriptions of the tests, given in a later section of Binet and Simons' article, are not included in these readings.—Editor)

Three years

Show eyes, nose, mouth
Name objects in a picture
Repeat 2 figures
Repeat a sentence of 6 syllables
Give last name

Four years

Give sex
Name key, knife, penny
Repeat 3 figures
Compare 2 lines

Five years

Compare 2 boxes of different weights
Copy a square
Repeat a sentence of 10 syllables
Count 4 sous
Put together two pieces in a game of "patience"

Six years

Repeat a sentence of 16 syllables
Compare two figures from an esthetic point of view
Define by use only, some simple objects
Execute 3 simultaneous commissions
Give one's age
Distinguish morning and evening

Seven years

Indicate omissions in drawings
Give the number of fingers
Copy a written sentence
Copy a triangle and a diamond
Repeat 5 figures
Describe a picture
Count 13 single sous
Name 4 pieces of money

Eight years

Read selection and retain two memories
Count 9 sous. (3 single and 3 double)
Name four colors
Count backward from 20-9
Compare 2 objects from memory
Write from dictation

Nine years

Give the date complete (day, month, day of the month, year)
Name the days of the week
Give definitions superior to use
Retain 6 memories after reading
Make change, 4 sous from 20 sous
Arrange 5 weights in order

Ten years

Name the months
Name 9 pieces of money
Place 3 words in 2 sentences
Answer 3 comprehensive questions
Answer 5 comprehensive questions

Eleven years

Criticize sentences containing absurdities
Place 3 words in 1 sentence
Find more than 60 words in 3 minutes
Give abstract definitions
Place disarranged words in order

Twelve years

Repeat 7 figures
Find 3 rhymes
Repeat a sentence of 26 syllables
Interpret pictures
Problem of facts

Thirteen years

Paper cutting
Reversed triangle
Give differences of meaning

The use of the measuring scale of intelligence

Our principal conclusion is that we actually possess an instrument which allows us to measure the intellectual development of young children whose age is included between three and twelve years. This method appears to us practical, convenient and rapid. If one wishes to know summarily whether a child has the intelligence of his age, or if he is advanced or retarded, it suffices to have him take the tests of his age; and the performance of these tests certainly does not require more than thirty minutes which should be interrupted by ten minutes rest if one thinks this necessary for the child.

Furthermore when one wishes to be more precise, or to make a closer approximation, one may make many more tests; if the child is seven years old, he may attempt the tests of eight, nine and ten years for example. One would also be able after an interval of several days to substitute analogous tests.

One question remains to be examined. To what purpose are these studies? In reading the reflections which we have interspersed in the course of our treatise, it will be seen that a profound knowledge of the normal intellectual development of the child would not only be of great interest but useful in formulating a course of instruction really adapted to their aptitudes. We fear that those who have drawn up the programs actually in force, are educated men who in their work have been led more by the fancies of their imaginations than by well-grounded principles. The pedagogical principle which ought to inspire the authors of programs seems to us to be the following: the instruction should always be according to the natural evolution of the child, and not precede it by a year or two. In other words the child should be taught only what he is sufficiently mature to understand; all precocious instruction is lost time, for it is not assimilated. We have cited an example of it in regard to the date, which is taught in the Maternal School, but which is not known and assimilated before the age of nine years. This is only one example, but it is eloquent; it shows the error of what has hitherto been done; it suggests a method which will enable us to improve upon the past,—a method less literary, less rapid, and even extremely laborious, for it demands that one establish by careful investigation the normal evolution of a child's intelligence, in order to make all our programs and methods of instruction conform to that evolution, when it is once known. If by this labor we have succeeded in showing the necessity for a thorough investigation conducted after this plan, our time has not been lost. But we are far from flattering ourselves that we have inaugurated a reform. Reforms in France do not succeed except through politics, and we cannot readily imagine a secretary of state busying himself with a question of this kind. What is taught to children at school! As though legislators could become interested in that!

It now remains to explain the use of our measuring scale which we consider a standard of the child's intelligence. Of what use is a measure of intelligence? Without doubt one could conceive many possible applications of the process, in dreaming of a future where the social sphere would be better organized than ours; where every one would work according to his known aptitudes in such a way that no particle of psychic force should be lost for society. That would be the ideal city. It is indeed far from us. But we have to remain among the sterner and the matter-of-fact realities of life, since we here deal with practical experiments which are the most commonplace realities.

We are of the opinion that the most valuable use of our scale will not be its application to the normal pupils, but rather to those of inferior grades of intelligence.

It is well known, as we have often affirmed, that the alienists are not agreed on the definitions of the words *idiot, imbecile* and *moron*. There are as many definitions as writers. Moreover the formulae employed and the processes of diagnosis in use, are so vague that the most conscientious author is not sure of remaining constantly consistent with himself. How, for instance, can one make use of formulae of diagnosis, founded on difference of degree, when these differences are not measured? Finally, the most serious criticisms that one can make of the actual medical practice is that if by chance, a child of normal intelligence were presented at a clinic, the alienist would not be able to know that he is dealing with a normal child. He will be unable for a very simple reason; he does not know what is necessary in order for a child to be normal; let us add that everyone is equally ignorant of how an individual intelligence can be studied and measured.

During the past year one of us examined 25 children who for various reasons had been admitted to Sainte-Anne and later confined at the Bicetre, at Salpetriere, or at other places. We applied the procedure of our measuring scale to all these children, and thus proved that *three of them were at age in intelligence, and two others were a year advanced beyond the average.*

On reflection, these cases should not surprise us; and it is not necessary to be in touch with questions of mental medicine to inveigh against arbitrary segregation. One ought to confine a child of normal intelligence, or even super-normal, if he has epilepsy, or irresistible impulses which constitute a danger to his neighbors or to himself. But it is none the less true that the doctors who were obliged to diagnose these cases, have had to judge the degree of intelligence of these children; it is very interesting to show the errors of diagnosis which have been committed in this regard. To two of these children who showed normal intelligence we regret to say that the term *mental debility* had been applied without consideration. The third had received the term, truly extraordinary of its kind, of *"enfant idiot."* The child was named T————, aged seven years. A doctor had written concerning him, "Idiotic, with attacks of furious anger. Wishes to bite. Does not know how to read or write." This last is a little too naive. Since the normal child does not know how to read and write at seven years, to be astonished that T———— who is just seven is still illiterate, is like reproaching a three year old baby for not knowing how to play the piano. Finally, one of these children who was a year in advance, was classed as a moron; and as to the other nothing was said concerning his mentality. Nothing could show more clearly, that with the means which it has at its command, the mental clinic is not in a position to diagnose correctly a child's intelligence.

In terminating this account, it will suffice to make a very brief allusion to the appreciation of penal responsibility; there also our scale will render service. The problems of penal responsibility such as are actually placed before the tribunals, are most complex and recently have caused discussions that are highly curious on account of the attention which has been paid to words rather than to things. We have scarcely the space here to make the multiple distinctions which would be necessary in making clear the real situation. It will suffice to remark that in certain cases experts have to give their opinion on the degree of intelligence of an accused person; and that according to their customary point of view which consists in distinguishing health from illness they are preoccupied in learning if the accused should or should not enter the group of feeble-minded. It is strange that so far, no other criterion than a subjective impression can guide them; they weigh each case with their good sense, which presupposes in the first place that everybody's good sense is equal to every other person's.

We suggest to them that they should use the six differentiating tests that we have described above. By the methodical employment of these tests, they will arrive at precise and controllable conclusions, which at the same time cannot help but enhance in the mind of the judges the value of the medico-legal appraisement of the alienists.

These examples to which we could add many others show that the methods of measuring the individual intelligence have not a speculative interest alone; by the direction, by the organization of all the investigations, psychology has furnished the proof (we do not say for the first time but in a more positive manner than ever before), that it is in a fair way to become a science of great social utility.

23

DUDLEY KIDD (1858-1916)

African childhood (1906)

This selection explores a new domain. In general the previous sections have assumed, and sometimes stated, that child behavior is the same the world over, but in fact they have dealt only with children in Europe or the United States who were members of a common Western culture. Even James Mitchell, Laura Bridgman and Helen Keller conformed in many ways to the Euro-American ethos.

Dudley Kidd was the first person to find it worthwhile to study non-European and non-American children. It may be true that some aspects of child behavior are universal, but some are not, and it is necessary to distinguish the universal from the local.

Kidd makes only a beginning but it is a notable beginning. He made his observations when for many years he was a government representative in South Africa.

His study is the first psychological and cultural study of Negro children. Of particular interest are his descriptions of the reactions of African Negro children to white men.

The excerpts here reprinted are from his book Savage Childhood: A Study of Kafir Childhood, *published in London by Adam and Charles Black, 1906.*

The baby is fed on sour milk . . . for the first few days of life. . . .
It is difficult to make the small babies drink the sour milk and so the mother adopts the following method of persuasion. She places the baby on her lap and pours some clotted milk into the palm of her own hand; she then applies the edge of her palm to the baby's mouth, and slowly raises up her hand till the baby's mouth is covered by the sour milk. But even then it refuses to drink the nauseous stuff. So the mother holds the baby's nose between her thumb and finger, till it is forced to capitulate and drink the milk. As a rule there is tremendous spluttering and cough-

ing as the result of this operation, and the baby's face and body become covered with mess. The mother calls up a dog, since she has no such things as napkins or pocket-handkerchiefs, and tells the dog to lick the baby clean.

* * *

Each morning the mothers give their babies a primitive sort of bath, but generally wait till the air is warm. The mother takes a calabash, and allows the water to trickle from it in a thin stream over the baby, which she holds up by one arm. If there should be no vessel handy, the mother fills her mouth with water which she squirts out slowly over the baby; the child always resents this indecorous treatment. . . .

Babies are carried in several ways. The commonest method adopted is as follows: the mother, or tiny sister who has to act as nurse, fastens her blanket round her hips and shoulders, allowing the blanket to form a pouch over the small of her back. The mother then lifts the infant by one of its arms, swings it round her head and plumps the naked baby into the pouch in the blanket, placing the baby next to her own skin. The child is soothed by a gentle motion, the mother rotating the upper part of her body round her hips. If the baby is troublesome, the mother hits the baby with her arm at the end of each swing. The mother does not feel the weight of the baby when it is carried thus, and can work all day in the sun with the baby strapped on to her back. The baby does not seem to experience any discomfort from the fact that its head lolls out of the pouch of blanket and so gets exposed to the rays of the sun. . . .

* * *

Women frequently carry children in another fashion; the baby is placed, either inside or outside the blanket, straddle-legged across one of the nurse's hips. . . .

Children are very fond of sucking their fingers or thumbs (especially the index finger), a habit the mothers like, for they say it makes the child feel comfortable, and so not anxious to be suckled too much.

* * *

The baby feeds, sleeps and crawls about the hut; it learns to walk and talk at about the same age as in the case of European children.

* * *

A child—perhaps about a year old—was sitting naked on the mud floor of a hut in which I was spending the night. Close to the baby there was a Kafir pot which had been removed but recently from the fire, but which had not yet cooled down completely. The lid of the pot was sufficiently hot to be painful to the touch, though not hot enough to burn the skin. There was a strangely thoughtful expression on the face of the chubby little fellow. It is not uncommon to see this expression on the face of a Kafir child as it sits bolt upright on the floor, looking out on the world from its wide eyes with an expression that is meditative, pensive, brooding.

* * *

By accident the hand of the baby came into contact with the hot lid of the pot; the hand was withdrawn at once—evidently by reflex action, for the child was not disturbed in its reverie. The action, which seemed purposeful, was probably as void of conscious effort as though it had been the action of a limb of a "pithed" frog that had touched the hot iron. The child showed no conscious perception of its action. The attention of the child was called away to something happening in another part of the hut, when again its hand accidentally touched the hot lid of the pot. This time the child withdrew the hand more quickly, as though it had a vague and dawning consciousness that something had gone wrong somewhere. The child evidently did not grasp the fact that the painful sensation was caused by the contact of the finger with the hot iron. But, to judge from the expression on the face, a dim suspicion that this might possibly account for the sensation dawned on the child, for after a few moments of meditation, the baby, evidently with the idea of inquiry, put out its first finger and deliberately touched the pot. Having done this it as deliberately withdrew its hand and looked at its finger with surprise; it then looked at the pot and seemed puzzled. The child seemed to grasp the facts that there was some connection between its finger and itself, and that something unpleasant was experienced when its finger touched the pot. The expression of the face was so striking that it was impossible to doubt what was going on in the child's mind, for one could almost see slowly dawning on the mind of the child the new idea that the finger was not an alien thing, but a part of itself. . . .

No sooner had the child recovered from this expression of surprise than it deliberately put out its finger once more and pressed it firmly against the lid of the pot. A short period elapsed in which nerve-currents were traveling to the brain and then the baby set up a piteous howl and was promptly seized by its mother, who removed it from the danger-zone.

When a Kafir child has learned this first lesson, he has still much difficulty in recognizing the fact that his pains and aches arise within "the frame that binds him in." Take, for example, a headache. One of the most intelligent Kafirs I know told me that he could quite well remember his first headache during childhood. He said he was conscious that something was wrong somewhere, but did not dream that the pain was within his head. The pain might just as well have been in the roof of his hut as in the roof of his head; and it was only when his mother told him that his head was aching that this fact dawned upon him.

* * *

The Kafir just referred to also said that he was very puzzled when he first took up his father's pipe and smoked it. He seemed to encounter a bitter taste, and was sorely puzzled to know wherever this unpleasant experience came from, or where it was located; it took repeated sucks at the pipe for the child to realize the fact that the taste came from the stem of the pipe, and that it was located in his own mouth.

* * *

And just as a Kafir is slow in locating pain which is being experienced in his own body, so is he slow in imagining what others are suffering. A grown-up Kafir told me with great amusement, that when he was a small boy his father threatened him with a beating if he did something or other. The child was puzzled as to whatever sort of thing a beating could be, for though he had often seen his bigger brothers being beaten, his imagination was unable to work *in vacuo*, and to reconstruct the experiences of another into terms of his own sensation. When his father threatened him, the child simply laughed at him, for he had not the remotest idea as to what a beating really meant. It took a very short time for our young gentleman to extend the boundaries of his knowledge. Swift retribution followed this unpardonable sin of showing disrespect to a father. As the children roam about stark naked there was no delay even for a preliminary stripping. The father took up a stick and applied it with astonishing vigor to the proper places before the child had an inkling as to what was happening. As the man said to me, "I remember that when the tears and smarting were over, I sat down and thought to myself, 'Well now I know what father means by a beating; I don't see the reason of it, but anyhow I now know what sort of thing a beating is.'"

* * *

When Kafirs are questioned as to their earliest remembered impressions they usually state that these were connected with the senses of taste and smell. The next things they remember are connected with the sense of color; then impressions of sound and of form seem to follow last of all. It is true that sight-impressions existed alongside of those of taste and smell, but all the Kafirs I have questioned agree in saying that the impressions of taste and smell were much more powerful than those of sight. In the early days of infancy the protecting care of the mother renders of comparatively little value sensations other than those of taste and smell; but later on, when the child begins to crawl, it gets exposed to a hundred new dangers, and consequently impressions of sight, and especially those of color and of movement, become of increased importance. Of course, even in infancy, stimuli arising from color, motion and sound, stream continually into the brain of the child, and are of the greatest possible importance in the development of the whole organism. It is suggestive also that amongst the first senses to be awakened is that of taste, which is perhaps the least aggressively localized of the sensations....

* * *

Little children of course pester their mothers at times with endless questions as to the origin of babies, and the Kafir mother has her stock answers ready for all occasions, The mothers tell the children that babies are found in the reeds, which fits in with the nursery-tales of the people. If this should not satisfy the inquisitive children, the mothers say that fabulous monsters bring the babies to the kraal at night, and that the infants are found outside the hut in the morning. At other times they say that babies are found by mothers at watersprings, and that the women bring them back with them when they return from fetching the day's water. Consequently, many a little child hunts for babies in the reeds or peeps out of the hut in the morning to see if some fabulous monster has left a baby over-night; at other times the children, with beating hearts, hunt over the veld looking for babies; and then return to the kraal with disappointed faces to tell of their fruitless task, much to the merriment of the grown-up people. . . .

* * *

The absence of self-consciousness in the case of very small Kafir children is most delightful. I shall never forget the impression stamped on the memory by watching some children dancing. The special dance was a very slow one, in which the children lifted their feet up rhythmically, pausing when their legs were in the air before they brought their feet down with a stamp at a certain note in the chant. A small child that could only just walk, was standing in the brilliant sunshine clothed with a little bead-work. The bigger brothers and sisters were leading the dance, and this infant was joining in with the most serious air, utterly unconscious that a white man and several adult Kafir women were watching it with suppressed amusement. The way in which the little child lifted its leg in the air, adjusting its balance with great difficulty while the leg had to be kept raised till the rhythm of the chant should indicate the point at which the leg should be lowered; the way in which the child ponderously stamped its foot on the earth as if it were occupied with the most serious business imaginable; and the way in which it then turned its chubby body round on its axis, so as to be ready for the next step in the dance, was one of the drollest things I have ever seen, and will never fade from the memory.

* * *

It has been said that the children are nearly always laughing or grinning; but there are times when they cry, and then they look the most woe-begone creatures imaginable. They are not expected to control their feelings at a very tender age, and no one laughs at them for crying. But when once they have their second teeth and join the society of the boys, they have to pull themselves together. The tears of the children are as short lived as the rain from an April sky. The tears give way to smiles.

As a rule but few mutilations are practised on the small children at this age. The ears may be pierced, but this is done in most tribes at a later date; tatooing may be performed on children, but this also is generally delayed till later years. Circumcision does not take place till a few years after puberty. The teeth are not filed in the Southern tribes, though it is done on the Zambesi. This custom is said to be done with a view to make the person like the totem of the clan in appearance. It would be natural for clans whose totem is the crocodile to file the front teeth.

* * *

Discipline seems to cause no trouble to Kafirs. They are inherently submissive to constituted authority. Respect for old men, and especially for a father, is most marked. The parents are very fond of their children, and treat them very well on the whole, never fussing about trifles. They seem to have the knack of keeping children in order. Every child knows quite well twhat it may and may not do—for Kafirs are not, as a rule, apt to threaten punishment and then weakly to gloss over disobedience—and there are no faddy and officious grown-up relations who interfere with a man's children. Old maiden aunts do not exist amongst the Kafirs, for as a rule every girl is married long before she is twenty; the aunt is a person of absolutely no importance in a kraal. The parents and relations are not demonstratively affectionate—a thing most children find tiresome, and which makes them restless and difficult to manage.

* * *

Mothers do not punish their children much till they are about four years old; before that they humour the children when they are cross, but as soon as they can really understand what is said to them—generally said to be between three and four years of age—the mothers bite them when they cry needlessly. This soon cures the evil.

* * *

Very young children do not in the least understand what a dream is: it is only slowly that they come to distinguish between a dream-experience and a waking one; little by little the distinction dawns on them, and yet even in adult life the people imagine that dream-experiences are real, though of a different order from ordinary waking experiences. A child will talk of its dream in such a way that even the mother does not know whether it is referring to a dream or to a real experience. Boys and girls as they grow up begin to distinguish their dreams from their waking experiences, though they think the dreams were real in a certain sense.

* * *

The dreams which boys have turn chiefly on the subject of fighting, herding cattle, squabbling about sweethearts, and other details of their daily life. Nightmares generally take the form of troubled dreams in which the boys think they have lost the cattle which they were herding, and that their fathers are trashing them. They are very delighted to find out on waking up that the thing was only a dream.

* * *

The smallest children are taught to be polite, and this constitutes their first lesson. Obedience to parents hardly needs to be taught, for the children notice how every one in the kraal is obedient to the old men; the children catch this spirit without knowing it. I never remember seeing a small child distinctly and definitely disobedient to its father. Were a child to be disobedient—and of course, it sometimes occurs—he would be so severely punished that he would not forget it for many a day.

* * *

A large number of prohibitions have the effect of preventing children from becoming unduly familiar with their betters. Young girls are told to give way to their betters when fetching water or firewood, when crossing streams, and so forth. It is the younger girl who should proffer the kiss to the elder. But other prohibitions apply to personal habits. Thus girls are told that it is very unseemly to sit with their legs parted; they are told to keep their knees in contact, and not to separate their legs, but to bend them both a little to one side. The very greatest stress is laid on this rule, which, owing to the scanty dress, is a proof of delicacy of feeling. Small boys are allowed to part their legs a little, whilst only old men are supposed to sit with their legs widely parted.

* * *

On entering a stream for washing, a boy or man, as a rule, begins by rubbing the feet with a small stone. . . . Then the men wade into the stream and wash the head first, after that the arms and trunk, and lastly the legs. The women reverse this order, and having washed their legs first, continue to wash in an upward direction. (Sometimes women wash the head first; but then they proceed to wash the legs and not the arms.) Small children take to the right order of washing without any instruction; they do so in imitation of their fellows. A little boy who washed his legs first would be laughed at, and would be called a girl in derision. Natives never use towels where-with to dry themselves, for the sun and dry air render them unnecessary; similarly, when even small children get wet in the rain their mothers do not get anxious and dry them carefully: they are allowed to run about and dry spontaneously; not being bothered with clothing they never catch cold during the process.

* * *

Curiosity or inquisitiveness is not developed much in early years. Black children do not pester their mothers at an early age to the extent that white children do; and if a child should ask a very awkward question, it is put off with the usual formula of "We do not know," or else "It is our custom." The children . . . soon find out . . . that it is not much use pestering their mothers with questions. A child soon comes to see that a custom is one of those fundamental things which it is useless to examine. A custom is its own justification.

* * *

When one asks Kafir parents whether their children are afraid of the dark, they laugh at the absurdity of the question; of course they are not afraid of it. As a rule the night fears of children are, as Lamb has told us, the product of an excitable imagination; but that is the very last thing a Kafir child suffers from. A Kafir child's mind is so placid, and is so little stuffed with terrifying ideas by nurserymaids, that the child does not lie awake in the dark fancying things (though sometimes the mothers frighten naughty children by talking about fabulous monsters, or about white men). This freedom from fear of the dark is also prevented by the fact that the whole family lives in the same hut, and by the fact that a fire is generally kept burning on the floor. The one fear that lurks in the darkness is the fear of wild animals; and this fear was well justified when the country was infested with lions, tigers, elephants, and other animals. Most of these animals have been killed off in the districts south of Delagoa Bay, but the memory of them is still fresh; in the more northern tribes the fears are only too well justified still. It is noticeable that children in these northern tribes *are* afraid when left alone in the dark.

Last night (let us say) an uncle was carried off from the kraal by a lion. All day the chubby little boys have been teased by their big brothers, who declare that lions are specially fond of small fat boys, and always take them in preference to big bony men. All day the little fellows have been pestering their mothers as to whether this is really true or not. The flimsy hut made of a few poles, a little grass, and some mud, offers but poor protection against a tiger or a lion. The grown-up people in the kraal have been discussing all day how to join in killing the lions which are expected again at night; and the stray ends of conversation picked up by the children only intensify the natural fears.

* * *

Fear of white men is a growing force in the lives of the children. In olden days the children showed but little fear in the presence of Europeans. There is, of course, the primitive and initial dislike of a difference of colour. Kafir children think a white skin very ugly, and sometimes even revolting. When a very small black child shakes hands with a white man, it instinctively looks at its hand to see whether "the white" has come off and soiled its black hand; it seems very surprised when it finds that the colour does not come off. As they grow older, the children lose their first idea that the black man is essentially superior to a white man; and though they do not often wish to have white skins, yet they covet the wisdom and knowledge of the race, which they feel forced to admit is the superior. It is a long time before they lose their idea that white and black men constitute two entirely different orders of beings, and that the black is the superior in everything but skill and knowledge. When once they become educated, and see how vast is the chasm which separates the two races, they not infrequently long to become white.

The chief factor that is increasing the fear of white men as felt by Kafir children is the talk they overhear when men return to their kraals from working on farms, railways and mines. Every little Kafir boy regards his father as the strongest and wisest person in the world, and in this matter cannot be beaten even by the small English schoolboy at a dame-school, who maintains against the world that his father is the most wonderful person living; that he is the richest, most powerful and cleverest of men. Consequently when Kafir children hear their much-venerated fathers describing how the white men thrashed them and knocked them about, they feel a fear and hatred of the monsters who could dare to touch their fathers. It is therefore most fortunate when a Kafir child meets with a white man who shows kindliness to black children, for the fact makes an indelible impression on the mind for life. A native told me that the first impression in life that he could remember was in connection with a white man who was fond of black children. He said he could remember with perfect clearness this white man romping about, and allowing children to take hold of his coat-tails and feel in his pockets for sweetmeats. The wild delirious joy of holding on to the coat-tails while the man ran about the place, and the delight of the taste of the sweetmeats clings to that child in his manhood, and gives him a kindly feeling towards white men; and though, of course, every white man cannot romp with black children, yet many could do a little to lessen the gulf between black and white in South Africa.

* * *

The ambitions of the boys are distinctly and frankly practical; unfortunately there are no railway engines, hansom cabs, or watering-carts in native territories, and so the boys cannot aspire to the height of driving such things. Boys brood a good deal on how to become rich, how to grow big, how to become brave and strong; and they long above all things for the day to come when they shall be circumcised, and so shall be regarded as men. They are keen to be able to fight well, to be brave, and sometimes even wish to be good cattle-herds. They dream of the day when they will have many cattle of their own, and a number of wives to work for them and bear them many children; for then they will have large kraals, and be men of great importance. They love to think of the days to come when they will be able to sit down and do no work, and have plenty of beer to drink and be treated with great respect.

* * *

With regard to the ambitions of girls, the following points need to be noted. A little girl longs for the day to come when she will be initiated into womanhood and will reach a marriageable age. She desires above all things to be the great wife of a chief, or to have a husband who will pay a large number of cattle for her; she longs to have many daughters, so that when she is old, and these daughters are given in marriage, there may be plenty of cattle at her kraal, and consequently plenty of karosses for her in her old age. Girls talk a great deal about their future husbands, and speak with a frankness that would shock European ears. A Kafir girl longs for a husband who can fight and sing well. Every girl hopes her husband will be the son of a great and rich man; she also longs to have a husband who will help her in her work in the gardens, and who will provide her with plenty of beads. With regard to personal appearance the following list of qualities shows what Kafir girls think desirable. Girls like in their lovers fine white teeth, a dark but not too black skin, eyes that are not yellowish in the "whites," small ears, a small flat nose, and a moderate amount of dressiness. They do not, as a rule, like their lovers to be too much dandified, for they think that men who pay too much attention to their personal appearance are sure to turn out drunken husbands. Yet foolish and giddy girls are not lacking who are inordinately attracted by dressy men.

24

N. S. KRASNOGORSKI (1882-1962)

The formation of conditioned reflexes in young children (1907)

Pavlov discovered the conditioned reflex in 1902 while studying the functioning of the digestive glands in dogs. The research possibilities of this technique for the study of the activity of the nervous system was immediately apparent to Pavlov and the activities of his laboratory shifted in this new direction.

Although Pavlov's own researches for many years continued to be with dogs, one of his early students, Krasnogorski, was the first person to condition a normal child experimentally. Needless to say, for many prior centuries, children had been conditioned outside of the laboratory without the aid of a psychologist.

The present translation, by Yvonne Brackbill, first appeared in Behavior in Infancy and Early Childhood *edited by Yvonne Brackbill and George E. Thompson and published by the Free Press in 1967. It is reprinted here with the permission of the translator and the publisher.*

Krasnogorski's paper appeared in Russkii Vrach, 36, *(1907): 1245–1246.*

The recent studies of Professor I. P. Pavlov and his students have opened to investigation a vast region in the psychic life of animals—a region of so-called artificial conditioned reflexes. By using a strictly objective method of research, i.e., by renouncing the imposition of his own psychic state on the object of experimentation, Professor I. P. Pavlov has succeeded in a short time in attaining interesting results and—what is more important—in opening a vast field for further study of complex-nervous (psychic) phenomena.

As an objective method of research I. P. Pavlov proposed using, as is well-known, the secretion of the salivary glands, having shown that the secretion of saliva has the most intimate relation with the activity of the cortex and that it serves as an index of this activity. In another publication I will review the literature that has come from Professor I. P. Pavlov's laboratory and that relates to this question. In the present article I wish only to point out the possibilities for the study of complex-nervous phenomena in infants and the related facts that have been observed in our laboratory.

The research itself I carried out on a fourteen-month-old child always in the same isolated, quiet room, and on the same table, in an effort to preserve identity in the situation. After some trials in which the child was stimulated by feeding, I was convinced that there was the beginning of an increase in glottal movements elicited by the heightened secretion of saliva. There were also motor reactions, particularly sucking movements of the mouth, which were so clearly expressed that there is no doubt they can serve as a convenient and relatively precise measure in the study of conditioned reflexes in infants—especially since it is impossible to have an artificial salivary fistula. Since in the child a most insignificant accumulation of saliva in the mouth, 0.5 cc, accompanies the act of swallowing, then by the number of swallows one can successfully judge the strength of secretion. Our attempts gave the following results. The child, somewhat satiated, was shown a little glass with the food (milk) in it which served as a visual conditional stimulus in order to observe the increased frequency in number of swallows, sucking movements, approaches, openings of the mouth, words—in short, none other than conditioned reflexes. The number of such movements in response to the sight of the milk increased from session to session.

Having obtained the conditioned reflex from stimulating the child by food shown at a distance, I tried to get it from a sound stimulus. For this purpose I combined food with the sound of a bell. After a certain number of combinations of the food with the bell I at last succeeded in that the bell alone began to elicit a clearly increased frequency of swallowing and motor reactions. In Table 1 are presented the results of three sessions—following the combination of food with bell and during which the child was lying quietly—showing the number of swallows for a period of time of 3 to 5 minutes up to and during the sound of the bell.

It must be noted that the excretion of saliva during the action of the conditional stimulus is, generally speaking, related in both quality and quantity to the excretion of saliva resulting from the action of the un-

Table 1. Number of swallows in successive 3-minute periods

Session number	Before bell sounded	During sound bell
1	3, 4, 2, 2, 0	6
2	3, 3, 2	5
3	5, 4, 4	8

conditioned stimulus. Therefore, if we had tried as an unconditioned stimulus a substance which produces much saliva, e.g., an acid, then we would have received, after stimulation by the conditional stimulus, a still sharper increase in the frequency of swallowing.

In order to observe the artificial conditioned reflex formed to the sound of the bell, I did the following. After a preliminary combination of food and bell we held a small glass of food in front of the child. The child began to make swallowing and sucking movements; he licked his lips (a conditioned reflex to the sight of the food), but very shortly thereafter still not having received the food, he began to cry; then little by little, he quieted down, losing interest in the glass and turning away from it. Suddenly the bell sounded. His head quickly turned toward the glass, his gaze was avidly directed toward the food, and he began to swallow and suck with energy. It is perhaps unnecessary to point out that crying is a highly inauspicious influence on the appearance of conditioned reflexes; therefore, it behooves one to carry out stimulation when the child is quiet.

There is no doubt whatsoever that the ringing of the bell after its combination with the unconditioned stimulus became a conditional stimulus, nor that I observed in the child an artifically formed conditioned reflex.

I will report at a later date evidence concerning the extinction of conditioned reflexes in children, the times of their appearance, the possibility of getting them by such stimuli as scratching, cold, warmth, light, and so on. In any event, by the method described above, it is possible with complete objectivity to study many aspects of the development of complex nervous activity in the child. I think also that for a solution to the question of the earliest time at which the child hears, sees, and so on, the method described herein, using sucking movements, will yield a more objective answer than will any other method.

SIGMUND FREUD (1856-1939)

Infantile sexuality (1910)

In 1909 G. Stanley Hall assembled a notable company of men at Worcester, Mass., on the occasion of the twentieth anniversary of the founding of Clark University.

Those giving lectures related to psychology and psychiatry were Sigmund Freud, Carl G. Jung, William Stern, E. B. Titchener, Franz Boas, H. S. Jennings, and Adolph Meyer. Their lectures were printed in 1910 in a volume by Clark University. They also appeared in the American Journal of Psychology, *founded and edited by G. Stanley Hall.*

Freud's lectures were the occasion of his only visit to America, and they aroused considerable interest in psychoanalysis in the United States. The lectures (he gave five) were entitled "The origin and development of psychoanalysis." In these lectures Freud said little he had not said before; rather he attempted to systematize what he had written previously. Reprinted here is what he said about infantile sexuality in his fourth lecture as it appeared in the Clark University volume.

Ladies and Gentlemen: At this point you will be asking what the technique which I have described has taught us of the nature of the pathogenic complexes and repressed wishes of neurotics.

One thing in particular: psychoanalytic investigations trace back the symptoms of disease with really surprising regularity to impressions from the sexual life, show us that the pathogenic wishes are of the nature of erotic impulse-components *(Triebkomponente)*, and necessitate the assumption that to disturbances of the erotic sphere must be ascribed the greatest significance among the etiological factors of the disease. This holds of both sexes.

I know that this assertion will not willingly be credited. Even those investigators who gladly follow my psychological labors, are inclined to think that I overestimate the etiological share of the sexual moments. They ask me why other mental excitations should not lead to the phenomena of repression and surrogate-creation which I have described. I can give them this answer; that I do not know why they should not do this, I have no objection to their doing it, but experience shows that they do not possess such a significance, and that they merely support the effect of the sexual moments, without being able to supplant them. This conclusion was not a theoretical postulate; in the *Studien über Hysterie,* published in 1895 with Dr. Breuer, I did not stand on this ground. I was converted to it when my experience was richer and had led me deeper into the nature of the case. Gentlemen, there are among you some of my closest friends and adherents, who have travelled to Worcester with me. Ask them, and they will tell you that they all were at first completely sceptical of the assertion of the determinative significance of the sexual etiology, until they were compelled by their own analytic labors to come to the same conclusion.

The conduct of the patients does not make it any easier to convince one's self of the correctness of the view which I have expressed. Instead of willingly giving us information concerning their sexual life, they try to conceal it by every means in their power. Men generally are not candid in sexual matters. They do not show their sexuality freely, but they wear a thick overcoat—a fabric of lies—to conceal it, as though it were bad weather in the world of sex. And they are not wrong; sun and wind are not favorable in our civilized society to any demonstration of sex life. In truth no one can freely disclose his erotic life to his neighbor. But when your patients see that in your treatment they may disregard the conventional restraints, they lay aside this veil of lies, and then only are you in a position to formulate a judgment on the question in dispute. Unfortunately physicians are not favored above the rest of the children of men in their personal relationship to the questions of the sex life. Many of them are under the ban of that mixture of prudery and lasciviousness which determines the behaviour of most *Kulturmenschen* in affairs of sex.

Now to proceed with the communication of our results. It is true that in another series of cases psychoanalysis at first traces the symptoms back not to the sexual, but to banal traumatic experiences. But the distinction loses its significance through other circumstances. The work of analysis which is necessary for the thorough explanation and complete cure of a case of sickness does not stop in any case with the experience of the time of onset of the disease, but in every case it goes back to the adolescence and the early childhood of the patient. Here only do we hit upon the impressions and circumstances which determine the later sickness. Only the childhood experiences can give the explanation for the sensitivity to later traumata and only when these memory traces, which almost always are forgotten, are discovered and made conscious, is the power developed to banish the symptoms. We arrive here at the same conclusion as in the investigation of dreams—that it is the incompatible, repressed wishes of childhood which lend their power to the creation of symptoms. Without these the reactions upon later traumata discharge normally. But we must consider these mighty wishes of childhood very generally as sexual in nature.

Now I can at any rate be sure of your astonishment. Is there an infantile sexuality? you will ask. Is childhood not rather that period of life which is distinguished by the lack of the sexual impulse? No, gentlemen, it is not at all true that the sexual impulse enters into the child at puberty, as the devils in the gospel entered into the swine. The child has his sexual impulses and activities from the beginning, he brings them with him into the world, and from these the so-called normal sexuality of adults emerges by a significant development through manifold stages. It is not very difficult to observe the expressions of this childish sexual activity; it needs rather a certain art to overlook them or to fail to interpret them.

As fate would have it, I am in a position to call a witness for my assertions from your own midst. I show you here the work of one Dr. Sanford Bell, published in 1902 in the *American Journal of Psychology*. The author was a fellow of Clark University, the same institution within whose walls we now stand. In this thesis, entitled "A Preliminary Study of the Emotion of Love between the Sexes," which appeared three years before my "Drei Abhandlungen zur Sexualtheorie," the author says just what I have been saying to you: "The emotion of sex love . . . does not make its appearance for the first time at the period of adolescence as has been thought." He has, as we should say in Europe, worked by the American method, and has fathered not less than 2,500 positive observations in the course of fifteen years, among them 800 of his own. He says of the signs by which this amourous condition manifests itself: "The unprejudiced mind, in observing these manifestations in hundreds of couples of children, cannot escape referring them to sex origin. The most exacting mind is satisfied when to these observations are added the confessions of those who have as children experienced the emotion to a marked degree of intensity, and whose memories of childhood are relatively distinct." Those of you who are unwilling to believe in infantile sexuality will be most astonished to hear that among those children who feel in love so early not a few are of the tender ages of three, four, and five years.

It would not be surprising if you should believe the observations of a fellow-countryman rather than my own. Fortunately a short time ago from the analysis of a five-year-old boy who was suffering from anxiety, an analysis undertaken with correct technique by his father, I succeeded in getting a fairly complete picture of the bodily expressions of the impulse and the mental productions of an early stage of childish sexual life. And I must remind you that my friend, Dr. C. G. Jung, read you a few hours ago in this room an observation on a still younger girl who from the same cause as my patient—the birth of a little child in the family—betrayed certainly almost the same secret excitement, wish and complex-creation. Accordingly I am not without hope that you may feel friendly toward this idea of infantile sexuality that was so strange at first. I might also quote the remarkable example of the Zurich psychiatrist, E. Bleuler, who said a few years ago openly that he faced my sexual theories incredulous and bewildered, and since that time by his own observations had substantiated them in their whole scope. If it is true that most men, medical observers and others, do not want to know anything about the sexual life of the child, the fact is capable of explanation only too easily. They have forgotten their own infantile sexual activity under the pressure of education for civilization and do not care to be reminded now of the repressed material. You will be convinced otherwise if you begin the investigation by the self-analysis, by an interpretation of your own childhood memories.

Lay aside your doubts and let us evaluate the infantile sexuality of the earliest years. The sexual impulse of the child manifests itself as a very complex one, it permits of an analysis into many components, which spring from different sources.... It is entirely disconnected from the functions of reproduction which it is later to serve. It permits the child to gain different sorts of pleasure sensations, which we include, by the analogues and connections which they show, under the term sexual pleasures. The great source of infantile sexual pleasure is the auto-excitation of certain particularly sensitive parts of the body; besides the genitals are included the rectum and the opening of the urinary canal, and also the skin and other sensory surfaces. Since in this first phase of child sexual life the satisfaction is found on the child's own body and has nothing to do with any other object, we call this phase after a word coined by Havelock Ellis, that of "auto-erotism." The parts of the body significant in giving sexual pleasure we call "erogenous zones." The thumb-sucking (Ludeln) or passionate sucking (Wonnesaugen) of very young children is good example of such an auto-erotic satisfaction of an erogenous zone. The first scientific observer of this phenomenon, a specialist in children's diseases in Budapest by the name of Lindner, interpreted these rightly as sexual satisfactions and described exhaustively their transformation into other and higher forms of sexual gratification. Another sexual satisfaction of this time of life is the excitation of the genitals by masturbation, which has such a great significance for later life and, in the case of many individuals, is never fully overcome. Besides this and other auto-erotic manifestations we see very early in the child the impulse-components of sexual pleasure, or as we may say, of this libido, which presupposes a second person as its object. These impulses appear in opposed pairs, as active and passive. The most important representatives of this group are the pleasure in inflicting pain (sadism) with its passive opposite (masochism) and active and passive exhibition-pleasure (Schaulust). From the first of these later pairs splits off the curiosity for knowledge, as from the latter the impulse toward artistic and theatrical representation. Other sexual manifestations of the child can already be regarded from the view-point of object-choice, in which the second person plays the prominent part. The significance of this was primarily based upon motives of the impulse of self-preservation. The difference between the sexes plays, however, in the child no very great role. One may attribute to every child, without wronging him, a bit of the homosexual disposition.

The sexual life of the child, rich, but dissociated, in which each single impulse goes about the business of arousing pleasure independently of every other, is later correlated and organized in two general directions, so that by the close of puberty the definite sexual character of the individual is practically finally determined. The single impulses subordinate themselves to the overlordship of the genital zone, so that the whole sexual life is taken over into the service of procreation, and their gratification is now significant only so far as they help to prepare and promote the true sexual act. On the other hand, object-choice prevails over auto-erotism, so that now in the sexual life all components of the sexual impulse are satisfied in the loved person. But not all the original impulse-components are given a share in the final shaping of the sexual life. Even before the advent of puberty certain impulses have undergone the most energetic repression under the impulse of education, and mental forces like shame, disgust and morality are developed, which like sentinels, keep the repressed wishes in subjection. When there comes, in puberty, the high tide of sexual desire it finds dams in this creation of reactions and resistances. These guide the outflow into the so-called normal channels, and make it impossible to revivify the impulses which have undergone repression.

The most important of these repressed impulses are coprophilism, that is, the pleasure in children connected with the excrements; and, further, the tendencies attaching themselves to the persons of the primitive object-choice.

A sentence of general pathology says that every process of development brings with it the germ of pathological dispositions in so far as it may be inhibited, delayed, or incompletely carried out. This holds for the development of the sexual function, with its many complications. It is not smoothly completed in all individuals, and may leave behind either abnormalities or disposition to later diseases by the way of later falling back or regression. It may happen that not all the partial impulses subordinate themselves to the rule of the genital zone. Such an impulse which has remained disconnected brings about what we call a perversion, which may replace the normal sexual goal by one of its own. It may happen, as has been said before, that the auto-erotism is not fully overcome, as many sorts of disturbances testify. The originally equal value of both sexes as sexual objects may be maintained and an inclination to homosexual activities in adult life result from this, which, under suitable conditions, rises to the level of exclusive homosexuality. This series of disturbances corresponds to the direct inhibition of development of the sexual function, it includes the perversions and the general infantilism of the sex life that are not seldom met with.

The disposition to neuroses is to be derived in another way from an injury to the development of the sex life. The neuroses are related to the perversions as the negative to the positive; in them we find the same impulse-components as in perversions, as bearers of the complexes and as creators of the symptoms; but here they work from out the unconscious. They have undergone a repression, but in spite of this they maintain themselves in the unconscious. Psychoanalysis teaches us that overstrong expression of the impulse in every early life leads to a sort of fixation (Fixirung), which then offers a weak point in the articulation of the sexual function. If the exercise of the normal sexual function meets with hindrances in later life, this repression, dating from the time of development, is broken through at just that point at which the infantile fixation took place.

You will now perhaps make the objection: "But all that is not sexuality." I have used the word in a very much wider sense than you are accustomed to understand. This I willingly concede. But it is a question whether you do not rather use the word in much too narrow a sense when you restrict it to the realm of procreation. You sacrifice by that the understanding of perversions; of the connection between perversion, neurosis, and normal sexual life; and have no means of recognition, in its true significance, the easily observable beginning of the somatic and mental sexual life of the child. But however you decide about the use of the word, remember that the psychoanalyst understands sexuality in that full sense to which he is led by the evaluation of infantile sexuality.

Now we turn again to the sexual development of the child. We still have much to say here, since we have given more attention to the sematic than to the mental expressions of the sexual life. The primitive object-choice of the child, which is derived from his need of help, demands our further interest. It first attaches to all persons to whom he is accustomed, but soon these give way in favor of his parents. The relation of the child to his parents is, as both direct observation of the child and later analytic investigation of adults agree, not at all free from elements of sexual accessory-excitation (Miterregung). The child takes both parents, and especially one, as an object of his erotic wishes. Usually he follows in this the stimulus given by his parents, whose tenderness has very clearly the character of a sex manifestation though inhibited so far as its goal is concerned. As a rule, the father prefers the daughter, the mother the son; the child reacts to this situation, since, as son, he wishes himself in the place of his father, as daughter, in the place of the mother. The feelings awakened in these relations between parents and children, and, as a resultant of them, those among the children in relation to each other, are not only positively of a tender, but negatively of an inimical sort. The complex built up in this way is destined to quick repression, but it still exerts a great and lasting effect from the unconscious. We must express the opinion that this with its ramifications presents the nuclear complex of every neurosis, and so we are prepared to meet with it in a not less effectual way in the other fields of mental life. The myth of King Oedipus, who kills his father and wins his mother as a wife is only the slightly altered presentation of the infantile wish, rejected later by the opposing barriers of incest. Shakespeare's tale of Hamlet rests on the same basis of an incest complex, though better concealed. At the time when the child is still ruled by the still unrepressed nuclear complex, there begins a very significant part of his mental activity which serves sexual interest. He begins to investigate the question of where children come from and guesses more than adults imagine of the true relations by deduction from the signs which he sees. Usually his interest in this investigation is awakened by the threat to his welfare through the birth of another child in the family, in whom at first he sees only a rival. Under the influence of the partial impulses which are active in him he arrives at a number of "infantile sexual theories," as that the same male genitals belong to both sexes, that children are conceived by eating and born through the opening of the intestine, and that sexual intercourse is to be regarded as an inimical act, a sort of overpowering.

But just the unfinished nature of his sexual constitution and the gaps in his knowledge brought about by the hidden condition of the feminine sexual canal, cause the infant investigator to discontinue his work as a failure. The facts of this childish investigation itself as well as the infant sex theories created by it are of determinative significance in the building of the child's character, and in the content of his later neuroses.

It is unavoidable and quite normal that the child should make his parents the objects of his first object-choice. But his libido must not remain fixed on these first chosen objects, but must take them merely as a prototype and transfer from these to other persons in the time of definite object-choice. The breaking loose (Ablosung) of the child from his parents is thus a problem impossible to escape if the social virtue of the young individual is not to be impaired. During the time that the repressive activity is making its choice among the partial sexual impulses and later, when the influence of the parents, which in the most essential way has furnished the material for these repressions, is lessened, great problems fall to the work of education, which at present certainly does not always solve them in the most intelligent and economic way.

26

LEWIS M. TERMAN (1877–1956)

The measurement of intelligence (1916)

Terman received his Ph.D. in psychology a Clark University under G. Stanley Hall. His dissertation, which had to do with the intellectual processes of seven bright and seven dull boys, was completed in 1905. The first Binet-Simon scale appeared in the same year, and Terman was immediately interested. In 1911 he published an article based upon his impressions from the use of the Binet-Simon tests, and in 1912 he published a tentative revision and extension of it. In 1913 another article by Terman on the revising, extending, and supplementing of the Binet tests appeared, as did one on the principles underlying the Binet-Simon scale. In 1916 Terman's own revision, entitled the Stanford-Binet, because Terman was at Stanford, was published. With further revisions, it has been the standard individual intelligence test in the United States since 1916.

The following selection is taken from Terman's The Measurement of Intelligence *(1916) pages 51–56 and 65–67 with the permission of the Houghton Mifflin Company.*

NATURE OF THE STANFORD REVISION AND EXTENSION

Although the Binet scale quickly demonstrated its value as an instrument for the classification of mentally-retarded and otherwise exceptional children, it had, nevertheless, several imperfections which greatly limited its usefulness. There was a dearth of tests at the higher mental levels, the procedure was so inadequately defined that needless disagreement came about in the interpretation of data, and so many of the tests were misplaced as to make the results of an examination more or less misleading, particularly in the case of very young subjects and those near the adult level. It was for the purpose of correcting these and certain other faults that the Stanford investigation was planned.

Sources of data

Our revision is the result of several years of work, and involved the examination of approximately 2300 subjects, including 1700 normal children, 200 defective and superior children, and more than 400 adults.

Tests of 400 of the 1700 normal children had been made by Childs and Terman in 1910–11, and of 300 children by Trost, Waddle, and Terman in 1911–12. For various reasons, however, the results of these tests did not furnish satisfactory data for a thoroughgoing revision of the scale. Accordingly a new investigation was undertaken, somewhat more extensive than the others, and more carefully planned. Its main features may be described as follows:

1. The first step was to assemble as nearly as possible all the results which had been secured for each test of the scale by all the workers of all countries. The result was a large sheet of tabulated data for each individual test, including percentages passing the test at various ages, conditions under which the results were secured, method of procedure, etc. After a comparative study of these data, and in the light of results we had ourselves secured, a provisional arrangement of these was prepared for try-out.

2. In addition to the tests of the original Binet scale, 40 additional tests were included for try-out. This, it was expected, would make possible the elimination of some of the least satisfactory tests, and at the same time permit the addition of enough new ones to give at least six tests, instead of five, for each age group.

3. A plan was then devised for securing subjects who should be as nearly as possible representative of the several ages. The method was to select a school in a community of average social status, a school attended by all or practically all the children in the district where it was located. In order to get clear pictures of age differences the tests were confined to children who were within two months of a birthday. To avoid accidental selection, all the children within two months of a birthday were tested, in whatever grade enrolled. Tests of foreign-born children, however, were eliminated in the treatment of results. There remained tests of approximately 1000 children, of whom 905 were between 5 and 14 years of age.

4. The children's responses were, for the most part, recorded verbatim. This made it possible to re-score the records according to any desired standard, and thus to fit a test more perfectly to the age level assigned it.

5. Much attention was given to securing uniformity of procedure. A half-year was devoted to training the examiners, and another half-year to the supervision of the testing. In the further interests of uniformity all the records were scored by one person (the writer).

Method of arriving at a revision

The revision of the scale below the 14-year level was based almost entirely on the tests of the above-mentioned 1,000 unselected children. The guiding principle was to secure an arrangement of the tests and a standard of scoring which would cause the median mental age of the unselected children of each group to coincide with the median chronological age. That is, a correct scale must cause the average child of 5 years to test exactly at 5, the average child at 6 to test exactly at 6, etc. Or, to express the same fact in terms of intelligence quotient, a correct scale must give a median intelligence quotient of unity, or 100 per cent, for unselected children of each age.

If the median mental age resulting at any point from the provisional arrangement of tests was too high or too low, it was only necessary to change the location of certain of the tests, or to change the standard of scoring, until an order of arrangement and a standard of passing were found which would throw the median mental age where it belongs. We had already become convinced, for reasons too involved for presentation here, that no satisfactory revision of the Binet scale was possible on any theoretical considerations as to the percentage of passes which an individual test ought to show in a given year in order to be considered standard for that year.

As was to be expected, the first draft of the revision did not prove satisfactory. The scale was still too hard at some points, and too easy at others. In fact, three successive revisions were necessary, involving three separate scorings of the data and as many tabulations of the mental ages, before the desired degree of accuracy was secured. As finally revised, the scale gives a median intelligence quotient closely approximating 100 for the unselected children of each age from 4 to 14.

Since our school children who were above 14 years and still in the grades were retarded left-overs, it was necessary to base the revision above this level on the tests of adults. These included 30 business men and 150 "migrating" unemployed men tested by Mr. H. E. Knollin, 150 adolescent delinquents tested by Mr. J. Harold Williams, and 50 high-school students tested by the writer.

The extension of the scale in the upper range is such that ordinary intelligent adults, little educated, test up to what is called the "average adult" level. Adults whose intelligence is known from other sources to be superior are found to test well up toward the "superior adult" level, and this holds whether the subjects in question are well educated or practically unschooled. The almost entirely unschooled business men, in fact, tested fully as well as high-school juniors and seniors.

The following method was employed for determining the validity of a test. The children of each age level were divided into three groups according to intelligence quotient, those testing below 90, those between 90 and 109, and those with an intelligence quotient of 110 or above. The percentages of passes on each individual test at or near that age level were then ascertained separately for these three groups. If a test fails to show a decidedly higher proportion of passes in the superior IQ group than in the inferior IQ group, it cannot be regarded as a satisfactory test of intelligence. On the other hand, a test which satisfies this criterion must be accepted as valid or the entire scale must be rejected. Henceforth it stands or falls with the scale as a whole.

When tried out by this method, some of the tests which have been most criticized showed a high degree of reliability; certain others which have been considered excellent proved to be so little correlated with intelligence that they had to be discarded.

After making a few necessary eliminations, 90 tests remained, or 36 more than the number included in the Binet 1911 scale. There are 6 at each age level from 3 to 10, 8 at 12, 6 at 14, 6 at "average adult," 6 at "superior adult," and 16 alternative tests. The alternative tests, which are distributed among the different groups, are intended to be used only as substitutes when one or more of the regular tests have been rendered, by coaching or otherwise, undesirable.

Of the 36 new tests, 27 were added and standardized in the various Stanford investigations. Two tests were borrowed from the Healy-Fernald series, one from Kuhlmann, one was adapted from Bonser, and the remaining five were amplifications or adaptations of some of the earlier Binet tests.

ANALYSIS OF 1000 INTELLIGENCE QUOTIENTS

An extended account of the 1000 tests on which the Stanford revision is chiefly based has been presented in a separate monograph. This chapter will include only the briefest summary of some of those results of the investigation which contribute to the intelligent use of the revision.

The distribution of intelligence

The question as to the manner in which intelligence is distributed is one of great practical as well as theoretical importance. One of the most vital questions which can be asked by any nation of any age is the following: "How high is the average level of intelligence among our people, and how frequent are the various grades of ability above and below the average?" With the development of standardized tests we are approaching, for the first time in history, a possible answer to this question.

Most of the earlier Binet studies, however, have thrown little light on the distribution of intelligence because of their failure to avoid the influence of accidental selection in choosing subjects for testing. The method of securing subjects for the Stanford revision makes our results on this point especially interesting. It is believed that the subjects used for this investigation were as nearly representative of average American-born children as it is possible to secure.

The intelligence quotients for these 1000 unselected children were calculated, and their distribution was plotted for the ages separately. The distribution was found fairly symmetrical at each age from 5 to 14. At 15 the range is on either side of 90 as a median, and at 16 on either side of 80 as a median. That the 15- and 16-year-olds test low is due to the fact that these children are left-over retardates and are below average in intelligence.

The IQ's were then grouped in ranges of ten. In the middle group were thrown those from 96 to 105. The ascending groups including in order

212 Lewis M. Terman

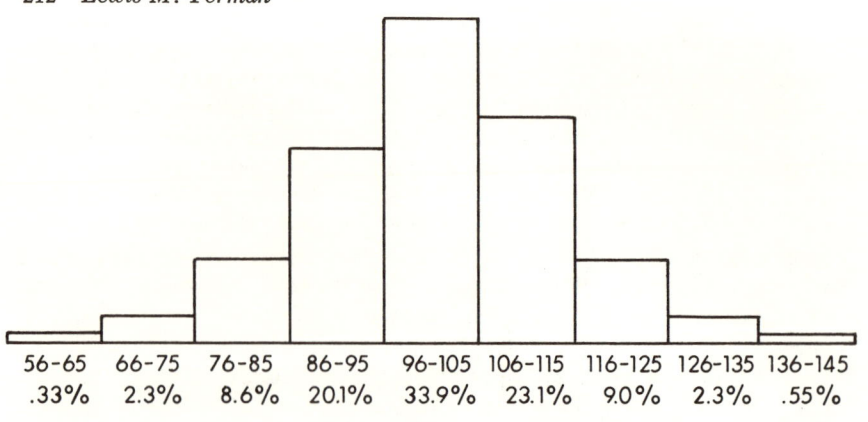

| 56-65 | 66-75 | 76-85 | 86-95 | 96-105 | 106-115 | 116-125 | 126-135 | 136-145 |
| .33% | 2.3% | 8.6% | 20.1% | 33.9% | 23.1% | 9.0% | 2.3% | .55% |

Figure 1. Distribution of IQ's of 905 unselected children 5–14 years of age.

the IQ's from 106 to 115, 116 to 125, etc.; correspondingly with the descending groups. Figure 1 shows the distribution found by this grouping for the 905 children of ages 5 to 14 combined. The subjects above 14 are not included in this curve because they are left-overs and not representative of their ages.

The distribution for the ages combined is seen to be remarkably symmetrical. The symmetry for the separate ages was hardly less marked, considering that only 80 to 120 children were tested at each age. In fact, the range, including the middle 50 per cent of IQ's, was found, practically constant from 5 to 14 years. The tendency is for the middle 50 per cent to fall (approximately) between 93 and 108.

Three important conclusions are justified by the above facts:

1. Since the frequency of the various grades of intelligence decreases gradually and at no point abruptly on each side of the median, it is evident that there is no definite dividing line between normality and feeblemindedness, or between normality and genius. Psychologically, the mentally defective child does not belong to a distinct type, nor does the genius. There is no line of demarcation between either of these extremes and the so-called "normal" child. The number of mentally defective individuals in a population will depend upon the standard arbitrarily set up as to what constitutes mental deficiency. Similarly for genius. It is exactly as if we should undertake to classify all people into the three groups: abnormally tall, normally tall, and abnormally short.

2. The common opinion that extreme deviations below the median are more frequent than extreme deviations above the median seems to have no foundation in fact. Among unselected school children, at least, for every child of any given degree of deficiency there is another child as far above the average IQ as the former is below. We have shown elsewhere the serious consequences of neglect of this fact.

3. The traditional view that variability in mental traits becomes more marked during adolescence is here contradicted, as far as intelligence is concerned, for the distribution of IQ's is practically the same at each age

from 5 to 14. For example, 6-year-olds differ from one another fully as much as do 14-year-olds.

The validity of the intelligence quotient

The facts presented above argue strongly for the validity of the IQ as an expression of a child's intelligence status. This follows necessarily from the similar nature of the distributions at the various ages. The inference is that a child's IQ, as measured by this scale, remains constant. Re-tests of the same children at intervals of two to five years support the inference. Children of superior intelligence do not seem to deteriorate as they get older, nor dull children to develop average intelligence. Knowing a child's IQ, we can predict with a fair degree of accuracy the course of his later development.

The mental age of a subject is meaningless if considered apart from chronological age. It is only the ratio of retardation or acceleration to chronological age (that is, the IQ) which has significance.

It follows also that if the IQ is a valid expression of intelligence, as it seems to be, then the Binet-Simon "age-grade method" becomes transformed automatically into a "point-scale method," if one wants to use it that way. As such it is superior to any other point scale that has been proposed, because it includes a larger number of tests and its points have definite meaning.

Sex differences

The question as to the relative intelligence of the sexes is one of perennial interest and great social importance. The ancient hypothesis, the one which dates from the time when only men concerned themselves with scientific hypotheses, took for granted the superiority of the male. With the development of individual psychology, however, it was soon found that as far as the evidence of mental tests can be trusted the average intelligence of women and girls is as high as that of men and boys.

If we accept this result we are then confronted with the difficult problem of finding an explanation for the fact that so few of those who have acquired eminence in the various intellectual fields have been women. Two explanations have been proposed: (1) That women become eminent less often than men simply for lack of opportunity and stimulus; and (2) that while the average intelligence of the sexes is the same, extreme variations may be more common in males. It is pointed out that not only are there more eminent men than eminent women, but that statistics also show a preponderance of males in institutions for the mentally defective. Accordingly it is often said that women are grouped closely about the average, while men show a wider range of distribution.

Many hundreds of articles and books of popular or quasi-scientific nature have been written on one aspect or another of this question of sex difference in intelligence; but all such theoretical discussions taken together are worth less than the results of one good experiment. Let us see what our 1000 IQ's have to offer toward a solution of the problem.

1. When the IQ's of the boys and girls were treated separately there was found a small but fairly constant superiority of the girls up to the age of 13 years. At 14, however, the curve for the girls dropped below that for boys.

The supplementary data, including the teachers' estimates of intelligence on a scale of five, the teachers' judgments in regard to the quality of the school work, and records showing the age-grade distribution of the sexes, were all sifted for evidence as to the genuineness of the apparent superiority of the girls age for age. The results of all these lines of inquiry support the tests in suggesting that the superiority of the girls is probably real even up to and including age 14, the apparent superiority of the boys of this age being fully accounted for by the more frequent elimination of 14-year-old girls from the grades by promotion to the high school.

2. However, the superiority of girls over boys is so slight (amounting at most ages to only 2 to 3 points in terms of IQ) that for practical purposes it would seem negligible. This offers no support to the opinion expressed by Yerkes and Bridges that "at certain ages serious injustice will be done individuals by evaluating their scores in the light of norms which do not take account of sex differences."

3. Apart from the small superiority of girls, the distribution of intelligence in the two sexes is not different. The supposed wider variation of boys is not found. Girls do not group themselves about the median more closely than do boys. The range of IQ including the middle fifty per cent is approximately the same for the two sexes.

4. When the results for the individual tests were examined, it was found that not many showed very extreme differences as to the per cent of boys and girls passing. In a few cases, however, the difference was rather marked.

The boys were decidedly better in arithmetical reasoning, giving differences between a president and a king, solving the form board, making change, reversing hands of clock, finding similarities, and solving the "induction test." The girls were superior in drawing designs from memory, aesthetic comparison, comparing objects from memory, answering the "comprehension questions," repeating digits and sentences, tying a bow-knot, and finding rhymes.

Accordingly, our data, which for the most part agree with the results of others, justify the conclusion that the intelligence of girls, at least up to 14 years, does not differ materially from that of boys either as regards the average level or the range of distribution. It may still be argued that the mental development of boys beyond the age of 14 years lasts longer and extends farther than in the case of girls, but as a matter of fact this opinion received little support from such tests as have been made on men and women college students.

The fact that so few women have attained eminence may be due to wholly extraneous factors, the most important of which are the following: (1) The occupations in which it is possible to achieve eminence are for the most part only now beginning to open their doors to women. Women's career has been largely that of home-making, an occupation in which eminence, in the strict sense of the word, is impossible. (2) Even of the small number of women who embark upon a professional career, a majority marry and thereafter devote a fairly large proportion of their energy to bearing and rearing children. (3) Both the training given to girls and the general atmosphere in which they grow up are unfavorable to the inculcation of the professional point of view, and as a result women are not spurred on by deep-seated motives to constant and strenuous intellectual endeavor as men are. (4) It is also possible that the emotional traits of women are such as to favor the development of the sentiments at the expense of innate intellectual endowment.

Intelligence of the different social classes

Of the 1000 children, 492 were classified by their teachers according to social class into the following five groups: very inferior, inferior, average, superior, and very superior. A comparative study was then made of the distribution of IQ's for these different groups.

The data may be summarized as follows:

1. The median IQ for children of the superior social class is about 7 points above, and that of the inferior social class about 7 points below, the median IQ of the average social group. This means that by the age of 14 inferior class children are about one year below, and superior class children one year above, the median mental age for all classes taken together.

2. That the children of the superior social classes make a better showing in the tests is probably due, for the most part, to a superiority in original endowment. This conclusion is supported by five supplementary lines of evidence: (a) the teachers' rankings of the children according to intelligence; (b) the age-grade progress of the children; (c) the quality of the school work; (d) the comparison of older and younger children as regards the influence of social environment; and (e) the study of individual cases of bright and dull children in the same family.

3. In order to facilitate comparison, it is advisable to express the intelligence of children of all social classes in terms of the same objective scale of intelligence. This scale should be based on the median for all classes taken together.

As regards their responses to individual tests, our children of a given social class were not distinguishable from children of the same intelligence in any other social class.

The relation of the IQ to the quality of the child's school work

The school work of 504 children was graded by the teachers on a scale of five grades: very inferior, inferior, average, superior, and very superior. When this grouping was compared with that made on the basis of IQ, fairly close agreement was found. However, in about one case out of ten there was rather serious disagreement; a child, for example, would be rated as doing average school work when his IQ would place him in the very inferior intelligence group.

When the data were searched for explanations of such disagreements it was found that most of them were plainly due to the failure of teachers to take into account the age of the child when grading the quality of his school work. When allowance was made for this tendency there were no disagreements which justified any serious suspicion as to the accuracy of the intelligence scale. Minor disagreements may, of course, be disregarded, since the quality of school work depends in part on other factors than intelligence, such as industry, health, regularity of attendance, quality of instruction, etc.

The relation between IQ and grade progress

This comparison, which was made for the entire 1000 children, showed a fairly high correlation, but also some astonishing disagreements. Nine-year intelligence was found all the way from grade 1 to 7, inclusive; 10-year intelligence all the way from grade 2 to 7; and 12-year intelligence all the way from grade 3 to grade 8. Plainly the school's efforts at grading fail to give homogeneous groups of children as regards mental ability. On the whole, the grade location of the children did not fit their mental ages much better than it did their chronological ages.

When the data were examined, it was found that practically every child whose grade failed to correspond fairly closely with his mental age was either exceptionally bright or exceptionally dull. Those who tested between 96 and 105 IQ were never seriously misplaced in school. The very dull children, however, were usually located from one to three grades above where they belonged by mental age, and the duller the child the more serious, as a rule, was the misplacement. On the other hand, the very bright children were nearly always located from one to three grades below where they belonged by mental age, and the brighter the child the more serious the school's mistake. The child of 10-year mental age in the second grade, for example, is almost certain to be about 7 or 8 years old; the child of 10-year intelligence in the sixth grade is almost certain to be 13 to 15 years of age.

All this is due to one fact, and one alone: the school tends to promote children by age rather than ability. The bright children are held back, while the dull children are promoted beyond their mental ability. The retardation problem is exactly the reverse of what we have thought it to be. It is the bright children who are retarded, and the dull children who are accelerated.

The remedy is to be sought in differentiated courses (special classes) for both kinds of mentally exceptional children. Just as many special classes are needed for superior children as for the inferior. The social consequences of suitable educational advantages for children of superior ability would no doubt greatly exceed anything that could possibly result from the special instruction of dullards and border-line cases.

Special study of the IQ's between 70 and 79 revealed the fact that a child of this grade of intelligence never does satisfactory work in the grade where he belongs by chronological age. By the time he has attended school four or five years, such a child is usually found doing "very inferior" to "average" work in a grade from two to four years below his age.

On the other hand, the child with an IQ of 120 or above is almost never found below the grade for his chronological age, and occasionally he is one or two grades above. Wherever located, his work is always "superior" or "very superior," and the evidence suggests strongly that it would probably remain so even if extra promotions were granted.

Correlation between IQ and the teacher's estimates of the children's intelligence

By the Pearson formula the correlation found betweenn the IQ's and the teachers' rankings on a scale of five was .48. This is about what others have found, and is both high enough and low enough to be significant. That it is moderately high in so far corroborates the tests. That it is not higher means that either the teachers or the tests have made a good many mistakes.

When the data were searched for evidence on this point, it was found, that the fault was plainly on the part of the teachers. The serious mistakes were nearly all made with children who were either over age or under age for their grade, mostly the former. In estimating children's intelligence, just as in grading their school success, the teachers often failed to take account of the age factor. For example, the child whose mental age was, say, two years below normal, and who was enrolled in a class with children about two years younger than himself, is often graded "average" in intelligence.

The tendency of teachers is to estimate a child's intelligence according to the quality of his school work in the grade where he happens to be located. This results in over-estimating the intelligence of older, retarded children, and underestimating the intelligence of the younger, advanced children. The disagreements between the tests and the teachers' estimates are thus found, when analyzed, to confirm the validity of the test method rather than to bring it under suspicion.

The validity of the individual tests

The validity of each test was checked up by measuring it against the scale as a whole. For example, if 10-year-old children having 11-year intelligence succeed with a given test decidedly better than 10-year-old children who have 9-year intelligence, then either this test must be accepted as valid or the scale as a whole must be rejected. Since we know, however, that the scale as a whole has at least a reasonably high degree of reliability, this method becomes a sure and ready means of judging the worth of a test.

When the tests were tried out in this way it was found that some of those which have been most criticized have in reality a high correlation with intelligence. Among these are naming the days of the week, giving the value of stamps, counting thirteen pennies, giving differences between president and king, finding rhymes, giving age, distinguishing right and left, and interpretation of pictures. Others having a high reliability are the vocabulary tests, arithmetical reasoning, giving differences, copying a diamond, giving date, repeating digits in reverse order, interpretation of fables, the dissected sentence test, naming sixty words, finding omissions in pictures, and recognizing absurdities.

Among the somewhat less satisfactory tests are the following: repeating digits (direct order), naming coins, distinguishing forenoon and afternoon, defining in terms of use, drawing designs from memory, and aesthetic comparison. Binet's "line suggestion" test correlated so little with intelligence that it had to be thrown out. The same was also true of two of the new tests which we had added to the series for try-out.

Tests showing a medium correlation with the scale as a whole include arranging weights, executing three commissions, naming colors, giving number of fingers, describing pctures, naming the months, making change, giving superior definitions, finding similarities, reading for memories, reversing hands of clock, defining abstract words, problems of fact, bow-knot, induction test, and comprehension questions.

A test which makes a good showing on this criterion of agreement with the scale as a whole becomes immune to theoretical criticisms. Whatever it appears to be from mere inspection, it is a real measure of intelligence. Henceforth it stands or falls with the scale as a whole.

The reader will understand, of course, that no single test used alone will determine accurately the general level of intelligence. A great many tests are required; and for two reasons: (1) because intelligence has many aspects; and (2) in order to overcome the accidental influences of training or environment. If many tests are used no one of them need show more than a moderately high correlation with the scale as a whole. As stated by Binet, "Let the tests be rough, if there are only enough of them."

27

JOHN B. WATSON (1878-1958)

Watson on fear (1919)

No book on the history of child psychology could possibly omit John B. Watson, in spite of the fact that he made few permanent contributions to child psychology.

Watson began his career as a researcher in animal psychology. His first publication, based on his Ph.D. dissertation, was dated 1903. Between 1903 and 1912 all of his publications were in the animal psychology field, and were very good; his work in animal psychology continued until 1915. His first major theoretical paper, "Psychology as a Behaviorist Views It," was published in 1913. After that he became more noted as a theorist than as an investigator and wrote many theoretical articles. During World War I, as a major in the U.S. Army, he engaged in applied research dealing with such novel (for him) topics as the affect of oxygen deprivation upon handwriting, and (with Lashley!) the effect of sex education upon the incidence of venereal disease.

Only in 1918 did he begin his work in child psychology, and in 1920 he was forced to give up his academic position at the Johns Hopkins University because of a divorce that today would attract little attention. Consequently, his research career in child psychology was brief, and his investigations limited. However, he wrote prolifically and pontifically about child rearing, influencing a generation of students and mothers. There can be no doubt that if he had had the opportunity to observe children as carefully as he had observed noddy and sooty terns his permanent contributions to child psychology would have been of great value. As it happened, he popularized views, most of which have since been shown to be erroneous.

The limited nature of his objective studies of children are shown by the following excerpts from his general textbook, Psychology from the Standpoint of a Behaviorist *(1919), pages 199-213. They are reproduced by permission of the J. B. Lippincott Co.*

EARLY TYPES OF EMOTIONAL REACTIONS

After observing a number of infants, especially during the first months of life, we suggest the following group of emotional reactions as belonging to the original and fundamental nature of man: *fear, rage* and *love* (using *love* in approximately the same sense that Freud uses *sex*). We use these terms which are current in psychology with a good deal of hesitation. The student is asked to find nothing in them which is not fully statable in terms of situation and response. Indeed, we should be willing to call them emotional reaction states X, Y, and Z. They are far more easily observable in animals than in infants.

Fear

What stimulus apart from all training will call out fear responses; what are these responses, and how early may they be called out? The principal situations which call out fear responses seem to be as follows: (1) To suddenly remove from the infant all means of support, as when one drops it from the hands to be caught by an assistant (in the experiment the child is held over a bed upon which has been placed a soft feather pillow); (2) by loud sounds; (3) occasionally when an infant is just falling asleep or is just ready to waken, a sudden push or a slight shake is an adequate stimulus; (4) when an infant is just falling asleep, occasionally the sudden pulling of the blanket upon which it is lying will produce the fear responses. (2) and (3) above my be looked upon as belonging under (1). The responses are a sudden catching of the breath, clutching randomly with the hands (the grasping reflex invariably appearing when the child is dropped), sudden closing of the eye-lids, puckering of the lips, then crying; in older children possibly flight and hiding (not yet observed by us as "original" reactions). In regard to the age at which fear responses first appear, we can state with some sureness that the above mentioned group of reactions appears at birth. It is often stated that children are instinctively afraid in the dark. While we shall advance our opinion with the greatest caution we have not so far been able to gather any evidence to this effect. When such reactions to darkness do appear they are due to other causes; darkness comes to be associated with absence of customary stimulation, noises, etc. (they should be looked upon as conditioned fear reactions). From time immemorial children have been "scared" in the dark, either unintentionally or as a means of controlling them (this is especially true of children reared in the South).

Rage

In a similar way the question arises as to what is the original situation which brings out the activities seen in rage. Observation seems to show that the *hampering of the infant's movements* is the factor which apart from all training brings out the movements characterized as rage. If the face or head is held, crying results, quickly followed by screaming. The body stiffens and fairly well-coordinated slashing or striking movements of the hands and arms result; the feet and legs are drawn up and down; the breath is held until the child's face is flushed. In older children the slashing movements of the arms and legs are better coordinated, and appear as kicking, slapping, pushing, etc. These reactions continue until the irritating situation is relieved, and sometimes do not cease then. Almost any child from birth can be thrown into a rage if its arms are held tightly to its sides; sometimes even if the elbow joint is clasped tightly between the fingers the response appears; at times just the placing of the head between cotton pads will produce it. This was noticed repeatedly when testing eye coordinations in infants under ten days of age. The slight constraint put upon the head by the soft pads would often result in a disturbance so great that the experiment had to be discontinued for a time.

Love

The original situation which calls out the observable love responses seems to be the stroking or manipulation of some erogenous zone, tickling, shaking, gentile rocking, patting and turning upon the stomach across the attendant's knee. The response varies. If the infant is crying, crying ceases, a smile may appear, attempts at gurgling, cooing, and finally, in slightly older children, the extension of the arms, which we should class as the forerunner of the embrace of adults. The smile and the laugh which Freud connects with the release of repression (we are not denying in the case of adults this may be true) we should thus class as original reaction tendencies intimately connected from infancy with the stimulation of, in our opinion at least, the erogenous zones.

These types fit fairly well the general formulation. There is a reaction pattern; there is a definite stimulus, which has its peculiarly exciting character (the reason for which must be sought in biology); the radius of action is small; no particular adjustment is made to any object in the environment. It is admitted, however, that the responses contain both explicit and implicit components, that is, involve the skeletal musculature, the visceral system, the smooth muscles and glands. It is probable, though, that if the exciting stimulus were sufficiently strong—strong enough to produce "shock"—or if continued for a sufficient length of time, the subject would tend to take on more and more the purely vegetative type of existence illustrated by the example of the young tern. In rage, the child becomes so stiff, and holds its breath for such a long time, that it is often necessary to soothe it. The final stage in any great emotion would seem to be paralysis or the "death feint." Approximations to this condition are seen in the paralysis of fear, in the fainting under strong emotional excitement, in the stereotyped reactions of the stoics and martyrs when they unflinchingly endured the torch. Individuals on the battlefield, likewise, are able to withstand operations, wounds, and injuries without complaint. It must be admitted that there is a constant tendency for the organized habit response of the individual to disappear under the extremes of emotion. So far as we can see, this tendency towards stereotypy, paralysis or the death feint under the immediate effect of a strong emotional excitement has no biological or adaptive value. . . . The organism exhibiting it is at the mercy of its enemies, whether on the battlefield or in the struggle for food among savage tribes, and is at a disadvantage in the race for a much-sought-after woman, or in the fight for business and scientific reputation.

Negative results of experimental study

Three babies from the Harriet Lane Hospital were put into various situations, the types of which are illustrated below, for the purpose of finding out whether there is a wider range of stimuli that may arouse an emotional reaction than the one we cited a moment ago. These babies represented splendid, healthy types. Their mothers were the wet nurses belonging to the hospital. They were 165, 126 and 124 days of age. The first two, whose ages are given, were put through the more numerous tests. The experiments are interesting for the reason that the babies had never been out of the hospital and had never seen an animal. A summary of the tests on Thorne, a girl 165 days of age, is given below.

A very lively, friendly *black cat* was allowed to crawl near the baby. She reached for it with both hands at once. The cat was purring loudly. She touched its nose, playing with is with her fingers. It was shown three times. Each time she reached with both hands for it, the left hand being rather more active. She reached for it when it was placed on a lounge before her but out of reach.

Then a *pigeon* in a paper bag was laid on the couch. The pigeon was struggling, and moving the bag on the couch and making a loud rattling noise. The baby watched it intently but did not reach for it. The pigeon was taken out of the bag on the couch before her, cooing and struggling in the experimenter's hands. She reached for it again and again, and failing, of course, to get hold of it put her hands in her mouth each time. She was allowed to touch its head. The pigeon moved its head about with quick, jerking movements. It was then held by its feet and allowed to flap it wings near the baby's face. She watched it intently, showing no tendency to avoid it, but did not reach for it. When the bird became quiet she reached for it, and caught hold of its beak with her left hand.

Test with a rabbit. The animal was put on a couch in front of her. (The child was sitting on her mother's lap.) She watched it very intently but did not reach for it until the experimenter held it in his hands close to her; then she reached for it immediately, catching one of its ears in her left hand, and attempting to put it into her mouth.

The last animal presented to her was a *white rat*. She paid little attention to it, only fixating it occasionally. She followed it with her eyes somewhat when it moved about the couch. When held out to her on the experimenter's arm, she turned her head away, no longer stimulated.

April 24, 172 days old. The baby was taken into a dark room with only an electric light behind her, not very bright (faint illumination). A stranger held the baby. The mother sat where she could not be seen. A dog was brought into the room and allowed to jump up on the couch beside her. The baby watched intently every move the dog made but did not attempt to reach for it. Then she turned her head aside. The front light was then turned up and the dog again exhibited. The infant watched very closely every move the dog and the experimenter made, but did not attempt to catch the dog. Exhibited no fear reactions, no matter how close the dog was made to come to her.

The *black cat* was then brought in (both lights on). The cat rubbed against the baby's feet and put her front paws in the baby's lap, touching its nose to her hand. The baby watched intently and reached for it with her left hand. The front light was then turned out. The experimenter held the cat closer to her, and she reached for it with both hands.

Rabbit. She reached for it with both hands as soon as the experimenter came into the room with it in his arms. The front light was turned on. The rabbit was held out to her. She reached for it at once with both hands, trying to put her fingers in its eyes. She caught hold of a piece of fur above the rabbit's eye and pulled hard.

Pigeon. The front light was turned out. She reached for the bird with her left hand before the experimenter was ready to present it to her. The pigeon's wings were released and it fluttered violently just in front of the baby's eyes. She continued to reach for it with both hands, even when the wings brushed her face. When the bird was quiet it was presented to her again. She reached for it even more vigorously. She tried to take hold of the pigeon's beak with her left hand, but failed, because the bird continually bobbed its head. The front light was then turned on. The pigeon again flapped wildly. The baby looked at it intently with widely opened eyes, but this time did not reach. She showed no fear, however. It was then held out to her again when it had become quiet. She reached for it at once with both hands, held the feathers and tried to put her fingers into its eyes.

April 27, 175 days old. The baby was placed in a small chair and tied in, and put behind a screen, so that she could not see any of the people in the room. The dog was allowed to walk suddenly around the screen in front of her. She showed no fear when the dog rubbed against her legs. She did not reach for him, however. While she was still in the same position, the experimenter held the pigeon in front of her and allowed it to flap its wings. She reached for it with both hands the moment it was presented to her, and did not withdraw her hands while the bird was flapping its wings. She continued to reach as the bird was moved out of her range.

The cat was then brought around the screen and placed on the couch just in front of the baby's chair. She did not reach for it, but followed it with her eyes. It was held very close to her. She reached for it with her left hand and touched its head. The cat was then moved away, but she continued to reach for it. Then the cat put its front feet in her lap. She reached with her left hand and followed with her right, touching its ears.

Rabbit. She reached with her left hand at once when the rabbit was still too far away to touch. When it came close to her she reached with her left hand and touched it.

She was then taken into the dark room with both lights turned out and seated in a small chair. A newspaper was lighted before her and allowed to burn in a large metal bucket. She watched it intently from the moment the match was struck until the flames died down. She showed no fear, but did not attempt to reach.

While being tested in the large room for eye-hand coordination, the dog suddenly began to bark at some one entering the room. He was quite near the baby. He barked loudly and jumped about at the end of the leash. The baby became perfectly still, watching intently with widely opened eyes, blinking at each bark, but did not cry.

May 1, 178 days old. She was taken out to Druid Hill Park in an automobile for the first time in her life. She was wide awake the whole time. She was carried rather rapidly through the grounds of the small zoo at the park. The camel was braying and came up to the fence as we approached, rubbing rather violently against the fence, coming within a few feet of the baby. This produced no fear reaction and no constant fixation. She was then taken to the cages containing the cinnamon and black bears. She gazed at them from time to time, but with no constant fixation. We then took her into the monkey house which contained also a large number of parrots and other smaller birds. The monkeys came to the sides of the cage, and from time to time attacked the wires. Three or four times they came up and made threatening movements, and actually caught the experimenter by the arm. The child did not seem to be in the least afraid. The peacocks were making their rather uncanny sounds within twenty feet of her, but she did not turn her eyes towards the source of the sound. She was then taken back to the camel yard, and the camel again "performed" nicely. Two camels came up to each other and rubbed noses and put their heads over the dividing fence. The baby was within two or three inches of the camel's nose on several occasions, but while she followed the movements with her eyes, she showed no pronounced reactions of any kind. She was then taken to the Shetland pony, who put his nose through the wires and showed his teeth. She was within a few inches of his mouth. Outside of following movements of the eyes, no reactions were observable. She was taken near two zebras. They came to the edge of the fence, within a few inches of the baby. The zebras were possibly followed slightly more intently with the eyes, but there was no other observable reaction. While the baby was watching the zebras an ostrich came close to her and brought its head to the wire but did not strike the wire violently. During approximately half of the experiment the baby was carried by her mother and the rest of the time by the experimenter's secretary. She had never been carried by this individual before. At times the mother was kept out of the range of the baby's vision.

Baby Nixon, a girl, 126 days of age, had just learned the eye-hand coordination. She was put through exactly the same series of situations. Slight differences appeared, *e.g.,* when the cat rubbed its head against the baby's stomach, there was a distinct start, a tendency to stiffen. While the experimenter was out of the room getting the rabbit, three persons were left with the baby in the dark room (dim light). All were sitting very quietly. She was being held by a stranger. Suddenly the baby began to cry, and had to be given to the mother for a few moments. She quieted down immediately. Again when the pigeon flapped its wings near the baby's face, she gave a distinct jump, but did not cry or show other signs of fear. When the dog was made to bark (lighted room), the baby blinked her eyes at every bark, but gave no other reaction. She smiled throughout most of the situations. She smiled all through the burning of the paper in the dark room.

It is thus seen that this unusual opportunity of testing children's reactions to their first sight of animals yielded few positive results. At least we can say that the older statements which maintain that violent emotions appear must be very greatly modified. Of course, it is always possible that the children were too young, but this has not very much weight, since we have tested children from birth through to 200 days. These children left the hospital shortly after the tests and further experimentation could not be made. As a control test, similar observations were made upon a colored baby girl (Lee) 200 days of age, who had been under observation from birth. She lived in the city under the usual environmental conditions. Exactly the same results were obtained. There was practically no evidence of fear.

Are there other original emotional patterns?

It is thus seen that so far our attempts to bring out emotional patterns distinct from those enumerated [earlier] have been barren of result. If it were possible to continue such experiments through a much longer span of a child's life, and if we could face him with a much larger number of situations that more nearly touched his daily life activities, it might be possible to extend the list. It is realized that we are working here with very young members of the human species. A good deal of organization and development takes place after two hundred days. Some very complex situations have yet to be faced, such as masturbation (and in boys especially, the first masturbation after puberty); the first menstruation period in girls; complex situations connected with family life, such as quarrels between the parents, corporal punishment and the death of loved ones, all of which have to be met with for a first time.

* * *

Substitution of stimulus: attachments and detachments

Under the action of environmental factors situations which originally did not call out emotional response come later to do so.

* * *

The ... phenomenon is clearly observable in children. As was brought out above, they show little fear of animals. If, however, one animal succeeds in arousing fear, any moving furry animal thereafter may arouse it. In one observed case a child at 180 days had a small dog tossed into its carriage. She became terrified and thereafter showed marked reactions not only to dogs but even to rapid mechanically moving toy animals. At 600 days she was placed on the floor near her mother and father and two children with whom she had been playing. A very tame white mouse was placed on the floor near her. She watched it for a moment, her lips puckered, she shook slowly from side to side, squirmed, retracted hands and arms, and broke into a cry, scrambled to her feet and fell headlong into her father's arms.

The emotional transfers begin very early in life. The following diary of one of the infants under observation in the laboratory is clearly expressive of the process:

Lee, 67, 80 and 87 days of age. When first laid on the couch (where grasping reflex was tested) she would smile and gurgle on each of the above dates, but after testing the grasping reflex, she would cry the moment she was put back on the couch. When picked up she would stop, and when put down she would start to cry. If left on the couch for any length of time, she would stop crying, but if the experimenter approached her or touched her hands with the grasping rod, she would immediately start to cry.

94 days of age. She was laid on the couch by her mother. She gurgled and smiled. The mother then took her up and held her for a few minutes and again put her down. Again she smiled and gurgled. The experimenter then tried out the grasping reflex upon each hand. She cried loudly and struggled. As the experimenter first approached her with the rod to make this test she did not cry, but when the rod was put into her hand she began to whimper and actually cried before lifting was begun. After the test the mother took her up and held her until she became quiet. She was laid down, but immediately began to cry. The mother again took her up and quieted her and put her down, with the same result. Repeated, with the same result.

101 days of age. The above conditioned reflex did not carry over completely for the week. When her mother first laid her on the couch she did not cry. She was quite restless, however. The first contact of the rod in the left hand caused only a whimper. This became stronger on touching her right hand. She cried outright as soon as the rod was raised and before she had supported very much of her weight.

115 days of age. As soon as the mother was seated with the baby in her lap, the experimenter entered the room and tried to put a piece of candy in her hand (earlier tests had been made upon the eye-hand coordination). She began immediately to whimper and then to cry. This in all probability was the carrying over of the conditioned reflex, *i.e.,* the visual stimulus of the experimenter was enough to set off the crying reflex.

The fear reactions we see in the dark, in graveyards at night, at lightning, and in many other definite situations, probably belong in the conditioned emotional reaction class. We would put all of the definite phobias (where the reaction is to a definite situation or object) in this class. Such reactions are more numerous in individuals of the unstable emotional type, and especially among frontier and primitive people where every crackling of a twig or cry of an animal or shaking of a bough may be fraught with danger.

28

HUGH GORDON (1863-1934)

Mental and scholastic tests among retarded children (1923)

Terman, in order to standardize the Stanford-Binet test, chose children from typical American, white, largely urban, environments. He was inclined to believe that most of the differences in intelligence which he found were genetically determined. For the population from which his norms were derived, his belief was probably correct. In his groups the environment varied little, but genes varied considerably.

In the editor's opinion, Gordon's study is very important because it shows what happens to Stanford-Binet scores when the environment is much different from that in which the "standardization" has occurred.

Gordon's study, while occasionally referred to, has not been widely read. Because of bureaucratic publishing policies, it has not been readily accessible. It does not bear Gordon's name, although Gordon is the author. It is listed as Educational Pamphlet No. 44 of the Board of Education of London, *published under the authority of His Majesty's Stationery Office, 1923. The "prefatory note" says, "The following pamphlet contains a series of memoranda written by Mr. Hugh Gordon, one of His Majesty's Inspectors of Schools, upon investigations made by him, mostly in the Metropolitan area, in the course of his official work. The Board have published the memoranda in view of the interest and value of the contribution which they made to the discussion of a very difficult subject. For the view expressed in the memoranda the author alone is responsible."*

The editor is indebted to James Drever, Principal of the University of Dundee, for procuring a photostatic copy of this report.

The report is long, nearly 100 pages. What is reprinted below is greatly abridged. It contains only the sections dealing with canal boat children and they are abbreviated. Little is reprinted concerning "educational tests" which were one-minute tests of arithmetic and spelling.

The report is centered somewhat on "education." This emphasis was probably due to Gordon's position. There was much besides the absence of schooling which could have contributed to the poor performance of canal boat children on the Stanford-Binet. The intellectual level of their illiterate parents, while sufficient to stimulate the intelligence of young children, may not have sustained its growth, causing the observed decline of intelligence with age.

If this report had been widely read, it is possible that the controversy about intelligence tests would have subsided more quickly. Heredity influences the IQ. Environment influences the IQ. These statements are not contradictory, because intelligence at any moment is the result of the joint outcome of the two.

TESTS AMONG CANAL BOAT CHILDREN

In order to test the effect of a lack of schooling on the responses to "intelligence" tests, a school was chosen attended by children who had had little or no schooling—a special school for Canal Boat children.

The following quotations from a report on living-in on canal boats gives a good description of the life and education of these children. The report was drawn up in May 1921, and contains many facts of interest in connection with the present investigation.

Referring to the Canal Boat population generally, the report states:

> . . . but the majority of witnesses have agreed that, so far as health, cleanliness, morality, feeding and clothing are concerned, they are fully equal, if not superior, to town dwellers of a similar class.

In reference to the health of the children, it further says:

> . . . but taking the evidence as a whole, we cannot assert that the health of Canal Boat children is worse than that of those who live in the crowded dwellings of our large cities. Probably the open-air life during the day does something to counteract the conditions at night. Certainly the children do not appear to be nearly so liable to infectious diseases as those who live on shore, and this is in accordance with what we should naturally expect, as they must be less exposed to infection.

As regards child labour the Committee considers that without doubt these children are useful to the boatmen, particularly when they are 12 years of age and upwards.

As to education, the report continues:

> There remains the question of education, and here the evidence is overwhelming and practically unanimous that under the present circumstances Canal Boat children are scandalously under-educated. When their manner of life is considered, it is not surprising; their only opportunities for schooling occur when the boats are tied up for

loading or discharging, and the fact that many of the adult boat population are themselves unable to read or write has a tendency to make them lax in seeing that their children take full advantage of their opportunities.

It was calculated that in one part of the system half the children had not put in twenty half-day attendances in the year. From other statistics it appeared that 532 children averaged only forty-six half-day attendances during a period of sixteen months, and that if those children who lived on shore part of the time were eliminated the average of the remaining 354 was only twenty-two half-days. How small this attendance really is may be well judged when it is compared with the 360 half-day attendances in the year of the child in the ordinary Elementary School.

From the registers of the school under review it appears that the children only attend about once a month for one to perhaps two and a half days. The maximum continuous attendance of any child was five half-days, and such a number of attendances was very exceptional. It is true that in between their attendances here they have the opportunity of attending other schools, e.g., in Birmingham and elsewhere. It is unnecessary to emphasise the difficulties of teaching such children.

In referring to the future careers of the children, the report adds:

> It may be pointed out in this connection that want of education practically ties these children down to the occupation of their fathers, and, however useful this may be from the point of view of the industry, we cannot bring ourselves to consider it as a serious argument in comparison with the prospects of the children.

As to the number of Canal Boat children statistics are very meagre. It was estimated by the Board of Education that for the year 1919 there were 1,112 children of school age. In another estimate the number of children was given as 1,343, of whom 726 were of school age. Of these, 629 had either never been to school or had practically no education; there appeared to be only 97 whose education could be considered good or fair.

The following additional information, which seems to be reliable, may be of interest. The Canal Boat population as a rule, is born, lives and dies on the boats. It is stated that at least £4 a week is earned on an average, even in bad times; at other times considerably more. Some of the men even own their own boats. These people appear to live very isolated lives with very little social intercourse. To quote once more from the report:

> Life on board these boats appears to be of an almost patriarchal character, and there was a general agreement among witnesses that the presence of the wife and mother on board helps to preserve a high standard of morality among the men, and a kindly but efficient discipline among the children.

When the boats remain in a town for loading and unloading, the children do not appear to mix readily with other children; they attend places of entertainment, such as cinemas, etc., and have money to spend. Many of the children are well dressed, clean and appear fairly intelligent, although some of the older ones are undoubtedly very dull. The majority were found to be anxious to talk, but it was often difficult to understand what they said owing to their indistinct articulation and their use of unrecognisable words. As can be well imagined, the teacher of such a school has a most difficult task, for one day she may have thirty children aged from 5 to 14 years, half of whom can neither read nor do the simplest calculation; on the next day she may have but one pupil. The discipline during the inspections was excellent; the children were interested, and anxious to do their best.

To sum up, these children in respect to health, cleanliness, morality, feeding, etc., are fully equal, if not superior, to town dwellers of a similar character. That they are not mentally defective, as is generally understood by that term, is shown by the life and wages of their parents, who in many cases have had no education and can neither read nor write. Their intellectual life, on the other hand, is of most meagre description, owing to their lack of education and also owing to their social isolation.

The tests

The tests used in these investigations were those described by L. M. Terman, in his "Measurement of Intelligence," 1919. They are called "The Stanford Revision and Extension Tests" and are based on the Binet-Simon Scale, but with considerable revisions and extensions. Full details and explanations are given in the book. The instructions and scoring in the book and record booklet were followed as closely as possible. A few necessary changes were made. For example, in VIII_3 (c), "What's the thing to do if a playmate hits you without meaning to do it?" for "playmate," "boy" or "girl," as the case may be, was substituted; in III_4 (b), "An apple and a peach. In what way are they alike?" for "peach" was substituted "orange"; in XIV_6 "Change places" was substituted for "trade places." In IX_3, "pennies" was substituted for "cents"; the absurdity of the question as thus altered was never noticed; it was thought better, however, to keep the questions arithmetically as near as possible to the original. In the same question "shopkeeper" was used in place of "storekeeper."

In the first school tested (School B) the "abbreviated scale" was used. As the results were interesting, and unexpectedly subnormal, the full scale was used for School A. All the children present in the two schools were tested. The result of the two scales were carefully compared, and it was found on calculation that there was on the average a difference of less than a week in M.A. between them. Throughout the following report by the term "intelligence" is meant "intelligence" as found by the tests—nothing more unless otherwise stated. Whether this is real intelligence as is understood by the common use of the term is quite another matter.

In addition to these Stanford revision tests, standardised tests in the speed of reading (discontinuous), in the speed of adding, and in the speed of subtracting were given to all. These tests, standardised for age, were the only ones available when the investigation was begun. A full account of them is given in "Mental Tests" by P. B. Ballard (1920, pages 136, 187). They are one-minute tests and occupy very little time.

* * *

Results of the tests

Two facts became very evident as the tests proceeded:
(i) The lowness of the "intelligence" of these children.
(ii) The decided decrease of "intelligence" with an increase of age.

Mental and scholastic quotients

In Table 1 are given the results obtained in [B] school.

The average I.Q. for the remaining 40 children was 67.9.

The correlation between the mental and educational quotients for the 36 children was 0.715, P.E. ± 0.054. For 57 per cent of the children the difference between the I.Q. and educational quotient was only five points or less, and for 83 per cent ten points or less.

The average I.Q. (69.6) for the 76 children is very low; it is, in fact, only a little higher than that found by Burt in schools for mentally defective children (63.3). As in the schools for physical defectives, the girls test considerably lower than the boys (65.6 compared with 75.1). This difference, however, is probably to a large extent due to the girls being more than a year older than the boys on an average, i.e., 9 years 10 months, compared with 8 years 9 months of boys, for, as has already been explained, the older the children the worse they tested. The educational quotients of the thirty-six children who could be tested in reading, adding and subtracting was 70.4; slightly less than their I.Q., 71.5. In spelling the

Table 1. Average mental and educational quotients of those who could do all the educational tests

	No.	I.Q.	E.Q.*
Boys	14	77.6	70.8
Girls	22	67.6	70.1
Boys and Girls	36	71.5	70.4

*The "educational quotient" (E.Q.) is the average of the three subjects: reading, adding, and subtracting.

quotient (63.0) was considerably less than that of any of the other tests, the girls being especially weak in this subject, although they were slightly better than the boys in reading. The I.Q. of the forty children, who had no scholastic attainments, was 67.9, a quotient that is slightly lower than that of the other children.

It is evident that the low educational quotient is due to the lack of schooling. It is no so clear, however, why the I.Q. is so much below that of ordinary Elementary School children, unless the majority are "mentally defective," or unless the "intelligence" tests used depend on school attainments, or on the mental exercises given in schools.

Before, however, considering this question further, it is necessary to deal more precisely with the question of age and "intelligence." The correlation between the I.Q.'s and age—i.e., the correlation by rank, the children in order of ages, the oldest first and the youngest last—was as follows;

	No.	Observed Correlation	P.E.
ρ (calc. from)	76	−.755	±.033

That is to say, the older the child the less his "intelligence." This negative correlation is remarkably high, but still more remarkable is the result shown in Table 2, in which are given the ages and I.Q.'s of children in the same family. There are twenty-two cases in which two or more

Table 2. I.Q.'s and ages of children in the same family*

Family	Sex and age	I.Q.	Sex and age	I.Q.	Sex and age	I.Q.	Sex and Age	I.Q.
1	g. 13–1	59	b. 10–1	72	g. 8–0	75	b. 6–4	98
2	b. 10–6	74	g. 8–4	72	g. 6–5	74	b. 4–7	87
3	g. 10–7	38	b. 9–1	71	g. 7–5	64	g. 5–1	79
4	g. 12–9	78	g. 10–0	62	g. 8–5	82	g. 5–8	79
5	g. 13–8	58	g. 11–6	65	b. 9–6	76	b. 7–3	100
6	g. 12–1	43	b. 10–10	64	b. 6–10	84		
7	g. 12–2	67	g. 8–7	78	g. 6–2	93		
8	b. 10–1	70	b. 7–7	82	b. 6–2	97		
9	g. 12–1	58	b. 10–9	41	g. 9–7	38		
10	b. 12–1	58	b. 10–0	62	g. 7–10	70		
11	g. 12–8	75	b. 9–10	79	g. 5–1	83		
12	g. 11–6	65	b. 8–4	72				
13	g. 10–7	68	b. 6–6	96				
14	g. 9–3	70	b. 6–11	90				
15	b. 13–6	51	g. 11–4	68				
16	g. 11–0	68	b. 9–7	90				
17	b. 11–1	63	g. 5–9	82				
18	b. 7–5	77	g. 4–11	76				
19	g. 13–0	51	g. 10–3	63				
20	g. 13–11	43	g. 9–11	63				
21	g. 11–11	55	g. 8–3	70				
22	g. 14–0	33	b. 6–5	85				

*g. = girl; b. = boy. Age is given in years and months.

children of the same family are attending this school—eleven families with two children, six with three children and five with four children.

With one or two exceptions, an increase of age is found to be associated in the same family with a decrease in I.Q. Family No. 9 is one of the exceptions; the children are dirty and of a low-grade type, and all are very dull. The oldest (12–1) could read a little (reading age 6–10), could add 1 + 2 and 4 + 1 but could get no further, and could not take 1 from 2. The other two in the family could not read any of the words in the list, neither could they add or subtract any of the numbers given in the tests. One significant fact is noticeable in many of the families, and it is that in the same family the mental ages are practically the same, although the chronological ages differ very considerably, e.g., 7–0, 6–3, 6–0; 5–6, 5–6; 6–9, 6–6; 6–0 and 6–3. This peculiarity seems to indicate that for children associating only with uneducated brothers and sisters there is a tendency to equalisation of mental ages.

Figure 1 gives these results graphically. The average age and I.Q. of all the oldest children were calculated and then entered at the appropriate point—there were twenty-two, their average age was 11.6 years, their average I.Q. was 60: so with the second children in a family, etc. Again, in the case of the youngest of four in a family: there were five such children, with an average age of 5.7 years and an average I.Q. of about 87.

Summary and conclusions

1. Life, habits and education of Canal Boat children. Canal Boat population live an isolated life, almost patriarchal in character. In health, morals, etc., they compare favourably with town dwellers of the same class. The children are "scandalously under-educated"; their attendance at school

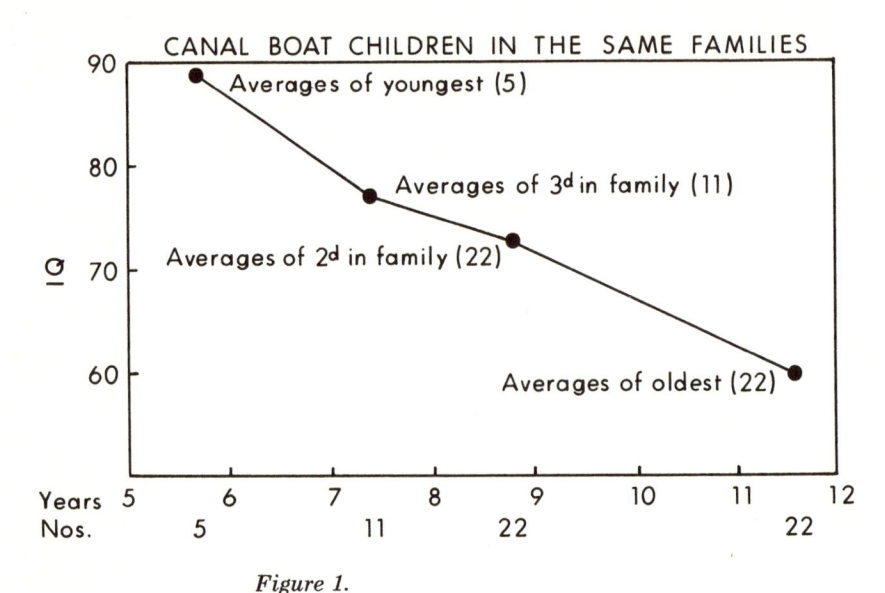

Figure 1.

averages about 4 to 5 per cent., compared with the 88 per cent of children in ordinary Elementary Schools.

2. The abbreviated scale of the Stanford revision tests was used, together with standardised tests in the speed of reading, adding and subtracting, and at a subsequent period a standardised test in spelling.

3. The average I.Q. of the seventy-six children tested was 69.6—a very low I.Q. when compared with those found in ordinary Elementary Schools. In a very superior (socially) school the I.Q. is 112; in a very poor school, 87; in schools for physically defective children, 85; and in schools for mentally defective children, 63.

4. The boys tested considerably higher than the girls, the latter being roughly a year more retarded than the boys. This retardation, however, may be accounted for, at all events in part, by the greater average age of the girls (9 years 10 months, against 8 years 9 months of the boys), for it has been shown that the older the children the less their "intelligence" as found by the tests.

5. The educational quotient of the thirty-six children who could do the simple scholastic tests was only slightly lower than the I.Q. (70.4 and 71.5 respectively); the educational quotients of both boys and girls was practically the same (70.8 and 70.1). Whereas in the case of the girls their educational quotient was slightly higher than their I.Q.; in the case of the boys it was considerably lower.

6. Spelling was the weakest subject, especially among the girls, whose spelling quotient was 60.9 compared with 66.0 of the boys.

7. The correlation (r) between the mental and educational quotients was .715, P.E. .054—a high correlation.

8. The correlation between "intelligence" (test) and age was –.755, P.E. ± .033—a very high negative correlation, indicating unquestionably that with an increase of age there was a corresponding decrease in "intelligence." The same conclusion was to be drawn from a comparison of the I.Q. of the children in the same family. Here also it is evident that even in the same family the older the child the less "intelligence" he has. This result makes it almost certain that the low average "intelligence" of the children in this school is not due to heredity, seeing that the youngest children test more or less normally, *i.e.*, are of average "intelligence."

The fact that there is a marked decrease in "intelligence" with an increase of age, and that this is especially noticeable among children in the same family, suggests very convincingly that the low average "intelligence" of these children is not due to heredity. It may be due to environment, or to the lack of schooling, or to both combined. But as it has been shown that the correlation between the results of the mental and scholastic tests is very high, and further that the average quotients for these two sets of tests are approximately the same, it may be assumed with some reasonableness that the lack of schooling has affected both "mental" and scholastic attainments to the same extent. In other words, without education (schooling) children are very much handicapped when tested by the "intelligence" tests used in this investigation—in fact, to nearly the same extent as when tested by purely scholastic tests. It is clear, however, that for very young children there cannot be any educational tests, as such children have, as a rule, no so-called scholastic attainments, and for this reason the "mental" tests are necessarily not of the same character as those for older children, and in consequence the children test normally. Without the mental effort or mental exercises associated with schooling it would appear that there has been very little mental development on the intellectual side. How far there has been a similar lack of development among these children in connection with problems touching their own especial environment, it is difficult to say and, without tests especially devised and standardised for children in such surroundings, impossible to measure.

29

JEAN PIAGET (B. 1896)

The language and thought of the child (1923)

Piaget is perhaps today's most famous child psychologist. Part of his fame is due to his productivity: a recent bibliography of Piaget's writings prepared on the occasion of his seventieth birthday filled thirty-five pages. But his productivity stems to a large extent from the fertility of his ideas.

In his autobiography in History of Psychology in Autobiography, *Volume IV, the most taciturn of his publications, Piaget indicates that he began scientific publication at age ten. There has been no let-up since.*

His first interest was in animal taxonomy. This shifted, at about age 23, to what may be called the taxonomy of child thought. Piaget is a master at conceptualizing and describing the categories of thought which occur in psychological development.

No one selection can do justice to the multiplicity of Piaget's contributions in psychology. The article presented here is taken from Piaget's first book Language and Thought in the Child, *which was published in French in 1923 and in English in 1926. It shows how Piaget at age 26 was able to manage such unmanageable material as children's conversations.*

We have chosen excerpts from his book which refer to only two children. Additional studies, reported in the same book, show that Lev and Pie are not unusual in their use of language. This book immediately received the attention of child psychologists.

The excerpts are reprinted with the permission of Routledge and Kegan Paul, London, and the Humanities Press, New York.

THE MATERIAL

The method we have adopted is as follows. Two of us followed each a child (a boy) for about a month at the morning class at the *Maison des*

Petits de l'Institut Rousseau, taking down in minute detail and in its context everything that was said by the child. In the class where our two subjects were observed the scholars draw or make whatever they like; they model and play at games of arithmetic and reading, etc. These activities take place in complete freedom; no check is put upon any desire that may manifest itself to talk or play together; no intervention takes place unless it is asked for. The children work individually or in groups, as they choose; the groups are formed and then break up again without any interference on the part of the adult; the children go from one room to another (modelling room, drawing room, etc.) just as they please without being asked to do any continuous work so long as they do not themselves feel any desire for it. In short, these school-rooms supply a first-class field of observation for everything connected with the study of the social life and of the language of childhood.

We must anticipate at once any objection that may be advanced on the plea that since these children were used as subjects they were not observed in natural conditions. In the first place, the children, when they are in the play-room with their friends, talk just as much as they would at home, since they are allowed to talk all day long at school, and do not feel censured or constrained in any way whatsoever. In the second place, they do not talk any more at school than they would at home, since observation shows that up to a certain age, varying between 5 and 7½, children generally prefer to work individually rather than in groups even of two. Moreover, as we have taken down in its entirety the context of our two subjects' conversations, especially when it was addressed to an adult, it will be quite easy to eliminate from our statistics all that is not spontaneous talk on the part of the children, *i.e.,* all that may have been said in answer to questions that were put to them.

Once the material was collected, we utilized it as follows. We began by numbering all the subjects' sentences. As a rule the child speaks in short sentences interspersed with long silences or with the talk of other children. Each sentence is numbered separately. Where the talk is a little prolonged, the reader must not be afraid of reckoning several consecutive sentences to one number, so long as to each sentence containing a definite idea only one number is affixed. In such cases, which are rare enough, the division is necessarily arbitrary, but this is of no importance for statistics dealing with hundreds of sentences.

Once the talk has been portioned out into numbered sentences, we endeavour to classify these into elementary functional categories. It is this method of classification which we are now about to study.

1. An example of the talk taken down

Let us first of all give one complete example of the documents collected in this way, and let us examine it in all its complexity:

> 23. Pie (to Ez who is drawing a tram-car with carriages in tow): *But the trams that are hooked on behind don't have any flags.* (No answer.)

24. (Talking about his tram). *They don't have any carriages hooked on*... (He was addressing no one in particular. No one answers him.)

25. (To Béa), *'T'sa tram that hasn't got no carriages.* (No answer.)

26. (To Hei), *This tram hasn't got no carriages, Hei, look, it isn't red, d'you see*... (No answer.)

27. (Lev says out loud, 'A funny gentleman' from a certain distance, and without addressing himself to Pie or to anyone else). (Pie: *A funny gentleman!* Goes on drawing his tram.)

28. *I'm leaving the tram white.*

29. (Ez who is drawing next to him says, 'I'm doing it yellow'), *No, you musn't do it all yellow.*

30. *I'm doing the stair-case, look.* (Béa answers, 'I can't come this afternoon, I've got a Eurhythmic class.')

31. *What did you say?* (Béa repeats the same sentence.)

32. *What did you say?* (Béa does not answer. She has forgotten what she said, and gives Ro a push.)

33. (To Béa), *Leave him alone.*

34. (Mlle B. asks Ez if he would like to come with her), *Come here Ez, it isn't finished.* 34 bis. *Please teacher, Ez hasn't finished.*

35. (Without addressing himself to anyone,) *I'm doing some black stones....*

36. (Id), *Pretty... these stones.*

37. (To Ez), *Better than you, eh?* (No answer. Ez had not heard the previous remark.)

We have chosen this example from Pie (6½ years) because it is taken during the most sociable activity of which this child is capable: he is drawing at the same table as his bosom friend, Ez, and is talking to him the whole time. It would therefore be natural in a case of this kind if the sole function of speech were to communicate thought. But let us examine the matter a little more closely. It will be seen that from the social point of view the significance of these sentences or fragments of sentences is extremely varied. When Pie says: *"They don't have... etc."* (24), or *"I'm doing... etc."* (35) he is not speaking to anyone. He is thinking aloud over his own drawing, just as people of the working classes mutter to themselves over their work. Here, then, is a first category which should be singled out, and which in future we shall designate as *monologue*. When Pie says to Hei or to Béa: *"'T'sa tram... etc."* (25) or *"This tram ... etc."* (26) he seems on this occasion to want to make himself understood; but on closer examination it will be seen that he cares very little who is listening to him (he turns from Béa to Hei to say exactly the same thing) and, furthermore, that he does not care whether the person he addresses has really heard him or not. He believes that someone is listening to him; that is all he wants. Similarly, when Béa gives him an answer devoid of any connexion with what he has just been saying (30), it is obvious that he does not seek to understand his friend's observation nor to make his own remark any clearer. Each one sticks to his own idea and is perfectly satisfied (30–32). The audience is there simply as a stimulus. Pie talks about himself just as he does when he soliloquizes, but with the added pleasure of feeling himself an object of interest to other people. Here then is a new category which we shall call the *collective monologue*. It is to be distinguished from the preceding category and also from those in which thoughts are actually exchanged or information given. This last case constitutes a separate category which we shall call *adapted information,* and to which we can relegate sentences 23 and 34b. In this case the child talks, not at random, but to specified persons, and with the object of making them listen and understand. In addition to these practical and objective forms of information, we can distinguish others of a more subjective character consisting of commands (33), expressions of derision or criticism, or assertions of personal superiority, etc. (37). Finally, we may distinguish mere senseless repetitions, questions and answers.

Let us now establish the criteria of these various categories.

2. The functions of child language classified

The talk of our two subjects may be divided into two large groups—the *ego-centric* and the *socialized*. When a child utters phrases belonging to the first group, he does not bother to know to whom he is speaking nor whether he is being listened to. He talks either for himself or for the pleasure of associating anyone who happens to be there with the activity of the moment. This talk is ego-centric, partly because the child speaks only about himself, but chiefly because he does not attempt to place himself at the point of view of his hearer. Anyone who happens to be there will serve as an audience. The child asks for no more than an apparent interest, though he has the illusion (except perhaps in pure soliloquy if even then) of being heard and understood. He feels no desire to influence his hearer nor to tell him anything; not unlike a certain type of drawing-room conversation where every one talks about himself and no one listens.

Ego-centric speech may be divided into three categories:

1. *Repetition (echolalia):* We shall deal only with the repetition of words and syllables. The child repeats them for the pleasure of talking, with no thought of talking to anyone, nor even at times of saying words that will make sense. This is a remnant of baby prattle, obviously devoid of any social character.

2. *Monologue:* The child talks to himself as though he were thinking aloud. He does not address anyone.

3. *Dual or collective monologue:* The contradiction contained in the phrase recalls the paradox of those conversations between children which we were discussing, where an outsider is always associated with the action or thought of the moment, but is expected neither to attend nor to understand. The point of view of the other person is never taken into account; his presence serves only as a stimulus.

In *Socialized speech* we can distinguish:

4. *Adapted information:* Here the child really exchanges his thoughts with others, either by telling his hearer something that will interest him

and influence his actions, or by an actual interchange of ideas by argument or even by collaboration in pursuit of a common aim.

Adapted information takes place when the child adopts the point of view of his hearer, and when the latter is not chosen at random. Collective monologues, on the other hand, take place when the child talks only about himself, regardless of his hearers' point of view, and very often without making sure whether he is being attended to or understood. We shall examine this criterion in more detail later on.

5. *Criticism:* This group includes all remarks made about the work or behaviour of others, but having the same character as adapted information; in other words, remarks specified in relation to a given audience. But these are more affective than intellectual, *i.e.*, they assert the superiority of the self and depreciate others. One might be tempted in view of this to place this group among the ego-centric categories. But "ego-centric" is to be taken in an intellectual, not in an ethical sense, and there can be no doubt that in the cases under consideration one child acts upon another in a way that may give rise to arguments, quarrels, and emulation, whereas the utterances of the collective monologue are without any effect upon the person to whom they are addressed. The shades of distinction, moreover, between adapted information and criticism are often extremely subtle and can only be established by the context.

6. *Commands, requests* and *threats:* In all of these there is definite interaction between one child and another.

7. *Questions:* Most questions asked by children among themselves call for an answer and can therefore be classed as socialized speech, with certain reservations to which we shall draw attention later on.

8. *Answers:* By these are meant answers to real questions (with interrogation mark) and to commands. They are not to be compared to those answers given in the course of conversation (categ. 4), to remarks which are not questions but belong to "information."

These, then, are the eight fundamental categories of speech. It goes without saying that this classification, like any other, is open to the charge of artificiality. What is more important, however, is that it should stand the test of practical application, *i.e.*, that any reader who has made himself familiar with our criteria should place the same phrases more or less in the same categories. Four people have been engaged in classifying the material in hand, including that which is dealt with in the next chapter, and the results of their respective enquiries were found to coincide within 2 or 3 per cent.

Let us now return to one of these categories in order to establish the constants of our statistical results.

3. Repetition (Escholalia)

Everyone knows how, in the first years of his life, a child loves to repeat the words he hears, to imitate syllables and sounds, even those of which he hardly understands the meaning. It is not easy to define the function of this imitation in a single formula. From the point of view of behaviour, imitation is, according to Claparède, an ideomotor adaptation by means of which the child reproduces and then simulates the movements and ideas of those around him. But from the point of view of personality and from the social point of view, imitation would seem to be, as Janet and Baldwin maintain, a confusion between the I and the not-I, between the activity of one's own body and that of other people's bodies. At his most imitative stage, the child mimics with his whole being, identifying himself with his model. But this game, though it seems to imply an essentially social attitude, really indicates one that is essentially ego-centric. The copied movements and behaviour have nothing in them to interest the child, there is no adaptation of the I to anyone else; there is a confusion by which the child does not know that he is imitating, but plays his game as though it were his own creation. This is why children up to the age of 6 or 7, when they have had something explained to them and are asked to do it immediately afterwards, invariably imagine that they have discovered by themselves what in reality they are only repeating from a model. In such cases imitation is completely unconscious, as we have often had occasion to observe.

This mental disposition constitutes a fringe on the child's activity, which persists throughout different ages, changing in contents but always identical in function. At the ages of our two children, many of the remarks collected partake of the nature of pure repetition or echolalia. The part played by this echolalia is simply that of a game; the child enjoys repeating the words for their own sake, for the pleasure they give him, without any external adaptation and without an audience. Here are a few typical examples:

>(Mlle E. teaches My the word 'celluloid') Lev, busy with his drawing at another table: *"Luloïd ... le le loid ..."* etc.
>(Before an aquarium Pie stands outside the group and takes no interest in what is being shown. Somebody says the word 'triton'). Pie: *"Triton ... triton."* Lev (after hearing the clock strike 'coucou'): *"Coucou ... coucou."*

These pure repetitions, rare enough at the age of Pie and Lev, have no interest for us. Their sudden appearance in the midst of ordinary conversation is more illuminating.

>Jac says to Ez: "Look, Ez, your pants are showing." Pie, who is in another part of the room immediately repeats: *"Look, my pants are showing, and my shirt, too."*

Now there is not a word of truth in all this. It is simply the joy of repeating for its own sake that makes Pie talk in this way, *i.e.*, the pleasure of using words not for the sake of adapting oneself to the conversation, but for the sake of playing with them.

>We have seen ... the example of Pie hearing Lev say: "A funny gentleman," and repeating this remark for his own amusement al-

though he is busy drawing a tram-car (27). This shows how little repetition distracts Pie from his class-work. (Ez says: "I want to ride on the train up there"), Pie: *"I want to ride on the train up there."*

There is no need to multiply examples. The process is always the same. The children are occupied with drawing or playing; they all talk intermittently without listening very much to each other; but words thrown out are caught on the bounce, like balls. Sometimes they are repeated as they are, like the remarks of the present category, sometimes they set in action those dual monologues of which we shall speak later on.

The frequency of repetition is about 2% and 1% for Pie and Lev respectively. If the talk be divided into sections of 100 sentences, then in each hundred will be found repetitions in the proportion of 1%, 4%, 0%, 5%, 3%, etc.

4. Monologue

Janet and the psycho-analysts have shown us how close in their opinion is the bond which originally connected word and action, words being so packed with concrete significance that the mere fact of uttering them, even without any reference to action, could be looked upon as the factor in initiating the action in question.

Now, independently of the question of origins, it is a matter of common observation that for the child words are much nearer to action and movement than for us. This leads us to two results which are of considerable importance in the study of child language in general and of the monologue in particular. 1. The child is impelled, even when he is alone, to speak as he acts, to accompany his movements with a play of shouts and words. True, there are silences, and very curious ones at that, when children work together as in the *Maison des Petits*. But, alongside of these silences, how many a soliloquy must take place when a child is alone in a room, or when children speak without addressing themselves to anyone. 2. If the child talks even when he is alone as an accompaniment to his action, he can reverse the process and use words to bring about what the action of itself is powerless to do. Hence the habit of romancing or inventing, which consists in creating reality by words and magical language, in working on things by means of words alone, apart from any contact either with them or with persons.

These two varieties belong to the same category, that of the monologue. It is worth noting that the monologue still plays an important part between the ages of 6 and 7. At this age the child soliloquizes even in the society of other children, as in the class-rooms where our work has been carried on. We have sometimes seen as many as ten children seated at separate tables or in groups of two or three, each talking to himself without taking any notice of his neighbour.

Here are a few examples of simple monologue (the first variety) where the child simply accompanies his action with sentences spoken aloud.

Lev sits down at his table alone: "*I want to do that drawing, there ... I want to draw something, I do. I shall need a big piece of paper to do that.*"

Lev knocks over a game: "*There! everything's fallen down.*"

Lev has just finished his drawing: "*Now I want to do something else.*"

Lev is a little fellow who is very much wrapped up in himself. He is always telling every one else what he is doing at the moment. In his case, therefore, monologue tends in the direction of collective monologue, where every one talks about himself without listening to the others. All the same, when he is alone he goes on announcing what he is going to do, with no other audience than himself. It is in these circumstances that we have the true monologue.

In the case of Pie, the monologue is rarer, but more true to type; the child will often talk with the sole aim of marking the rhythm of his action, without exhibiting a shade of self-satisfaction in the process. Here is one of Pie's conversations with context, where monologue is interspersed with other forms of talk:

53. Pie takes his arithmetic copy-book and turns the pages: "*1, 2 ... 3, 4, 5, 6, 7 ... 8 ... 8, 8, 8, 8 and 8 ... 9. Number 9, number 9, number 9* (singing) *I want number 9*. (This is the number he is going to represent by a drawing).

54. (Looking at Béa who is standing by the counting-frame but without speaking to him): *Now I'm going to do 9, 9, I'm doing 9, I'm doing 9.* (He draws).

55. (Mlle. L. passes by his table without saying anything). *Look, teacher, 9, 9, 9 ... number 9.*

56. (He goes to the frame to see what colour to choose for his number so that it should correspond to the 9th row in the frame). *Pink chalk, it will have to be 9.* (He sings).

57. (To Ez as he passes): *I'm doing 9, I am*—(Ez) What are you going to do?—*Little rounds.*

58. (Accident to the pencil) *Ow, ow!*

59. *Now I've got to 9.*"

The whole of this monologue has no further aim than to accompany the action as it takes place. There are only two diversions. Pie would like to inform someone about his plans (sentences 55 and 57). But in spite of this the monologue runs on uninterrupted as though Pie were alone in the room. Speech in this case functions only as a stimulus, and in nowise as a means of communication. Pie no doubt enjoys the feeling of being in a room full of people, but if he were alone, his remarks would be substantially the same.

At the same time it is obvious that this stimulus contains a certain danger. Although in some cases it accelerates action, it also runs the risk of supplanting it. "When the distance between two points has to be traversed, a man can actually walk it with his legs, but he can also stand still and shout: 'On, on! ...' like an opera singer." Hence the second variety child soliloquy where speech serves not so much to accompany and accelerate action as to replace it by an illusory satisfaction. To this last group belong certain cases of word magic; but these, frequent as they are, occur only in the strictest solitude. What is more usual is that the child takes so much pleasure in soliloquizing that he forgets his activity and does nothing but talk. The word then becomes a command to the external world. Here is an example of pure and of collective monologue ... where the child gradually works himself up into issuing a command to physical objects and to animals:

> *"Now then, it's coming* (a tortoise). *It's coming, it's coming, it's coming. Get out of the way, Da, it's coming, it's coming, it's coming. ... Come along, tortoise!"*
> A little later, after having watched the aquarium, soliloquizing all the time: *"Oh, isn't it* (a salamander) *surprised at the great big giant* (fish)," he exclaims, *"Salamander, you must eat up the fishes!"*

In short, we have here the mechanism of solitary games, where, after thinking out his action aloud, the child, under the influence of verbal excitement as much as of any voluntary illusion, comes to command both animate and inanimate beings.

In conclusion, the general characteristic of monologues of this category is that the words have no social function. In such cases speech does not communicate the thoughts of the speaker, it serves to accompany, to reinforce, or to supplement his action. It may be said that this is simply a side-tracking of the original function of language, and that the child commands himself and external things just as he has learned to command and speak to others. There can be no doubt that without originally imitating others and without the desire to call his parents and to influence them, the child would probably never learn to talk; in a sense, then, the monologue is due only to a repercussion of words acquired in relation to other people. It should be remembered, however, that throughout the time when he is learning to speak, the child is constantly the victim of a confusion between his own point of view and that of other people. For one thing, he does not know that he is imitating. For another, he talks as much to himself as to others, as much for the pleasure of prattling or of perpetuating some past state of being as for the sake of giving orders. It is therefore impossible to say that the monologue is either prior to or later than the more socialized forms of language; both spring from that undifferentiated state where cries and words accompany action, and then tend to prolong it; and both react one upon the other at the very outset of their development.

But as we pass from early childhood to the adult stage, we shall naturally see the gradual disappearance of the monologue, for it is a primitive and infantile function of language. It is remarkable in this connexion that in the cases of Pie and Lev this form should still constitute about 5% and

15% respectively of their total conversation. This percentage is considerable when the conditions in which the material was collected are taken into account. The difference in the percentages, however, corresponds to a marked difference in temperament, Pie being of a more practical disposition than Lev, better adapted to reality and therefore to the society of other children. When he speaks, it is therefore generally in order to make himself heard. It is true, as we saw, that when Pie does talk to himself his monologue is on the whole more genuine than Lev's, but Pie does not produce in such abundance those rather self-satisfied remarks in which a child is continually announcing his plans to himself, and which are the obvious sign of a certain imaginative exuberance.

5. Collective monologue

This form is the most social of the ego-centric varieties of child language, since to the pleasure of talking it adds that of soliloquizing before others and of interesting, or thinking to interest, them in one's own action and one's own thoughts. But as we have already pointed out, the child who acts in this manner does not succeed in making his audience listen, because, as a matter of fact, he is not really addressing himself to it. He is not speaking to anyone. He talks aloud to himself in front of others. This way of behaving reappears in certain men and women of a puerile disposition (certain hysterical subjects, if hysteria be described as the survival of infantile characteristics) who are in the habit of thinking aloud as though they were talking to themselves, but are also conscious of their audience. Suppress the slightly theatrical element in this attitude, and you have the equivalent of the collective monologue in normal children.

The examples . . . should now be re-read if we wish to realize how socially ineffectual is this form of language, *i.e.*, how little impression it makes upon the person spoken to. Pie makes the same remark to two different persons (25 and 26), and is in nowise astonished when he is neither listened to nor answered by either of them. Later on he asks Béa twice, "What did you say?" (31 and 32), but without listening to her. He busies himself with his own idea and his drawing, and talks only about himself.

Here are a few more examples which show how little a child is concerned with speaking to anyone in particular, or even with making himself heard:

> Mlle L. tells a group of children that owls cannot see by day. Lev: *"Well, I know quite well that it can't."*
> Lev (at a table where a group is at work): *"I've already done 'moon' so I'll have to change it."*
> Lev picks up some barley-sugar crumbs: *"I say, I've got a lovely pile of eye-glasses."*
> Lev: *"I say, I've got a gun to kill him with. I say, I am the captain on horseback. I say, I've got a horse and a gun as well."*

The opening phrase, "I say, I" which occurs in most of these sentences is significant. Every one is supposed to be listening. This is what distinguishes this type of remark from pure monologue. But with regard to its contents it is the exact equivalent of the monologue. The child is simply thinking out his actions aloud, with no desire to give anyone any information about it.

We shall find in the next chapter examples of collective monologues no longer isolated or chosen from the talk of two children only, but taken down verbatim from all-round conversations. This particular category need not therefore occupy us any longer.

The collective monologue represents about 23% of Lev's and 30% of Pie's entire conversation. But we have seen that it is harder to distinguish the pure from the collective monologue in Lev's case than in Pie's. Taking therefore the two types of monologue together, we may say that with Lev they represent 38%, and with Pie 35% of the subject's sum of conversation.

6. Adapted information

The criterion of adapted information, as opposed to the pseudo-information contained in the collective monologue, is that it is successful. The child actually makes his hearer listen, and contrives to influence him, *i.e.*, to tell him something. This time the child speaks from the point of view of his audience. The function of language is no longer merely to excite the speaker to action, but actually to communicate his thoughts to other people. These criteria, however, are difficult of application, and we shall try to discover some that admit of greater precision.

It is adapted information, moreover, that gives rise to dialogue. The dialogues of children deserve to be made the object of a special and very searching investigation, for it is probably through the habit of arguing that, as Janet and Baldwin have insisted, we first become conscious of the rules of logic and the forms of deductive reasoning. We shall therefore attempt in the next chapter to give a rough outline of the different stages of conversation as it takes place between children. In the meantime we shall content ourselves with examining adapted information (whether it takes place in dialogue or not) in relation to the main body of talk indulged in by our two subjects, and with noting how small is the part played by this form of language in comparison to the ego-centric forms and those socialized forms of speech such as commands, threats, criticisms, etc., which are not connected with mere statement of fact.

The form in which adapted information first presents itself to us, is that of simple information. Here are a few clear examples:

> Lev is helping Geo to play Lotto: *"I think that goes here."* Geo points to a duplicate card. Lev: *"If you lose one, there will still be one left."* Then: *"You've got three of the same,"* or: *"You all see what you have to do."*
> Mlle R. calls Ar "Roger." Pie: *"He isn't called Roger."*

Such remarks as these are clearly very different from dual monologues. The child's object is definitely to convey something to his hearer.

It is from the latter's point of view that the subject speaks, and no longer from his own. Henceforward the child lays claim to be understood, and presses his claim if he does not gain his point; whereas in the collective monologue words were thrown out at random, and it little mattered where they fell.

In adapted information the child can naturally talk about himself as about any other subject of conversation. All that is needed is that his remarks should be "adapted" as in the following examples:

> Ez and Pie: "I shall have one to-morrow (a season-ticket on the tram-way)—*I shall have mine this afternoon.*"
>
> Ez and Pie are building a church with bricks: *"We could do that with parallels too. I want to put the parallels on."*

We are now in a position to define more closely the distinction between the collective monologue and adapted information. The collective monologue takes place whenever the child talks about himself, except in those cases where he does so during collaboration with his hearer (as in the example just given of the church building game), and except in cases of dialogue. Dialogue, in our view, occurs when the child who has been spoken to in a proposition, answers by talking about something that was treated of in this proposition... and does not start off on some cock-and-bull story as so often happens in collective monologue.

In conclusion, as soon as the child informs his hearer about anything but himself, or as soon as in speaking of himself, he enters into collaboration or simply into dialogue with his hearer, there is adapted information. So long as the child talks about himself without collaborating with his audience or without evoking a dialogue, there is only collective monologue.

These definitions and the inability of collective monologue to draw others into the speakers sphere of action render it all the more remarkable that with Pie and Lev adapted information numbers only half as many remarks as collective monologue. Before establishing the exact proportion we must find out what sort of things our two subjects tell each other, and what they argue about on those rare occasions when we can talk of arguments taking place between children.

On the first point we may note the complete absence between the children of anything in the nature of explanation, if by this word we mean causal explanation, *i.e.*, an answer of the form "for such a reason" to the question "why?" All the observed cases of information which might be thought to resemble explanation are statements of fact or descriptions, and are free from any desire to explain the causes of phenomena.

Here are examples of information which simply state or describe:

> Lev and Pie: *"That's 420." "It isn't 10 o'clock." "A roof doesn't look like that"* (talking of a drawing). *"This is a village, a great big village,"* etc.

Even when they talk about natural phenomena, the information they give each other never touches on causality.

The language and thought of the child 249

Lev: "Thunder rolls—*No, it doesnt roll*—It's water—*No, it doesn't roll*—What is thunder?—*Thunder is . . .*" (He doesn't go on.)

This absence of causal explanations is remarkable, especially in the case of machines, motors, bicycles, etc., which the subjects occasionally discuss, but always from what we may call the factual point of view.

Lev: *"It's on the same rail. Funny sort of cart, a motor cart—A bicycle for two men."*

Now each of these children taken separately is able to explain the mechanism of a bicycle. Pie does so imperfectly, but Lev does so quite well. Each has a number of ideas on mechanics, but they never discuss them together. Causal relations remain unexpressed and are thought about only by the individual, probably because, to the child mind they are represented by images rather than by words. Only the underlying factual element finds expression.

* * *

CONCLUSIONS

Having defined, so far as was possible the various categories of the language used by our two children, it now remains for us to see whether it is not possible to establish certain numerical constants from the material before us. We wish to emphasize at the very outset the artificial character of such abstractions. The number of unclassifiable remarks, indeed, weighs heavily in the statistics. . . . But these difficulties are immaterial. If among our results some are definitely more constant than others, then we shall feel justified in attributing to these a certain objective value.

10. The measure of ego-centrism

Among the data we have obtained there is one, incidentally of the greatest interest for the study of child logic, which seems to supply the necessary guarantee of objectivity: we mean the proportion of ego-centric language to the sum of the child's spontaneous conversation. Ego-centric language is, as we have seen, the group made up by the first three of the categories we have enumerated—*repetition, monologue* and *collective monologue.* All three have this in common that they consist of remarks that are not addressed to anyone, or not to anyone in particular, and that they evoke no reaction adapted to them on the part of anyone to whom they may chance to be addressed. Spontaneous language is therefore made up of the first seven categories, *i.e.*, of all except *answers.* It is therefore the sum total of all remarks, *minus* those which are made as an answer to a question asked by an adult or a child. We have eliminated this heading as being subject to chance circumstances; it is sufficient for a child to have come in contact with many adults or with some talkative companion, to undergo a marked change in the percentage of his answers. Answers given, not to definite questions (with interrogation mark) or commands, but in the course of the dialogue, *i.e.*, propositions answering to other propositions, have naturally been classed under the heading *information and dialogue*, so that there is nothing artificial about the omission of questions from the statistics which we shall give. The child's language *minus* his answers constitutes a complete whole in which intelligence is represented at every stage of its development.

The proportion of ego-centric to other spontaneous forms of language is represented by the following fractions:

$$\frac{Eg.\ L}{Sp.\ L} = 0\cdot47 \text{ for Lev, } \frac{Eg.\ L}{Sp.\ L} = 0\cdot43 \text{ for Pie.}$$

(The proportion of ego-centric language to the sum total of the subject's speech, including answers, is 39% for Lev and 37% for Pie.) The similarity of result for Lev and Pie is a propitious sign, especially as what difference there is corresponds to a marked difference of temperament. (Lev is certainly more ego-centric than Pie.) But the value of the result is vouched for in yet another way.

If we divide the 1400 remarks made by Lev during the month in which his talk was being studied into sections of 100 sentences, and seek to establish for each section the ratio $\frac{Eg.\ L}{Sp.\ L}$, the fraction will be found to vary only from 0·40 to 0·57, which indicates only a small maximum deviation. On the contrary, the *mean variations, i.e.*, the average of the deviations between each value and the arithmetical average of these values, is only 0·04, which is really very little.

If Pie's 1500 remarks are submitted to the same treatment, the proportions will be found to vary between 0·31 and 0·59, with an average variation of 0·06. This greater variability is just what we should expect from what we know of Pie's character, which at first sight seems more practical, better adapted than Lev's, more inclined to collaboration (particularly with his bosom friend Ez). But Pie every now and then indulges in fantasies which isolate him for several hours, and during which he soliloquizes without ceasing.

We shall see in the next chapter, moreover, that these two coefficients do actually represent the average for children between the ages of 7 and 8. The same calculation based on some 1500 remarks in quite another class-room yielded the result of 0·45 (a. v. = 0·05).

This constancy in the proportion of ego-centric language is the more remarkable in view of the fact that we have found nothing of the kind in connexion with the other coefficients which we have sought to establish. We have, it is true, determined the proportion of social factual language (*information* and *questions*) to socialized non-factual language (*criticism, commands,* and *requests*). But this proportion fluctuates from 0·72 to 2·23 with a mean variation 0·71 for Lev (as compared with 0·04 and 0·06 as the coefficients of ego-centrism), and between 0·43 and 2·33 with a mean variation of 0·42 for Pie. Similarly, the relation of ego-centric to socialized factual language yields no coefficient of any constancy.

Of all this calculation let us bear only this in mind, that our two subjects of 6½ have each an ego-centric language which amounts to nearly half of their total spontaneous speech.

The following table summarizes the functions of the language used by both these children:

	Pie	Lev
1 Repetition	2	1
2 Monologue	5	15
3 Collective Monologue	30	23
4 Adapted Information	14	13
5 Criticism	7	3
6 Commands	15	10
7 Requests	13	17
8 Answers	14	18
Ego-centric language	37	39
Spontaneous Socialized language	49	43
Sum of Socialized language	63	61
Coefficient of Ego-centrism	0.43±0.06	0.47±0.04

We must once more emphasize the fact that in all these calculations the number of remarks made by children to adults is negligible. By omitting them we raise the coefficient of ego-centrism to about 0·02, which is within the allowed limits of deviation. In future, however, we shall have completely to eliminate such remarks from our calculations, even if it means making a separate class for them. We shall, moreover, observe this rule in the next chapter where the coefficient of ego-centrism has been calculated solely on the basis of remarks made between children.

11. Conclusion

What are the conclusions we can draw from these facts? It would seem that up to a certain age we may safely admit that children think and act more ego-centrically than adults, that they share each other's intellectual life less than we do. True, when they are together they seem to talk to each other a great deal more than we do about what they are doing, but for the most part they are only talking to themselves. We, on the contrary, keep silent far longer about our action, but our talk is almost always socialized.

Such assertions may seem paradoxical. In observing children between the ages of 4 and 7 at work together in the classes of the *Maison des Petits,* one is certainly struck by silences, which are, we repeat, in no way imposed nor even suggested by the adults. One would expect, not indeed the formation of working groups, since children are slow to awake to social life, but a hubbub caused by all the children talking at once. This is not what happens. All the same, it is obvious that a child between the ages of 4 and 7, placed in the conditions of spontaneous work provided by the educational games of the *Maison des Petits,* breaks silence far oftener than does the adult at work, and seems at first sight to be continuously communicating his thoughts to those around him.

Ego-centrism must not be confused with secrecy. Reflexion in the child does not admit of privacy. Apart from thinking by images or autistic symbols which cannot be directly communicated, the child up to an age, as yet undetermined but probably somewhere about seven, is incapable of keeping to himself the thoughts which enter his mind. He says everything. He has no verbal continence. Does this mean that he socializes his thought more than we do? That is the whole question, and it is for us to see to whom the child really speaks. It may be to others. We think on the contrary that, as the preceding study shows, it is first and foremost to himself, and that speech, before it can be used to socialize thought, serves to accompany and reinforce individual activity. Let us try to examine more closely the difference between thought which is socialized but capable of secrecy, and infantile thought which is ego-centric but incapable of secrecy.

The adult, even in his most personal and private occupation, even when he is engaged on an enquiry which is incomprehensible to his fellow-beings, thinks socially, has continually in his mind's eye his collaborators or opponents, actual or eventual, at any rate members of his own profession to whom sooner or later he will announce the result of his labours. This mental picture pursues him throughout his task. The task itself is henceforth socialized at almost every stage of its development. Invention eludes this process, but the need for checking and demonstrating calls into being an inner speech addressed throughout to a hypothetical opponent, whom the imagination often pictures as one of flesh and blood. When, therefore, the adult is brought face to face with his fellow-beings, what he announces to them is something already socially elaborated and therefore roughly adapted to his audience, *i.e.*, it is comprehensible. Indeed, the further a man has advanced in his own line of thought, the better able is he to see things from the point of view of others and to make himself understood by them.

30

LEWIS M. TERMAN (1877–1956) AND ASSOCIATES

Mental and physical traits of a thousand gifted children (1925)

It has been mentioned earlier (in selection 26) that Terman's doctoral dissertation in psychology was concerned in part with gifted children. His interest in the gifted continued throughout his life.

About 1922 he began a long-term study of highly intelligent children, most of the subjects he chose having IQ's of 140 or above. The following selection consists of excerpts from his first report on this long-term study which was published by the Stanford University Press under the title listed above. The book comprises 648 pages. The pages which follow are from the preface and from the summary. They are reprinted by permission of the Stanford University Press.

Subsequent to this first report several volumes of follow-up studies of the same individuals as older children and as adults have been published. After Terman's death his associates at Stanford continued this extraordinary longitudinal project, and obtained data on some of the grandchildren of the original "children."

The work of Terman and his associates has greatly changed the popular image of the intellectually gifted child, who in 1925 was generally conceived to be an undersized weakling, ill adapted to life. While such children exist among the gifted, Terman has shown that the majority of them are healthy and do well in this world. Probably their grandchildren also will do well.

The reader may compare the study of one thousand gifted children by Terman and his associates with the study of Mozart by Barrington (selection 2) to see how far psychology had progressed in about two hundred years.

It should go without saying that a nation's resources of intellectual talent are among the most precious it will ever have. The origin of genius, the

253

natural laws of its development, and the environmental influences by which it may be affected for good or ill, are scientific problems of almost unequaled importance for human welfare. Many philosophers and scientists, from Plato and Aristotle to the present day, have recognized the truth of this. A number of factors, however, have worked together to postpone until our own time the inauguration of research in this field. Among these may be mentioned the following: (1) the influence of current beliefs, partaking of the nature of superstitions, regarding the essential nature of the Great Man, who has commonly been regarded by the masses as qualitatively set off from the rest of mankind, the product of supernatural causes, and moved by forces which are not to be explained by the natural laws of human behavior; (2) the widespread belief, hardly less superstitious in its origin, that intellectual precocity is pathological; (3) the vigorous growth of democratic sentiment in Western Europe and America during the last few hundred years, which has necessarily tended to encourage an attitude unfavorable to a just appreciation of native individual differences in human endowment; and (4) the tardy birth of the biological sciences, particularly genetics, psychology, and education.

The publication of Galton's *Hereditary Genius*, in 1869, marks the beginning of a new era. Since that date the interest in individual differences and their causes has grown until these promise to become national issues on such problems as selective immigration, the evils of differential birth rates, special training for the gifted, and the economic reward of creative talent. Both scientific and popular interest along these lines has been greatly intensified by recent developments in the psychological methods of measuring intelligence, which have furnished conclusive proof that native differences in endowment are a universal phenomenon and that it is possible to evaluate them. Educators, especially, have been quick to appreciate the practical significance of such differences, first for the training of backward and defective children and more recently for the education of the gifted. Twice in the last four years the National Society for the Study of Education has devoted a yearbook to the gifted child.

The problems of genius are chiefly three: its nature, its origin, and its cultivation. This volume is concerned primarily with the nature of genius, insofar as this is indicated by the mental and physical traits of intellectually superior children. On the origin of such children it has only a few facts of rather general nature to present, for it has thus far not been possible to make a thoroughgoing study of the heredity of our subjects. On the education of the gifted it is hoped that the data presented throw considerable light, since educational procedure to be sound must always be based upon an analysis of the raw material with which it deals. Before the present investigation was undertaken, no large group of gifted children had ever been studied. Our positive knowledge of the physical, mental, and personality traits of such children has been extremely limited, and until this knowledge is available there can be no basis for intelligent educational procedure. It is hardly too much to say that this field at present is the "Darkest Africa" of education. To what extent genius can be created or destroyed by right or wrong training is entirely unknown.

The purpose of the present investigation has been, therefore, to determine in what respects the typical gifted child differs from the typical child of normal mentality. Data have been collected on more than 1,400 children, each of whom ranks well within the top one per cent of the unselected school population of corresponding age. The greater part of this report, however, is devoted to 643 such children, who constitute a typical group for whom the data at hand are most extensive. Less extensive material is reported for a second group of 309 subjects, making a total, in round numbers, of nearly 1,000 gifted subjects for whom data have been analyzed. On many points control data have been secured for 600 to 800 unselected children. The aim has been to collect, so far as possible, information of objective nature, although it has not seemed wise to reject, altogether, methods subject to the influence of the personal equation. In the main, however, the conclusions are based upon well defined experimental procedures which can be repeated ad libitum for purposes of verification or refutation. Whatever erroneous conclusions have been drawn from the data at hand, and it would be vain to hope that such have been altogether avoided, should in time be corrected.

* * *

CONCLUSIONS AND PROBLEMS

It will be recalled that the primary purpose of the investigations which have been recounted in this volume was to determine, if possible, what traits may be said to characterize children of markedly superior intellectuality. "Superior intellectuality" is here arbitrarily defined as ability to make a high score on such intelligence tests as the National, the Terman Group, and the Stanford-Binet. It is not necessary to assume that the criterion of intellectual superiority is wholly adequate, or that the superiority itself is either hereditary or abiding. The adequacy of the criterion and the degree of permanence of the superiority which has been found can later be judged in the light of follow-up studies in which the promise of youth is compared with the performance of manhood and womanhood.

Regardless of the results which such follow-up studies may yield, it is unquestionably a matter of considerable importance to ascertain the *present* traits of children earning high intelligence scores. The nature of many of these traits has been indicated in considerable detail in preceding chapters, and the numerous chapter summaries render an inclusive summarization at this point unnecessary. It remains only to bring together a few of the outstanding results of the study and to suggest problems for further investigation.

First, however, the reader is cautioned to bear in mind the variability which obtains in the so-called gifted group with respect to the various traits that have been rated or measured. The group has been described throughout in terms of the deviation of its average from the average of unselected children. It does not follow that what is true of the group is true of all its individual members. Where it could be done without unduly extending the report, complete distributions of both the gifted group and the control group have been given. Where this was not feasible the amount of dispersion from the central tendency has ordinarily been indicated. In most cases the amount of overlapping of the two groups can readily be computed from the data given, where such computations have not already been made.

Doubtless a more compelling realization of the lack of homogeneity of the group in physical, mental, and personality traits could be had from clinical descriptions of appropriately selected cases. At another time it may be possible to prepare a series of case studies; their exclusion from the present volume has been a matter of necessity.

The validity of the generalizations made regarding the traits which characterize gifted children hinges upon the representative nature of the group studied. We have been at considerable pains to insure that the group would not be to any considerable extent unrepresentative of that entire portion of the child population which is capable of earning an intelligence quotient of 140 or above. We believe that our efforts in this direction have been reasonably successful. It is unlikely that more than 20 per cent of the cases have been missed, out of the total number of children who could have qualified in the school population canvassed. The loss may not have exceeded 10 per cent. Granted that the cases missed might for some traits have yielded distributions differing appreciably from those actually found, there is no likelihood that their inclusion would have modified in any important respect the nature of the conclusions that have been drawn. So far as the traits which have been measured are concerned, one is justified in believing that the characterizations which hold for the experimental group hold for gifted children in general.

It is perhaps more important to bear in mind the limits of the field covered by the various tests and measurements that have been applied. For example, it cannot be supposed that the intelligence of our subjects has been measured in all its aspects by the two intelligence tests used, that the full scope and depth of interests have been measured by the interest data, or that the available samplings of character and personality traits tell all it would be worth while to know about this group of trait-complexes. The twenty-five traits which have been rated by the parents and teachers are so many out of possible hundreds, although it is hoped they are among the most important. The physical measurements and medical examinations were exceptionally complete, but they leave altogether untouched a great many things that one would like to know about the physical correlates of superior mentality.

Nevertheless, incomplete and fragmentary as our data are when compared with the many-sided richness of a child's total mental and physical equipment, it may justly be claimed that they carry us well beyond the bounds of previously established fact. Character analyses and case descriptions based upon the subjective evaluation of the best data to be had from ordinary observation can never take the place of quantitative measurements even of the cruder sort. If our data are incomplete, they are at any rate, for the most part, objective and verifiable. No degree of completeness could possibly make good the fault of subjectivity and unverifiableness. If the methods that have been employed have at times led to erroneous conclusions, these in time will be discovered and corrected. One who suspects error at any point has only to apply the same or demonstrably better objective methods to test the justness of his suspicions. It is to be hoped that sooner or later all our conclusions will thus be put to trial. The ultimate value of our study will be measured more by the investigations which it stimulates or provokes others to make than by the amount of its factual data that later experiments may verify.

What are the outstanding characteristics of this group of gifted children? Space is available for mention of but a few, and the temptation to extended discussion must be resisted.

The group contains an unexpectedly large proportion of cases in the upper IQ ranges. Assuming the standard deviation of the IQ distribution for unselected children to be between 15 and 18, there is an appreciable excess of 150 IQ cases, or better, over and above the theoretical expectation. Above 160 IQ the number of cases found increases out of all proportion to the theoretically expected number and by IQ 170 exceeds it several times. Unless this discrepancy can be explained as due to the imperfection of the IQ technique it would appear that the distribution of intelligence in the child population departs considerably from that described by the normal probability curve.

The group contains a significant though not overwhelming preponderance of boys. This finding is not in harmony with any expectations that could be based upon a comparison of the mean scores earned in intelligence tests by unselected boys and girls of corresponding age. No thoroughly convincing explanation can be formulated from the data at hand, although an examination of various hypotheses suggests that the cause may possibly lie in the greater variability of boys. The fact that the excess of boys over girls is far greater in the high school group than in the younger gifted group raises the question whether the mental growth of boys tends to continue somewhat beyond the level which marks the mental maturity of girls.

In physical growth and in general health the gifted group unquestionably rates on the whole somewhat above par. There is no shred of evidence to support the widespread opinion that typically the intellectually precocious child is weak, undersized, or nervously unstable. Insofar as the gifted child departs at all from the average on these traits it is pretty certainly in the other direction, but the fact seems to be that his deviation from the norm on physical traits is in most cases very small indeed in comparison with his deviation in intellectual and volitional traits. Even the slight superiority that he enjoys with respect to physical equipment may or may not be due primarily to endowment. It might be accounted for mainly if not entirely by such factors as diet, medical care, and other environmental influences.

To explain by the environment hypothesis the relatively much greater deviation of our group from unselected children with respect to intellectual and volitional traits appears difficult if not impossible. Our data, however, offer no convincing proof, merely numerous converging lines of evidence.

There is a marked excess of Jewish and of Northern and Western European stock represented. The number of highly successful, even eminent, relatives is impressively great. The fact that in a State which justly prides itself on the equality of educational opportunity provided for its children of every class and station an impartially selected gifted group should draw so heavily from the higher occupational levels and so lightly from the lower, throws a heavy burden upon the environment hypothesis. In spite of all our effort to equalize educational opportunity, the 10 year old child of the California laborer competes for high IQ rank no more successfully than the laborer's son competed for the genius rank in Europe a hundred years ago. This statement is based upon a comparison of the relative number in our group and in the Galton-de Candolle-Ellis genius-groups of individuals whose parents belonged to the unskilled or semi-skilled labor classes. Previous studies had only demonstrated the superiority of the higher occupational and social class with respect to the number of finished geniuses produced, and it was only natural that many should prefer to explain this superiority on the ground of educational opportunity. We have demonstrated that the superiority of the same occupational and social classes is no less decisive when the compared offspring are at an age at which educational opportunity is about as nearly equalized as an enlightened democracy can make it.

Two possible environmental causes of the intellectual superiority of our gifted group are definitely excluded by the data that have been presented: (1) formal schooling, and (2) parental income. It has been shown that within a given age group, the intelligence and achievement scores earned are totally uncorrelated with length of school attendance. The median family income does not greatly exceed that for the general population of the cities in question. The families of some of our most gifted subjects are in financial circumstances below the level of moderate comfort.

In a majority of cases the superiority of the gifted child is evidenced at a very early age. Among the most commonly mentioned indications are intellectual curiosity, wealth of miscellaneous information, and desire to learn to read. The frequent presence of such traits among our subjects in the pre-school period suggests strongly the influence of endowment. Although in a small minority of cases attempts at forced culture may have contributed to the result, it is manifestly impossible to account for the general superiority of the group by any such influence.

There are, nevertheless, many persons who believe that intelligence quotients can be manufactured to order by the application of suitable methods of training. There are even prominent educators and psychologists who are inclined to regard such a pedagogical feat as within the realm of possibility, and no one knows that it is not. If it is possible it is time we were finding it out. Conclusive evidence as to the extent to which IQ's can be artifically raised could be supplied in a few years by an experiment which would cost a few hundred thousand or at most a few million dollars. The knowledge would probably be worth to humanity a thousand times that amount.

Although a majority of our children have had the advantage of superior cultural influences in the home, their more formal educational opportunities have been entirely commonplace, in no way superior to those enjoyed by the children from the humblest families of Los Angeles, San Francisco, and Oakland. At school they have studied and played with the children of the generality. The school has provided for them no special program of instruction. It has given no form of individual treatment except an occasional extra promotion. Such promotions have usually been doubly or trebly earned, for it has been demonstrated by reliable and extensive achievement tests that the average child of our group had already mastered the subject matter of the curriculum two or three grades beyond that in which he was located. More accurately, this promotional "slack" amounts on the average to about 25 per cent of the child's age. Perhaps because of this fact, the superiority of the group in achievement is only two-thirds or three-fourths as great as its superiority in intelligence. It is evidently a rare experience for a gifted child to be given work of a grade of difficulty commensurate with his intellectual abilities.

The excess in achievement above the norm for the gifted child's actual grade status is general rather than special, although it is somewhat less marked in spelling and arithmetic than in general information, reading, and language. The amount of specialization or unevenness in the abilities of our group was made the subject of extended study by Dr. De Voss. His results show that in respect to measurable disparity of abilities the gifted child differs little if at all from children in general. The "one-sidedness" of precocious children is mythical. The fact is that a considerable proportion of all children show appreciable specialization in their achievements. The gifted child has only his share of this common human trait. Nevertheless, the measurable disparities found are such as to show clearly the necessity of taking them into account in any scheme of vocational or educational guidance for children of every grade of intelligence. It will be one of the important problems in the follow-up of these gifted children to work out the degree of correlation between the specialized achievement in adult life and the special aptitudes discovered in this investigation.

The matter of interests was deemed of sufficient importance to warrant investigation from several angles. As would be expected, the interests of gifted children reflect in many ways their intellectual superiority. The school subjects which they like best are for the most part the subjects which unselected children find the most difficult. The vocations which they prefer rank fairly high in the occupational hierarchy with respect to the intellectual demands they make.

The reading of gifted children surpasses that of unselected children both in quantity and quality. The typical gifted child of seven years reads more books than the unselected child reads at any age up to fifteen years. Gifted children have more than the usual interest in books of science, history, biography, travel, and informational fiction, and less in books of adventure, mystery, and emotional fiction.

The common opinion that intellectually superior children are characterized by a deficiency of play interests has been shown to be wholly unfounded. The mean play-information quotient of the gifted group is 136.

The typical gifted child of nine years has a larger body of definite knowledge about plays and games than the average child of twelve years. If he devotes somewhat fewer hours per week to play activities it is because his play interests must compete with a wealth of other interests which are no less compelling. Another finding of considerable importance in this connection is that the play interests of the gifted boy are above rather than below the norm in degree of "masculinity."

The experiment carried out for the purpose of measuring the strength of interests along intellectual, social, and activity lines is perhaps one of the most significant reported in the entire study, whether considered from the point of view of methodology or results. It is probable that the type of instrument which Mrs. Wyman designed for this purpose will be found capable of unlocking many hitherto inaccessible regions of human personality and interest. Adaptations of her method might be devised which would aid in the discovery of special aptitudes and in the diagnosis of pre-delinquent and pre-psychotic tendencies. In the present instance the Wyman test has given a fairly precise measure of three important aspects of interest. It has shown that in strength of intellectual interest 90 per cent of our gifted children surpass the average of a control group, that the superiority of the gifted in strength of social interests is well-nigh as great, and that in activity interests the two groups are practically indistinguishable.

That our gifted surpass unselected children in tests of honesty, trustworthiness, and similar moral traits, will probably surprise no observant judge of human character. Few have ever denied that there is at least a certain amount of positive correlation between intelligence and character. The Cady-Raubenheimer tests show that it is considerable. Considering total score on the seven character tests used, one can say that the gifted child of nine or ten years has reached a stage of moral development which is not attained by the average child until the age of thirteen or fourteen. Approximately 85 per cent of the gifted surpass the average of unselected children. The test results on this point are confirmed by the testimony of special class teachers of gifted children. The tests in question are measures of untrustworthiness, of dishonesty of report, of tendency to overstatement, of objectionable social-moral attitudes, and of interest in questionable books and questionable companions.

A modification of Woodworth's test of psychotic tendencies showed approximately 75 per cent of the gifted above the average of unselected children. Comparison of later mental troubles and conduct disorders with the results of these tests will be of surpassing interest.

It should be emphasized, however, that one could find in the gifted group numerous exceptions to the general rule with respect to character, personality, and emotional stability. The gifted are not free from faults, and at least one out of five has more of them than the average child of the general population. Perhaps one out of twenty presents a more or less serious problem in one or another respect.

The ratings secured from parents and teachers on the twenty-five mental, moral, social, and physical traits are of value chiefly in their confirmation of the results secured by the method of test. These ratings undoubtedly have a very low reliability for an individual subject, but when used as a basis for comparing the relatively large gifted and control groups they yield reasonably dependable results. For example, one can say with considerable assurance that gifted children excel the average most of all in intellectual and volitional traits, next in emotional and moral traits, and least in physical and social traits.

The purpose and form of this report have tended almost inevitably to center attention upon the traits of the gifted group rather than upon the control groups with which they have been compared. To an extent this is unfortunate. A volume could well have been devoted to fuller treatment and discussion of the data collected for unselected children, including sex and age differences in each of the following: scholastic and occupational interests, play interest and play information, reading interests, teachers' ratings of scholastic abilities, interest tests, character and personality tests, and ratings by teachers and parents on the twenty-five selected traits. . . .

A study of superior talent inevitably raises a host of pedagogical problems. It has been no part of our purpose, however, to exploit any theory as to the educational methods best adapted to the gifted child. About the culture of genius next to nothing is known, although new light may in time be expected from the rapidly increasing experimentation with differentiated curricula, classification by ability, and methods of individual instruction. Traditional methods have ignored the problem; their influence is negative rather than positive; the best that can be hoped for them is that they may not be as bad as they seem. The present neglect of superior talent is sufficiently indicated by the inability of teachers to recognize it. One of the most astonishing facts brought out in this investigation is that one's best chance of identifying the brightest child in a schoolroom is to examine the birth records and select the youngest, rather than to take the one rated as brightest by the teacher.

Follow-up covering the first two years after the subjects were located are encouraging. Grade progress and quality of school work indicate that general ability is being fully maintained. The previous good record of school deportment has been improved, and difficulties in the field of social adjustment are clearing up. It is probably very significant that the children who received the greatest number of extra promotions are in general the ones whose school work has most improved in quality.

Prediction as to the probable future of these children would be profitless. We can only wait and watch. It should be pointed out, however, that to expect all or even a majority of the subjects to attain any considerable degree of eminence would be unwarranted optimism. In the first place, eminence is a poor measure of success. In the second place, success even in the best sense is largely a product of fortunate chance combinations of personal merits and environmental circumstances. In the third place, the group itself, although far superior to the average, is nothing like as highly selected as the groups of genius-adults studied by Galton, de Candolle, Ellis, Castle, Cattell, and others. Each of Galton's subjects, for example, ranked in eminence at least as high as the first in four thousand adults of the general population. To qualify for our gifted group it was only necessary for a child to rate as high as the first in two hundred. Only about one of our subjects in twenty, or about fifty in the group of one thousand, would rank as the first in four thousand of a random selection. About one man in a thousand in the generality finds his way into *Who's Who*. Twenty per cent of our boys rank as high in IQ as the first in a thousand taken at random, but we should hardly expect so large a proportion to attain *Who's Who* distinction. Perhaps no one would contend that this or any similar type of eminence is more than moderately correlated with general intelligence. In a city of 25,000 population there are, say, 5,000 males above the age of thirty years. It is with the most distinguished 25 to 50 of such a group that our gifted boys could be most fairly compared a few decades hence.

It is hoped that some of the later volumes which are planned for this series of *Genetic Studies of Genius* will add at least something to our present knowledge about the origin of exceptional talent, the methods of culture adapted to insure its fullest development, and the social and governmenal policies that will conserve and utilize it to the best advantage of all. These are the great problems of genius; they are outranked in importance by few if any of the issues that confront mankind; they cannot be solved except in the light of psychological, biological, and educational researches along lines that are still almost wholly unexplored.

31

BRONISLAW MALINOWSKI (1884–1942)

The social and sexual life of Trobriand Children (1929)

One way to do an exceedingly thorough piece of field research is to become stuck for four years in an isolated spot by a world war. This is what happened to anthropologist Malinowski in World War I in the Trobriand Islands, off the coast of New Guinea. It happened also to Köhler and his chimpanzees on Tenerife off the coast of Portugal.

The result in Malinowski's case was that the publication of several important anthropological books. The following selection is reproduced from one of them, published under the rather unfortunate title of The Sexual Life of Savages. The Trobriand Islanders are not savages. The selection is reproduced with the permission of Halcyon House.

Malinokski's field work was done between 1914–1918 and thus precedes by a decade Margaret Mead's field trip to Samoa. It was published however, one year later than Coming of Age in Samoa. It is one of the important early contributions to cross-cultural research.

THE SEXUAL LIFE OF CHILDREN

Children in the Trobriand Islands enjoy considerable freedom and independence. They soon become emancipated from a parental tutelage which has never been very strict. Some of them obey their parents willingly, but this is entirely a matter of the personal character of both parties: there is no idea of a regular discipline, no system of domestic coercion. Often as I sat among them, observing some family incident or listening to a quarrel between parent and child, I would hear a youngster told to do this or that, and generally the thing, whatever it was, would be asked as a favour, though sometimes the request might be backed up by a threat of violence. The parents would either coax or scold or ask from one equal to another.

A simple command, implying the expectation of natural obedience, is never heard from parent to child in the Trobriands.

People will sometimes grow angry with their children and beat them in an outburst of rage; but I have quite as often seen a child rush furiously at his parent and strike him. This attack might be received with a good-natured smile, or the blow might be angrily returned; but the idea of definite retribution, or of coercive punishment, is not only foreign, but distinctly repugnant to the native. Several times, when I suggested, after some flagrant infantile misdeed, that it would mend matters for the future if the child were beaten or otherwise punished in cold blood, the idea appeared unnatural and immoral to my friends, and was rejected with some resentment.

Such freedom gives scope for the formation of the children's own little community, an independent group, into which they drop naturally from the age of four or five and continue till puberty. As the mood prompts them, they remain with their parents during the day, or else join their playmates for a time in their small republic. And this community within a community acts very much as its own members determine, standing often in a sort of collective opposition to its elders. If the children make up their minds to do a certain thing, to go for a day's expedition, for instance, the grown-ups and even the chief himself, as I often observed, will not be able to stop them. In my ethnographic work I was able and was indeed forced to collect my information about children and their concerns directly from them. Their spiritual ownership in games and childish activities was acknowledged, and they were also quite capable of instructing me and explaining the intricacies of their play or enterprise.

Small children begin also to understand and to defer to tribal tradition and custom; to those restrictions which have the character of a taboo or of a definite command of tribal law, or usage or propriety.

The child's freedom and independence extend also to sexual matters. To begin with, children hear of and witness much in the sexual life of their elders. Within the house, where the parents have no possibility of finding privacy, a child has opportunities of acquiring practical information concerning the sexual act. I was told that no special precautions are taken to prevent children from witnessing their parents' sexual enjoyment. The child would merely be scolded and told to cover its head with a mat. I sometimes heard a little boy or girl praised in these terms: "Good child, he never tells what happens between his parents." Young children are allowed to listen to baldly sexual talk, and they understand perfectly well what is being discussed. They are also themselves tolerably expert in swearing and the use of obscene language. Because of their early mental development some quite tiny children are able to make smutty jokes, and these their elders will greet with laughter.

Small girls follow their fathers on fishing expeditions, during which the men remove their pubic leaf. Nakedness under these conditions is regarded as natural, since it is necessary. There is no lubricity or ribaldry associated with it. Once, when I was engaged in the discussion of an obscene subject, a little girl, the daughter of one of my informants, joined our group. I asked the father to tell her to go away. "Oh, no," he answered, "she is a good girl, she never repeats to her mother anything that is said among men. When we take her fishing with us we need not be ashamed. Another girl would describe the details of our nakedness to her companions or her mothers. Then these will chaff us and repeat what they have heard about us. This little girl never says a word." The other men present enthusiastically assented, and developed the theme of the girl's discretion. But a boy is much less in contact with his mother in such matters, for here, between maternal relations, that is, for the natives, between real kindred, the taboo of incest begins to act at an early age, and the boy is removed from any intimate contact of this sort with his mother and above all with his sisters.

There are plenty of opportunities for both boys and girls to receive instruction in erotic matters from their companions. The children initiate each other into the mysteries of sexual life in a directly practical manner at a very early age. A premature amorous existence begins among them long before they are able really to carry out the act of sex. They indulge in plays and pastimes in which they satisfy their curiosity concerning the appearance and function of the organs of generation, and incidentally receive, it would seem, a certain amount of positive pleasure. Genital manipulation and such minor perversions as oral stimulation of the organs are typical forms of this amusement. Small boys and girls are said to be frequently initiated by their somewhat older companions, who allow them to witness their own amorous dalliance. As they are untrammelled by the authority of their elders and unrestrained by any moral code, except that of specific tribal taboo, there is nothing but their degree of curiosity, of ripeness, and of "temperament" or sensuality, to determine how much or how little they shall indulge in sexual pastimes.

The attitude of the grown-ups and even of the parents towards such infantile indulgence is either that of complete indifference or that of complacency—they find it natural, and do not see why they should scold or interfere. Usually they show a kind of tolerant and amused interest, and discuss the love affairs of their children with easy jocularity. I often heard some such benevolent gossip as this: "So-and-so (a little girl) has already had intercourse with So-and-so (a little boy)." And if such were the case, it would be added that it was her first experience. An exchange of lovers; or some small love drama in the little world would be half-seriously, half-jokingly discussed. The infantile sexual act, or its substitute, is regarded as an innocent amusement. "It is their play to *kayta* (to have intercourse). They give each other a coconut, a small piece of betel-nut, a few beads or some fruits from the bush, and then they go and hide, and *kayta*." But it is not considered proper for the children to carry on their affairs in the house. It has always to be done in the bush.

The age at which a girl begins to amuse herself in this manner is said to coincide wtih her putting on the small fibre skirt, between, that is, the ages of four and five. But this obviously can refer only to incomplete practices and not to the real act. Some of my informants insisted that such small female children actually have intercourse with penetration.

Remembering, however, the Trobriander's very strong tendency to exaggerate in the direction of the grotesque, a tendency not altogether devoid of a certain malicious Rabelaisian humour, I am inclined to discount those statements of my authorities. If we place the beginning of real sexual life at the age of six to eight in the case of girls, and ten to twelve in the case of boys, we shall probably not be erring very greatly in either direction. And from these times sexuality will gradually assume a greater and greater importance as life goes on, until it abates in the course of nature.

Sexual, or at least sensuous, pleasure constitutes if not the basis of, at least an element in, many of the children's pastimes. Some of them do not, of course, provide any sexual excitement at all, as for instance those in imitation of the grown-up economic and ceremonial activities or games of skill or childish athletics; but all sorts of round games, which are played by the children of both sexes on the central place of the village, have a more or less strongly marked flavour of sex, though the outlets they furnish are indirect and only accessible to the elder youths and maidens, who also join in them. Indeed, we shall have to return later to a consideration of sex in certain games, songs, and stories, for as the sexual association becomes more subtle and indirect it appeals more and more to older people alone and has, therefore, to be examined in the contexts of later life.

There are, however, some specific games in which the older children never participate, and into which sex directly enters. The little ones sometimes play, for instance, at house-building, and at family life. A small hut of sticks and boughs is constructed in a secluded part of the jungle, and a couple or more repair thither and play at husband and wife, prepare food and carry out or imitate as best they can the act of sex. Or else a band of them, in imitation of the amorous expeditions of their elders, carry food to some favourite spot on the sea-shore or in the coral ridge, cook and eat vegetables there, and "when they are full of food, the boys sometimes fight with each other, or sometimes *kayta* (copulate) with the girls." When the fruit ripens on certain wild trees in the jungle they go in parties to pick it, to exchange presents, make *kula* (ceremonial exchange) of the fruit, and engage in erotic pastimes.

Thus it will be seen that they have a tendency to palliate the crudity of their sexual interest and indulgence by associating it with something more poetic. Indeed, the Trobriand children show a great sense of the singular and romantic in their games. For instance, if a part of the jungle or village has been flooded by rain, they go and sail their small canoes on this new water; or if a very strong sea has thrown up some interesting flotsam, they proceed to the beach and inaugurate some imaginative game around it. The little boys, too, search for unusual animals, insects, or flowers, and give them to the little girls, thus lending a redeeming æsthetic touch to their premature eroticisms.

In spite of the importance of the sexual motive in the life of the youngest generation, it must be kept in mind that the separation of the sexes, in many matters, obtains also among children. Small girls can very often be seen playing or wandering in independent parties by themselves.

Little boys in certain moods—and these seem their more usual ones—scorn the society of the female and amuse themselves alone. Thus the small republic falls into two distinct groups which are perhaps to be seen more often apart than together; and, though they frequently unite in play, this need by no means be necessarily sensuous.

It is important to note that there is no interference by older persons in the sexual life of children. On rare occasions some old man or woman is suspected of taking a strong sexual interest in the children, and even of having intercourse with some of them. But I never found such suspicions supported even by a general consensus of opinion, and it was always considered both improper and silly for an older man or woman to have sexual dealings with a child. There is certainly no trace of any custom of ceremonial defloration by old men, or even by men belonging to an older age class.

Age divisions

I have just used the expression "age class," but I did so in a broad sense only: for there are no sharply distinguished age grades or classes among the Trobriand natives. The following table of age designations only roughly indicates the stages of their life; for these stages in practice merge into one another.

Designation of age

1. *Waywaya* (fœtus; infant till the age of crawling, both male and female) 2. *Pwapwawa* (infant till the stage of walking, male or female) 3. *Gwadi* (child, till puberty, male or female) 4. *Monagwadi* (male child)	4. *Inagwadi* (female child)	I. Stage: *Gwadi*—Word used as a generic designation for all these stages 1-4, meaning *child*, male or female, at any time between birth and maturity
5. *To'ulatile* (youth from puberty till marriage) 6. *Tobubowa'u* (mature man) 6a. *Tovavaygile* (married man)	5. *Nakapugula* or *Nakubukwabuya* (girl from puberty till marriage) 6. *Nabubowa'u* (ripe woman) 6a. *Navavaygile* (married woman)	II. Stage: Generic designations—*Ta'u* (man), *Vivila* (woman)
7. *Tomwaya* (old man) 7a. *Tomwaya* (old honoured man)	7. *Numwaya* (old woman)	III. Stage: Old age

The terms used in this table will be found to overlap in some instances. Thus a very small infant may be referred to as *waywaya* or *pwapwawa* indiscriminately, but only the former term as a rule would be used in speaking of a fœtus or referring to the pre-incarnated children from Tuma. Again, you might call a few months old child either *gwadi* or *pwapwawa*, but the latter term would be but seldom used except for a very small baby. The term *gwadi* moreover can be used generically, as "child" in English, to denote anything from a fœtus to a young boy or girl. Thus, it will be seen that two terms may encroach on each other's field of meaning, but only if they be consecutive. The terms with sex prefixes (4) are normally used only of elder children who may be distinguished by their dress.

There are, besides these more specific subdivisions, the three main distinctions of age, between the ripe man and woman in the full vigour of life and the two stages—those of childhood and of old age—which limit manhood and womanhood on either side. The second main stage is divided into two parts, mainly by the fact of marriage. Thus, the words under (5) primarily designate unmarried people and to that extent are opposed to (6a), but they also imply youthfulness or unripeness, and in that respect are opposed to (6).

The male term for old age, *tomwaya* (7) can also denote rank or importance. I myself was often so addressed, but I was not flattered, and much preferred to be called *toboma* (literally "the tabooed man"), a name given to old men of rank, but stressing the latter attribute rather than the former. Curiously enough, the compliment or distinction implied in the word *tomwaya* becomes much weaker, and almost disappears in its feminine equivalent. *Numwaya* conveys that tinge of scorn or ridicule inseparable from "old woman" in so many languages.

The amorous life of adolescence

When a boy reaches the age of from twelve to fourteen years, and attains that physical vigour which comes with sexual maturity, and when, above all, his increased strength and mental ripeness allow him to take part, though still in a somewhat limited and fitful manner, in some of the economic activities of his elders, he ceases to be regarded as a child (*gwadi*), and assumes the position of adolescent (*ulatile* or *to'ulatile*). At the same time he receives a different status, involving some duties and many privileges, a stricter observance of taboos, and a greater participation in tribal affairs. He has already donned the pubic leaf for some time; now he becomes more careful in his wearing of it, and more interested in its appearance. The girl emerges from childhood into adolescence through the obvious bodily changes: "her breasts are round and full; her bodily hair begins to grow; her menses flow and ebb with every moon," as the natives put it. She also has no new change in her attire to make, for she has much earlier assumed her fibre skirt, but now her interest in it from the two points of view of elegance and decorum is greatly increased.

At this stage a partial break-up of the family takes place. Brothers and sisters must be segregated in obedience to that stringent taboo which plays such an imporant part in tribal life. The elder children, especially the males, have to leave the house, so as not to hamper by their embarrassing presence the sexual life of their parents. This partial disintegration of the family group is effected by the boy moving to a house tenanted by bachelors or by elderly widowed male relatives or friends. Such a house is called *bukumatula*, and in the next section we shall become acquainted with the details of its arrangement. The girl sometimes goes to the house of an elderly widowed maternal aunt or other relative.

As the boy or girl enters upon adolescence the nature of his or her sexual activity becomes more serious. It ceases to be mere child's play and assumes a prominent place among life's interests. What was before an unstable relation culminating in an exchange of erotic manipulation or an immature sexual act becomes now an absorbing passion, and a matter for serious endeavour. An adolescent gets definitely attached to a given person, wishes to possess her, works purposefully towards this goal, plans to reach the fulfilment of his desires by magical and other means, and finally rejoices in achievement. I have seen young people of this age grow positively miserable through ill-success in love. This stage, in fact, differs from the one before in that personal preference has now come into play and with it a tendency towards a greater permanence in intrigue. The boy develops a desire to retain the fidelity and exclusive affection of the loved one, at least for a time. But this tendency is not associated so far with any idea of settling down to one exclusive relationship, nor do adolescents yet begin to think of marriage. A boy or girl wishes to pass through many more experiences; he or she still enjoys the prospect of complete freedom and has no desire to accept obligations. Though pleased to imagine that his partner is faithful, the youthful lover does not feel obliged to reciprocate this fidelity.

We have seen in the previous section that a group of children forming a sort of small republic within the community is conspicuous in every village. Adolescence furnishes the community with another small group, of youths and girls. At this stage, however, though the boys and girls are much more bound up in each other as regards amorous interests, they but rarely mix in public or in the daytime. The group is really broken up into two, according to sex.... To this division there correspond two words, *to'ulatile* and *nakubukwabuya*, there being no one expression—such as there is to describe the younger age group, *gugwadi*, children—to define the adolescent youth of both sexes.

The natives take an evident pride in this, "the flower of the village," as it might be called. They frequently mention that "all the *to'ulatile* and *nakubukwabuya* (youths and girls) of the village were there." In speaking of some competitive game, or dance or sport, they compare the looks or performance of their own youths with those of some other village, and always to the advantage of their own. This group leads a happy, free, arcadian existence, devoted to amusement and the pursuit of pleasure.

Its members are so far not claimed by any serious duties, yet their greater physical strength and ripeness give them more independence and a wider scope of action than they had as children. The adolescent boys participate, but mainly as free-lances, in garden work, in the fishing and hunting and in oversea expeditions; they get all the excitement and pleasure, as well as some of the prestige, yet remain free from a great deal of the drudgery and many of the restrictions which trammel and weigh on their elders. Many of the taboos are not yet quite binding on them, the burden of magic has not yet fallen on their shoulders. If they grow tired of work, they simply stop and rest. The self-discipline of ambition and subservience to traditional ideals, which moves all the elder individuals and leaves them relatively little personal freedom, has not yet quite drawn these boys into the wheels of the social machine. Girls, too, obtain a certain amount of the enjoyment and excitement denied to children by joining in some of the activities of their elders, while still escaping the worst of the drudgery.

Young people of this age, besides conducting their love affairs more seriously and intensely, widen and give a greater variety to the setting of their amours. Both sexes arrange picnics and excursions and thus their indulgence in intercourse becomes associated with an enjoyment of novel experiences and fine scenery. They also form sexual connections outside the village community to which they belong. Whenever there occurs in some other locality one of the ceremonial occasions on which custom permits of licence, thither they repair, usually in bands either of boys or of girls, since on such occasions opportunity of indulgence offers for one sex alone.

It is necessary to add that the places used for love-making differ at this stage from those of the previous one. The small children carry on their sexual practices surrepititiously in bush or grove as a part of their games, using all sorts of makeshift ararngements to attain privacy, but the *ulatile* (adolescent) has either a couch of his own in a bachelors' house, or the use of a hut belonging to one of his unmarried relatives. In a certain type of yam-house, too, there is an empty closed-in space in which boys sometimes arrange little "cosy-corners," affording room for two. In these, they make a bed of dry leaves and mats, and thus obtain a comfortable *garçonnière*, where they can meet and spend a happy hour or two with their loves. Such arrangements are, of course, necessary now that amorous intercourse has become a passion instead of a game.

But a couple will not yet regularly cohabit in a bachelors' house (*bukumatula*), living together and sharing the same bed night after night. Both girl and boy prefer to adopt more furtive and less conventionally binding methods, to avoid lapsing into a permanent relationship which might put unnecessary restraint upon their liberty by becoming generally known. That is why they usually prefer a small nest in the *sokwaypa* (covered yam-house), or the temporary hospitality of a bachelors' house.

We have seen that the youthful attachments between boys and girls at this stage have ripened out of childish games and intimacies. All these young people have grown up in close propinquity and with full knowledge of each other. Such early acquaintances take fire, as it were, under the influence of certain entertainments, where the intoxicating influence of music and moonlight, and the changed mood and attire of all the participants, transfigure the boy and girl in each other's eyes. Intimate observation of the natives and their personal confidences have convinced me that extraneous stimuli of this kind play a great part in the love affairs of the Trobrianders. Such opportunities of mutual transformation and escape from the monotony of everyday life are afforded not only by the many fixed seasons of festivity and permitted license, but also by that monthly increase in the people's pleasure-seeking mood which leads to many special pastimes at the full of the moon.

Thus adolescence marks the transition between infantile and playful sexualities and those serious permanent relations which precede marriage. During this intermediate period love becomes passionate and yet remains free.

As time goes on, and the boys and girls grow older, their intrigues last longer, and their mutual ties tend to become stronger and more permanent. A personal preference as a rule develops and begins definitely to overshadow all other love affairs. It may be based on true sexual passion or else on an affinity of characters. Practical considerations become involved in it, and, sooner or later, the man thinks of stabilizing one of his liaisons by marriage. In the ordinary course of events, every marriage is preceded by a more or less protracted period of sexual life in common. This is generally known and spoken of, and is regarded as a public intimation of the matrimonial projects of the pair. It serves also as a test of the strength of their attachment and extent of their mutual compatibility. This trial period also gives time for the prospective bridegroom and for the woman's family to prepare economically for the event.

Two people living together as permanent lovers are described respectively as "his woman" (*la vivila*) and "her man" (*la ta'u*). Or else a term, also used to describe the friendship between two men, is applied to this relationship (*lubay-*, with pronominal suffixes). In order to distinguish between a passing liaison and one which is considered preliminary to marriage, they would say of the female concerned in the latter: *"la vivila mokita; imisiya yambwata yambwata"*—"his woman truly; he sleeps with her always always." In this locution the sexual relationship between the two is denoted by the verb "to sleep with" (*imisiya*), the durative and iterative form of *masisi*, to sleep. The use of this verb also emphasizes the lawfulness of the relation, for it is used in talking of sexual intercourse between husband and wife, or of such relations as the speaker wishes to discuss seriously and respectfully. An approximate equivalent in English would be the verb "cohabit." The natives have two other words in distinction to this. The verb *kaylasi*, which implies an illicit element in the act, is used when speaking of adultery or other forms of non-lawful intercourse. Here the English word "fornicate" would come nearest to rendering the native meaning. When the natives wish to indicate the crude, physiological fact, they use the word *kayta*, translatable, though pedantically, by the verb "copulate with."

The pre-matrimonial, lasting intrigue is based upon and maintained by personal elements only. There is no legal obligation on either party. They may enter into and dissolve it as they like. In fact, this relationship differs from other liaisons only in its duration and stability. Towards the end, when marriage actually approaches, the element of personal responsibility and obligation becomes stronger. The two now regularly cohabit in the same house, and a considerable degree of exclusiveness in sexual matters is observed by them. But they have not yet given up their personal freedom; on the several occasions of wider licence affianced couples are invariably separated and each partner is "unfaithful" with his or her temporary choice. Even within the village, in the normal course, the girl who is definitely going to marry a particular boy will bestow favours on other men, though a certain measure of decorum must be observed in this; if she sleeps out too often, there will be possibly a dissolution of the tie and certainly friction and disagreement. Neither boy nor girl may go openly and flagrantly with other partners on an amorous expedition. Quite apart from nocturnal cohabitation, the two are supposed to be seen in each other's company and to make a display of their relationship in public. Any deviation from the exclusive liaison must be decent, that is to say, clandestine. The relation of free engagement is the natural outcome of a series of trial liaisons, and the appropriate preliminary test of marriage.

32

ARNOLD L. GESELL (1880–1961)

Maturation and infant behavior pattern (1929)

Gesell, who was both a pediatrician and a psychologist, was for years the head of the Psycho-Clinic of Child Development at Yale. He was a pioneer in the development of mental tests for children, and, in addition, conducted and directed many studies in child psychology. His emphasis was upon the role of maturation in child development, although he did not rule out the effects of experience. The following selection was chosen to represent Gesell because it shows the variety of projects in which he was engaged in the most active part of his career. It is reprinted in full from the Psychological Review, *36 (1929): 307–319, by permission of the American Psychological Association.*

Gesell's autobiography is in Volume IV of History of Psychology in Autobiography.

The influence of conditioning on the human infant has been so forcibly asserted from the standpoint of behaviorism, that it may be desirable to examine the influence of sheer maturation on his patterns of behavior.

The behavior of the infant, by nature, is obedient to pattern. Never does the picture of normal behavior become as diffuse and formless as a drifting cloud. Even the random movements of the month-old child are not utterly fortuitous. The closer one studies them the more configuration they assume. There is indeed no such thing as utter randomness in infant behavior. Accordingly the "random activity" of the two months infant is distinct from that of the month-old. It is distinctive because it has its own pattern.

Likewise with the fœtus. Its behavior is in no sense amorphous, but, as the studies of Minkowski have shown, manifests itself in fairly well-defined reflexes—long, short, diagonal, and trot reflexes; postural reflexes; rhythmical and inhibitive phenomena. These patterns of behavior follow an orderly genetic sequence in their emergence. Genetic sequence is itself an expression of elaborate pattern. And the relative stability of both prenatal and postnatal ontogenesis under normal and even unusual conditions must be regarded as a significant indication of the fundamental rôle of maturational factors in the determination of behavior.

Again take the fœtus. The uterus is the normal environment of the fœtus till the end of a gestation period of 40 weeks. But birth with survival, may exceptionally occur as early as 24 weeks and as late as 48 weeks, an enormous range of variation in natal age amounting to 6 lunar months. Variation with a range of 3 lunar months is common and yet this considerable variation does not impose a corresponding deviation on the complex of behavior. Our normative studies of both premature and postmature infants have shown repeatedly that the growth course of behavior tends to be obedient to the regular underlying pattern of genetic sequence, irrespective of the irregularity of the birth event. Refined studies will doubtless reveal that such irregularity does subtly modify many details of behavior; but as a point of departure for the discussion of maturation, nothing is more comprehensive in implication than the general stability of the trend and the tempo of development, in spite of precocious or postponed displacement of birth. The patterns of genetic sequence insure a basically similar growth career for full term, pre-term, and post-term infants. It is as though Nature has provided a regulatory factor of safety against the stress of extreme variations of environment. In the mechanisms of maturation this regulation operates.

The term *growth* may be construed to embrace the total complex of ontogenetic development. Maturation refers to those phases and products of growth which are wholly or chiefly due to innate and endogenous factors. It is our purpose to assemble in a summary manner, diverse evidences of behavior maturation, based upon our clinical, experimental and normative observations.

These evidences are drawn from several sources as follows:

1. The development of prehension.
2. Developmental correspondence in identical twins.
3. The limitations of training.
4. The restricted influence of physical handicap.
5. Developmental progression in emotional behavior.

1. The development of prehension

The development of prehension throughout the first year of life displays significant progressive changes in behavior pattern. These changes raise searching doubts concerning the influence of experience and training upon these patterns. We have studied these changes with particular reference to a pellet 8 millimeters in diameter. The characteristic eye-hand reactions of an infant confronted with this tiny pellet may be recapitulated in the following which is a genetic order:

a. No visual regard for the pellet.
b. Transient regard for the pellet.

c. More prolonged and definite fixation upon the pellet with slight postural changes (16 weeks).
   d. Visual fixation with crude bilateral or unilateral hand approach (20 weeks).
   e. Unilateral pronated hand approach with scratching in vicinity of the pellet (24 weeks).
   f. Pronated hand approach with occasional raking flexion resulting in palmar prehension (28 weeks).
   g. Pronated hand approach with extension of index finger and partial suppression of other digits resulting in poking or prehension by index finger with partial thumb opposition.
   h. Rotation of wrist in hand approach, with pincer-like prehension of pellet by index finger and thumb (40 weeks).
   i. Perfection and further delimitation of pincer-like response.

All these changes mature with subtle but significant accompanying changes in head posture, body posture, hand and arm attitude and associated visual behavior. It seems quite erroneous to say that the child learns to prehend the pellet in the traditional sense of the learning process. Crudely, but nevertheless effectively, he prehends the pellet by gross palmar approach as early as the age of 28 weeks. The refinement of his eye-hand behavior comes not by the alleged utilization of snatches of successful random activity, but by the progressive acquisition and consolidation of a hierarchy of behavior patterns which are the result of developmental decrements and increments rather than the stamping in or chaining of satisfying, successful reflexes. The defective child shows retardation in the acquisition of these patterns even though he may, in a durational sense, have a larger fund of prehensory experience. It is not improbable that many of these developmental changes in the pattern of prehension would be realized even if the prehensory hand were altogether swaddled and deprived of activity. When the prehensory mechanism is damaged by restricted birth injury to the brain, resulting in extensive athetosis, the propensity to prehend or reach may still assert itself at the proper genetic level. Even though the propensity is aborted its presence is highly suggestive of the potency of maturational determination.

2. Developmental correspondence in twins

During the past year we have gathered extensive detailed data on the development of prehension in a pair of identical infant twins. These twins were identical not only with regard to their skin patterns but also to a remarkable degree, with regard to their behavior patterns. Nowhere was this more objectively shown than in their prehensory reactions to cubes and pellets under controlled observational conditions. At 28 weeks both of these twins, being somewhat retarded in their development, were visually unheedful of the pellet, though they definitely regarded a cube. At 38 weeks they addressed themselves in an identical manner to the pellet. The hands were in full pronation, the fingers, spread apart in a fan-like manner, were fully extended. The thumb was fully extended almost at right angles. The photographic record of their attack upon the pellet, in the motion pictures, shows an almost uncanny degree of identity in the details of postural attitude, hand attitude and mechanism of grasp. Time does not permit the further specifications of these details.

At 40 weeks each twin made a crude raking attack upon the pellet, with occasional awkward but completed prehension in which the palm and all of the digits participated. The form of the prehension pattern was again remarkably similar in the two children. At 42 weeks they were again examined in the same situation. Although there had been no special instruction or conditioning in the interval, these 2 weeks imposed a palpable and strikingly similar change upon the prehension picture. Simultaneous flexion of the digits was very neatly displaced by a preferential flexion of the index finger. The raking approach was replaced by a poking with the tip of the index finger. Such an interesting inflection of the prehensory pattern surely could not have been induced so precisely and so simultaneously in both of these children without the presence of controlling factors of organic maturation. Of similar significance is the fact that comparable changes in prehension pattern appeared coincidentally throughout the course of their development.

The correspondences in behavior patterns in these twins were literally uncountable. However, the records of 13 developmental examinations were analyzed and 612 separate comparative ratings of behavior items were made from these records in order to determine items of correspondence and disparity. There were 99 items of minor disparity and 513 items of identical or nearly identical correspondence. The parity of behavior patterns was overwhelming.

A brief example of behavior correspondence may be cited from the 44 weeks examination record. The twins were confronted with a test performance box with its three holes. The common method of approach of the two children, their preferred regard for the edge of the performance box, the fleeting regard for the holes, the exploitation of the vertical surface of the performance box by scratching, simultaneous flexion of the digits, the failure to place a round rod into any of the holes, the brushing of the surface of the performance box with the rod, the transfer of the rod from one hand to the other, and finally an almost simultaneous peculiar, clicking vocalization in both twins—altogether constituted a very complicated behavior pattern, but one which bristled with numerous identities of spatial and dynamic detail. One can give due weight to the significance of this correspondence only by reflecting on the myriad of behavior exploitations of the situation which the twins *might* have adopted. But in spite of this multitude of exploitational possibilities, the twins were apparently under a common inner compulsion to adopt those very similarities of behavior which have been noted.

Many convincing examples of behavior correspondence might be cited. We content ourselves with a few much abbreviated illustrations. Here is one which seems to us to have experimental control, even though it deals with nothing more than the reaction of two infants when placed in exactly the same manner upon a flat platform to observe their postural control in the sitting position. Both children showed precisely the same kind and degree of difficulty in equilibrium at the age of 28 weeks. In both there was a tendency to sway to the right; in both it was impossible, even by spreading the legs, to make the body lean forward sufficiently to establish a passive balance. In the case of each child there was an antagonistic tension which made the body rebound backward in an automatic manner resembling a sharp spring-like action of a knife blade snapping into position. We have never seen precisely this kind of reaction in an infant at this age. It is inconceivable that the response arose out of some identical conditioning factor in the environment. It is reasonable to suppose that this distinctive behavior pattern reflected a maturity level and a synchronous neural organization shared by both children because of their common genetic origin.

Within a week this reaction disappeared. Four days later the twins were placed upon a large blotter on the platform of a clinical crib and maintained the sitting position by leaning forward. Simultaneously they attacked the blotter with the hand in full pronation, and simultaneously, with vocalization, they continued to scratch the blotter, leaving visible marks. Here again was a dramatic bit of correspondence all the more impressive because displayed simultaneously. The complexity and nature of these two behavior patterns again suggest the determining rôle of maturation. If it is argued that extrinsic factors determine the form and the incidence of these simultaneous patterns it is necessary to demonstrate in detail the cunning arrangements of environment and of conditioning stimuli which could design so precisely, and in duplicate, the configuration of behavior. How can the environment, even of twins, accomplish such architectonic miracles?

Still another, and very pretty example of identity was disclosed in the pellet and bottle test at 48 weeks. This test involved a bit of learning as well as perception and prehension. Three trials were made with each child. The examiner dropped a pellet into a small glass bottle and then gave the bottle to the child. Both children watched the dropping of the pellet with the same transfixed attention. Both children, on the first trial and on the second trial too, seized the bottle apparently heedless of the contained pellet. Both children on the third trial pursued the pellet by poking at it against the glass. Here the details of behavior pattern extended even into the marginal zone of adaptation through learning.

In passing it should be noted that although these observations on twins are comparative, they are objective. They have an objective, quantitative validity. It must be insisted that it would be very difficult to devise a more complicated and in some senses a more delicate instrument of behavior measurement than one twin used in juxtaposition with an identical co-twin as a standard of reference and comparative observation.

3. Limitations of training

While the positive results of training and conditioning have somewhat obscured the factors of maturation, the limitations of training may be adduced to show the existence of these factors. Such limitations were put to experimental study in the same pair of twins (Twin T and Twin C) whom we have just cited. At the age of 46 weeks, when the thorough-going mental and physical identity of the twins had been well established, it was decided to determine the influence of training confined to one twin, by using an experimental method which we have designated *the method of co-twin control*. T became the trained twin; C was reserved as a control.

Very briefly, Twin T was systematically trained for 20 minutes daily over a period of 6 weeks, in two fields of behavior, stair climbing and cube behavior, including prehension, manipulation and constructive play with a dozen one-inch red cubes. An experimental staircase arrangement of 5 treads was used, and for 10 minutes daily Twin T was put through her paces. At 48 weeks she scaled the stairs for the first time with slight assistance. At the conclusion of the 6 weeks training period (age one year) she was a relatively expert climber. At that age her untrained Co-twin C, would not yet scale the staircase, even with assistance. At the age of 53 weeks however, when C was again confronted with the staircase she climbed to the top without any assistance and without any previous training whatsoever. In this sense the form and the efficiency of her pattern of climbing were almost purely a function of the maturation of the appropriate neural counterparts.

Twin C was then given an experimental course of training in stair climbing, two weeks in length. At the end of this period (age 55 weeks) she approached Twin T in her climbing skill. By means of the motion picture it was possible to make a comparison of the climbing ability of C at 55 weeks (after 2 weeks of training) with that of T at 52 weeks (after 6 weeks of training). This comparison introduced an interesting form of relativity into the investigation and brought out the significant fact that although T had been trained three times longer and seven weeks earlier, this advantage was more than overcome by the three weeks of C's added age. Again the powerful influence of maturation on infant behavior pattern is made clear. Early training altered slightly the form of the pattern, and hastened the acquisition of facility, but left no considerable or decisive locomotor advantage in favor of Twin T.

In the field of cube play the experiment clearly showed that training had no significant effects upon the patterns of prehension, manipulation and constructive exploitation. Although Twin C had enjoyed no special opportunities in the handling of cubes, her cube behavior was fully equal to that of T after a 6 weeks training period. The similarity in temporal and spatial details of pattern was confirmed in this case by a time-space analysis of the behavior patterns by means of the cinema record. This does not mean, however, that there were no changes in the patterns of cube behavior during the training period from 46 weeks to 52 weeks. On the contrary, the records, when analyzed, show consistent and incontrovertible weekly increments. Indeed, a day by day analysis of the diurnal records of cube behavior satisfied us that there was a daily drift toward progressive changes in the cube performance patterns. These changes were developmentally achieved by steady processes of decrement and increment rather than by a saltatory or zigzag course. There may be spurts and plateaus and rhythms in the development of other fields of behavior, but at this stage of the life cycle there was a relatively constant trend toward daily change. This progressive daily changing apparently occurs by a process of continuous emergence which tends to lift the level of development slowly and steadily as though by tide action rather than by rhythmic spurt. We would explain the resistance of the patterns of cube behavior to the influences of training and conditioning by the fact that these patterns are basically under the stress and the regulation of the intrinsic organic factors of muturation. The very fact that there is a growth trend toward daily change of pattern makes the behavior less susceptible to stereotypy and to conditioning.

4. The restricted influence of physical handicap

This subject opens up the vast field of experimental etiology in which the conditions of disease and environmental abnormality may be analyzed to determine the influence of extrinsic factors upon the complex of growth. In many instances these extrinsic factors seem to be much less powerful than one might suppose. Even grave degrees of malnutrition, correlated with excessive subnormality of weight, are usually incompetent to inflict any drastic changes upon the forms of fundamental behavior patterns and upon the genetic order of their sequence. While it must be granted that certain food deficiencies, for example in the field of calcium metabolism, may definitely influence the general picture of behavior, the nervous system itself is remarkably resistant to general adversity, even to malnutrition. When certain areas of the nervous system are actually damaged by disease or injury, maturation cannot make amends, but the maturation of the nervous system seems to proceed toward the optimum in the areas unimpaired, even though lacking the stimulus of exercise of the functions controlled by the impaired areas. It is for this reason that certain clinical types of profound motor disability attain none the less considerable approximation to normality in certain patterns of behavior.

In this context we may also mention the high degree of autonomy which the nervous system maintains even in extreme cases of *puberty praecox*. We have investigated one case in which there was a precocious displacement of puberty amounting to a whole decade. This girl became physiologically mature at the age of 3½ years. In spite of this extreme developmental alteration, the course of her behavior development in the fields of intelligence, language and locomotion has been relatively normal and stable.

Here, also, should be mentioned the general developmental course of the healthy infant born after an abnormally short or an abnormally long gestation period. A premature postnatal environment and a protracted uterine environment must be considered as drastic deviations from normal environmental influence. The relative immunity of the behavior patterns from these environmental deviations again bespeaks the potency of maturation factors.

5. Developmental progression in emotional behavior

The role of maturation in the control of emotional behavior has had scant recognition. The primary emotions have been discussed as though they were elementary stable phenomena subject only to the changes of social conditioning. This is the implication in much that has been written concerning the emotion of fear. It seems to us that the problem has been over-simplified. Fear may be an original tendency, but it is subject to the genetic alterations of organic growth as well as to organization by environmental conditioning. Such conditioning may determine the orientation and reference of fears, but the mode of fearing undergoes change as a result of maturation. Fear is neither more nor less of an abstraction than prehension. It is not a simple entity. It waxes and alters with growth. It is shaped by intrinsic maturation as well as by experience, certainly during the period of infancy.

Consider for example the reactions of an infant to confinement in a small enclosed space, approximately 2 x 3 x 4 feet. In a physical sense the situation is entirely harmless. The space is ample in size, it is ventilated, it is illuminated, it is open at one end. In a personal sense however, the space may have elements of novelty and unusualness. The infant is not accustomed to lie in such a small space which shuts him off from his accustomed environment. What are his reactions, even when he is gently introduced into this enclosed chamber? At 10 weeks he may accept the situation with complete complaisance; at 20 weeks he may betray a mild intolerance, a dissatisfaction, persistent head turning and social seeking which we may safely characterize as mild apprehension; at 30 weeks his intolerance to the same situation may be so vigorously expressed by crying that we describe the reaction as fear or fright. Here then are three gradations of response: first, no disquietude; second, mild disquietude; third, robust disquietude. Is not this a genetic gradation of fear behavior which is based upon maturational sequence rather than upon an historical sequence of extrinsic conditioning factors? Such factors may account for specific aspects of fear behavior, but not for the organic pattern beneath such behavior. This pattern, we would suggest, is as much the product of organic growth as the various stages in the elaboration and perfection of prehension. Incidentally it may be said that the observation of duplicate twins will tend to substantiate the existence of maturational factors in the development of emotion. Although the tendency towards developmental divergence in identical twins is probably greater in the field of personality make-up than in any other sphere of behavior, there is, during infancy, an impressive tendency toward identity of emotional behavior. Twins T and C, already referred to, showed a highly significant degree of correspondence in their manifestations of initial timidity, in their responsiveness to social games in their reactions to the mirror image, in their gestures of avoiding and refusing, in their seeking and begging gestures, in their laughter and crying. The relatively simultaneous and progressive nature of these changes in the field of emotional behavior suggests the influence of organic maturational factors as opposed to purely extrinsic factors in the determination of behavior pattern.

The extreme versions of environmentalist and conditioning theories suffer because they explain too much. They suggest that the individual is fabricated out of the conditioning patterns. They do not give due recognition to the inner checks which set metes and bounds to the area of conditioning and which happily prevent abnormal and grotesque consequences which the theories themselves would make too easily possible. Although it is artificial to press unduly a distinction between intrinsic and extrinsic factors, it must after all, be granted that growth is a function of the organism rather than of the environment as such. The environment furnishes the foil and the milieu for the manifestations of development, but these manifestations come from inner compulsion and are primarily organized by inherent inner mechanics and by an intrinsic physiology of development. The very plasticity of growth requires that there be limiting and regulatory mechanisms. Growth is a process so intricate and so sensitive that there must be powerful stabilizing factors, intrinsic rather than extrinsic, which preserve the balance of the total pattern and the direction of the growth trend. Maturation is, in a sense, a name for this regulatory mechanism. Just because we do not grant complete dichotomy of internal and external factors, it is necessary to explain what keeps the almost infinite fortuities of physical and social environment from dominating the organism of the developing individual.

The organismal concept requires that the individual shall maintain an optimum or normal integrity. The phenomena of maturation suggest the stabilizing and inexpugnable factors which safeguard the basic patterns of growth. Just as the respiration of the organism depends upon the maintenance of constant hydrogen-ion concentration, so probably on a vastly more intricate scale, the life career of the individual is maintained by the physiological processes of maturation—processes which determine in such large measure the form and the sequence of infant behavior pattern, that the infant as an individual is reasonably secure against extreme conditioning, whether favorable or unfavorable.

33

WILLIS C. BEASLEY (B. 1901)

Visual pursuit in white and Negro infants (1933)

Early psychological studies of Negro children in the United States were primarily studies of intelligence test scores which showed that Negro children were retarded, and which often were given an interpretation in terms of hereditary race differences. None of these is presented here because it is now clear that intelligence test scores can be greatly influenced by environment. (See Hugh Gordon's study of Canal Boat and Gypsy Children, selection 28, which shows that underprivileged white group score as low as any underprivileged Negro group). It is also clear from other studies that present day Negro scores are higher than those obtained from Negroes several decades ago, and that there were marked changes in the intelligence scores of both Negro and white soldiers between World War I and World War II.

Since the early studies of Negro intelligence, many American psychologists appear to have leaned over backward in an attempt to correct their errors. The impression one gets from reading social psychologists is that there are no *racial differences in behavior.*

It is true that most *differences between races are ethnic, that is, of cultural origin, and are not biological. But the physical differences are biological, and there is no reason to deny that there may be behavioral differences between races.*

Beasley's careful study of visual pursuit in newborn infants shows that the ocular-motor responses of American Negro neonates is superior, on the average, to that of newly-born whites. It is difficult if not impossible to explain this in terms of pre-natal environment, where no light penetrates to the fetus. The subsequent importance, if any, of this racial difference is to be determined.

This selection is abridged from an article in Child Development, *4 (1933): 106–120 by permission of the Society for Research in Child Development.*

This report is the first of a series concerned with investigations of related problems in the vision of newborn infants. The problem of research being conducted by the writer is directed toward a solution of some of the problems arising from the following considerations:

At what stage of development are the various oculo-motor processes during the first few hours subsequent to delivery? The "various processes" include: (a) negative movements of the eye-balls to light, (b) protective eye-lid reactions, (c) iris reflexes, (d) accommodation of the lens, (e) squint, or incoordinate binocular movements, (f) binocular fixation of stationary objects, (g) binocular fixation of successively displaced objects, (h) binocular convergence (adaptive of changing distance of object), (i) binocular pursuit of continuously moving objects. There are quite possibly other important functions, which will arise in the course of investigation applied to these. To what extent are significant individual differences exhibited at this early period, and if they are marked with what known factors can they be correlated? Certain of these possible factors are: (a) race, (b) good stock as indicated by the "vitality" or more specific organic or glandular characteristics of the parents, (c) nutritional factors of the mother during term, (d) conditions of delivery. These are only suggestive of pertinent items, which may yield important relationships.

At what age levels do significant changes from the birth condition occur? Which processes develop first, most rapidly? What intercorrelations between these processes and other behavior obtain? What influence has early practice upon accelerating the development of these functions? For example, does practicing binocular pursuit reduce the age at which certain standards of pursuit are attained? Or does lack of practice advance the age at which certain standards of performance are usually reached? Problems are here in large number; they are definite and important. They are practically untouched, insofar as systematic research is concerned. In the literature one finds only occasional sampling taken with reference to each of the problems and processes mentioned above. The fundamental problems remain unsolved.

* * *

Although the writer has accumulated data on several hundred infants for several of the functions mentioned above, the present report is concerned with visual pursuit. The infants were examined in a special experimental cabinet measuring 30 inches wide by 42 inches long by 40 inches high inside. Only one side was open, over which a curtain was hung. This cabinet was mounted on a table of approximately the same breadth and length as the outside dimensions of the cabinet, the whole structure being painted white. The legs of the table were equipped with 4 inches by 1 inch rubber-tired casters, so that the experimental set-up could be moved from one floor of the hospital to another. Inside the cabinet was placed a crib-like platform, measuring 22 inches by 30 inches by 4 inches, and having a concave surface. On this was placed appropriate padding to insure comfort for the infant which would be equivalent to that supplied by the nursery crib. The cabinet was wired for interior overhead illumination.

The procedure for studying visual pursuit in these infants was designed so as to make possible (a) measurements on a large number of subjects, (b) comparisons of pursuit with directly transmitted and reflected light with either a dark field or an illuminated one, (c) designation of definite standards of pursuit so that other investigators who so desire can duplicate the measurements, (d) the inclusion of three types of motion of the object with reference to the median plane of the infant's head, i.e., horizontal, vertical and circular, (e) a variation of the rate of motion of the object and its distance from the infant's head, (f) the designation for tabulation purposes of what constitutes a single "test."

Since funds were not available for building apparatus with automatic controls and recording units, the very simplest sort of means were utilized for fulfilling the above requirements. Three stimulus objects were used always in the same way. For the tests of pursuit with directly transmitted light in a dark field a small fountain-pen flashlight was used within the darkened cabinet. Over the bulb in the end of the flashlight three layers of tissue paper were tied, so that the stimulus object in the dark appeared as a faint circular spot of diffuse light about 1.5 cm. in diameter. The second test object may be characterized as fluttering, flickering or moving fingers. The experimenter's hand was moved across the field, the fingers executing alternating movements continuously. The third object was a dark blue cylinder, 2 cm. in diameter and seven inches long. The second and third test objects were always presented in a faintly illuminated field. A single 25 watt Edison Mazda bulb which had been dipped in ordinary theater blue dye was used in a socket in the top of the cabinet 32 inches above the infant's face and 12 inches to the infant's left.

For making records of pursuit elicited a simple schematization was devised. The records were written on standard 6 inches by 9 inches cardboard filing cards, immediately following each test. In recording instances of horizontal pursuit, a vertical line one inch long was drawn on the record card to represent the sagittal plane of the infant's head. Horizontal lines were then drawn with reference to this vertical one to indicate through what extent of the field from extreme right to left or vice versa the pursuit continued. For example, if the infant followed the object across the field from a position immediately in front of his face when he was looking up to the extreme right, the object being moved in a circular arc having its center at the infant's nose, a line was drawn on the card from the vertical reference line to the right. Above the line was written 90°, indicating that the infant had followed the object all the way down to the plane of the crib on which he was lying. This pursuit would require several successive eye fixations and from two to four head adjustments. It was not at all difficult to observe the number of head adjustments, and some of the eye adjustments could be directly counted. Along the line a check mark was placed for each eye adjustment observed, and an x mark for each head adjustment. The records are in error in so far as they do not contain all that happened. What was recorded had happened, but no doubt movements, especially small adjustments of the eye-balls occurred which could not be observed directly by the experimenter. If the infant followed an object from the center of the field to the extreme right and back to the center continuously, arrow heads were placed on the record lines to indicate that the pursuit had been continuous in two directions, one following the other. A similar technique was used for recording vertical pursuit, except that the reference line was horizontal and the pursuit lines were vertical. In recording circular pursuit, a circle was sketched on the record card to indicate the path of the moving object. Crossmarks indicated the positions in the field at which pursuit was begun and terminated. Checks were placed in the positions where eye fixations were observed, and x's again where head adjustments occurred.

The procedure in making a test of horizontal pursuit was as follows: in the case of a test with the flashlight, the spot was moved slowly in the region where the infant's eyes were apparently "looking" until apparent fixation of the object was obtained. It was then moved to the right, usually at a rate of approximately one inch per second at a distance of from six to fourteen inches directly in front of the infant's eyes, then back to the left then to the right through short distances (one to two inches). This was done until successive fixation was obtained. If the infant's eyes followed for a movement of one or two inches, the object was moved further in the same direction. If when this was done, the infant did not continue to follow the object, more bracketing back and forth was done until another indication of pursuit appeared. This sort of procedure was repeatedly carried out for several minutes, sometimes eight to ten minutes, with no pursuit beyond one or two slight successive fixations exhibited. And, frequently, when the experimenter was at the point of dispensing with the subject at hand and obtaining another one or two more trials would be given and 90° pursuit or more elicited. It is certain that from the procedures required in these experiments in order to elicit pursuit, if an automatically controlled continuously moving stimulus object were set moving in the field, even at this slow rate, very few instances of pursuit would be elicited. The most crucial part of the procedure is to obtain fixation of the object and then not to move it in the field too rapidly following this. Once continuous pursuit is obtained for several successive eye and head adjustments, the object is moved to the extreme right then back to the extreme left, the "test" ending when pursuit ceases. It is important also *not* to maintain the distance of the object from the infants eyes constant. There are interesting suggestions in this fact. It was repeatedly observed that some infants followed the object better at twelve to fourteen inches, others at from six to eight inches. Is it not likely that there are variations in accommodation present at this age that would determine partly at least optimal distances for objects of any size? A similar procedure was used for horizontal pursuit tests with the moving fingers and with the dark cylinder. The latter test object was always held so that its long axis was parallel to the sagittal plane of the head during horizontal tests.

An identical procedure was used for tests of vertical pursuit with simply a change in the directions of motion of the test objects. The dark cylinder in vertical pursuit was held so that its long axis was perpendicular to the sagittal plane of the infant's head. The same specifications apply to tests of circular pursuit. The circular path through which the test objects were moved had a radius of about ten inches centering at the infant's nose. Usually, some type of horizontal or vertical pursuit preceded the circular. Although the path of motion of the stimulus is designated as circular, it was not so in the actual mathematical sense. The actual path probably was more that of the outline of a six or eight pointed star. Deviations from the circular path were necessitated by the tendency of the infants to make fixations out of line with the circle. The experimenter in this case would move the object in or out, really assisting the infant's pursuit.

In the tables which follow, 4 types of pursuit have been designated which are based upon the following quantitative considerations characterizing each "Type."

Type A. This type of pursuit is characterized qualitatively as excellent. From the record cards, all instances of pursuit which exhibit the following minimum requirements have been classified as Type A. (1) In horizontal pursuit a minimum of 90° across the field, involving several successive eye fixations and several successive head adjustments correlated with the direction of motion of the stimulus object and a *return* in the opposite direction of an equivalent extent. There were numerous instances of pursuit where the infant would follow the object 180° across the field two or three successive times back and forth, turning the head completely to the right or to the left. A well-known experimental psychologist observed this one day with a two-day old infant and remarked, "I would never have believed it." (2) In vertical pursuit a minimum of several successive eye fixations and several head adjustments in the same direction followed by several in the opposite direction continuously correlated with the direction of motion of the stimulus. (3) In circular pursuit a minimum of continuous following of the object until it has completed the circuit around the field, involving both eye and head adjustments.

Type B. (1) In horizontal pursuit a minimum of 90° across the field in one direction, involving both eye and head adjustments in the direction of the moving stimulus. (2) In vertical pursuit several successive head and eye adjustments in the same direction of the moving stimulus. (3) In circular pursuit, continuous following for at least half the circuit around the field. This type of pursuit has been designated qualitatively as good.

Type C. (1) A minimum of 3 successive eye fixations of the object without head adjustments for horizontal, and (2) the same for vertical. (3) For circular, several successive eye fixations with one or two head adjustments, but failure to pursue the object for more than one-fourth of the circuit around the field.

None. In all instances where less than three successive fixations correlated with the direction of motion of the stimulus were elicited, the responses were classified as "fixation" but not pursuit.

Pursuit tests were given altogether to 109 White infants and to 142 Negro infants, ranging in age from 2½ hours to 12 days. Attention should be called to the fact that the infants in this study which are classified as "Negro" are so termed because they were born in the Negro Clinic. The writer is perfectly cognizant of the problems involved here in racial intermixture. In most cases, the mothers were uncertain of their own family history beyond one or two generations. Physical traits became the only index in such cases, and unfortunately we do not have infallible standards in this respect. Skin color, eye color and hair type seem to supply the most reliable index to purity of stock. Data on each of these factors have been taken for all of the infants used in this study.... Roughly, about 30 per cent of the Negro infants used in this study exhibit the three features mentioned in a manner characteristic of the newborn in "pure" stocks.

Table 1 exhibits the complete data on pursuit in the White infants, and table 2 that for the "Negroes." Reading across the first row of tabulations in table 1, one makes the following interpolation: seven infants were examined for the first time 5 hours or less after delivery. None of these seven was re-examined within this period. These seven infants were given 17 tests with the flashlight (FL), of which 6 were for horizontal (H) pursuit, six for vertical (V), and five for circular (Cr); they were given 9 tests with the moving fingers (MF), of which 3 were for horizontal pursuit, 3 for vertical, and 3 for circular; they were given 12 tests with the dark cylinder (DC), of which 4 were for horizontal pursuit, 4 for vertical, and 4 for circular. A total of 38 tests was given to these 7 infants within 5 hours after delivery. Of these, 13 were for H pursuit, 13 for V, and 12 for Cr. Of the 13 H tests, 6 were FL, 3 were MF, and 4 were DC. All together, at this age level with the seven White infants, there were 5 cases of Horizontal Type A (Excellent) pursuit responses elicited (5H-Type A) from a total of 13 H-tests. Of these 5H-Type A responses, there were 2 FL, 1 MF and 2 DC. From the remaining 9 H-tests at this age level, there were 3 H-Type B, 3 H-Type C pursuit responses elicited. There were 2 failures as listed under "None" horizontal. This example should make clear the procedure in reading the tables.

The row of "Totals" in table 1 yields the following information: there were 109 different White infants tested, 95 of whom were re-tested. There were 829 tests given, the computed number of tests per subject being 7.6. Of these tests, 315 (39 per cent) were FL, 255 (30 per cent) were MF, and 259 (31 per cent) were DC. From the 829 tests, there were 320 instances (39 per cent of the cases) in which *no* pursuit was elicited, and 509 instances (61 per cent of the cases) in which *some* type of pursuit was elicited. Equivalent interpolations from table 2 show that 142 different Negro infants, of whom 81 were re-tested, were given a total of 1,111 tests, the computed number of tests per subject being 7.8. Of these tests 420 (38 per cent) were FL, 350 (31 per cent) were MF, and 341 (31 per cent) were DC. Therefore, each stimulus object was used a comparable number of times in each racial group. From the 1,111 tests in the Negro group, there were 213 instances (19 per cent, compared with 39 per cent for the Whites) in which *no* pursuit was elicited, and 898 instances (81 per cent, compared with 61 per cent for the Whites) in which some type of pursuit was elicited. For all subjects at all age levels for all kinds of pursuit, then, the Negro infants excelled the Whites.

Comparative details in types of pursuit are interesting. Of the 509

Table 1. Pursuit data from 829 tests given to 109 white newborn infants

Age groups	Number infants first examined by age groups	Number infants re-examined	Total number examined at each age level	Flashlight, FL	Moving fingers, MF	Dark cylinder, DC	Test totals	Stimulus object
Up to 5 hrs	7	0	7	17	9	12	38	FL MF DC
6—12 hrs.	10	0	10	30	24	21	75	FL MF DC
13—24 hrs.	25	0	25	71	42	40	153	FL MF DC
2 days	11	12	23	26	21	19	66	FL MF DC
3 days	9	6	15	21	12	14	47	FL MF DC
4 days	7	13	20	18	24	18	60	FL MF DC
5 days	13	26	39	42	39	36	117	FL MF DC
6—8 days	20	23	43	60	60	66	186	FL MF DC
9—12 days	7	15	22	30	24	33	87	FL MF DC
Totals	109	95	204	315	255	259	829	

*See text for quantitative definition of each "type" of pursuit. These data are not "qualitive."

	Pursuit elicited* (frequency)											Test totals by type of stimulus motion used		
Type A "excellent"			Type B "good"			Type C "poor"			None						
Horizontal	*Vertical*	*Circular*	*Horizontal*	*Vertical*	*Circular*	*Horizontal*	*Vertical*	*Circular*	*Horizontal*	*Vertical*	*Circular*	*Horizontal*	*Vertical*	*Circular*
2	1	0	1	0	0	1	1	0	2	4	5	6	6	5
1	1	0	1	0	0	1	1	1	0	1	2	3	3	3
2	2	0	1	1	0	1	0	1	0	1	3	4	4	4
3	2	1	6	2	1	2	3	1	0	2	7	11	9	10
3	3	1	3	1	1	1	1	1	1	3	5	8	8	8
4	2	1	3	2	1	0	3	1	0	0	4	7	7	7
7	4	0	4	4	1	6	3	5	4	10	23	21	21	29
5	3	0	3	4	0	6	2	4	1	6	8	15	15	12
5	3	0	3	5	0	6	2	3	1	5	7	15	15	10
4	1	0	2	2	0	0	2	1	2	2	10	8	7	11
4	1	0	1	2	0	1	1	1	2	3	5	8	7	6
4	1	0	1	1	0	0	1	1	2	3	5	7	6	6
1	1	0	1	1	1	1	1	0	4	4	6	7	7	7
0	0	0	1	1	1	2	2	0	1	1	3	4	4	4
1	0	0	2	1	1	1	1	0	1	2	4	5	4	5
4	3	1	1	1	0	0	0	3	1	2	2	6	6	6
4	3	1	1	1	0	0	0	3	3	4	4	8	8	8
3	3	1	1	1	0	0	0	3	2	2	2	6	6	6
7	6	0	4	4	2	1	0	2	2	4	10	14	14	14
7	7	0	3	4	2	2	1	2	1	1	9	13	13	13
6	6	0	4	3	2	0	1	2	2	2	8	12	12	12
12	9	1	2	2	2	3	4	3	3	5	14	20	20	20
11	12	1	4	0	5	3	3	3	2	5	11	20	20	20
15	11	0	3	2	3	2	3	5	2	6	14	22	22	22
8	2	0	1	1	1	1	0	1	0	7	8	10	10	10
6	5	0	1	2	2	1	0	2	0	1	4	8	8	8
7	5	0	0	2	2	3	0	2	1	4	7	11	11	11
136	97	8	58	50	28	45	36	51	40	90	190	279	273	277

Table 2. Pursuit data from 1,111 tests given to 142 negro newborn infants

Age groups	Number infants first examined by age groups	Number infants re-examined	Total number examined at each age level	Flashlight, FL	Moving fingers, MF	Dark cylinder, DC	Test totals	Stimulus object
Up to 5 hrs.	3	0	3	10	6	9	25	FL MF DC
6—12 hrs.	10	0	10	30	27	24	81	FL MF DC
13—24 hrs.	34	0	34	97	87	84	268	FL MF DC
2 days	16	8	24	42	30	30	102	FL MF DC
3 days	5	10	15	15	9	9	33	FL MF DC
4 days	5	14	19	17	14	17	48	FL MF DC
5 days	33	6	39	94	92	88	274	FL MF DC
6—8 days	22	31	53	58	45	43	146	FL MF DC
9—12 days	14	12	26	57	40	37	134	FL MF DC
Totals	142	81	223	420	350	341	1,111	

*See text for quantitative definition of each type of pursuit. These data are not "qualitive."

Pursuit elicited* (frequency)

| \multicolumn{3}{c|}{Type A "excellent"} | \multicolumn{3}{c|}{Type B "good"} | \multicolumn{3}{c|}{Type C "poor"} | \multicolumn{3}{c|}{None} | \multicolumn{3}{c}{Test totals by type of stimulus motion used} |

Horizontal	Vertical	Circular	Horizontal	Vertical	Circular	Horizontal	Vertical	Circular	Horizontal	Vertical	Circular	Horizontal	Vertical	Circular
2	1	1	0	1	0	1	1	2	0	0	1	3	3	4
1	1	1	0	0	0	1	1	0	0	0	1	2	2	2
1	1	1	1	1	0	1	1	1	0	0	1	3	3	3
3	0	0	2	5	1	4	5	5	1	1	3	10	11	9
1	0	0	3	4	1	4	5	3	1	1	4	9	10	8
0	0	0	3	3	1	3	4	3	2	2	3	8	9	7
15	13	6	4	3	4	7	8	11	7	8	11	33	32	32
13	11	2	5	5	5	6	7	13	5	6	9	29	29	29
12	10	2	5	4	4	6	8	13	5	6	9	28	28	28
10	8	6	0	1	0	1	1	4	4	6	14	14	14	
7	4	2	0	2	1	0	1	2	3	3	5	10	10	10
7	5	3	0	1	1	0	1	1	3	3	5	10	10	10
5	4	2	0	1	1	0	0	2	0	0	0	5	5	5
3	2	0	0	1	1	0	0	2	0	0	0	3	3	3
3	2	0	0	1	1	0	0	2	0	0	0	3	3	3
5	5	3	0	0	0	1	1	1	0	0	1	6	6	5
4	4	1	0	1	0	1	1	1	0	0	1	5	6	3
5	5	2	0	1	0	1	1	1	0	0	1	6	7	4
17	14	8	9	9	5	2	6	8	3	3	10	31	32	31
17	13	7	10	8	6	3	7	7	2	2	10	32	30	30
16	13	7	9	8	5	2	7	9	2	2	8	29	30	29
14	11	9	2	2	2	4	3	3	1	2	5	21	18	19
11	8	5	2	1	3	1	3	3	2	2	4	16	14	15
10	9	6	1	1	2	2	3	4	1	1	3	14	14	15
12	11	7	2	3	2	2	1	5	3	4	5	19	19	19
9	7	3	2	2	1	1	3	5	1	2	4	13	14	13
8	7	2	2	2	1	1	3	6	1	1	3	12	13	12
211	169	86	62	71	49	54	82	114	47	53	113	374	375	362

instances of pursuit by the Whites, there were 241 instances (47 per cent) of Type A pursuit, 136 instances (27 per cent) of Type B, and 132 instances (26 per cent) of Type C. Of the 898 instances of pursuit by the Negroes, there were 466 instances (52 per cent) of Type A pursuit, 182 instances (20 per cent) of Type B, and 250 instances (28 per cent) of Type C. This comparison yields no discernible difference between the racial groups.

Of the 829 tests given to the Whites, 279 (34 per cent) were for H pursuit, 273 (33 per cent) for V, and 277 (33 per cent) for Cr. This is an excellent frequency distribution of test types. Of the 279 instances of H pursuit tests, there were 40 instances (14 per cent) in which *no* pursuit was elicited, and 239 instances (86 per cent) in which *some* type of pursuit was elicited. Of the 239 instances of H pursuit, there were 136 instances (57 per cent) of Type A pursuit, 58 instances (24 per cent) of Type B, and 45 instances (19 per cent) of Type C. Of the 273 instances of V pursuit tests, there were 90 instances (33 per cent) in which *no* pursuit was elicited, and 183 instances (67 per cent) in which *some* type of pursuit occurred. Of these 183, 97 instances (53 per cent) were Type A, 50 instances (27 per cent) were Type B, and 36 instances (20 per cent) were Type C. Of the 277 instances of Cr pursuit tests, there were 190 instances (69 per cent, compared with 14 per cent for H, and 33 per cent for V) in which *no* pursuit was elicited, and 87 instances (31 per cent, compared with 86 per cent for H, and 67 per cent for V) in which *some* type of pursuit was elicited. Of these 87 instances of Cr pursuit, there were 8 instances (9 per cent) of Type A, 28 instances (32 per cent) of Type B, and 51 (59 per cent) of Type C.

A comparison of the data on the Negroes for the same items presents some similarities, but also striking differences. Of the 1,111 tests in the Negro group, 374 (34 per cent) were for H pursuit, 375 (34 per cent) were V, and 362 (32 per cent) were Cr. Again, a well-balanced frequency distribution. Of the 374 tests of H pursuit, there were 47 instances (13 per cent, compared with 14 per cent for Whites) in which *no* pursuit was elicited, and 327 instances (87 per cent, compared with 86 per cent for Whites), in which some type of pursuit was elicited. Of these 327 instances of H pursuit by the Negroes, 211 (65 per cent) were Type A, 62 (19 per cent) Type B, and 54 (16 per cent) Type C. The respective percentages for Whites were 57 per cent, 24 per cent, and 19 per cent. Although the Negroes here show a slightly higher proportion of Type A pursuit, the difference is not marked. Of the 375 tests for V pursuit with the Negroes, there were 53 instances (14 per cent, compared with 33 per cent for the Whites) in which no pursuit was elicited, and 322 instances (86 per cent, compared with 67 per cent for the Whites) in which *some* type of V pursuit was obtained. This difference is significant. Of these 322 instances of V pursuit by the Negroes, 160 (53 per cent) were Type A, 71 (22 per cent) were Type B, and 82 (25 per cent) were Type C. The corresponding percentages for the Whites were 53 per cent, 27 per cent, and 20 per cent. Thus, in vertical pursuit the Negroes exhibit a greater proportion of pursuit responses, even though the relative frequency of each Type is equivalent for the two groups. But in the case of circular pursuit, a marked difference is presented. Of the 362 Cr tests given the Negroes, there were 113 instances (31 per cent, compared with 69 per cent for Whites) in which *no* Cr pursuit was elicited, and 249 instances (69 per cent, compared with 31 per cent for Whites) in which some type of Cr pursuit was elicited. Of these 249 instances of Cr pursuit by the Negroes, 86 (34 per cent, compared with 9 per cent for Whites) were Type A, 49 (20 per cent, compared with 32 per cent for Whites) were Type B, and 114 (46 per cent, compared with 59 per cent for Whites) were Type C. In the case of ability to pursue an object traversing a circular path in the visual field, then, the Negroes show a striking superiority to the Whites.

It is usually maintained that infants do not pursue objects "Visually," but merely execute a sort of heliotropic orientation to light, and that, consequently, they can pursue a "light" but not ordinary objects. The present data affords an opportunity to compare the relative efficacy of the 3 stimulus objects in eliciting pursuit from the infants. Of the 829 tests given to the White infants, 315 (38 per cent) were with the flashlight, 255 (31 per cent) with the moving fingers, and 259 (31 per cent) with the dark cylinder. This is an excellent apportionment with reference to stimulus objects. In 143 (45 per cent) of the FL tests, 87 (34 per cent) of the MF tests, and 90 (35 per cent) of the DC tests, *no* pursuit was elicited. For the White infants, then, there was a slightly greater tendency for pursuit to occur in the MF and DC tests than in the FL tests, although the difference is perhaps not significant. Another question, which can be answered here, is whether the type of stimulus object influences the relative frequency of the different types of pursuit. Of the 172 instances of pursuit in the FL tests, 80 (47 per cent) were Type A, 47 (27 per cent) were Type B, and 45 (26 per cent) were Type C. Of the 168 instances of pursuit in the MF tests, 79 (47 per cent) were Type A, 44 (26 per cent) were Type B, and 45 (27 per cent) were Type C. Of the 169 instances of pursuit in the DC tests, 82 (48 per cent) were Type A, 45 (27 per cent) were Type B, and 42 (25 per cent) were Type C. There is clearly no tendency for the White infants to show better pursuit for either of the stimulus objects.

In the Negro group there were 1,111 tests, of which 420 (38 per cent) were FL, 350 (31 per cent) were MF, and 341 (31 per cent) were DC. In the FL tests there were 83 instances (20 per cent), in the MF there were 68 instances (19 per cent), and in the DC there were 62 instances (18 per cent) in which *no* pursuit was elicited. Here, again, the tendency of the Negro infants to exhibit a greater relative frequency of pursuit is shown, but the tendency is not influenced differentially by the type of stimulus object used. With respect to the quality of pursuit for the several stimulus objects, no apparent difference is shown with the Negro infants. Of the 337 instances of pursuit with FL tests, 192 (57 per cent) were Type A, 60 (18 per cent) were Type B, and 85 (25 per cent) were Type C. Of the 282 instances of pursuit with MF tests, 137 (49 per cent) were Type A, 64 (23 per cent) were Type B, and 81 (28 per cent) were Type C. Of the 279 instances of pursuit with DC tests, 137 (49 per cent) were Type A, 58 (21 per cent) were Type B, 84 (30 per cent) were Type C. Although there is a slightly greater proportion of Type A pursuit with the flashlight, the difference is probably not significant.

In any investigation centered upon the early development of responses, the question of improvement is always vital. Although the present data cannot be graphed in the manner of the conventional "learning curve," when the data are assembled as in table 3 unambiguous signs of "development," "learning," "maturation," or functional improvement are shown. For the purposes of this table, the three age groups of tables 1 and 2 under the captions "Up to 5 hours," "6–12 hours" and "13–24 hours" have been summed and listed under "1 day;" and those designated as "2 days," "3 days," "4 days" and "5 days" have been summed and included under the single group "2–5 days" in table 3. Similarly, the groups labelled "6–8 days" and "9–12 days" in tables 1 and 2 are included in the single group "6–12 days" in table 3. Although the time distributions are not equal in this arrangment, any one familiar with the literature on infant behavior will recognize the stages as ones in which usually differentiations in behavior occur. Moreover, a fairly comparable sampling of different infants in the present data is obtained by this grouping. The former reason for the grouping is more important.

From table 3 it is seen that of the 829 tests given to White infants, 266 (32 per cent) were with infants less than 24 hours old, 290 (35 per cent) were with infants in the 2–5 day group, and 273 (33 per cent) were with the 6–12 day group. Of the 1,111 tests given to Negroes, 374 (34 per cent) were with the 1 day group, 457 (41 per cent) were with the 2–5 day group, and 280 (25 per cent) were with the 6–12 day group. Although the relative frequencies are distributed better with the Whites, in both racial groups there is a representative number of tests given at each age level segregated in the table. Comparisons of the two groups with respect to the percentages of the total number of tests for each age group which yielded *no* pursuit and each type of pursuit affords an immediate indication of any marked tendencies in the direction of functional improvement.

An analysis of the percentage data in the table shows that (1) of the 266 tests given to White infants in the 1 day group, in 40 per cent of the

Table 3. Percentages of the total number of tests for each age group for each race yielding failures and each type of pursuit

Age Group days	Type of Pursuit								Number of tests given			Number of Subjects		
	A		B		C		None		Both races	W	N	Both races	W	N
	W	N	W	N	W	N	W	N						
1	21	26	18	18	21	33	40	23	640	266	374	89	42	47
2—5	28	48	18	19	12	16	42	17	747	290	457	194	97	97
6—12	39	53	13	12	14	19	34	16	553	273	280	144	65	79

cases no pursuit was elicited, in 21 per cent Type A pursuit was obtained, in 18 per cent Type B, and in 21 per cent Type C; (2) of the 374 tests given to Negroes in the 1 day group, in 23 per cent of the cases no pursuit was elicited, in 26 per cent Type A pursuit was obtained, in 18 per cent Type B, and in 33 per cent Type C; (3) of the 290 tests given to White infants in the 2–5 day group, 42 per cent yielded no pursuit, 28 per cent Type A, 18 per cent Type B, and 12 per cent Type C; (4) of the 457 tests given to Negroes in the 2–5 day group. 17 per cent yielded no pursuit, 48 per cent Type A, 19 per cent Type B, and 16 per cent Type C; (5) of the 273 tests given to White infants in the 6–12 day group, 34 per cent yielded no pursuit, 39 per cent yielded Type A, 13 per cent Type B, and 14 per cent Type C; (6) of the 280 tests given to Negroes in the 6–12 day group, 16 per cent yielded no pursuit, 53 per cent yielded Type A, 12 per cent Type B and 19 per cent Type C. The Negro infants exhibited a greater percentage of pursuit responses on the first day (Negro: 77 per cent; White: 60 per cent); both racial groups showed marked functional improvement as indicated by the increased percentage of Type A pursuit throughout the three age levels; the Negroes not only began at a higher level of excellence, but also showed a more rapid improvement as indicated by greater increases in the percentage of Type A pursuit (Negroes: 26 per cent, 48 per cent, 53 per cent; Whites: 21 per cent, 28 per cent, 39 per cent). These data favor the conclusion that functional development is more advanced in the Negroes at birth than in the Whites, at least with respect to the responses under consideration.

The method employed in these experiments has justified itself in yield. Numerous problems have arisen in the course of this work which require more refined methods, including photographic recording, for their solution, as well as optical instruments of precision. The most important development besides the amassing of response data has been a segregation of the optimal conditions for eliciting pursuit responses in newborn infants.

A second equally important result from this experimentation has been the development of a method and apparatus for studying visual acuity, absolute and relative sensitivity, and color vision in the newborn. Throughout this past year the writer has devoted considerable time to the testing of various optical systems for producing the following controls: the projection of a large field approximately twenty inches by thirty inches, on which forms of any *type* and *size* can be projected (lines, circles, or any irregular form); the independent variation of the *brightness* and *hue* of the field and the form, so that the form can be reduced to any relative level of brightness *above* and *below* that of the field; the maintenance of the field in a stationary condition, with the spot moving in a linear path, back and forth, across any axis of the field, or in a *circular* path of any desirable radius within the limits of the field size.

Seven different combined optical systems have been tested, and one finally developed which is entirely satisfactory. . . .

The theoretical basis for the method involves simply the assumptions (1) that if the subject pursues a "form" across the field and returns, the movement being spatially and temporally directly correlated with the successive positions of the spot in the field, then the subject "sees" the form; (2) the seen characteristics of the form can be approximated through indirect inference from measures of acuity of absolute and relative brightness discrimination, and of hue discrimination; (3) acuity can be determined by, for example, using a line of considerable width and reducing the width to the point where pursuit is no longer elicited. This measurement would require the use of various contrasts between the field and the line, as well as various brightness levels of the field. (4) Absolute sensitivity could be determined by using a black field and raising by small steps the energy of the spot until pursuit is elicited. The critical reader can readily infer the applications to the other processes. The details of the optical system selected, and further specifications of methodology, will be assigned to a forthcoming article.

It is obvious, also, that the method is equally applicable with reference to the same functions in older infants, children, adults, as well as to animals. The method is quantitative and subject to precision measurements, and the response criteria are simple and direct, not involving round about methods, such as formation of discrimination habits, which are tremendously time-consuming and involve numerous ambiguities yielding uncertainty of results.

HORATIO H. NEWMAN (1875–1957),
FRANK N. FREEMAN (1880–1961) AND
KARL J. HOLZINGER (1892–1954)

Twins: A study of heredity and environment (1937)

This cooperative study by Newman, a biologist, Freeman, an educational psychologist, and Holzinger, a statistician, is a projection of the research on twins undertaken by Galton in 1875 (selection 10). The amount of data gathered by Newman, Freeman, and Holzinger was immense. Chosen for presentation here are primarily the data from identical twins separated in infancy and reared apart. These data are widely considered to be the most important contributions of their book.

Through intensive efforts, the authors were able to find 19 pairs of identical twins reared apart who met their severe criteria. Data on another case contributed by another investigator is often included in their data, making a total of 20 cases.

The excerpts which follow are presented with the permission of the University of Chicago Press which published the book by Newman, Freeman and Holzinger in 1937.

It is now ten years since the three authors agreed to pool their intellectual resources in an attack upon the much-debated nature-nurture problem, using twins as the most favorable weapons for such an attack. It was thought that the three of us together—a psychologists, a statistician, and a specialist in the biology of twins—might be able to go more deeply into this problem than could one person with one particular type of training.

Originally the plan was to compare, in as many ways as we could, a group of identical twins reared together with an equivalent group of fraternal twins reared together. Subsequently, when we began to secure for study a number of pairs of identical twins reared apart, it seemed advisable to postpone an attempt to arrive at final conclusions until the number of twins reared apart became sufficiently large to have statistical value. These cases came in slowly, . . .

* * *

In the faint hope of possibly securing information about as many as four or five cases of such twins, one of us (Newman) wrote a short article about our studies of twins in which an urgent appeal was made for information about any cases of identical twins reared apart. Among the scores of replies to this request were four or five that seemed promising. Incidentally, it might be intimated that this matter of opening up the channels for public correspondence is not without its drawbacks. Letters were received from scores of proud mothers of twins and from twins themselves telling how similar they were, how utterly different, or how remarkable in various ways. . . .

The first case studied by us of identical twins reared apart gained considerable publicity through no fault of ours, for the twins themselves gave their photograph and their life-stories to an enterprising local reporter, who sent his news story to an American newspaper, from which it was copied far and wide. Since our name and address were given, we were again deluged with all sorts of letters from twins and about twins, a few of which furnished valuable clues.

The second pair of separated twins studied by us desired publicity in the hope that it might be the means of bringing them information about their unknown parents. So a little story with a cut of the twins was given to Chicago newspapers. This brought a further deluge of letters—some of value but most of no scientific significance. . . .

To come back to the actual gathering of cases, it has been intimated that newspaper publicity of a discreet sort had brought some results. Four or five cases were secured for study in this way. But newspapers were far less effective than radio. Two radio talks were given on national hookups, and information from that source came in very rapidly. We thus got into correspondence with about ten new cases—all apparently of the desired type. It was one thing, however, to locate cases but quite another and much more difficult one to bring the cases to Chicago for study. . . . In two cases we had to go to them, but this is not so satisfactory, for we work better in our own quarters and with our full corps of specialists.

The one most important factor in our ultimate success in securing the last nine cases within a few months was the Century of Progress Exposition. Pair after pair, who had previously been unmoved by appeals to the effect that they owed it to science and to society to permit us to study them, could not resist the offer of a free, all-expense-paid trip to the Chicago Fair. For a time we had a pair every week-end, and once, inadvertently, two pairs on the same weekend. So we are grateful to the Fair for enabling us to reach our goal of twenty cases—a number far exceeding our earlier hopes. No one who has not tried to get together many cases of identical twins reared apart can realize the amount of sustained effort required. Yet we believe this collection is worth the effort. . . . We have at the present time no further promising clues. All the good cases known to us have been studied. On this account, if for no others, we have decided to let this be our definitive collection of cases. Another generation of students of twins may pick up another ten or twenty cases of such separated twins, but we feel that our task for the present is accomplished.

Proofs of the monozygocity of the separated pairs

Because of the great expense involved in bringing these separated twins to Chicago, no chances were taken that any of them might prove to be fraternal twins. In every case an affirmative answer to the following questions was required before twins were asked to come to us for study:

1. Are you or have you been at some time so strikingly similar that even your friends or relatives have confused you?
2. Do you yourselves believe that you are far more alike than any pair of brothers or sisters you know of?
3. Can you send us a good photograph of yourselves, taken together in about the same positions?

In all of our nineteen cases these questions were answered in the affirmative, and in every case the photographs, sometimes several for one pair of twins, showed such striking similarity that we could be fairly sure on the ground of the photographs alone that they were monozygotic twins.

After the twins arrived they were examined in great detail as to genetic correspondences, and in not a single case has there been a marked genetic discrepancy between the two members of any pair. We looked for and frequently found concordances in many rare and peculiar characteristics, such as moles and other birthmarks, eye defects, finger and toe peculiarities, strange habits, and other oddities.

In addition, it should be said that, in eighteen out of nineteen of our own pairs, the palm and finger patterns would in themselves have afforded sufficient evidence of monozygocity for one familiar with these materials.

On the whole, it would be fair to say that our collection of nineteen pairs of identical twins reared apart average as similar physically as those reared together and can be as definitely diagnosed as monozygotic as were the latter.

The similarity method of diagnosis of monozygocity

The same methods of diagnosis have been used as for the twins reared together.... When the twins have been found to correspond almost exactly in a great many separately inherited genetic characters, such as hair color, hair form, hair texture, eye color and shape, ear shape and set, features, shape and arrangement of teeth, form of hands and fingers, shape of fingernails, general body build, and, in addition, exhibit correspondences in a number of unusual peculiarities, we might be satisfied that they are monozygotic; but we have gone even farther in order to make the diagnosis doubly sure. The procedure may again be reviewed.

The final check on monozygocity, after all the ordinary methods have been favorable, involves the detailed study of palm prints and fingerprints.

Age of twins at time of separation

In order, however, to eliminate from our studies the possibility that similar or identical environments during childhood might tend to cast twins in the same mold and thus bring about similarities, we decided at the outset to study only those cases of identical twins that were separated in infancy. Several cases came to our attention in which the separation occurred at the age of eight to twelve years, but such cases appeared to us at the time to be of little value and were not followed up.

We have adhered consistently in eighteen out of nineteen cases to the rule that the separation must have occurred in real infancy, but we weakened a little in the nineteenth case. This case, which had been on our list for some time, was finally accepted in order to round out the second block of ten cases (the first block of ten including Muller's case). In this pair, our Case XIX, the twins were separated at six years, somewhat late for our purposes; but we had information that the environments of the twins had been so markedly different since separation that we decided to add the case to our collection. In justification of this apparent relaxation of our standards, it might be said that we had not a single clue as to the existence of any more cases, so, if we were to round out our second block of ten cases, it was this case or none. Moreover, it seemed to us that a marked difference in environment with a relatively late separation might be about as good for our purposes as an earlier separation with no marked contrast in environments. . . .

Duration of separation

The actual ages when separated range in our twenty cases from two weeks to six years. . . . Twelve out of twenty cases were separated before the end of the first year of life, five cases were separated during the second year, one during the third year, one during the fourth year, and one during the seventh year. The duration of separation ranged from 11 to about 53 years, the actual durations being: 11, 12, 12, 13, 16, 17, 18, 19, 19, 22, 26, 27, 28, 29, 32, 33, 34, 34, 35, and 53 years. These periods of separation include a large part of the periods of infancy, childhood, and youth in all cases, and in several of the cases the first meeting did not occur until the twenties or thirties. There is no apparent correlation between the extent of the periods of separation and the extent of mental, temperamental, and physical differences found.

Degree of completeness of separation

The separated twins differed greatly in the degree of completeness of separation during the critical period. In a number of cases the separation was complete for a long period after they first parted company. In other cases there has been visiting at intervals throughout the entire period, or there has been at least some communication during that period.

The most extreme instances of complete separation are those in which twins had never heard of each other's existence until they were brought together by some curious freak of circumstances. There are six such cases. In several cases the twins have always been known to each other, but there has been visiting between them only at long intervals. Most of the cases are of this sort. Two of the pairs, Cases IV and IX, are cases where the twins lived very close together and saw each other frequently, though living in different families and in different environments.

It is a question whether complete separation is in itself an important factor when there are involved no pronounced differences in the environment. Complete separation of a pair of twins guarantees that they shall have in common none of the random and casual experiences of childhood and shall have no friends and acquaintances in common, but it does not preclude the possibility that they may have been brought up in environments and lived through experiences which, if not specifically, at least generally, are the same. . . .

General summary and interpretation

The general purpose of this study is to secure evidence on the extent to which characteristics of human beings, especially their ability and behavior, are determined by their genetic constitution and the extent to which these characteristics are influenced by the conditions of the environment. The authors have at no time conceived their problem to be to discover whether heredity or environment determines the development of the individual, nor even to derive a ratio to express, in any universal or final sense, the relative potency of the two sets of factors. The first statement of the problem is meaningless since development is always a function both of genetic constitution and of environmental conditions. The second is indeterminate since such a ratio depends upon the type of trait and the amount of variation which exists in both the genetic and the environmental factors which are compared.

It may be possible to estimate roughly how much variation in ability or behavior may be expected to accompany such a range of difference in genetic constitution as occurs in a given community of people, assuming a uniform environment or, on the other hand, to estimate the variation accompanying the range of difference in environment which is to be found in a given community, assuming a uniform genetic constitution. The evidence we have gathered enables us to take a step in the direction of such an estimate but hardly gives the basis for making it definite. We shall undertake to formulate as general a statement as we can after reviewing our procedure and results.

The two parts of our study represent the two possible approaches to the problem. Each approach seeks to trace the variations in individuals which accompany variations in one of the two sets of factors when the other is held constant. Thus, we may compare individuals who are brought up under the same environment (so far as possible) but differ by specified degrees in genetic constitution. This was the procedure of the first part of our study, in which we compared the resemblances (or differences) between identical twins and fraternal twins when both types were reared together. On the other hand, we may compare individuals who are genetically the same but are subjected to different environments. This was done in the second part of the study, in which we compared the resemblances (or differences) of identical twins reared in environments differing in varying amounts with those reared together. In both cases the comparisons are complicated, and the inferences which may be drawn from them are subject to qualification and open to some difference of opinion.

* * *

It is significant as an essential condition of some of the statistical calculations, and interesting as a general fact about twins, that both groups of twins were found to be normal in intelligence and in educational achievement. This is shown both in the average scores of the two groups and in their standard deviations. The only marked differences in the averages of the two groups occur in the case of number of finger ridges, and possibly intelligence, the identical twins in both cases yielding the higher average. On the whole, the two groups are remarkably alike both in average score and in spread of scores. Twins, according to our findings, are neither superior nor inferior to people in general.

Assuming that identical and fraternal twins differ in origin and that the one type has exactly the same heredity, whereas the other shares the same heredity to the extent of 50 per cent on the average, we have compared the degree of likeness of these two classes of twins. It will be recalled that both sets of twins have been reared together and that a difference in environment is doubtless not a major cause of difference in traits, though it may be a minor cause, as we shall see.

The likeness between the two types of twins is expressed in the form both of correlations and of differences. They amount to the same thing, and the correlations will be used in this summary. We may first make simple comparisons of the correlations and consider their significance.

In most of the traits measured the identical twins are much more alike than the fraternal twins, as indicated by the higher correlations. This is true of physical dimensions, of intelligence, and of educational achievement. The only group of traits in which identical twins are not much more alike consists of those commonly classified under the head of personality. For the rest it is obvious that the twins who have the same inheritance are the more alike. By and large, this indicates, since the environment is similar for both groups, that genetic constitution is a large factor in physical dimensions (as well as appearance and qualitative differences), mental ability, and educational achievement. This conclusion seems clearly warranted.

The difference in resemblance of the two classes of twins, however, is not the same in the different groups of traits. In general, the contrast is greater in physical traits, next in tests of general ability (intelligence), less in achievement tests, and least in tests of personality or temperament. In certain instances, viz., arithmetic, nature study, history and literature, tapping, will-temperament, and neurotic disposition, the correlations of identical twins are but little higher than those of fraternal twins. This seems to indicate that inheritance is a greater factor relatively in producing likeness or difference in some traits than in others.

Because earlier investigators have compared the resemblance of younger and older twins but have not distinguished adequately between identical and fraternal twins, we made this comparison. We are in some doubt concerning the bearing of this comparison on the general problem, but we present the results for what they are worth. Our chief contribution lies in a difference which appears between the two types of twins. The identical twins become neither more nor less alike as they grow older. This is true of both physical and mental traits. The fraternal twins behave differently, but only in the mental traits. In physical traits they remain as much alike as they grow older. In mental traits, however, they grow less alike. This would seem to be due to the fact that fraternal twins pursue somewhat different paths as they grow older and that the diverging environment affects their abilities and behavior. If the divergence were due to genetic factors, it would seem that it would affect the physical as well as the mental traits and the identical as well as the fraternal twins. It is reasonable to support that fraternal twins fall under the influence of more widely different environments than identical twins and that it is this influence which increases the difference between them.

* * *

There is one feature of the results which is not affected seriously by either the uncertainty of the assumptions or the limitation of the circumstances under which the correlations are found. This is the relative share of the genetic and the environmental factors in the different classes of traits. By this more rigid method, as by the simple comparison of differences between the correlations for the two types of twins, it appears that the physical characteristics are least affected by the environment, that intelligence is affected more; educational achievement still more; and personality or temperament, if our tests can be relied upon, the most. This finding is significant, regardless of the absolute amount of the environmental influence.

Our index shows that about 25 or 30 per cent of the variance in intelligence in fraternal twins reared together may be attributed to environmental influence. To what extent is this estimate sound, and, if sound, to what extent may it be generalized?

The soundness of the estimate rests on the correctness of the assumptions. One assumption in question is that a part of the differences between identical twins may be attributed to the effect of environment.... If the environment includes all nongenetic factors, this assumption is merely another expression of the theory that identical twins are derived from a single zygote, all parts of which, of course, have the same heredity. If, however, by environment is meant *postnatal* environment, then the question is raised whether a large share of the variance may not be due to *prenatal* environment, which is not subject to human control.

The biologist, in general, is inclined to attribute a larger share to prenatal factors than is the psychologist, who emphasizes the possibilities of postnatal differences, even in the case of identical twins reared together....

General biological facts suggest that ... prenatal conditions produce differences of significant magnitude in the physical characteristics of identical twins and possibly, therefore, in the organic substrate of mental abilities and personality. For example, identical-twin embryos differ more in size than do fraternal-twin embryos, and identical twins differ as much as fraternal twins at birth. The prenatal mortality rate of identical twins is several times as high as that of fraternal twins, and very frequently one member of an identical-twin pair dies before birth, showing symptoms of injury from lack of nutrition. There is an exchange of blood supply between identical-twin fetuses which frequently produces an imbalance of blood exchange to the disadvantage of one twin. Conjoined twins (Siamese twins) show marked differences in height, weight, features, and intelligence. The differences between completely separated identical twins may have the same origin as those differences. These considerations predispose the biologist to attribute to prenatal factors the predominant share in the causation of differences between identical twins reared together.

How far the postnatal environment of identical twins may differ and how far this difference may affect them is, at present, a speculative question. Doubtless their environment is more alike than that of fraternal twins or siblings. Our finding that identical twins retain their likeness in mental traits whereas fraternal twins grow less alike in mental traits bears this out. Still, it may differ sufficiently to affect behavior. For example, we have noticed that one twin usually takes the lead in social intercourse, while the other accepts the follower's position. A slight initial difference may produce a habitual difference in attitude and behavior which grows out of the very circumstances that might be expected to produce similarity, namely, the twins' intimate association with each other. The situation may be stated generally by saying that each twin is a part of the environment of the other, and a part which, while it does not differ much in original nature, comes to different more because of the differentiation in attitude and behavior growing out of their mutual association. This argument is admittedly hypothetical and perhaps fine spun, but it seems to contain a possibility.

* * *

This brings us to the separated cases, in which we have attempted to trace the effects of differences in the environment upon pairs of twins who are genetically identical. One obvious way to treat the data is to compare the average differences for the group as a whole with the average differences in the case of identical twins reared together. If the differences for the separated group are significantly greater than those for the unseparated group, we may conclude that the greater difference in traits has been produced by the greater difference in environment (allowing for the fact that the separated group may very likely be a somewhat biased sampling). In one of the physical traits, weight, and in intelligence and school achievement the differences are significantly greater, demonstrating the effect of environment on these traits. In height, head measures, and the score on the Woodworth-Mathews test, on the other hand, no significantly greater difference is found. This is important since it indicates, as does the comparison of identical and fraternal twins, that some characteristics are more susceptible to environmental influences than are others.

Whether the amount of this excess difference can be taken as a direct measure of the amount of postnatal environmental effect is a different question. One of the authors is inclined to treat the unseparated identical twins as a control group, assuming, since they have been brought up together, that their differences are due almost solely to prenatal factors and little if at all to postnatal environmental factors. This would mean that only the excess differences of the separated twins could be attributed to increased differences in postnatal environments. The other authors, while recognizing the impossibility of disproving this position, regard it as more probable, as was argued previously, that a considerable part of the differences of identical twins reared together is due to postnatal environmental factors and that this must therefore be added to the excess difference in order to obtain a measure of the total influence of the postnatal environment.

A further argument pointing to the limitation of the effect of the environment is that the differences between a majority of the separated twins, namely, those who have been brought up in similar environments, are no larger than are to be found among the unseparated pairs. In fact, if we eliminate some half-dozen pairs from the separated cases, the average differences of the remainder are about the same as those of the unseparated group. The differences in the environment between those separated pairs, so the argument runs, must be greater on the whole than are those of twins reared together; hence, small differences in the environment have no effect. This argument may be sound, as far as gross measures like general intelligence and school achievement are concerned, but it should be noted that the differences in environment between this group of separated pairs are small enough so that they cannot be detected or measured by a fairly careful study of the life-histories of the twins. Again, the argument has not quite the same significance if we regard the environment of twins reared together as differing by significant amounts as it would have if we regarded differences as zero in amount. It therefore seems safe to say that the measurable difference found in the separated cases, plus an undetermined amount corresponding to that portion of the difference in unseparated cases is attributable to the environment.

Besides comparing the separated and unseparated identical twins, we may compare the separated twins with fraternal twins. This may conveniently be done in terms of the correlations between pairs. In some of the physical characteristics, particularly height and head measurements, separated twins are more alike than fraternal twins and approximately as much alike as are unseparated identical twins. In weight, intelligence, and educational achievement, however, separated identical twins are, on the whole, as different as are fraternals. It is fair to say that, for these latter traits, if we average together the various amounts of environmental differences found in the separated identical twins, they just about balance in their effect the amount of hereditary difference which exists between fraternal twins.

The next comparison is not clouded by speculative difficulties but is clear and obvious in its implication. When the amount of difference between the separated twins is compared with the estimated amount of difference between their environments, highly significant correlations are found. They are closest between schooling and educational achievement (.91); somewhat less close between schooling and intelligence (.40 to .79) and social environment and intelligence (.32 to .53); and about the same between physical environment and weight (.60) and Downey Will-Temperament (.47). No further comment seems necessary since only one interpretation is possible. The concomitance between the amount of difference in the environment and the amount of difference between the twins can only indicate that the environment has affected the characteristics in which the correspondence occurs. Differences produced by other factors, such as prenatal conditions, could have only a fortuitous relation to the environmental differences and could therefore not bring about a correlation with them. Moreover, there is no reason to suppose that these factors have operated any differently in twins reared apart from those reared together.

At the beginning of this chapter we said that any estimate of the relative influence of genetic and environmental factors must be made with certain qualifications and limitations in mind. These can best be discussed in the light of findings of both parts of the study, and it has therefore been deferred until this point.

In presenting the statistical estimates of the genetic and environmental factors in the differences between the fifty pairs of fraternal twins, we pointed out the fact that the variations which we studied are only such as occur within a family. This applies to both the genetic and the environmental factor. Specifically, the variation in the genetic factor is limited to that which occurs between siblings of the same sex, that is, brothers and sisters. This is much less than the variation occurring between pairs of persons at random, who in the vast majority of cases would not be related in any known way. (Of course, in a small stable community with much intermarriage the pairs of relatives would be more numerous.) This limits the effect of genetic differences since these differences would be greater if the pairs compared were less closely related.

The environmental differences are also severely limited in the comparison in question. It is obvious that the environmental differences of pairs of children picked from the same family are small as compared with those of pairs picked at random from the community. Again, the amount of such differences depends on the size and diversity of the community from which the pairs are chosen. A small, homogeneous New England town would yield relatively small differences, a large metropolitan city much greater differences, a whole nation still greater, and the whole world still greater. Can we say that, when our genetic and our environmental differences are such as exist within a family, the one or the other factor is more severely limited? This is a hard question.

Perhaps some light is thrown on the question by comparing the ratios which are found in the analysis of the separated cases with those obtained from the twins reared together.... One set of ratios is derived by comparing the differences between the identical twins reared together and those reared apart. The other is derived by comparing the identical twins reared apart and fraternal twins reared together. Perhaps it would not be far wrong to say that the one comparison gives greater scope to the range of environmental differences and the other to genetic differences.

In any case, the difference obtained by the two modes of comparison is striking. By the comparison of identical twins reared together with identical twins reared apart, the share of environment in determining weight is .87; by the comparison of identical with fraternal twins, it is only .21. Similarly, for Binet I. Q. the two methods give .59 and .31; for Otis I. Q., .64 and .16; and for Stanford Achievement, .87 and .36; respectively. In brief, if the environment differs greatly as compared with heredity, the share of environment in determining traits which are susceptible to environmental influence is large. If, on the other hand, there is large genetic difference and small environmental difference, the share of heredity is relatively large. This is what makes the solution of the question as to relative share of the two sets of factors indeterminate....

The correlations of measures of personality are of a different order from the correlations of measures of ability. This is shown in several ways. The correlations between identical twins in these measures is much lower than in the physical measures or the measures of ability. This seems hardly attributable mainly to a lower reliability of these measures since they have been shown in numerous studies to have fair reliability and since the correlations in the case of fraternal twins are not correspondingly lower. This general fact suggests that the forms of behavior measured may, in general, not be expressions of the genetic character of the organism to the same extent as abilities.

Again, the differences in the personality measures of separated twins have negligible correlation with differences in the environment, so far as they could be ascertained and estimated along a general scale. This suggests that such relations as exist between personality and environment are of a different sort than those between environment and ability.

Before suggesting any explanation of these differences in the results for personality and ability, let us remind ourselves of the evidence of the case studies that some type of relation appears to exist between the environment and personality. There are a number of instances in which a rather large difference exists between the personalities of twins as shown by the tests or by observation, or by both, in which a large difference also exists between their environments, and in which it seems plausible to infer a relation between the two sets of differences. The following may serve as examples:

Case I. Alice exhibits a constrained manner in comparison with her sister, has a more cramped style of writing, and differs in the Downey test. Correspondingly, she was brought up in a narrower, more restricted, and conventional type of environment.

Case IV. Mary has lived a sedentary town life in contrast to Mabel's active farm life. Correspondingly, Mary is more feminine in manner, more excitable, and shows large differences in handwriting and on the tests.

Case VIII. Mildred has had a free, stimulating social environment, and Ruth a restricted, impoverished one. Correspondingly, Mildred is spontaneous and vivacious in manner, is poised and self-confident, is stable as revealed by the tests, and writes a flourishing hand, whereas Ruth manifests the opposite characteristics.

Case X. Betty's home influence seems to have made her slightly more neurotic.

Case XI. Helen's very superior education has brought with it an easier manner of life, and this may be responsible for her higher scores on the "speed and fluidity" and greater "care and attention to detail" on the Downey test, more mature, more delicate, neater, and more feminine handwriting, and more feminine manner.

Case XIV. Esther was an adopted child brought up on a farm, has an adopted child, and is naturally left-handed but has been taught to write with her right hand. Ethel was brought up in a Catholic orphanage, has a child of her own, and is naturally right-handed. Esther is much more neurotic according to the Woodworth-Mathews and Pressey tests. There may be a connection.

Case XVII. James appears to be more neurotic and appeared to be glum and unhappy in the interview. His foster-home seems to have been somewhat less happy than that of Gene.

Case XVIII. These brothers, though brought up in widely different circumstances, are similar in manner and the measureable features of behavior. However, their conduct, from the point of view of its direction and social significance, differs very widely. We might expect them to act with equal vigor, decision or persistence, but one to a socially constructive and the other to a socially destructive end.

* * *

Conclusion

If, at the inception of this research project over ten years ago, the authors entertained any hope of reaching a definitive solution of the general nature-nurture problem or even of any large section of the subordinate problems involved, in terms of a simple formula, they were destined to be rather disillusioned. The farther one penetrates into the intricacies of the complex of genetic and environmental factors that together determine the development of individuals, the more one is compelled to admit that there is not one problem but a multiplicity of minor problems—that there is no general solution of the major problems nor even of any one of the minor problems. For any particular genetic and environmental setup it is possible by the methods presented in this book to determine what fraction of the variance is due to genetic or to environmental differences. In another setup this fraction will undoubtedly vary. . . .

While, then, we have not provided a comprehensive or final solution of the problems within our field of study, we have presented a body of evidence which we believe is more crucial than any previously available, and we have undertaken to analyze it as thoroughly as possible from the combined points of view of the biologist, the psychologist, and the statistician. The data themselves have been presented in sufficient detail to enable other workers in the field to evaluate our own interpretation and to seek for more inclusive interpretations of their own. We shall be satisfied if we have succeeded in tracing a few of the threads in the tangled web which constitutes the organism we call man.

MYRTLE M. MCGRAW (B. 1899)

The neuromuscular maturation of the human infant (1943)

Not all development is maturational but some behavioral change is. We are accustomed to think of infant development as consisting of the onset of a series of new items of behavior, many of which involve learning. McGraw shows that behavioral development also encompasses the dropping out of some items of behavior as the cortex assumes control over subcortical centers.

This selection is reprinted from pages 27–36 of a book by the title cited above with the permission of Dr. McGraw and Columbia University Press.

SUSPENSION GRASP BEHAVIOR

The ability to suspend the body weight by the force of hand grip on a rod is an infantile reaction which lends itself readily to numerical determinations. Simple stop-watch determinations of the time suspended provide values adequate to demonstrate the general course of development. This method was used in making 5,138 determinations on a group of children over a period of several years. The data were averaged over 10- or 20-day intervals during the first 300 days and over 200-day intervals thereafter. The trend of development during the first 300 days is shown by curves A in Figure 1. From these curves it is clear that the intensity of response tends to increase during the first 30 days, after which there is a gradual decline. Single-hand suspension is suppressed. Curves B in Figure 1 illustrate the course of development after the first 300 days. In general, suspension time is steadily increased. It might be said that the first 30 days represent an expansion in the development of nuclear centers governing this function. The subsequent decline probably corresponds to the onset of some inhibitory influence of cortical centers upon the activity of subcortical nuclei.

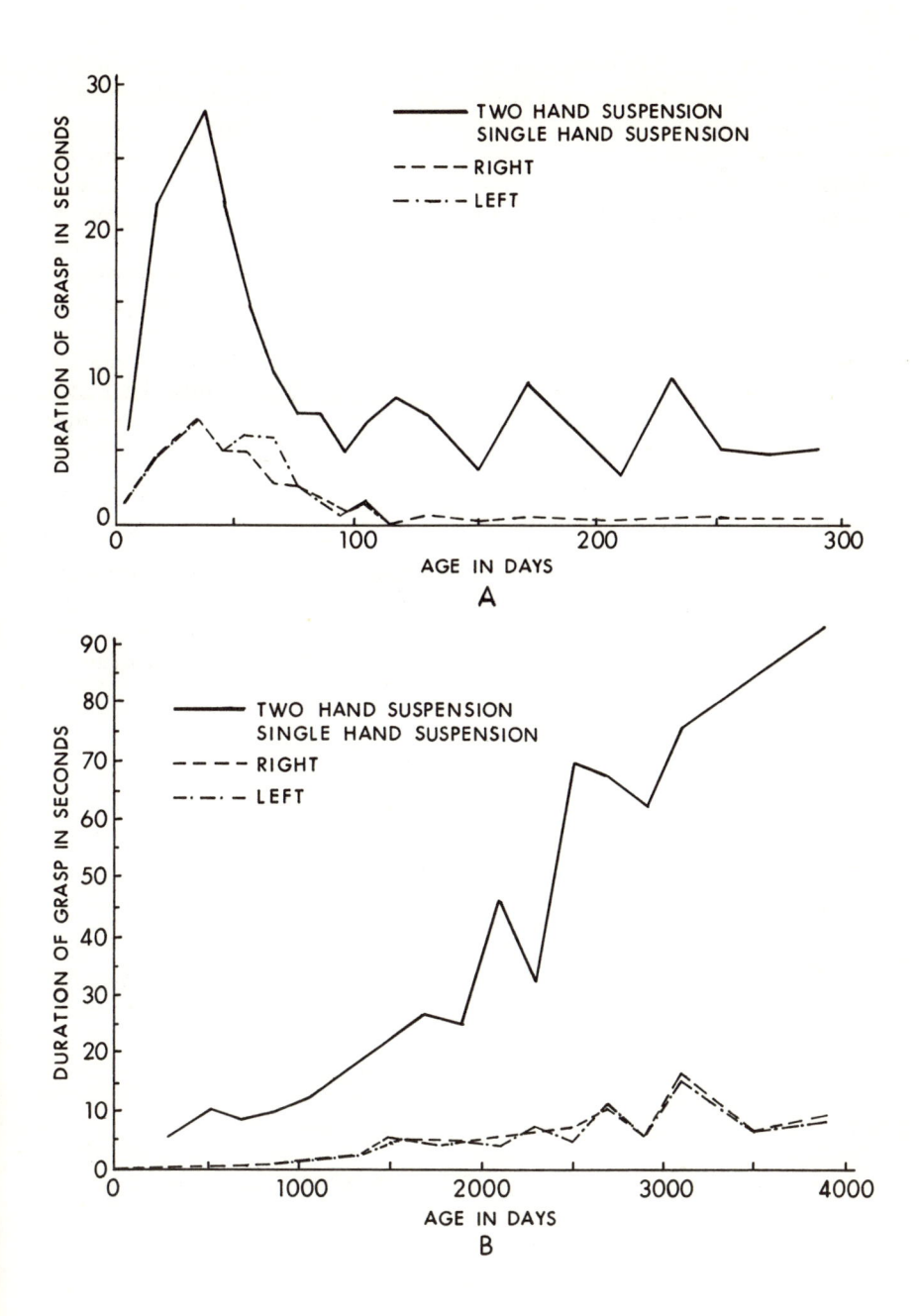

Figure 1. The suspension for the group of children: (A) suspension time averaged over 10-day intervals during the first four months and over 20-day intervals thereafter; (B) suspension time averaged over 200-day intervals after the age of three hundred days.

Later, as illustrated in curves B, the ability recurs, but at this time under the dominance of the cerebral cortex. The general course of development is even more graphically illustrated by the logarithmic curve in Figure 2, which covers a period of eight years. The phenomenon manifests an increase in intensity during the first few weeks, followed by a period of progressive diminution in intensity of response. It reasserts itself as an activity under cortical control. The reflex phase is controlled by nuclear or subcortical centers; the decline or extinction of the powers of suspension is interpreted as an indication of development in cortical cells which exercise an inhibitory influence on subcortical functioning. The recurrence or re-enforcement of the ability to suspend the body is regarded as evidence of maturation in those cells which activate or control neuromuscular movements and of their integration with neural centers which govern other factors involved in deliberate performances.

Procedures with other activities

Observations upon other neuromuscular functions of the infant were not so easily reduced to numerical values. However, observations were made and records were kept. It can be seen from the following accounts that the course of development of these more complex functions is not theoreti-

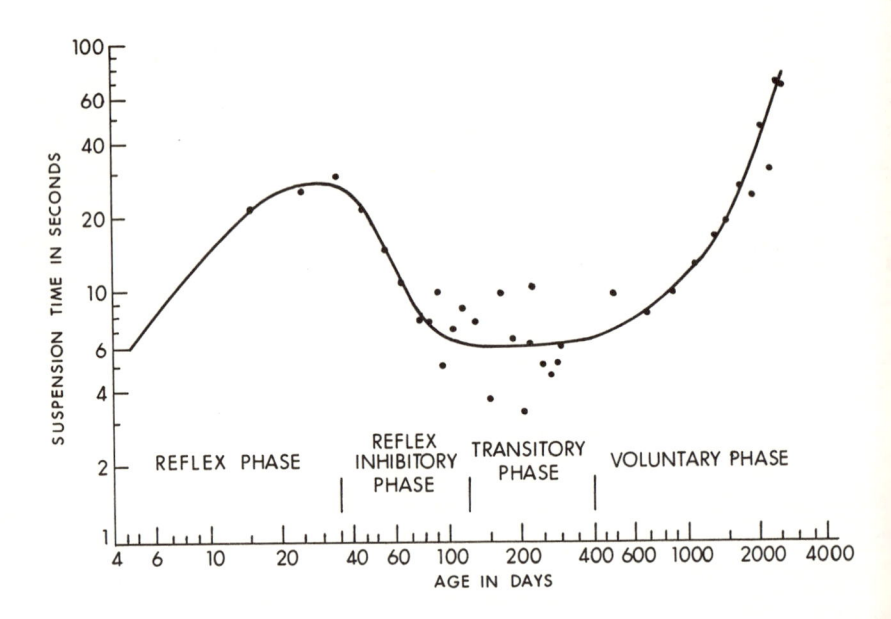

Figure 2. Suspension time for the group of children plotted on a logarithmic scale against chronological age, showing the trend of suspension behavior for all ages to eight years.

cally incompatible with the interpretations given to these simpler phenomena.

The procedure followed in studying other neuromuscular activities was fundamentally the same for each function. Observations were initiated immediately after birth of the baby or at the time of functional inception. Activities which were not a part of the newborn behavior repertoire could not be observed until some evidence of their emergence was indicated. Observations of each function in a number of children were made repeatedly until the activity attained a relative state of stability. Records were made on 16 mm. motion picture film or in protocols. Written descriptions were restricted to observable phenomena, with no attempt to inject interpretations. In addition to the sequential observations upon the group of children over a period of years, daily records were made of most of the performances of several babies in order to provide adequate longitudinal data of individual growth.

After the mass of data was accumulated, both the film and written records were analyzed for the purpose of selecting significant phases in the development of each function. In formulating the criteria for each phase of an activity it was realized that verbal descriptions of overt behavior only are not always adequate to differentiate voluntary from involuntary movements. That is, a report to the effect that an infant supported in an upright position engaged in progressive stepping movements does not distinguish stepping movements of the newborn infant from those which appear just prior to independent walking. Yet any moderately experienced observer can recognize the qualitative differences in such stepping. Furthermore, it was recognized that two babies may adopt movements which in pattern appear to be different but in fact reflect the same level of neural organization. For that reason a rationale based upon a theoretical interpretation of neural maturation was incorporated into the criteria formulated for appraising development in overt behavior.

Once the criteria were formulated for the phases of each function, it was possible to rate the many individual observations in accordance with developmental sequence. These ratings converted the descriptive data into a symbolic system so that the mass of data could be more easily manipulated. In making the ratings attention was focused upon those features common to the development of each function without specific regard for individual peculiarities. The method of rating was simple. A plus sign was ascribed to the phase most representative of the behavior as described or recorded on the film, and minus signs were assigned to other phases of the function. Because of the gradual process of growth a plus rating was on some occasions assigned to more than one phase in order to represent transitional periods more accurately. The number of phases in each function varied, as did also the number of observations, since some activities may attain relative stability within a few months, whereas the development of others extends over a period of years. A data sheet, after the ratings had been made on the observations of a particular child in a given function, is illustrated in Figure 3. Such a system of rating lends itself to the comparison of rates of development of different functions and also to an appraisal of

NAME	AGE IN DAYS		PHASE								
	Observation	Movies	A	B	C	D	E	F	G	H	I
BRIGGS, JAMES		2	+	−	−	−	−	−	−	−	−
	11		+	−	−	−	−	−	−	−	−
	18		+	−	−	−	−	−	−	−	−
	24		+	−	−	−	−	−	−	−	−
		30	+	+	−	−	−	−	−	−	−
	38		+	−	−	−	−	−	−	−	−
	44		+	−	−	−	−	−	−	−	−
	52		+	−	−	−	−	−	−	−	−
		62	+	+	−	−	−	−	−	−	−
	65		+	+	−	−	−	−	−	−	−
	74		−	+	−	−	−	−	−	−	−
	81		−	+	−	−	−	−	−	−	−
	89		+	+	−	−	−	−	−	−	−
		95	−	+	+	−	−	−	−	−	−
	102		−	+	−	−	−	−	−	−	−
	107		−	−	+	−	−	−	−	−	−
	118		−	+	+	+	−	−	−	−	−
		124	−	−	+	−	−	−	−	−	−
	128		−	−	+	−	−	−	−	−	−
	135		−	−	+	−	−	−	−	−	−
	142		−	−	+	−	−	−	−	−	−
	153		−	−	+	−	+	−	−	−	−
		156	−	−	−	+	−	−	−	−	−
	167		−	−	+	−	+	−	−	−	−
	170		−	−	+	−	+	−	−	−	−
	177		−	−	+	−	+	−	−	−	−
		186	−	−	−	+	+	+	−	−	−
	191		−	−	−	+	+	−	+	−	−
	193		−	−	−	−	−	+	−	−	−
	199		−	−	−	+	+	−	+	−	−
		202	−	−	−	+	+	+	−	−	−
		205	−	−	−	−	−	+	−	−	−
	213		−	−	−	−	−	+	+	−	−
	220		−	−	−	−	−	+	+	+	−
		221	−	−	−	−	−	+	+	−	−
	227		−	−	−	−	−	−	−	+	−
		229	−	−	−	−	−	−	+	−	−
		230	−	−	−	−	−	−	−	+	−
	235		−	−	−	−	−	−	+	+	−
		237	−	−	−	−	−	−	−	+	−
		243	−	−	−	−	−	−	−	+	−
		250	−	−	−	−	−	−	−	+	−

Figure 3. Typical data sheet showing the ratings on one child activity during the first 250 days of life.

an individual against a group of his contemporaries. However, our first concerns are the delineation of significant phases in the development of each function and a theoretical interpretation of the neural reorganization reflected in overt behavior. More specific correlation between structural and functional development must await further studies in neuroanatomy and neurophysiology; until these facts are available the organization of behavior data into a theoretical framework seems justifiable.

Swimming

After 445 observations of the aquatic behavior of 42 infants, ranging in age from eleven days to two and a half years, it became apparent that the significant developmental changes in such behavior could be conveniently classified into three phases, as follows:

Phase A, Reflex Swimming. When the newborn infant is submerged in a prone position the organization of neuromuscular activity is striking. The baby usually remains in the prone position; and definite rhythmical associated flexor-extensor movements in upper and lower extremities, together with a lateral flexion of the trunk corresponding to the flexor phase of the lower extremity, are usually manifested. These movements are ordinarily sufficiently forceful to propel the baby a short distance through the water. The movements involve the total musculature and are usually better organized than newborn crawling or stepping movements. Ingestion of water and coughing after removal from the water are less common among the reactions of the newborn than in older infants. Apparently some reflex still functions during the early weeks of life sufficiently to inhibit breathing efforts on the part of the submerged newborn infant. Line drawings

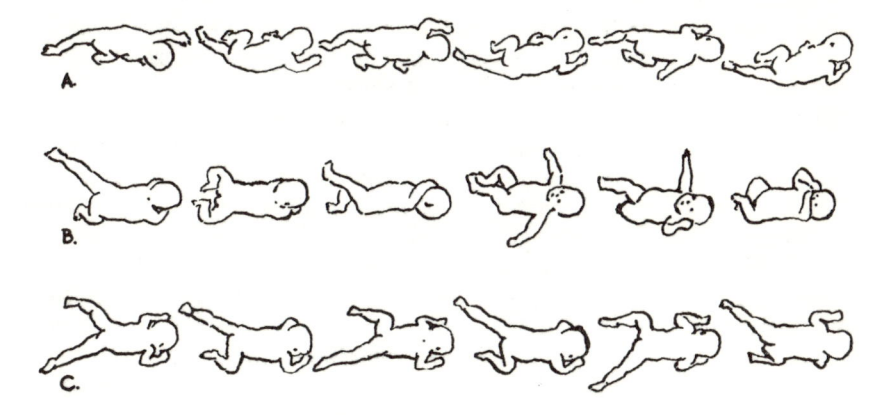

Figure 4. Three phases in the development of aquatic behavior of the human infant: (A) reflex swimming movements; (B) disorganized behavior; (C) voluntary or deliberate movements. These drawings were obtained by tracing successive frames of 16 mm. movie film illustrating the quality of consecutive movement at different made chronological or developmental stages.

A of Figure 4 illustrate the character and rhythmicity of reflex swimming movements. Since the cerebral cortex is not functioning appreciably at this time, it is reasonable to assume that these movements are under the control of subcortical nuclei.

Phase B, Disorganized Activity. After the first few months the rhythmicity and organization of pattern become somewhat dissipated when the infant is submerged in water. There follows a period when the baby tends to rotate from a prone to a dorsal position and movements of the extremities are of a struggling order. It may be that some awareness of the environment is expressed by the infant's bringing his hands to the water line on his face. Less control over the respiratory mechanisms is evidenced by coughing and the ingestion of water. Line drawings B of Figure 4 represent the character of movements commonly exhibited during this phase. This change in aquatic behavior seems to reflect the development of some neural mechanism which serves to disrupt the organization of reflex activity. During this period neither cortex nor subcortical nuclei function for the optimum benefit of the baby. It is a period of transition from reflex to a more voluntary type of activity.

Phase C, Deliberate or Voluntary Movements. At about the time when independent walking develops, another change is exhibited in the aquatic behavior of the child. Again the baby tends to remain submerged in the prone position, to engage in flexor-extensor movements of the extremities, especially the lower extremities, and to propel the body through the water. The quality of these movements differs from the rhythmical movements of the newborn; they are more deliberate and apparently voluntary. The child is not merely fighting; he is making purposeful movements, fairly well organized, but less automatic than the reflex movements, in order to reach the edge of the pool. The nature of neuromuscular movements of this order are illustrated by line drawings C of Figure 4. The quality of the movements and the child's awareness of his environment indicate that the cerebral cortex is participating in the activity. It is not until much later that the child gains the ability to raise his head above he water level in order to breathe. There is reason to believe that unless swimming experience is continued at this time, these deliberate movements characteristic of the ambulatory child will be abandoned as the horizon for sensory experience and judgment expands.

After the observations were rated in accordance with the above criteria, it was possible to calculate the developmental trend of each phase as demonstrated by the curves in Figure 5. Plus-minus ratings are too gross to demonstrate the rise in specificity of the reflex movements which occurs during the first three weeks or so of life. However, a great variety of response becomes available as the cortex comes into play. To some extent it can be assumed that this variability of response is shown on the curve by the increase in scatter during the later age periods.

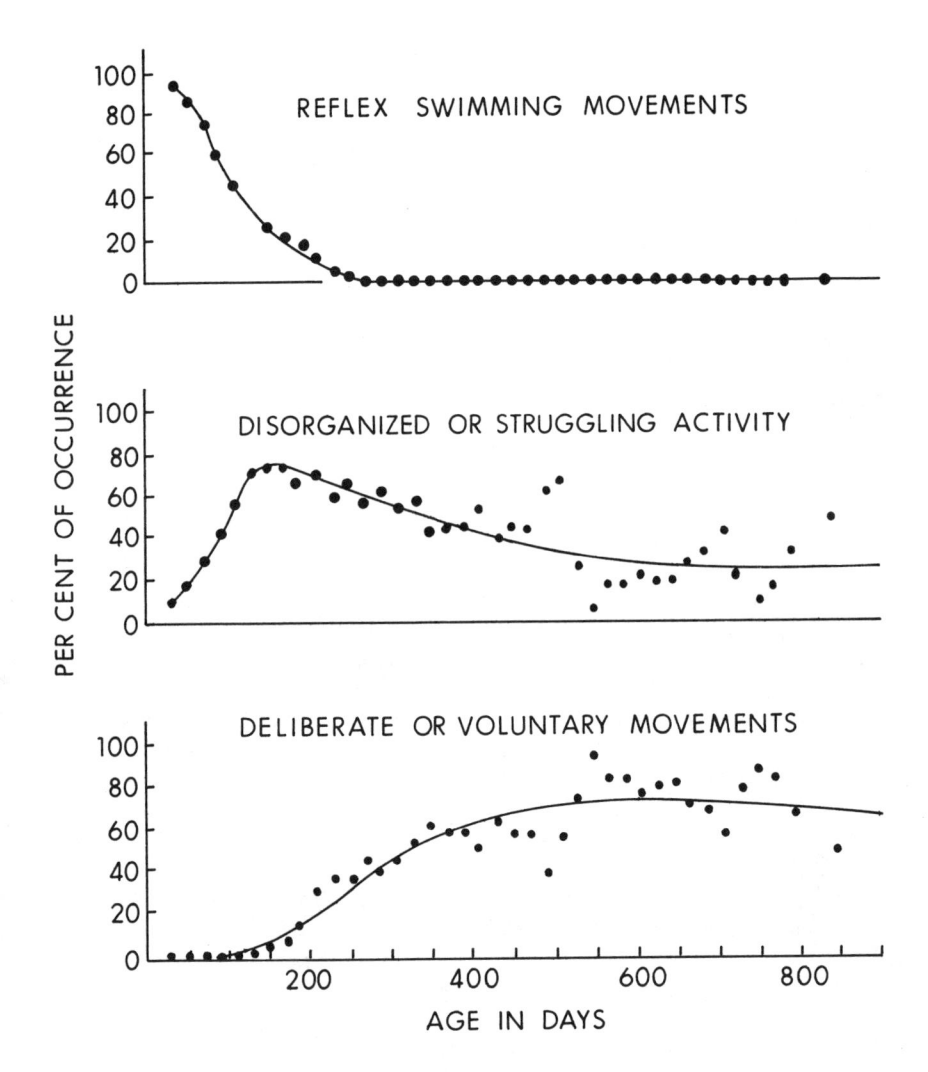

Figure 5. The incidence of three phases in the aquatic behavior of infants.

36

DONALD O. HEBB (B. 1904)

On the nature of fear (1946)

Many writers on human nature have dealt with the cause of fear, but few of them have done it successfully. Most accounts are written in terms of innate fears plus learning. Watson proposed that only fear of falling and of loud sounds are innate and that fear of all other things are the result of Pavlovian conditioning. It follows that if people are kept away from loud noises and high places they will fear nothing, which of course is pure nonsense. This simplistic theory was in the textbooks for many years. It has often been refuted, but what was needed was not refutation but a better explanation to replace it.

Hebb provided this. While, as his copious references show, not all that he says is new, no one had previously assembled such a large array of evidence concerning the nature of fear. Hebb's theory is derived in part from experiments with chimpanzees, but it applies to man and child as well.

Hebb's article appeared in the Psychological Review, 53 (1946) 259–276, *and is reprinted by permission of the author and the American Psychological Association.*

In the course of an experiment dealing with individual differences of behavior among chimpanzees, observations of fear were made which held an immediate interest. Besides extending the information concerning the causes of anthropoid fear which is provided by the work of Kohler (23), Jacobsen, Jacobsen and Yoshioka (17), Yerkes and Yerkes (42), Haslerud (10), McCulloch and Haslerud (31) and Hebb and Riesen (14), the new data brought up again the questions of mechanism. Analysis of the behavior leads, in the present discussion, to a review of the whole problem and an attempt to formulate an hypothesis of the causes and nature of fear.

Nature of the data

Validity and Reliability. The validity of naming fear in chimpanzees, or recognizing something in animals which can be identified with fear in man, and the reliability of naming have been discussed elsewhere (13). There it was shown that the recognition of emotion in an animal is possible in the same way as in another human being. Fear named in an animal means either that there was actual avoidance of some object or place, or that the observer inferred from incidental behavior ("associated signs") that avoidance was imminent and likely to appear with further stimulation. When such inferences are made with confidence by experienced observers, it appears that they are valid and reliable, the criterion being the animal's subsequent behavior.

Definition of Fear Behavior. The symbol "W," for withdrawal, was recorded when the animal actually moved away from a test object in such a way as to show that he did not move by coincidence, but was responding to the test situation. The evidence was of several kinds: (1) when change of position of the test object produced a corresponding movement of the animal, maintaining his distance from it; (2) when the original movement was abrupt and coincided exactly with the appearance of the test object; (3) when there was coincident evidence of unusual excitation, such as erection of hair, screaming, threatening gestures directed at the test object, or continued orientation of gaze at the object, while moving directly away from it. On occasions one of these three forms of evidence alone, if exceptionally clear, might provide the basis for an entry of "W" in the record; usually, at least two were present before the entry was made. In many instances the experimenter was certain that an animal would be afraid to approach the test object, but did not record his opinion since the formal behavioral criteria were not met.

Experimental method

The experimental procedures were part of a study of individual differences of emotionality and temperament, and not planned to meet the problem of defining the adequate stimulus to fear. Thus the range of test objects was limited, and the order in which they were presented does not permit an exact comparison of the excitatory value of each.

Test Objects. The test objects were representations of animals, from reptile to man, varying considerably in completeness and verisimilitude. They fall in three classes: picture, primate, and nonprimate objects. It was not expected that the pictures would induce fear—they were used for another purpose—but they were presented in the same way as the other objects and consequently are useful as control material.

Primate Objects. There were 9 objects representing primates. The responses to these are the main interest of the study.

1. An adult chimpanzee head, three-fifths life size, made of papier-mâché, and painted to appear reasonably lifelike.
2. An unclothed doll representing a human infant, one-half life size.
3. An infant chimpanzee's head and shoulders, nearly life size, modelled in wax and painted—about as lifelike as the adult chimpanzee head.

4. The cadaver of a chimpanzee infant, newborn, fixed in formalin.
5. A lifelike full-sized human head from a window display dummy.
6. The skull of a 5-year-old chimpanzee, with movable jaw controlled by a string.
7. The roughly mounted skin of a spider monkey, with head and shoulders movable by means of string.
8. An unpainted plaster of Paris cast of the visage of an adult chimpanzee without the ears or the rest of the head, made from a death mask.
9. The cured and flexible hide of a 5-year-old chimpanzee, somewhat denuded of hair; the proportions of the skin about the head and face were distorted out of recognition, but the hands and feet were recognizable.

The pictures are not described in detail, since they are important here only as 14 emotionally unexciting objects, presented in the same way as the others.

Nonprimate objects varied greatly in verisimilitude, from a careful replica of a snake to a bug which was a rectangular block of wood on coiled-spring legs.

1. A dog's head and forequarters, of cloth, slipped over the hand and manipulated from inside with the fingers; this common toy is surprisingly lifelike in its movements.
2. A model of an imaginary white grub, 4 inches long, with long white legs.
3. A grub identical in proportions and color, one-third as large.
4. A rubber tube, ½ inch in diameter, 24 inches long, with a roughly carved wooden snake's head at one end; so mounted, with string inside the tube, that it could be given a snakelike movement without apparent external agency.
5. A rectangular wooden bug, 6 inches long. It was capable of an oscillating movement, since it was mounted on six coiled-wire legs, and had oscillating antennae.
6. A grasshopper, a mechanical toy with moving legs.
7. A similar turtle.
8. A rubber dog, 3½ inches high.
9. A brightly colored cloth dog, 7 inches high.
10. A painted wax replica of a coiled 24-inch snake.

Procedure. Test objects were presented to the animals while they were in their own living cages. The animal or pair of animals was first brought to the front of the cage by an offer of a small amount of food. The hinged top and front of the presentation box (which was wheeled from cage to cage) was then lifted, exposing one test object to the chimpanzee. At the end of 15 seconds the test object was set in motion if it had movable parts; if not, it was moved forward about 6 inches nearer the animal. The presentation box was closed at the end of another 15 seconds; total exposure was thus 30 seconds. The box had three compartments, and three objects were shown in succession on each experimental period, once or twice a week. The objects were shown to all animals in the same order with the same time intervals.

Experimental results

With a fixed order of presentation to all subjects, there is a probability that the serial position of a test object will affect the degree of response to it, either by negative adaptation or cumulative effect. There were marked indications that such effects occurred. Some animals apparently learned that the test objects, at first terrifying, would not move out of the presentation box; others began to show fear in the later trials before the box was opened at all.

The total number of animals making fear responses to any object, therefore, is not a wholly satisfactory index of its relative effectiveness in provoking fear. However, there is evidence that the amount of such error is limited. In each group of three objects one or more pictures were included. The number of avoidance responses was consistently low for these pictures, while remaining high for objects, such as dog or snake, known from the work of others (Yerkes, Haslerud) to be fear provoking. This means that transfer or generalization effects were limited. Also there was no sign of a steady increase or decrease of fear responses as the experiment progressed. The animals' responses were highly selective. Preliminary observations, and tests made after the completion of the experiment, also make it clear that such objects as a head without the body attached are in themselves capable of eliciting panic, and that the number of fear responses to human or chimpanzee head, recorded experimentally, is not due to an association of these test objects with the others.

Table 1 presents the number of fear responses to each test object, separating primate, pictorial and nonprimate objects. The table gives the order of presentation and also shows which three objects were grouped together for each test period. It is assumed, partly on the basis of evidence not presented here, that what particular pictures were used is irrelevant and that the number of animals avoiding the pictures is an index of the "spread" of fear from exciting to neutral objects. From a total of 30 animals the mean number making fear responses to each primate test object was 9.6; to pictures, 0.9; to nonprimate objects, 6.7. These scores, it must be remembered, are the number of actual overt withdrawals which met the criteria set up in advance for a definable fear response. They take no account of signs of fear which were peculiar to an individual animal. Also, they are the number of such responses made while animal and test object were separated by a stout wire mesh. Tests in other circumstances show a higher percentage of avoidance, and show also that the relative effectiveness of two objects as causes of fear may vary somewhat according to the mode of presentation. In the conditions of the experiment, the following are the most effective stimuli, in descending order: *skull* (with moving jaw); painted wax *snake*; *monkey* (with

Table 1. Number of animals (from a total of 30) making fear responses to primate test objects, pictures, and nonprimate objects

		Primate		Picture		Nonprimate
Test	I	Adult ape head	7	0	dog head (M)*	10
	II	Doll	4	1	large grub	3
	III	Infant ape head	3	2	rubber tube (M)	3
	IV	Infant	1	1	wood-wire bug (M)	3
	V			0	mechanical grasshopper (M)	4
	VI	Human head	12	1	rubber dog	5
	VII	Skull (M)	24	0		
		Monkey (M)	16			
	VIII			4	small grub	2
	IX	Cast of ape visage	14	4	mechanical turtle (M)	8
	X	Ape hide	5	0	cloth dog	8
	XI			0		
				0		
				0	Cast of snake	21
	Total		86	13		67
	Mean		9.6	0.9		6.7

*(M) Indicates that the object was put in motion during the presentation period.

moving head); plaster cast of *chimpanzee visage;* and *human head.* Least exciting are, in ascending order: chimpanzee infant; small wax grub; infant chimpanzee head; large wax grub; moving rubber tube (snake); and moving wood-and-wire bug.

Supplementary observations

The chimpanzee's fear of toy animals and snakes is of course well known (*23, 42*). The data which are new and which were the occasion of this report are those showing that the chimpanzee is excited by, and avoids, parts of chimpanzee or human bodies. It was evident that such a conclusion had important implications, and that further observations would be desirable as a control of the data. Control observations, accordingly, were made after the formal experiment was completed. Their purpose was to discover whether some peculiarity of the actual experimental objects, or some detail of procedure, might have been the true cause of fear; or whether the behavior falls into a more general class related to the common human avoidance of a mutilated face and of dead bodies.

Preliminary experiments had already shown that all the adult chimpanzees were excited at the first sight of a chimpanzee head modelled in clay and carried in the hand from cage to cage. A majority showed avoidance, which was outright panic in five or six of the thirty subjects. In the supplementary observations an unpainted plaster cast of the clay model, and also an actual head from a dead chimpanzee, produced definite avoidance.

With different presentations the results were essentially the same, although intensity of response varied, in part with adaptation to sight of so many similar objects. Avoidance was observed when a head was carried by hand; when it was exposed by removing a cloth or opening a box; and when the head was first put in the chimpanzee's cage and the animal admitted afterward. In another observation the head was placed behind a small ledge, so that the actual termination of the neck was not visible (although the chimpanzee "knew" from familiarity with the cage in which the test was made that there was no space large enough for a body beneath the head). The chimpanzee was then admitted from a detaining inner room from which none of the preparations could be seen. A marked fear response occurred immediately, before the lapse of enough time to make the unresponsiveness of the head abnormal. Thus lack of movement in the test object did not determine the fear, nor yet an actual perception of the termination of the neck.

A painted human eye and eyebrow (sawn from a plaster manikin's head) produced marked avoidance.

Finally, observations were made with anesthetized chimpanzees as stimulus objects. Four adults were shown an anesthetized infant, two years old, carried by two members of the staff. The infant was recovering from nembutal, and made some spontaneous movements of an arm and hand. Three of the four adults were very excited and one at least afraid, in spite of the fact that they had often seen young chimpanzees being carried by the staff. A more deeply anesthetized adult was taken on a low, flat, two-wheeled barrow up to the cages of nine of the adults. Definite fear was shown by six, aggression (possibly related to fear) by two others, and the remaining animal was almost certainly afraid but remained at a distance without showing definable avoidance.

The fear evoked by a detached face or head in the formal experiment, therefore, was not a product of some uncontrolled detail of procedure or of the construction of the test objects. Any of a number of related stimuli have the same effect, in a number of situations.

From the data it appears that *either* lack of responsiveness in a whole animal, *or* an evident lack of a body when the head or part of the head is seen, can determine the fear. The first conclusion depends on the observations with anesthetized animals as stimuli. The second follows from the fact that avoidance of an isolated head was immediate and certainly was not delayed long enough for an unusual unresponsiveness, as such, to have become apparent before fear occurred.

Spontaneity of the fear

The fears observed must also have been spontaneous,[1] and not conditioned by some association of the test objects with a more primitive source of fear such as pain. This is shown by the following considerations.

There are two ways in which fear of a detached head or an anesthe-

---

[1] The term "spontaneous" is used here to mean that the fear is not built up by association, as a learned response. The term is not synonymous with "innate" since there are definite factors of past experience involved....

tized animal could be due to learning. Fear might occur (1) because the subjects recognized part of a whole which they had learned to fear in the past, or (2) because of an earlier association of a class of objects (detached heads, abnormally unresponsive chimpanzees) with a more primitive cause of fear.

1. The first explanation can be ruled out. The dummy human head represented an ordinary young man whom the adults of the colony might have teased or injured, as they often tend to do with strangers whose general appearance is similar to that of members of the laboratory staff, but whom they would not have feared. The cast of a face was a faithful replica of the chimpanzee Lita's, and made from a death mask. She had died not long before the experiment began, and certainly would not have been a source of fear to any of the other chimpanzees with cage wire intervening, as in the conditions of the experiment. The anesthetized infant in his normal state would not have been feared by an adult; and the anesthetized adult who was used as a stimulus object was Don, who is dominated by almost all of the other adults of the colony. The test object which aroused fear therefore did not do so because it was recognized as part of a whole which in its normal completeness would have caused the response.

2. The second possibility to be examined is that an association had been formed earlier between the class of stimulus objects and some event such as pain, loud noise, or a fall. For animals born in the bush and captured when their mothers were killed this was a real possibility. But nine of the adolescent and adult subjects of the experiment were born and reared in captivity and definitely had no opportunity to make such associations. None of these had seen a detached human or chimpanzee head; a few of them had seen a dead chimpanzee, but no more primitive cause of fear would be associated with the sight. The nine animals who are known not to have associations showed on the average rather more frequent and stronger avoidance than the remaining twenty-one animals.

These facts require the conclusion that the fears discussed are spontaneous. Further support for the conclusion is found in the behavior of human beings.

Human avoidance of mutilated and dead bodies

Human emotional responses to the dead and to such things as the sight of a major operation or of a badly mutilated face cannot reasonably be attributed to conditioning. The responses tend to be strongest on the first experience, which eliminates direct conditioning as an explanation and requires the supporting assumption of a preliminary verbal conditioning which forms the whole basis of the response. But if avoidance were so readily established, with on innate tendency toward fear of the conditioned stimulus itself, one could easily keep children from playing in dangerous places or train adults to drive automobiles carefully—by verbal instruction alone. This is the essence of Valentine's (39) brilliant criticism of Watsonian theory and my rejection of the explanation by conditioning rests upon his argument. What he did was to show how easy it is to condition fear of some things, how hard with others, and thus demonstrated the existence of emotional susceptibilities which are the basis of spontaneous and almost spontaneous fears.

Watson's (40) theory of fear has rightly had a profound effect upon psychological thought, and a radical departure from his ideas is not easily accepted. Yet the present situation is that the theory has been demolished, with no good substitute in sight. Jones and Jones' (22) experiment on the human fear of snakes constituted a strong and radical attack on Watson's theory. The evidence adduced by Valentine (39) reinforced the attack with evidence from a variety of fears. He has shown that there is a wide range of situations, not easily defined or classified, which have some tendency to evoke human fear. Finally, Hebb and Riesen (14) have shown the existence of a spontaneous fear of strangers in infant chimpanzees, where the customary appeal to the subject's unknown past experience is impossible and the explanation by conditioning ruled out.

Watson's work, consequently, provides no more than a starting point in determining the causes of fear and gives no reason to reject the conclusion that human fear of dead or mutilated bodies is spontaneous. The conclusion is also not affected by the fact that an almost complete adaptation to such stimuli is possible, nor by the fact that some persons may not have an emotional disturbance at their first sight of an operation, autopsy, or dissection. It has sometimes been assumed that if a fear is not general it must have been learned by those who do have it: that an innate fear should be found in all persons. This argument of course is quite invalid in view of the existence of individual genetic differences, and it has been seen that some of the chimpanzee fears discussed in this paper are not found in all animals and yet cannot be ascribed to learning.

The evidence, therefore, is that both in man and in chimpanzee there occur spontaneous fears of mutilated and unresponsive bodies. The chimpanzee knows nothing of anesthesia, has no abstract conception of death, and presumably may confuse a model of a head and the real thing. Considering the intellectual differences between the species and the extent to which man's behavior is influenced by speech, one must say that human and chimpanzee fear susceptibilities, with dismembered or inert bodies as stimulus objects, are remarkably similar. In this fact there is further support for the idea that such fears are spontaneous and not associative or conditioned.

So that this conclusion will be seen in the proper perspective, the reader is reminded that the importance of learning is not minimized. There are essential factors of past experience in the fears which have been discussed; and the hypothesis which is to be presented lays a good deal of emphasis on learning as an element in the development of any fear.

Central versus sensory factors determining fear

The first step in an analysis of fear is a better definition of the problem and of its relation to other psychological investigations.

It should be specified that the problem is not simply that of the subcortical motor integration of fear behavior. The earlier studies of Bard (2) had the effect of concentration attention on the hypothalamus, but it is now evident that more must be taken into account. The analysis by Lashley (24) and Masserman (32) has limited the emotional functions of the diencephalon to a motor integration. More recently, Bard (3) has described rage in a cat lacking *only* the hypothalamic region which he formerly considered to be essential to emotional activity. In view also of the marked differences of the stimuli which are effective in each case, and the absence of "after-discharge" in the decorticate preparation, it is evident that the processes of normal and decorticate emotions cannot be equated. Fear behavior has been demonstrated by Bard in the decorticate cat, but only with auditory stimuli. An essential problem remains in understanding cortico-subcortical interaction and the important role of perception in the fear responses of the normal animal.

The evidence presented has shown that the chimpanzee's fear of a detached head is in some way related to the physical lack of an attached body or of movement or both. But our real interest is not in the physical properties of the stimulus object but in the way they act on the organism. The first question to be asked concerns the existence of a sensory control of the response: can one find any property of the sensory excitation which in itself determines the occurrence and form of the response?

The answer seems to be no. In the first place, the physical lack in the stimulus object cannot be equated with a sensory lack by saying that the sight of a head without the normally associated sight of a body causes fear, for the statement would not be true. When a chimpanzee sees a man's head only, without movement and with the rest of the man's body out of sight behind a door, he is not afraid. There are certainly sensory cues which distinguish the two situations (i.e., detached head *vs.* attached head with body hidden) but I have not been able to find any generalization that distinguishes the purely sensory [2] event which causes fear from the one which does not. In the second place, it has been shown that the fears are spontaneous. If they were also sensorily determined, it would follow that there are innate connections from the sensory cells, excited in seeing any chimpanzee or human head, to the motor centers determining avoidance; or in a more gestalt formulation, that the dynamic properties of every such sensory excitation have an innately selective action on those particular motor centers. It would follow further that this sensori-motor relationship is consistently inhibited and nonfunctional throughout the animal's lifetime, no matter how many times he sees a human or chimpanzee head, unless by chance the head has been cut off from its owner. The improbability of such ideas is evident. They seem to be a product of the assumption (quite reasonable in itself) that the form of a response is fully determined by the sensory event that precipitates it;

[2] "Sensory" in the present discussion is defined as referring to activity, in afferent structures, which is directly determined by environmental events; roughly, activity in the receptor organ and afferent tracts, up to and including the corresponding sensory projection area.

since a physical lack in the stimulus object cannot excite receptor cells, the assumption means that the part of the stimulus object which is present is an adequate excitant of fear, and, since the whole object does not cause fear, that the part which is missing is normally an inhibitor or in some way prevents an innately determined response to the other part. Such reasoning will be found to lead rapidly to absurdities. Doubt is then cast on the original assumption, and the alternative conclusion is indicated that the determinant of certain strongly marked anthropoid fears is not any property of the sensory excitation alone but may have to be sought in some interaction of sensory events with other cerebral processes.

This argument depends on the accuracy of the analysis which has been made of the stimulating conditions in which fear of dismembered or inert bodies is observed. Other interpretations are possible, but seem either to beg the question or to amount of the same thing. (One might say, for example, that it is strangeness or mysteriousness that produces fear of a decapitated head and of an inert chimpanzee being carried by human beings. Actually, reference to strangeness only strengthens the preceding argument, as we shall see in a moment.) Nevertheless, it would be unwise to depend too strongly on the evidence of behavior into which so many complicating factors of experience may enter. Let us turn to fear of strangers (14) and of sudden noise (8). The theoretical interpretation suggested by fear of a dismembered body gains decisive support from these other observations and in turn makes their theoretical significance clearer.

The growing chimpanzee is persistently afraid of strange persons, objects and places, although the response is not always predictable in the individual case. Hebb and Riesen (14) have shown that the fear of strangers by chimpanzee infants is spontaneous and cannot be accounted for as a conditioned response. Also, a slight change of clothing may produce fear of a familiar attendant who was not feared before. To assume that the form of the response on seeing something strange is controlled alone by some property of the sensory event is to assume that *any* visual excitation is primarily a cause of fear and that other responses are substituted merely by repetition of the stimulation. Fear of strangers would mean that the visual excitation from any human or chimpanzee face (strange chimpanzees are feared as much as strange men) or any pattern of clothing is an innately adequate excitant of fear; for any pattern whatever may be strange, depending on accidents of experience. The idea seems absurd in itself, and is definitely contradicted by observations of the behavior of an infant chimpanzee blindfolded from birth to the age of four months, when the avoidance of strangers by normal animals is beginning (Nissen).[3] In Senden's (35) comprehensive review of the literature on persons born blind and given their sight after infancy, there is

---

[3] Personal communication from Dr. H. W. Nissen. The experiment was not an investigation of emotional behavior, and detailed records on this point were not kept. But it is known with certainty that there was no avoidance evoked by the chimpanzee's first visual perception of human beings.

no mention of fear aroused by the first visual form-perception; and Dennis (7) explicitly denies that fear occurs in these persons. Fear of a strange person is, therefore, not determined by a particular property of the sensory excitation, but by some discrepancy of the pattern from those which have been frequently experienced by the subject—by a complex relationship, that is, of the sensory event to preexistent cerebral processes.

A similar meaning lies in the fact noted by English (8) that a noise must be sudden to cause fear. When auditory intensity is built up gradually, the response is hard to elicit. The same is true of loss of support. An unexpected drop is the one that causes fear, not one for which preparation has been made verbally or by playful swinging of infant subjects. Jones (21) has shown that unexpectedness is an essential feature of a number of fear-provoking situations. In all such fears the major determinant cannot be the afferent excitation alone but involves a relationship of that excitation to concurrent cerebral activity.

These facts actually raise no new theoretical issue. Their effect is to sharpen the definition of a problem which has been formulated in various ways by other writers. That both sensory and central processes are involved in the control of behavior and must be distinguished for theoretical purposes is implied by the concept of "operants" (Skinner, 37) and of "stimulus trace" (Hull, 16) no less than the "expectancy" of Cowles and Nissen (6), Mowrer (34) and Hilgard and Marquis (15). It is the real problem of attention and of the selectivity of response to the several properties of a sensory event (Leeper, 27; Lashley, 26). The problem is made explicit by Hilgard and Marquis's "central process which seems relatively independent of afferent stimuli," Beach's (4) "central excitatory mechanism," and Morgan's (33) "central motive state." Every serious attempt in recent years to analyze the neural mechanisms of the more complex forms of behavior has found the need of distinguishing, as more or less independent factors, sensory and central states or processes; in other words, of denying that the direction of transmission of a sensory excitation is determined by the properties of that excitation alone, even when the stable changes of learning have been taken into account. This is thoroughly consistent also with modern electro-physiology. All parts of the brain are continuously active and there are reasons for believing that the activity may be self-maintaining, and even self-initiating (1, 18, 29, 30, 41). An afferent excitation does not arouse inactive tissue, but modifies an activity already in existence. The conclusion, therefore, that there are nonsensory factors in the determination of certain fears agrees with existing theory.

It must be added that the conclusion is not necessarily trivial. Current opinion recognizes the necessity of postulating central determinants of behavior but it has done so reluctantly, always with reference to a single, rather narrow aspect of behavioral theory, and apparently without recognizing how generally the necessity has actually cropped up in psychological analysis. The preceding discussion may do no more than suggest a change of emphasis, but the change is one which, as I shall try to show, has a considerable effect on theory. Besides drawing attention to facts of behavior which are usually forgotten, it reveals some order in the facts and makes possible a coherent hypothesis of the nature of fear.

Development of an hypothesis

Avoidance of strangers provides a possible starting point for a theory of the nature of fear. An essential feature of the stimulating conditions is the divergence of the object avoided from a familiar group of objects, while still having enough of their properties to fall within the same class. It is a most important fact that the fear or shyness does not develop at first vision, as the already cited data of Nissen, Senden (*35*), and Dennis (*7*) have shown. Common experience indicates also that the fear is minimized or absent if the growing infant has always been exposed to sight of a large number of persons. It is therefore dependent on the fact that certain perceptions have become habitual, a limited number of central neural reactions to the sight of human beings having been established with great specificity by repeated experience. The idea that there are such habits of perception was developed by Gibson (*9*) and further supported by later studies of the effect of set upon perception (*5, 27, 43*). A number of facts relating to the development of intelligence, and its changes with advancing age, have the same import (*11*, pp. 286, 289). From this point of view, it might be proposed that fear occurs when an object is seen which is like familiar objects in enough respects to arouse habitual processes of perception, but in other respects arouses incompatible processes.

Such a treatment of the fear of strangers would amount to an interference, incongruity, or conflict theory. It might subsume fear of mutilated bodies as well, by classifying them as strange objects, and could be extended to cover fears due to pain and sudden loud noise, which obviously tend to disrupt concurrent psychological processes. But farther than this such a conflict theory will not go. There might be some difficulty in applying it even to the fear of strange objects, when the strangeness is apparently due to incompleteness in a familiar object (as with the chimpanzee's fear of a detached head); and conflict cannot account for causes of fear such as darkness (*39*) in which a sensory deficit is the effective condition, or nutritional disturbance (*38*).

Moreover, a fundamental question would remain as to the meaning of "conflict," and why an incompatibility between two perceptions should produce the incoordinations of emotional behavior. This is the crucial question, and in trying to answer it I believe we can find the possibility of a more comprehensive hypothesis, according to which conflict is only one of several ways in which a true source of fear occurs. If two perceptual processes, which cannot coexist, cannot even alternate without producing gross disturbances of behavior (which is what the conflict notion implies), ordinary unemotional behavior must depend on an essential temporal integration in cerebral processes, and fear may be a direct result of their disorganization. Let us ask what such ideas would involve.

It has already been seen that sensory and central processes contribute separately to the control of behavior. For convenience, let us designate the specific pattern of cellular activity throughout the thalamo-cortical system, at any one moment, as a "phase." Behavior is directly correlated with a phase sequence which is temporally organized (4), in part by the inherent properties of the system (the constitutional factor) and in part by the time relations of various afferent excitations in the past (the factor of experience.) The spatial organization of each phase, the actual anatomical pattern of cells which are active at any moment, would be affected by the present afferent excitation also. Subjectively, the phase sequence would be identified with the train of thought and perception. Now each phase is determined by a neural interaction, between the preceding phase and the concurrent afferent excitations. Lorente De Nó's (29) discussion of the dynamics of neural action shows that two or more simultaneous neural events might reinforce each other's effects and contribute to a single, determinate pattern of subsequent cerebral activity; or on the contrary might be indeterminate, in the sense that slight changes of timing and intensity could lead to marked and sudden fluctuations of pattern. A phase sequence, that is, could be stable or unstable, and one can assume that vacillating, unpredictable, and incoordinated behavior is the expression of unstable cerebral activity. Also, the effect of learning in general is to increase the predictability and coordination of behavior. The element of learning in emotional behavior will be discussed more specifically, but in the meantime we may speak of the cerebral processes controlling predictable, coordinated behavior as "organized," and recognize the tendency of learning to establish and maintain cerebral organization.

Disorganization could occur in several ways, some of which may be called conflict. (1) A sensory event might disrupt the concurrent phase sequence. The event might be one whose facilitation has been integrated into other phase sequences, and disruptive only because it is "unexpected." If so the disruption would be brief, another well-organized phase sequence would be promptly established, and one would speak of the subject as having only been "startled." The disruption would be brief but it would occur; a well-organized phase could not be set up instantaneously, independent of facilitation from the preceding phase. On the other hand, the sensory event might fail to set up another organized sequence, and so initiate a prolonged disturbance; or might, like loud noise, and especially pain, tend persistently to break down cerebral organization. (2) Simultaneous sensory events might have facilitations which are enough unlike to make the following phase sequence unstable, even though each event separately might be capable of integration with the concurrent phase. Evidently (1) and (2) would be modes of conflict, one sensory-central, the other sensory-sensory.[4] But disorganization might also result (3) from the absence of a usually present sensory process. Cerebral

[4] Logically, another category of "central-central" conflict would be possible, which might have some meaning with regard to emotional disturbances and anxiety arising from a conflict of ideas or beliefs. Such a concept might be applied to fear of socialism or of catholics and emotional disturbances due to such purely intellectual ideas as those of Galileo or Darwin.

organization involves learning. If a sensory activity A has always been present during adaptation to a sensory event B, facilitation from A would necessarily affect the final pattern of cellular activities which constitutes the adaptaion to B, and might be essential to it. If so, B in the absence of A could again produce behavioral disturbance (if B without A occurs often enough, however, another adaptation would be established). Finally (4) metabolic and structural changes in the central nervous system could obviously be a source of disorganization, by changing the time relations between the activities of individual cells, apart from any unusual conflict or sensory deficiency.

Attention must now be turned to the way in which cerebral processes tend to maintain their organization, in order to round out the picture of fear behavior. Whatever else may be true of it, avoidance certainly averts or minimizes disruptive stimulation. When we distinguish between the disruption and the processes tending to avert it, and assume that the degree of disruption may vary, we obtain the valuable result of seeing how a single mechanism of fear could on different occasions produce perfectly coordinated flight, a less coordinated avoidance accompanied by trembling and so on, startle, or the paralysis of terror: When cerebral disruption is extreme, it might presumably prevent any coordinated action, even flight.

It seems evident that the so-to-speak homeostatic processes which maintain the dynamic equilibrium of unemotional behavior are to a great extent processes of learning, operating in either of two ways. On the one hand there is negative adaptation to strange objects, which implies that a sensory-central conflict may be banished by an effect of learning on the central organization alone. The sensory event remains the same, yet disturbance disappears. With still further exposure, the formerly strange object may become not merely tolerated but "liked" and "pleasant," which is to say that the originally disturbing sensory even now actively supports cerebral integration.

On the other hand, learning may contribute to this integration indirectly, by reinforcing a mode of behavior (avoidance) which minimizes or removes the disturbing sensations. The incoordinations of emotional behavior, its most characteristic feature, are unlearned; they are apt to be most marked on the first occasion on which they are aroused by any particular stimulus. But the coordinated element of the behavior tends to become more prominent on repetition of the stimulus and to increase, while the unlearned incoordination is decreasing. It thus appears that the coordinated avoidance which occurs in fear behavior of normal animals is mainly learned.

There is indeed a primitive innate avoidance (manifested e.g., in the flexion reflex of Sherrington's (36) spinal animals, and the cowering of Bard's (3) decerebrate cats), but the avoidance which operates most efficiently to maintain coordinated effector activity is acquired. In the normal mammal at least, simple avoidance appears as a conditioned response to cues which in the past have preceded a disruptive stimulation. When a disruptive event is sudden and without warning the response is never an uncomplicated avoidance, a smooth and economical cooperation of effector organs, but involves startle, trembling, sweating, vocalization, and so on. The optimum toward which behavior tends, with repetition of such disturbances, is a response (to premonitory cues) which completely averts the disturbing sensory event. At this final stage of learning, avoidance is fully effective in maintaining integrated cerebral action, and no emotional component is left in the behavior. Thus avoidance without fear occurs. In the avoidance that does involve fear the learning process is not complete or premonitory cues have not been available, and the belated avoidance appears side by side with the excess of effector activity that justifies the inference of cerebral disorganization.

The reciprocal relationship of learning to the disruption of integrated behavior is most simply illustrated by an adult's unemotional avoidance of a hot stove which as an infant he may once have feared. Another illustration is provided by observation of adult chimpanzees where the course of learning in a very unusual social situation could be followed from its beginning. The experimenter, disguised with a grotesque false face and a change of clothing, approached each animal's cage wearing heavy gloves and acted the part of a very aggressive individual, instead of the cautious role one ordinarily takes with the chimpanzee. The results suggested an interpretation similar to that of Bridges (cited by Jones, 21) who concluded that an infant's fear develops out of primitive undifferentiated excitement. The first response by a number of animals was a generalized excitement and marked autonomic activity. An animal might be "friendly" and viciously aggressive, almost in the same breath, or show erection of hair and scream and yet solicit petting. Attack, flight, and the friendly pattern alternated unpredictably. As the stimulus was repeated over a 5-week period, the autonomic activity decreased and one or other of the various patterns dominated. Eventually each animal's behavior became predictable, but it appeared often to be a matter of chance whether the original disturbance would develop into fear, aggression or (less often) friendliness. When avoidance became dominant, the animal would move back out of reach while the experimenter was still distant, with a marked decrease of the excessive effector activity. Learning was clearly involved. We shall also see that the possibility, suggested by this example, that the learning may take more than one form, has a bearing on the theoretical relation of fear to other emotional patterns.

The hypothesis implicitly developed in this discussion can now be made explicit. The immediate source of fear is a disruption of a coordination, principally acquired in the timing of cellular activities in the cerebrum. The disruption may be due to conflict, sensory deficit or constitutional change. With disruption there at once occur processes tending to restore the integration of cerebral activities; in fear these include either liminal or subliminal (13) activation of processes determining avoidance. Optimally, avoidance tends toward completely averting the cerebral disruption, and at this stage avoidance without fear would be said to occur.

Classification of specific fears

The value and limitations of the hypothesis will be clearer if we next see how it would be related to specific causes of fear.

1. *Fears Due to "Conflict."* Here may be included fears induced by pain, loud noise, dead or mutilated bodies, and strange persons and animals. Pain and loud noise appear to have a primitive disrupting action, not psychologically analyzable nor dependent on any previous experience. To this extent fear of such things is in a special class. It is also noteworthy that there is little adaptation of the repetition of pain and sudden intense noise except in very special conditions (28).

Fear of the strange and of dead and mutilated bodies is included under the heading of conflict on the assumption that strange objects arouse incompatible perceptual and intellectual processes. If it should be concluded however that the effective condition is a perceptual deficit, fear of the strange should be included in the following category (2). Finally, fear of snakes and certain small mammals may belong either in this or the following category. Although some basis for including them in the present category might be proposed it would be much too speculative, and it is best to let such fears stand for the present as not fully accounted for.

2. *Fears Due to Sensory Deficit.* Loss of support, darkness and solitude, as causes of fear, have in common an absence of customary stimulation.

Proprioceptive and pressure stimulation due to maintained position in space is practically alway present, and it is plausible to suppose that the afferent excitation form these sources would have an essential part in maintaining experientially organized, or habitual, modes of cerebral action. With loss of support, however, the proprioception accompanying maintenance of posture against gravity, and exteroception from the surfaces on which the body's weight rests, are decreased or abolished. Redistribution of blood pressure and changes of position of the viscera would no doubt also lead to positive stimulation, but it seems unlikely that this is an effective cause of fear in the infant. In the adult, of course, such stimulation would have become conditioned by experience. (If it should be true that positive visceral stimulation is the main cause of fear in an infant dropped for the first time, the fear should be classed in the preceding category 1, as one of those aroused by an unaccustomed stimulation.)

Fears induced by darkness and solitude (39) do not occur with time relations such that the emotional excitation can be attributed to the positive visual activity of the "off-effect." The response appears to be genuine reaction to deficit (25), intelligible only on the assumption of the present discussion that a "response" need have no direct *sensory* excitant. The violent attempts of the growing chimpanzee to avoid isolation, even in full daylight, seem to require a quite similar interpretation. Kohler (23) has shown that the effective condition here is the social deprivation, as such. Just as a few patterns of postural stimulation are a practically constant feature of the afferent influx to the brain, and visual stimulation during waking hours, so social perceptions are frequent (though intermittent) and might be expected to become an integral element in the organization of cerebral action patterns. It is important to note that this would be a function of experience, and that no fear of darkness or of being alone should be expected in the subject who has only infrequently experienced anything else. Such a subject would develop a different cerebral organization, in which the perceptions referred to would play no essential part. It is also implied that in early infancy neither darkness nor isolation would have any emotional effect; and that as psychological development continues the patterns of cerebral action might, toward maturity, become so stable as to be relatively independent of any particular set of perceptions. Some adults, or most adults in a particular culture, might have no fear of darkness and isolation.

3. *Constitutional Disturbances and Maturation.* Spies et al. (*38*) have provided exceptionally clear evidence that the psychotic fears so frequently found in pellegra are, in some instances at least, directly due to nutritional disturbance (see also Jolliffe, *20*). When the psychosis is acute (before irreversible neural damage has been done), fear of friends and relatives and of hallucinatory creatures may clear up dramatically upon administration of nicotinic acid. The patient regains insight rapidly, can recall his fears clearly, but also is puzzled at the lack of any incident that might have caused them. Controls made to exactly define the action of nicotinic acid rule out psychological influences as essential either to the mental illness or its cure. Such fears must be regarded as originating in a disturbance of the metabolism of the individual cell, changing (for example) the timing of its detonation cycle and thus its relationship to the activity of other cells. In other words, metabolic changes would have disrupted the orderly sequence of cerebral events which is postulated here as the basis of normal unemotional behavior.

It is also evident that endocrine factors might at times produce a similar effect, partly accounting for the increased shyness and emotional instability of adolescence. The gonadal hormones must be supposed to have a selective action on certain central neural cells (*4, 25*) changing their properties of excitability and thus disrupting to a greater or less degree the neural organizations into which those cells have entered. With the passage of time reorganization would occur and shyness would decrease.

I do not of course suggest that constitutional changes are the only cause of shyness, or even the main cause. In its most pronounced form it must be thought of simply as an avoidance of strangers, and the next most important factor, after the sight of a strange person, may well be the fact that as the child matures others begin to behave toward him in a different way, according to his age. The child is confronted by strange behavior, and situations which are strange to him. Thus shyness can be treated mainly as avoidance of the strange. It is not impossible however that structural and endocrine changes may also play a part in the emotional instabilities of youth. One thinks of maturation as slow and gradual, but there is actually little evidence on this point, and spurts of growth might well make a significant modification of cerebral organizations established by earlier experience. In general terms, such an approach makes intelligible the sporadic appearance of the "imaginative, subjective, or anticipatory fears" classified as such by Jersild and Holmes (19). The fears referred to by Jersild and Holmes are markedly subject to maturation during a period of rapid and irregular growth, and when one observes them in the growing child it is characteristically hard to discover any sufficient cause in experience.

The relationship of fear to rage and other states

Fear and rage are notoriously related, and it is impossible to frame any statement of the causes of rage (12) which would not on some points comprise causes of fear as well. The question, whether there is in fact any definite distinction, has been raised elsewhere (13). The hypothesis developed here suggests a kinship between the two emotions which may be put as follows.

The fundamental source of either emotion is of the same kind, a disruption of coordinated cerebral activity. Flight and aggression are two different modes of reaction tending to restore the dynamic equilibrium, or stability, of cerebral processes. The question may be left open at present whether there are different kinds of disturbance, one kind leading to rage, the other to fear. It seems almost certain that such a difference exists between extremes, but with no clear dichotomy; for in some situations, as I have suggested above, it appears to be a matter of chance whether aggression or flight will dominate behavior. Each of these modes of response tends to restore integrated cerebral action, one by modifying the disturbing source of stimulation, the other by removing the animal from it.

Fawning would be another mode of reaction which would tend to modify disruptive stimulation (by placating the source). It is evident also that the hypothesis of this paper opens a wide field of speculation concerning a number of socially and clinically familiar conditions, such as shame, grief, chronic depression and so on. To deal with these varied emotional disturbances the first step would be to classify the source of disturbance as modifiable by the subject's responses, or unmodifiable; and further to classify the modifiable according to the mode of overt reaction which would be effective. Thus shame or grief would arise from unmodifiable conditions; fear primarily from situations which are (or appear to the subject to be) modifiable by retreat; and so on. Finally, neurosis and some forms of psychosis would be regarded as a chronic condition of cerebral disorganization which according to the hypothesis might be initiated either by severe and prolonged conflict, or by a metabolic disturbance.

It would be idle at present to carry speculation farther, but it has been worthwhile observing that a theoretical relationship of fear to other emotional patterns is provided. If the proposed hypothesis is on the right track, the details of the relationship will become evident when more is known of the physiology of the cerebrum.

Conclusions

The conclusions of this paper may be put as follows:

1. Anthropoid fears of inert, mutilated, or dismembered bodies are spontaneous: that is to say, although experience of a certain kind is a prerequisite and learning is definitely involved, the avoidance of such objects is not built up by association with a more primitive cause of fear.

2. These and a number of other fears are evidently not determined by a sensory event alone, and the behavior is not intelligible except on the assumption that its control is a joint product of sensory and "autonomous" central processes. Consequently no amount of analysis of the stimulating conditions alone can be expected to elucidate the nature of fear, or to lead to any useful generalization concerning its causes.

3. An adequate hypothesis of the nature of fear cannot be framed in psychological terms alone, but must utilize physiological concepts of cerebral action. No common psychological ground can be discovered for all the various causes of fear. What is there in common, for example, between the characteristically high level of the auditory and low level of visual stimulation which induces fear in children? Or between fear of strangers, which decreases, and fear induced by pain, which tends to increase, with repetition?

The hypothesis developed here has made a considerable synthesis of formerly unrelated facts, although it remains vague on some crucial points. It proposes in brief that fear originates in the disruption of temporally and spatially organized cerebral activities; that fear is distinct from other emotions by the nature of the processes tending to restore cerebral equilibrium (that is, *via* flight); and classifies the sources of fear as involving (1) conflict, (2) sensory deficit, or (3) constitutional change. By distinguishing between processes which break down and those which restore physiological organization in the cerebrum, the variability of fear behavior is accounted for.

The conceptions of neurophysiological action on which this is based were developed originally as an approach to other problems.... When this is done, and the neurophysiological implications are made explicit, it may appear that a basis has been laid at last for an adequate theory of emotion and motivation—something which is lacking in psychology at present.

References

1. Adrian, E. D. Electrical activity of the nervous system. *Arch. neurol. Psychiatr.*, 1934, **32**, 1125–1136.
2. Bard, P. On emotional expression after decortication with some remarks on certain theoretical views. *Psychol. Rev.*, 1934, **41**, 309–329.

3. Bard, P. Neural mechanisms in emotional and sexual behavior. *Psychosom. Med.*, 1942, **4**, 171–172.
4. Beach, F. A. Analysis of factors involved in the arousal, maintenance and manifestation of sexual excitement in male animals. *Psychosom. Med.*, 1942, **4**, 171–198.
5. Carmichael, L., Hogan, H. P., & Walter, A. A. An experimental study of the effect of language on the reproduction of visually perceived form. *J. exp. Psychol.*, 1932, **15**, 73–86.
6. Cowles, J. T., & Nissen, H. W., Reward-expectancy in delayed responses of chimpanzees. *J. comp. Psychol.*, 1937, **24**, 345–358.
7. Dennis, W. Congenital cataract and unlearned behavior. *J. genet. Psychol.*, 1934, **44**, 340–350.
8. English, H. B. Three cases of the "conditioned fear response." *J. abnorm. soc. Psychol.*, 1929, **24**, 221–225.
9. Gibson, J. J. The reproduction of visually perceived forms. *J. exp. Psychol.*, 1929, **12**, 1–39.
10. Haslerud, G. M. The effect of movement of stimulus objects upon avoidance reactions in chimpanzees. *J. comp. Psychol.*, 1938, **25**, 507–528.
11. Hebb, D. O. The effect of early and late brain injury on test scores, and the nature of normal adult intelligence. *Proc. Amer, phil. Soc.*, 1942, **85**, 275–292.
12. Hebb, D. O. The forms and conditions of chimpanzee anger. *Bull. Canad. psychol. Assoc.*, 1945, **5**, 32–35.
13. Hebb, D. O. Emotion in man and animal: an analysis of the intuitive processes of recognition. *Psychol. Rev.*, 1946, **53**, 88–106.
14. Hebb, D. O., & Riesen, A. H. The genesis of irrational fears. *Bull. Canad. psychol. Assoc.*, 1943, **3**, 49–50.
15. Hilgard, E. R., & Marquis, D. G. *Conditioning and learning.* New York: Appleton-Century, 1940.
16. Hull, C. L. *Principles of behavior: an introduction to behavior theory.* New York: Appleton-Century, 1943.
17. Jacobsen, C. F., Jacobsen, M. M., & Yoshioka, J. G. Development of an infant chimpanzee during her first year. *Comp. Psychol., Monog.*, 1932, **9**, 1–94.
18. Jasper, H. H. Electrical signs of cortical activity. *Psychol. Bull.*, 1937, **34**, 411–481.
19. Jersild, A. T., & Holmes, F. B. *Children's fears.* New York: Teachers College Bureau of Publications, 1935.
20. Jolliffe, N. The neuropsychiatric manifestations of vitamin deficiencies. *J. Mt. Sinai Hosp.*, 1942, **8**, 658–667.
21. Jones, M. C. Emotional development. In C. Murchison (Ed.), *A handbook of child psychology.* (2nd ed.) Worcester, Mass.: Clark Univ. Press, 1933. Pp. 271–302.
22. Jones, H. E., & Jones, M. C. A study of fear. *Childhood Educ.*, 1928, **5**, 136–143.
23. Köhler, W. *The mentality of apes.* New York: Harcourt, Brace, 1925.

24. Lashley, K. S. The thalamus and emotion. *Psychol. Rev.*, 1938, **45**, 42–61.
25. Lashley, K. S. Experimental analysis of instinctive behavior. *Psychol. Rev.*, 1938, **45**, 445–471.
26. Lashley, K. S. An examination of the "continuity theory" as applied to discrimination learning. *J. gen. Psychol.*, 1942, **26**, 241–265.
27. Leeper, R. A study of a neglected portion of the field of learning: the development of sensory organization. *J. genet. Psychol.*, 1935, **46**, 41–75.
28. Liddell, H. S. Animal behavior studies bearing on the problem of pain. *Psychosom. Med.*, 1944, **6**, 261–263.
29. Lorente De Nó, R. Transmission of impulses through cranial motor nuclei. *J. Neurophysiol.*, 1939, **2**, 402–464.
30. Lorente De Nó, R. Cerebral cortex: architecture. In J. F. Fulton (Ed), *Physiology of the nervous system.* (2nd ed.) New York: Oxford Univ. Press, 1943. Pp. 274–301.
31. McCulloch, T. L., & Haslerud, G. M. Affective responses of an infant chimpanzee reared in isolation from its kind. *J. comp. Psychol.*, 1939, **28**, 437–445.
32. Masserman, J. H. The hypothalamus in psychiatry. *Amer. J. Psychiatr.*, 1942, **98**, 633–637.
33. Morgan, C. T. *Physiological psychology.* New York: McGraw-Hill, 1943.
34. Mowrer, O. H. Preparatory set (expectancy)—a determinant in motivation and learning. *Psychol. Rev.*, 1938, **45**, 62–91.
35. Senden, M. v. *Raum- und Gestaltauffassung bei operierten Blindgeborenen vor und nach der Operation.* Leipzig: Barth, 1932.
36. Sherrington, C. S. *Integrative action of the nervous system.* New York: Scribner's, 1906.
37. Skinner, B. F. *The behavior of organisms: an experimental analysis.* New York: Appleton-Century, 1938.
38. Spies, T. D., Aring, C. D., Gelperin, J., & Bean, W. B. The mental symptoms of pellagra: their relief with nicotinic acid. *Amer. J. med. Sci.*, 1938, **196**, 461–475.
39. Valentine, C. W. The innate bases of fear. *J. genet. Psychol.*, 1930, **37**, 394–419.
40. Watson, J. B. *Behaviorism.* New York: Norton, 1924.
41. Weiss, P. Autonomous versus reflexogenous activity of the central nervous system. *Proc. Amer. phil. Soc.*, 1941, **84**, 53–64.
42. Yerkes, R. M., & Yerkes, A. W. Nature and conditions of avoidance (fear) response in chimpanzee, *J. comp. Psychol.*, 1936, **21**, 53–66.
43. Zangwill, O. L. A study of the significance of attitude in recognition. *Brit. J. Psychol.*, 1937, **28**, 12–17.

37

ALFRED C. KINSEY (1894–1956),
WARDELL B. POMEROY (B. 1913) AND
CLYDE E. MARTIN (B. 1918)

The sexual behavior of boys (1948)

Many authors have written about sexual behavior in man, but it remained for Kinsey and his associates to reduce it to numbers. The present excerpts from the first book by Kinsey and his associates constitutes an abridgment of the section dealing with the sexual behavior of boys. The title of the book is Sexual Behavior in the Human Male. *It was published by the W. B. Saunders Co., and the excerpts are reprinted with the publisher's permission.*

The present selection provides abundant evidence of childhood sexuality reaffirming the observations of Freud (selection 25) and of Malinowski (selection 31).

EARLY SEXUAL GROWTH AND ACTIVITY

The present volume is concerned, for the most part, with the record of the frequency and sources of sexual outlet in the biologically mature male, *i.e.*, in the adolescent and older male. This chapter, however, will discuss the nature of sexual response, and will show something of the origins of adult behavior in the activities of the younger, pre-adolescent boy.

The sexual activity of an individual may involve a variety of experiences, a portion of which may culminate in the event which is known as orgasm or sexual climax. There are six chief sources of sexual climax. There is self stimulation (masturbation), nocturnal dreaming to the point of climax, heterosexual petting to climax (without intercourse), true heterosexual intercourse, homosexual intercourse, and contact with animals of other species. There are still other possible sources of organism, but they are rare and never constitute a significant fraction of the outlet for any large segment of the population.

339

Erotic arousal and orgasm

Sexual contacts in the adolescent or adult male almost always involve physiologic disturbance which is recognizable as "erotic arousal." This is also true of much pre-adolescent activity, although some of the sex play of younger children seems to be devoid of erotic content. Pre-adolescent sexual stimulation is much more common among younger boys than it is among younger girls. Many younger females and, for that matter, a certain portion of the older and married female population, may engage in such specifically sexual activities as petting and even intercourse without discernible erotic reaction.

Erotic arousal is a material phenomenon which involves an extended series of physical, physiologic, and psychologic changes. Many of these could be subjected to precise instrument measurement if objectivity among scientists and public respect for scientific research allowed such laboratory investigation. In the higher mammals, including the human, tactile stimulation is the chief mechanical source of arousal; but the higher mammal, especially the human, soon becomes so conditioned by his experience, or by the vicariously shared experiences of others, that psychologic stimulation becomes the major source of arousal for many an older person, especially if he is educated and his mental capacities are well trained. There is an occasional individual who comes to climax through psychologic stimulation alone.

Erotic stimulation, whatever its source, effects a series of physiologic changes which, as far as we yet know, appear to involve adrenal secretion, typically autonomic reactions, increased pulse rate, increased blood pressure, an increase in peripheral circulation and a consequent rise in the surface temperature of the body; a flow of blood into such distensible organs as the eyes, the lips, the lobes of the ears, the nipples of the breast, the penis of the male, and the clitoris, the genital labia and the vaginal walls of the female; a partial but often considerable loss of perceptive capacity (sight, hearing, touch, taste, smell); an increase in so-called nervous tension, some degree of rigidity of some part or of the whole of the body at the moment of maximum tension; and then a sudden release which produces local spasms or more extensive or all-consuming convulsions. The moment of sudden release is the point commonly recognized among biologists as orgasm.

* * *

The most important consequence of sexual orgasm is the abrupt release of the extreme tension which preceded the event and the rather sudden return to a normal or subnormal physiologic state after the event. In the mature male, ejaculation of the liquid secretions of the prostate and seminal vesicles, through the urethra of the penis, is a usual consequence of the convulsions produced by orgasm in those particular organs; and such ejaculation usually provides the most ready proof that the individual has passed through climax. But orgasm may occur without the emission of semen. This latter situation is, of course, the rule when orgasm occurs among pre-adolescent males and among females....

Among pre-adolescent boys... and among younger females, orgasm is not so readily recognized, partly because of the lack of an ejaculate, and partly because the inexperienced individual is without a background from which to judge the event. In the younger boy there is no ejaculate because the prostate and seminal vesicles are not yet functionally developed, and in the female those glands are rudimentary and never develop. Nevertheless, erotic arousal and organism where it occurs among younger boys and among females appears to involve the same sequence of physiologic events that has been described for the older, ejaculating males; and many of the younger boys and most of the older females who have contributed to the present study have been able to supply apparently reliable records of such experience.

* * *

Pre-adolescent sex play

It has been assumed that the development of sexual attitudes and the first overt sexual activities occur in the early history of the infant, but there have been few specific data available. Recently we have begun the accumulation of information through conferences with quite young children and with their parents; and in addition we now have material obtained by some of our subjects through the direct observation of infants and of older pre-adolescents. These histories emphasize the early development of the attitudes which largely determine the subsequent patterns of adult sexual behavior; but this material must be analyzed in a later volume, after we have accumulated a great many more specific data. For the time being we can report only on the specifically genital play and overt socio-sexual behavior which occurs before adolescence.

We are not in a position to discuss the developing child's more generalized sensory responses which may be sexual, but which are not so specific as genital activities are. Freud and the psychoanalysts contend that all tactile stimulation and response are basically sexual, and there seems considerable justification for this thesis, in view of the tactile origin of so much of the mammalian stimulation. This, however, involves a considerable extension of both the everyday and scientific meanings of the term sexual, and we are not now concerned with recording every occasion on which a babe brings two parts of its body into juxtaposition, every time it scratches its ear or its genitalia, nor every occasion in which it sucks its thumb. If all such acts are to be interpreted as masturbatory, it is, of course, a simple matter to conclude that masturbation and early sexual activity are universal phenomena; but it is still to be shown that these elemental tactile experiences have anything to do with the development of the sexual behavior of the adult.

* * *

Our own interviews with children younger than five, and observations made by parents and others who have been subjects in this study, indicate that hugging and kissing are usual in the activity of the very young child, and that self manipulation of genitalia, the exhibition of genitalia, the exploration of the genitalia of other children, and some manual and occasionally oral manipulation of the genitalia of other children occur in the two- to five-year olds more frequently than older persons ordinarily remember from their own histories. Much of this earliest sex play appears to be purely exploratory, animated by curiosity, and as devoid of erotic content as boxing, or wrestling, or other non-sexual physical contacts among older persons. Nevertheless, at a very early age the child learns that there are social values attached to the activities, and his emotional excitation while engaged in such play must involve reactions to the mysterious, to the forbidden, and to the socially dangerous performance, as often as it involves true erotic response. Some of the play in the younger boy occurs without erection, but some of it brings erection and may culminate in true orgasm.

In pre-adolescent and early adolescent boys, erection and orgasm are easily induced. They are more easily induced than in older males. Erection may occur immediately after birth and, as many observant mothers (and few scientists) know, it is practically a daily matter for all small boys, from earliest infancy and up in age. Slight physical stimulation of the genitalia, general body tensions, and generalized emotional situations bring immediate erection, even when there is no specifically sexual situation involved. The very generalized nature of the response becomes evident when one accumulates a list of the apparently non-sexual stimuli which bring erection. Ramsey (1943) has published such a list gathered from a group of 291 younger boys which he had interviewed, and his histories provide part of the data which we have used in the present volume. A complete tabulation, based on the total sample now available on all cases, is as follows:

NON-SEXUAL SOURCES OF EROTIC RESPONSE
AMONG PRE-ADOLESCENT AND YOUNGER ADOLESCENT BOYS

Chiefly Physical

Sitting in class
Friction with clothing
Taking a shower
Punishment
Accidents
Electric shock
Fast elevator rides
Carnival rides, Ferris wheel
Fast sled riding
Fast bicycle riding
Fast car driving
Skiing

Airplane rides
A sudden change in environment
Sitting in church
Motion of car or bus
A skidding car
Sitting in warm sand
Urinating
Boxing and wrestling
High dives
Riding horseback
Swimming

Chiefly Emotional

Being scared
Fear of a house intruder

Near accidents
Being late to school

Chiefly Emotional (Cont'd)

Reciting before a class
Asked to go front in class
Tests at school
Seeing a policeman
Cops chasing him
Getting home late
Receiving grade card
Big fires
Setting a field afire
Hearing revolver shot
Anger
Watching exciting games
Playing in exciting games
Marching soldiers
War motion pictures
Other movies
Band music
Hearing "extra paper" called
Harsh words
Fear of punishment
Being yelled at
Being alone at night
Fear of a big boy
Playing musical solo
Losing balance on heights
Looking over edge of building
Falling from garage, etc.
Long flight of stairs
Adventure stories
National anthem
Watching a stunting airplane
Finding money
Seeing name in print
Detective stories
Running away from home
Entering an empty house
Nocturnal dreams of fighting, accidents, wild animals, falling from high places, giants, being chased, or frightened

Among these younger boys, it is difficult to say what is an erotic response and what is a simple physical, or a generalized emotional situation.

Specifically sexual situations to which the younger boys respond before adolescence include the following:

SEXUAL SOURCES OF EROTIC RESPONSE AMONG 212 PRE-ADOLESCENT BOYS

Seeing females	107	Physical contact with females	34
Thinking about females	104	Love stories in books	32
Sex jokes	104	Seeing genitalia of other males	29
Sex pictures	89	Burlesque shows	23
Pictures of females	76	Seeing animals in coitus	21
Females in moving pictures	55	Dancing with females	13
Seeing self nude in mirror	47		

The above table is based on the histories of 212 boys who were pre-adolescent at the time of interview. Since the questions were not systematically put in all the pre-adolescent cases, the figures represent frequencies of answers in particular boys, and should not be taken as incidence figures for the population as a whole.

The record suggests that the physiologic mechanism of any emotional response (anger, fright, pain, etc.) may be the basic mechanism of sexual response. Originally the pre-adolescent boy erects indiscriminately to the whole array of emotional situations, whether they be sexual or non-sexual in nature. By his late teens the male has been so conditioned that he rarely responds to anything except a direct physical stimulation of genitalia, or to psychic situations that are specifically sexual. In the still older male even physical stimulation is rarely effective unless accompanied by such a psychologic atmosphere. The picture is that of the psychosexual emerging from a much more generalized and basic physiologic capacity which becomes sexual, as an adult knows it, through experience and conditioning.

The most specific activities among younger boys involve genital exhibition and genital contacts with other children. Something more than a half (57%) of the older boys and adults recall some sort of pre-adolescent sex play. This figure is much higher than some other students have found but it is probably still too low, for 70 per cent of the pre-adolescent boys who have contributed to the present study have admitted such experience, and there is no doubt that even they forget many of their earlier activities. It is not improbable that nearly all boys have some pre-adolescent genital play with other boys or with girls. Only about one-fifth as many of the girls have such play.

Most of this pre-adolescent sex play occurs between the ages of eight and thirteen, although some of it occurs at every age from earliest childhood to adolescence. For a quarter of the boys who have such play, the activity is limited to a single year (24.3%) or two (17.9%) or three (10.4%) in pre-adolescence. For many of them there is only a single experience. A third of the active males (36.2%) continue the play for five years or more. That the activity does not extend further is clearly a product of cultural restraints, for pre-adolescent sex play in the other anthropoids is abundant and continues into adult performance. Most of the play takes place with companions close to the subject's own age. On the other hand, the boy's initial experience is often (although not invariably) with a slightly older boy or girl. Older persons are the teachers of younger people in all matters, including the sexual. The record includes some cases of pre-adolescent boys involved in sexual contacts with adult females, and still more cases of pre-adolescent boys involved with adult males. Data on this point were not systematically gathered from all histories, and consequently the frequency of contacts with adults cannot be calculated with precision.

* * *

Homosexual Play. On the whole, the homosexual child play is found in more histories, occurs more frequently, and becomes more specific than the pre-adolescent heterosexual play. This depends, as so much of the adult homosexual activity depends, on the greater accessibility of the boy's own sex. In the younger boy, it is also fostered by his socially encouraged disdain for girls' ways, by his admiration for masculine prowess, and by his desire to emulate older boys. The anatomy and functional capacities of male genitalia interest the younger boy to a degree that is not appreciated by older males who have become heterosexually conditioned and who are continuously on the defensive against reactions which might be interpreted as homosexual.

About half of the older males (48%), and nearer two-thirds (60%) of the boys who were pre-adolescent at the time they contributed their histories, recall homosexual activity in their pre-adolescent years. The mean age of the first homosexual contact is about nine years, two and a half months (9.21 years).

The order of appearance of the several homosexual techniques is: exhibition of genitalia, manual manipulation of genitalia, anal or oral contacts with genitalia, and urethral insertions. Exhibition is much the most common form of homosexual play (in 99.8 per cent of all the histories which have any activity). It appears in the sex play of the youngest children, where much of it is incidental, definitely casual, and quite fruitless as far as erotic arousal is concerned. The most extreme development of exhibitionism occurs among the older pre-adolescents and the younger adolescent males who have discovered the significance of self masturbation and may have acquired proficiency in effecting orgasm. By that time there is a social value in establishing one's ability, and many a boy exhibits his masturbatory techniques to lone companions or to whole groups of boys. In the latter case, there may be simultaneous exhibition as a group activity. The boy's emotional reaction in such a performance is undoubtedly enhanced by the presence of the other boys. There are teen-age boys who continue this exhibitionistic activity throughout their high school years, some of them even entering into compacts with their closest friends to refrain from self masturbation except when in the presence of each other. In confining such social performances to self masturbation, these boys avoid conflicts over the homosexual. By this time, however, the psychic reactions may be homosexual enough, although it may be difficult to persuade these individuals to admit it.

Exhibitionism leads naturally into the next step in the homosexual play, namely the mutual manipulation of genitalia. Such manipulation occurs in the play of two-thirds (67.4%) of all the pre-adolescent males who have any homosexual activity. Among younger pre-adolescents the manual contacts are still very incidental and casual and without any recognition of the emotional possibilities of such experience. Only a small portion of the cases leads to the sort of manipulation which does effect arousal and possibly orgasm in the partner. Manual manipulation is more likely to become so specific if the relation is had with a somewhat older boy, or with an adult. Without help from more experienced persons, many pre-adolescents take a good many years to discover masturbatory techniques that are sexually effective.

Anal intercourse is reported by 17 per cent of the pre-adolescents who have any homosexual play. Anal intercourse among younger boys usually fails of penetration and is therefore primarily femoral. Oral manipulation is reported by nearly 16 per cent of the boys. Among younger boys, erotic arousal is less easily effected by oral contacts, more easily effected by manual manipulation. The anal and oral techniques are limited as they are because even at these younger ages there is some knowledge of the social taboos on these activities; and it is, in consequence, probable that the reported data are considerable understatements of the activities which actually occur.

Pre-adolescent homosexual play is carried over into adolescent or adult activity in something less than a half of all the cases. There are differences between social levels. In lower educational levels, the chances are 50–50 that the pre-adolescent homosexual play will be continued into adolescence or later. For the group that will go to college, the chances are better than four to one that the pre-adolescent activity will not be followed by later homosexual experience. In many cases, the later homosexuality stops with the adolescent years, but many of the adults who are actively and more or less exclusively homosexual date their activities from pre-adolescence. In a later volume these data will be examined in more detail, in connection with an analysis of the factors involved in the development of a heterosexual-homosexual balance.

Heterosexual Play. The average age for beginning pre-adolescent heterosexual play is about eight years and ten months (a mean of 8.81 years). This is approximately five months earlier than the average age for the beginning of homosexual play; but heterosexual activity, nonetheless, does not occupy quite as much of the attention of the pre-adolescent boys. It is found in 40 per cent of the pre-adolescent histories.

Just as with the homosexual, the heterosexual play begins with the exhibition of genitalia; and of those pre-adolescent boys who have any sex play with girls, about 99 per cent engage in such exhibition. For nearly 20 per cent of the boys, this is the limit of the activity. There is considerable curiosity among children, both male and female, about the genitalia of the opposite sex, fostered, if not primarily engendered, by the social restrictions on inter-sexual display. The boy is incited by the greater care which many parents exercise in covering the genitalia of the girls in the family—a custom which reaches its extreme in some other cultures where the boys may go completely nude until adolescence, while the girls are carefully clothed at least from the ages of four or five.

Of those pre-adolescent boys who have any heterosexual play, 81.4 per cent carry it to the point of manually manipulating the genitalia of the female. For many of the youngest boys this is even more incidental than the manual manipulation which occurs in homosexual contacts. Among certain groups, particularly in upper social levels, the children sometimes lack information on coitus, and there may be no comprehension that there are possibilities in heterosexual activity other than those afforded by manual contacts. There are vaginal insertions which involve objects of various sort, but most often they are finger insertions. Pre-adolescent attempts to effect genital union occur in nearly 22 per cent of all male histories, which is over half (55.3%) of the histories of the boys who have any pre-adolescent play. On this point, there are considerable differences between social levels. Three-quarters (74.4%) of the boys who will never go beyond eighth grade try such pre-adolescent coitus, but such experience is had by only one-quarter (25.7%) of the pre-adolescent boys of the group which will ultimately go to college.

The lower level boy has considerable information and help on these matters from older boys or from adult males, and in many cases his first heterosexual contacts are with older girls who have already had experience. Consequently, in this lower level, pre-adolescent contacts often involve actual penetration and the children have what amounts to real intercourse. The efforts of the upper level boys are less often successful, in many cases amounting to little more than the apposition of genitalia. With the lower level boy, pre-adolescent coitus may occur with some frequency, and it may be had with a variety of partners. For the upper level boy, the experience often occurs only once or twice, and with a single partner or two. These differences between patterns at different social levels, even in pre-adolescence, are of the utmost significance in any consideration of a program of sex education.

Oral contacts with females occur in only 8.9 per cent of the boys who have pre-adolescent heterosexual play. Oral contacts are more likely to occur where the girl is older, or where an adult woman is involved. There is considerable evidence that oral contacts are recognized as taboo, even at pre-adolescent ages.

Pre-adolescent heterosexual play is carried over into corresponding adolescent activities in nearly two-thirds of the cases. There is a somewhat higher carry-over of heterosexual petting, a lesser carry-over of heterosexual coitus. Again there are tremendous differences between social levels. If coitus is had by a pre-adolescent boy who will never go beyond eighth grade in school, the chances are three to one that he will continue such activity, without any major break, in his adolescent and adult years. If the boy who has pre-adolescent coitus belongs to the group that will ultimately go to college, the chances are more than four to one that the activity will not be continued in his adolescent years. Community attitudes on these matters are already exerting an influence on the pre-adolescent boy.

* * *

In the technical literature there seem to be only a few references to the possibility of the pre-adolescent child experiencing orgasm. But, as we have already indicated, organism is not at all rare among pre-adolescent boys, and it also occurs among pre-adolescent girls. Since this significant fact had not been well established in scientific publication, it will be profitable to record here the nature of the data for the male in some detail.

Pre-adolescent boys, since they are incapable of ejaculation, may be as uncertain as some inexperienced females in their recognition of orgasm. In consequence, the record on such early experience is incomplete in most of the histories, and it is as yet impossible to make any exact calculation of the incidence or frequency in the population as a whole. Nevertheless, some of the younger boys who have contributed to the present study have described what is unmistakably sexual orgasm in their pre-adolescent histories, and a larger number of adults remember such experience.

* * *

Orgasm has been observed in boys of every age from 5 months to adolescence. Orgasm is in our records for a female babe of 4 months. The orgasm in an infant or other young male is, except for the lack of an ejaculation, a striking duplicate of organism in an older adult. As described earlier in this chapter, the behavior involves a series of gradual physiologic changes, the development of rhythmic body movements with distinct penis throbs and pelvic thrusts, an obvious change in sensory capacities, a final tension of muscles, especially of the abdomen, hips, and back, a sudden release with convulsions, including rhythmic and anal contractions —followed by the disappearance of all symptoms. A fretful babe quiets down under the initial sexual stimulation, is distracted from other activities, begins rhythmic pelvic thrusts, becomes tense as climax approaches, is thrown into convulsive action, often with violent arm and leg movements, sometimes with weeping at the moment of climax. After climax the child loses erection quickly and subsides into the calm and peace that typically follows adult orgasm. It may be some time before erection can be induced again after such an experience. There are observations of 16 males up to 11 months of age, with such typical orgasm reached in 7 cases. In 5 cases of young pre-adolescents, observations were continued over periods of months or years, until the individuals were old enough to make it certain that true orgasm was involved; and in all of these cases the later reactions were so similar to the earlier behavior that there could be no doubt of the orgastic nature of the first experience.

While the records for very young boys are fewer than for boys nearer the age of adolescence, and while the calculations for these youngest cases are consequently less reliable, the data do show a gradual increase, with advancing age, in the percentage of cases able to reach climax: 32 per cent of the boys 2 to 12 months of age, more than half (57.1%) of the 2- to 5-year olds, and nearly 80 per cent of the pre-adolescent boys between 10 and 13 years of age (inclusive) came to climax. Half of the boys had reached climax by 7 years of age (nearly half of them by 5 years), and two-thirds of them by 12 years of age. The observers emphasize that there are some of these pre-adolescent boys (estimated by one observer as less than one-quarter of the cases), who fail to reach climax even under prolonged and varied and repeated stimulation; but, even in these young boys, this probably represents psychologic blockage more often than physiologic incapacity.

In the population as a whole, a much smaller percentage of the boys experience orgasm at any early age, because few of them find themselves in circumstances that test their capacities; but the positive record on these boys who did have the opportunity makes it certain that many infant males and younger boys are capable of orgasm, and it is probable that half or more of the boys in an uninhibited society could reach climax by the time they were three or four years of age, and that nearly all of them could experience such a climax three to five years before the onset of adolescence.

Erection is much quicker in pre-adolescent boys than in adults, although the speed with which climax is reached in pre-adolescent males varies considerably in different boys, just as it does in adults. There are two-year olds who come to climax in less than 10 seconds, and there are two-year olds who may take 10 or 20 minutes, or more. There is a similar range among pre-adolescents of every other age. The mean time required to reach climax was almost exactly 3 minutes, and the median time was under 2 minutes. From earliest infancy until the middle twenties there is no effect of age on this point, although beyond that older males slow up in speed of response.

The most remarkable aspect of the pre-adolescent population is its capacity to achieve repeated orgasm in limited periods of time. This capacity definitely exceeds the ability of teen-age boys who, in turn, are much more capable than any older males. Among 182 pre-adolescent boys on whom sufficient data are available, more than half (55.5%, 138 cases) readily reached a second climax within a short period of time, and nearly a third (30.8%) of all these 182 boys were able to achieve 5 or more climaces in quite rapid succession. It is certain that a higher proportion of the boys could have had multiple orgasm if the situation had offered. Among 64 cases on which there are detailed reports, the average interval between the first and second climaces ranged from less than 10 seconds to 30 minutes or more, but the mean interval was only 6.28 minutes (median 2.25 minutes). There are older males, even in their thirties and older, who are able to equal this performance, but a much higher proportion of these pre-adolescent males are so capable. Even the youngest males, as young as 5 months in age, are capable of such repeated reactions. The maximum observed was 26 climaces in 24 hours, and the report indicates that still more might have been possible in the same period of time.

* * *

These data on the sexual activities of younger males provide an important substantiation of the Freudian view of sexuality as a component that is present in the human animal from earliest infancy, although it gives no support to the Freudian concept of a pre-genital stage of generalized erotic response that precedes more specific genital activity; nor does it show any necessity for a sexually latent or dormant period in the later adolescent years, except as such inactivity results from parental and social repressions of the growing child. It would seem that analysts have been correct in considering these capacities for childhood sexual development, or their suppression, as prime sources of adult patterns of sexual behavior and of many of the characteristics of the total personality.

Name Index

Adrian, E. D., 336

Bach, J. D., 8
Baldwin, J. M., 247
Ballard, M., 101–105
Ballard, P. B., 232
Bard, P., 326, 331, 336, 337
Barratier, J., 9
Barrington, D., 5–10, 253
Bartholomai, Prof., 68
Baume, Dr., 87
Beach, F. A., 328, 337
Beasley, W. C., 282–296
Bell, A. G., 159
Bell, S., 203
Benjamin, R., 9
Binet, A., 41, 177–187, 208, 211
Bleuler, E., 203
Boas, F., 201
Brace, J., 63
Brackbill, Y., 198
Breuer, J., 202
Bridgman, L., 62–67, 78, 154, 182, 188
Bryan, W. L., 119
Buckland, F., 151
Burt, C., 232

Candolle, de A. L. P. P., 258, 261
Carmichael, L., 337
Castle, C. A., 261
Cattell, J. McK., 157, 261
Cheselden, W., 1–4, 16, 25, 50, 58, 117
Claparede, E., 242
Clark, E. H., 132
Cowles, J. T., 328, 337
Cox, C. M., 5

Darwin, C., 75–79, 85, 150, 161, 330
Dennis, W., 328, 337
d'Estrella, T., 102
De Voss, J. C., 258
Drever, J., 228

Ebbinghaus, H., 93, 144
Ellis, H., 258
English, H. B., 328, 337

Fite, E. S., 177
Freeman, F. H., 297–309
Freud, S., 201–207, 220, 339, 341, 349

Galileo, 330
Galton, F., 80–92, 93–100, 138, 144, 254, 258, 261, 297
Gesell, A. L., 119, 160, 273, 281
Gibson, J. J., 329, 337
Goddard, H. H., 119
Gordon, H., 228–236, 282

Hall, F. H., 63
Hall, G. S., 119–137, 148, 201, 208
Handel, G. F., 9, 10
Harris, W. T., 169, 174
Harte, B., 152
Haslerud, G. M., 318, 321, 337, 338
Hebb, D. O., 318–338
Heerman, G., 138, 140, 141, 142
Hilgard, E. R., 328, 337
Hogan, H. P., 337
Holmes, F. B., 335, 337
Holzinger, K. J., 297–309
Homer, 78
Howe, M., 63

351

Name Index

Howe, S. G., 62–67, 154
Hull, C. L., 328, 337
Humphrey, G., 32
Humphrey, M., 32

Itard, J. M. C., 32–49

Jacobs, J., 144–147
Jacobsen, C. F., 318, 337
Jacobsen, M. M., 318, 337
James, W., 101, 102, 119
Janet, P. M. F., 247
Jasper, H. H., 337
Jastrow, J., 138–143, 154–159
Jennings, H. S., 201
Jersild, A. T., 335, 337
Jolliffe, N., 334, 337
Jones, H. E., 325, 328, 337
Jones, M. C., 325, 337
Jung, C. J., 201, 203

Keller, H., 154–159, 182, 188
Kidd, D., 2, 188–197
Kinsey, A. C., 339–349
Kitto, D. I., 142
Kleinwächter, L., 81
Köhler, W., 33, 263, 318, 330, 337
Krasnogarski., N. I., 198–200

Langer, S., 12
Lashley, K. S., 219, 326, 328, 337
Leeper, R., 328, 338
Leuba, J. H., 119
Liddell, H. S., 338
Lindner, G., 204
Lorente De No, R., 330, 338

Magnus, H., 108
Malinowski, B., 263–272, 339
Marquis, D. G., 328, 337
Martin, C. E., 339–349
Masserman, J. H., 326, 338
McCulloch, T. L., 318, 338
McGraw, M. M., 148, 310–317
Mead, M., 263
Meyer, A., 201
Minkowski, M., 273
Mitchell, J., 50–61, 188
Moreau, J., 86
Morgan, C. T., 328, 338
Mowrer, O. H., 328, 338
Mozart, T. C. W. T., 5–10, 253
Muller, H. J., 300
Murchison, C., 12, 154
Murchison, P., 12
Münsterberg, H., 156

Newman, H. H., 297–309
Nissen, H. W., 327, 328, 329, 337

Paget, Prof., 87
Pavlov, R. P., 198, 318
Pearson, K., 217
Piaget, J., 12, 102, 160, 237–252
Pinel, P., 34, 35
Pomeroy, W. B., 339–349
Porter, S., 101
Preyer, W., 12, 106–116, 117–118, 160, 161, 162

Ramsey, G. V., 342
Riesen, A. H., 325, 327, 337
Robinson, L., 148–153
Romanes, G. J., 92

Schobert, K., 68
Senden, M. von, 3, 327, 329, 338
Sherrington, C. S., 331, 338
Shinn, M., 160–167
Simon, T., 177–187
Singh, J. A. L., 32
Skinner, B. F., 106, 328, 338
Spies, T. D., 334, 338
Stern, W., 201
Stewart, D., 61
Sullivan, A., 156, 158

Terman, L. M., 119, 208–218, 228, 231, 253–262
Thompson, G. E., 198
Thorndike, E. L., 168–176
Tiedemann, D., 11–31, 148, 160
Titchener, E. B., 201
Trousseau, A., 85

Valentine, C. W., 324, 325, 338

Wallace, A. R., 151
Walter, A. A., 337
Wardrop, J., 50–61
Watson, J. B., 148, 219–227, 318, 325, 338
Weiss, P., 338
Willman, O., 68
Woodworth, R. S., 260
Wyman, J. B., 260

Yerkes, A. W., 318, 338
Yerkes, R. M., 318, 321, 338
Yoshioka, J. G., 318, 337

Zangwill, O. L., 338
Zingg, R. M., 33

Subject Index

acephalic neonate, behavior of, 117, 118
animistic thinking, of
  Tiedemann's son, 30, 31*
  Melville Ballard, 103, 104
  Boston children, 128
association of ideas
  referred to, 16, 17, 23, 28, 70
  first study of, 93–99
  method of study, 93–96
  time required for, 96
  repetition in, 97
  age at formation, 99
  below level of consciousness, 100

Binet-Simon scale
  development of, 177–187
  purpose of, 177–178
  use of age norms, 179, 184, 185
  directions for administration, 182, 183
  usefulness of the test, 185–187
  criticism of by Terman, 208
biographical studies of normal children
  Tiedemann's son, 11–31
  Preyer's son, 106–116
  Shinn's niece, 160–167

Canal Boat children
  conditions of life of, 229
  school attendance of, 230
  intelligence of, 232–236
case studies of exceptional children
  Cheselden's subject, 1–4
  Mozart, 5–10
  wild boy of Aveyron, 32–49
  James Mitchell, 50–61
  Laura Bridgman, 62–67

Melville Ballard, 101–105
Helen Keller, 154–159
children's concepts
  role of experience in, 74
  of Berlin children, 68–74
  of Boston children, 119–137
  of Irish-American children, 135
  of boys vs. girls, 68–74
  of rural vs. urban, 124, 126
  affected by sound similarities, 126, 127
  religious, 104, 105, 130
color discrimination, 106–116, 127–128
color-sound associations, 132
conditional reflexes in infancy, 198–199, 225–227
congenital cataracts
  description of, 1, 2, 51, 58
  operations for, 2, 57, 58
  visual perception following surgery, 3, 4, 51, 58, 60
critical periods, 48, 138, 139, 140, 141, 142, 143
crying
  increased by reinforcement, 18
  causes of, 75, 76, 77
cup or spoon feeding, 13

deaf-blind children, studies of
  James Mitchell, 50–61
  Laura Bridgman, 62–67
  Helen Keller, 154–159
deaf-mute
  recollections of, 101–105
  animistic thinking of, 103–105
  concepts of, 103–105
  religious ideas of, 104, 105

* Subentries are arranged chronologically, in the order in which they appear in the book.

353

354 *Subject Index*

delayed reaction, 33, 37, 44
development of visual perception in normal children, 19, 22, 23, 160–167
  after surgery for cataracts, 3, 4, 51, 58, 60
  in wild boy of Aveyron, 34
digit span, as related to age, 145
  class standing, 146
dreams
  of the blind, 138–143
  of cripples, 141
  of the deaf, 141
  of color, 142
  of Kafir children, 93, 194

egocentric speech and thought, 237–252
erotic responses, causes of, 342–343

fears
  of falling, 21
  of darkness, 195
  of animals, 195
  of other races, 195
  Watson on fear, 218–227
  absence of fear of animals, 222–225
  tests of in chimpanzees, 319–323
  spontaneous fears, 323–324
  of dead and mutilated bodies, 324–325
  central factors in fear, 325–328
  Hebb's theory of fear, 329–332
  classification of fears, 333–335
  relationship to rage and other states, 335–336

gifted children
  importance of, 253–254
  how selected for study, 255–256
  preponderance of boys, 257
  health and growth of, 257
  racial and social origins of, 258
  formal education of, 259
  interests of, 259, 260
  personality and character of, 260
  probable future of, 261, 262
grasp reflex, 15, 148, 151–152, 220, 226, 310

human figure drawings, 133

imitation, 17, 25, 26
infantile sexuality
  Freud's lecture on, 201–207
  in the Trobriand islands, 263–272
  in the Kinsey report, 339–349
intelligence
  Binet's definition of, 182
  not measurable under age two years, 182
  Binet-Simon scale, 177–187
  Stanford-Binet scale, 208–217
  of Canal Boat children, 228–236
  of twins, 302
interest in sensory stimulation, shown by
  Cheselden's subject, 1–4
  Tiedemann's son, 14, 18, 21, 22, 23, 27
  wild boy of Aveyron, 36, 38, 40
  James Mitchell, 51–57, 59–60
  Shinn's niece, 163–166
  newborn infants, 282–297

jealousy, 27, 28, 29

Kafir children, observations on
  forced feeding, 188
  bathing, 189
  finger sucking, 189
  walking and talking, 189
  reaction to burn, 190
  reaction to beating, 191
  earliest memories, 191
  questions of, 192
  imitation, 192
  discipline and punishment, 193
  dreams, 193, 194
  curiosity, 194
  fears of white men, 195
  ambitions, 196–197
kindergarten training, effects of, 135

learning an arbitrary language, by
  the wild boy of Aveyron, 42–49
  Laura Bridgman, 65–67

maturation, effect upon
  motor sequences, 274–279
  emotional behavior, 280–281
  suspension grasp behavior, 310–312
  swimming, 315–317
memory span
  for numbers and letters, 144–147
  of Helen Keller, 154–159
moral judgments, 133

natural signs, used by
  wild boy of Aveyron, 40
  James Mitchell, 55, 57, 60
  Laura Bridgman, 64
  Melville Ballard, 102
Negro-white differences in visual pursuit, 282–296
newborn infants
  behavior of, 13, 14, 161–162
  acephalic, 117–118
  visual pursuit of, 282–296

Subject Index

orgasm
   causes of, 339–340
   physiological changes during, 340
   occurrence in infancy, 347–348
   frequency among boys, 348–349
original emotions, Watson's view, 220–221

performances of precocious children
   Mozart, 5–10
   Barratier, 9
   Rabbi Benjamin, 9
   Handel, 9, 10
prehension, development of, 274, 275
puberty, influence of upon
   the wild boy of Aveyron, 47, 48
   James Mitchell, 61
   Trobriand Island children, 263–273
   subjects of the Kinsey report, 345–349
puberty praecox, 279

recapitulation theory, 148
reinforcement
   by new clothing, 57, 59
   by patting, 57, 60, 64, 65
repression, 205
restraint, reactions to, 14, 16, 25, 56, 57

sequences of behavioral development, 13, 107, 160–167, 273–281, 310–312, 315–317
sex differences
   in frequency of concepts, 71, 135
   in intelligence, 213–215
   among the gifted, 257
   in sexual behavior, 344
sexual behavior in childhood
   Freud's account of, 201–207
   Watson's account of, 221
   in the Trobriand Islands, 263–272
   in the Kinsey report, 339–350
sexual etiology of neuroses, 202
sexual theories of children, 206–207
sibling rivalry, 23, 28, 206
skin color, reactions to, 3, 195
smiling and laughter, 15, 17, 18, 19, 20, 27, 35, 60, 78, 79

speech
   beginning of, 23
   sequence of speech sounds, 27
   sentence development, 29
   unsuccessful training of the wild boy of Aveyron, 38–40, 46
span of apprehension, 144–147
spontaneous conversations
   method of study of, 234–240
   functions of, 240–241
   types of, 241–249
   egocentric nature of, 249–252
Stanford-Binet test
   a revision of the Binet-Simon scale, 209–211
   distribution of scores, 211, 212
   constancy of the IQ, 213
   social class differences, 215
   sex differences, 213–215
   relation to school progress, 215–217
   used in Canal Boat study, 228–236
   used in study of gifted children, 253–262
   used in study of twins, 307
strangers, fear of, 149, 150, 325, 327, 333
sucking increased by reinforcement, 13

thought without language, 101–105
twins
   in the study of nature and nurture, 80–94, 297–309
   two kinds distinguished, 81–82, 299–300
   degree of similarity of identical twins, 82–88
   effects of varied environment upon, 91–92, 304
   developmental correspondence in, 275–277
   co-twin control experiments, 278–279
   one twin the leader, 304
   affected by prenatal environment, 304
   case studies of, 308

visual imagery of the blind, 138–143
visual perception
   development of, 166, 282–296